TAKE IT LIKE A
MAN

TAKE IT LIKE A
MAN

THE AUTOBIOGRAPHY OF
BOY
GEORGE

WITH SPENCER BRIGHT

HarperCollinsPublishers

Photographs follow pages 216 and 376.

This book was published in Great Britain in 1995 by Sidgwick & Jackson, an imprint of Macmillan General Books.

FIRST U.S. EDITION

Designed by Caitlin Daniels

Library of Congress Cataloging-in-Publication Data

Boy George, 1961–
 Take it like a man : the autobiography of Boy George / with Spencer Bright.
  p. cm.
 ISBN 0-06-017368-8
 1. Boy George, 1961– . 2. Rock musicians—England—Biography. I. Title.
ML420.B757A3 1995
782.42166' 092—dc20
[B]   95-22573

95 96 97 98 99 ❖/RRD 10 9 8 7 6 5 4 3 2 1

To my parents, Dinah and Jeremiah O'Dowd, and all the many twisted, gorgeous friends that have made my life colorful and this book very interesting.

ACKNOWLEDGMENTS

Boy George thanks Springs Hydro, Packington, Ashby-de-la-Zouch, Leicestershire, for comfort and sanctuary; Bruce Forrest for unwittingly lending us his Amiga computer to write this book; Eileen Schembri of Virgin Records; and Ana Maria Boto Silvestre for the loan of her home in Portugal; Tony Gordon and Jean Reynolds at Wedge Music.

Spencer Bright thanks his transcribers, Adrienne Banks, Hilary Bright, Susan Banks, Zanna Laws, Paul Vaughan-Phillips. Maurice Conroy for his cultural signposts, Amy Greenberger and Terri Howard at Tea with George USA for their chronological and video research. Mr. Hore, headmaster of Eltham Green School. For research and information: Keiko Imaizumi in Japan, Wyn Arthur in Australia, Emily Morrison in New York, Chrissie Wilson ex of Los Angeles, Valerie Dawes, Rosie Bartlett, Jerry Adamson at Gemini Travel, Bob Fierro at Zebra Marketing USA, Carole Burton-Fairbrother and Lisa Beatty at Virgin's video department, all at Virgin Records, Jonathan Morrish at Sony Records, Amanda Williams at WEA Records, Will Whitehorn at Virgin Atlantic, Limelight video; Chris Salewicz, Tim Hulse, Dave Wainwright, Daniel Hausermann, Jade Hausermann. Tina Moriarty and Peter Cuffy at the Royal Bank of Scotland. My agent Lavinia Trevor, and at Sidgwick & Jackson—Susan Hill, Helen Gummer, Ingrid Connell, William Armstrong—for going beyond patience. Roz Poland for her positive thinking, and heartfelt everythings to Chrissy Iley for her love and advice, and Poodle and Tugboat for their warm furryness.

PROLOGUE

When I was a little boy I wanted to be like Shirley Bassey. I longed for those rare occasions when my brothers were out of the bedroom so I could close the curtains, turn off the light, and put Shirley on the record player. I would strut around the room waving my arms, clenching my fists, stroking my curves, throwing my head from side to side.

I'd like to run away from you—and if I could,
You know I would,
But I would die.

My very first performances were on the front doorstep, or at the old people's home round the corner. I'd go and sing to the old dears.

My old man
Said follow the van,
And don't dilly dally on the way . . .

Music was my only friend, a way of escaping the isolation. The World of Pop seemed the perfect place for a boy like me. Boys at school called Marc Bolan and Mickey Finn "fucking queers." I collected pictures of them, they were my rock 'n' roll Romeo and Juliet.

I preferred the company of girls, swapping beads and broken jewelery, dreaming and scheming, singing the latest pop songs. Girls had a capacity for endless chat. They were a good audience too. I never wanted to give up the stage, always hogging the limelight. I hated football and climbing trees. I much preferred the Good Ship Lollipop. I would rush home from school to watch *Junior Showtime*. I even wrote letters trying to get an audition on *Opportunity Knocks*.

Dad found an old fifties record player and gave it to us for our room. Only my brother Richard and I used it. The others weren't into music. The first records I had were "Alexander Beetle" and "Brand New Key" by Melanie, "Yellow River" by Christie, "Gypsys, Tramps & Thieves" by Cher. I played them as loud as I could and sang along. Mum and Dad's old records too, Frank Sinatra, Pearl Bailey, Peggy Lee, Judy Garland. It didn't matter that they weren't in the charts. I learned the words to every song I heard. If they weren't audible I made up my own.

On Saturday afternoons I watched the old films, *The King and I*, *South Pacific*, the Busby Berkeley musicals, *Gold Diggers of 1933*, *42nd Street*. I loved Fred Astaire and Ginger Rogers, Alice Faye, Rosemary Clooney, Shirley Temple, Mickey Rooney, and Al Jolson. I'd dance around and sing.

I'm gonna wash that man right outta my hair.
And send him on his way . . .

I tried in vain to be like other kids. I couldn't hide my feminine nature.

My earliest memory is from when I was six. I was page boy at Uncle Davey and Auntie Jan's wedding—I wore knee-length red velvet trousers, black cummerbund, white ruffled shirt, and, best of all, black patent shoes with a huge silver buckle on the front. I was so proud of that outfit, strutting around like Little Lord Fauntleroy.

After the wedding my shoes were given to cousin Denise. I cried and cried. "Why couldn't I keep them? Why couldn't I wear them to school?" Everything in those days was recycled, passed down in the family or passed on to a relative. Of course, Mum couldn't let her little boy go to school in shoes like that. I wished every day was a wedding.

When I was eight or so I developed asthma. Mum said it was nerves, the local doctor put it down to dust, but there was more than dust blowing in our house. We all lived in fear of Dad's temper and Mum's tears, which seemed to affect me much more than the others. Monday mornings were prime time for an asthma attack: the thought of school brought panic. Mum had to hold me over the washing machine so I could inhale the steam. It was years before I received proper medication.

As kids we all had nicknames for each other. Mine were "poof" and "pansy" from as early as I can remember. Children can be cruel. They have an unsettling ability to poke you where it hurts. "You're a poof." Who tells them? Mum and Dad are quick to tell you about the pixies and the elves. But they never sit you down and say, "There are those that love women, and there are those that don't." Kids find these things out for themselves.

Georgie Porgie pudding and pie
Kissed the girls and made them cry
When the boys came out to play
He kissed them too
He likes it that way.

Being a "poof" was like having a contagious disease. The jokes, the jibes, the small talk, the unsubtle messages, blue for boys, pink for girls. From the womb to the tomb we are guided strategically up the procreative path. Parents never even consider their child might be gay. They plan for every other eventuality.

I thought there was no one else like me in the world. Later on that was to make me feel special; as a child it just made me lonely.

I was pretty. People said, "What's your daughter's name?"

Mum would snap back, "That's my son, Georgie."

She told them I was "sensitive, highly strung." It was her way of explaining me. I was the pink sheep of the family.

I had lots of girlfriends. I liked girls. I just couldn't respond to them physically. In all other ways I was the perfect boyfriend, jealous, possessive, selfish. But I was no good when it came to giving them what they really wanted, affection, kissing, cuddling—I was terrified of getting it wrong. I worried that I wouldn't enjoy it and they'd be able to tell—so I avoided close contact, thus avoiding failure—I knew I couldn't avoid it for ever.

Richard had his eighteenth birthday party at our house. We were really excited, even though he didn't want us there. I had my first drink—lager shandy—and my first French kiss. I was dragged into a corner and initiated by Brenda Ritchie, an eighteen-year-old Diana Dors type, big and motherly with bushy red hair and child-bearing lips—she almost swallowed me. I'd spent so much time worrying about it. I couldn't believe how easy it was. The next day I went shopping with Mum. We saw Brenda on the bus. She shouted, "Who's my favorite kisser, then?" I cringed, but I was quite proud of myself.

I was more interested in boys. They were the true objects of my desire. I'd been aware of that fact from a very early age.

Often I would lie awake at night thinking about boys, boys, boys—the godlike Edwards brothers; Barry Foley, the local heart-throb who was always playing with his zipper. There were boys at school all the girls were mad for, I was mad for them too.

I had a picture that I tore out of *Cosmopolitan* magazine, which I kept hidden under the mattress. It was of a naked man lifting himself out of a swimming pool. He had the most beautiful round muscly bottom. I drooled over that picture for months. And hoped one day I'd meet a man just like that.

I never trusted anyone totally. I was convinced everyone was laughing or talking about me. I trusted girls more than boys, unless they were like my friend Michael Crome. I was sure he was gay, he certainly showed all the signs, and was often the butt of cruel jokes himself. Michael was freckle-faced with Brillo pad hair. His lips were in a permanent pout and he sauntered around like a drunk catwalk model, with a large satchel slung over his shoulder. Kids would shout, "Like your handbag." Unlike me he was quiet, he never answered back. This saved him a lot of trouble.

I wondered whether Michael thought I was gay, I wondered whether he thought about it at all. It was something you couldn't discuss. Michael may have appeared gay, what if I'd got it wrong? What if he was just an artistic type? It was too big a risk to just come out and ask someone. You'd open yourself up to even greater persecution.

Michael lived a couple of streets away in Gregory Crescent. We went to the same primary school and Sunday school together. I was probably seduced by the free orange juice and fairy cakes. The O'Dowds were Roman Catholics in the loose sense, a picture of the Pope in the hall next to one of Muhammad Ali—everything was well balanced. We were taken to church a few times when we were very little. My brother Gerald pulled his trousers down during Sunday mass, and we never went back.

Going round to Michael's house was like entering another world, crisp and Christian. They were a "nice" family. I think they considered me a bad influence. One Sunday I went to collect Michael for Sunday school. I was wearing a large beige wedding hat and Richard's matching camel hair coat with one of Mum's floral headscarves tied around my neck. Michael's mother was much too polite to show her horror. Instead she made me a cup of tea and got straight on the phone to Mum suggesting my outfit "may be a little too loud for the Church of England." Mum's attitude was "Let him get on with it." She figured people would laugh and that would embarrass me into normality. That was a terrible miscalculation on her part.

Once, while buying me a school coat she tried painfully to convince me that a padded green hooded parka would be ideal. "Marc Bolan would wear it," she said. But I knew Marc had better taste.

When I left school I lost touch with Michael. His family moved to Chislehurst, a posher area two or three miles away from Eltham. Michael got in touch out of the blue and left a number. I called him and arranged a visit. I'd started wearing a little makeup by this time, my hair was dyed black and teased into spikes. Michael looked the same as ever. His parents told me he had almost been molested by a strange man on the train on his way to work. They were disgusted. "Poor Michael. He was off work for two weeks." Michael must be straight, I thought, passing up an opportunity like that.

Some years later, while walking in the West End, I spotted a lanky Nelly mincing toward me with a dog. As he got closer I realized it was the almost molested Michael, and if he wasn't out by now something was definitely wrong. All my suspicions were confirmed when he told me he was flat-sharing with a black man. Poor Michael indeed.

You hear your brothers and boys at school talking about girls all the time. Tits, tits, tits. This one's a slag, that one's a slag. The four Fs—Find 'em, Finger 'em, Fuck 'em, Forget 'em. Boys bragging about their sexual conquests, fannies and dicks, blow jobs and pricks. You join in, spinning a few of your own yarns, always wary of going too far in case you get caught out. No matter how hard I tried I could never be part of that masculine environment. There were times when I tried to join in at football or rugby, but the more I tried the more they pushed me out. Whenever the time came to choose a team for games no one would want me. They would shout, "He's useless. We don't want him." I was outcast, along with the fatties.

In my last year at school I got friendly with the Edwards brothers, Jimmy and Terry, they were bullyboy heartthrobs. I was at St. Peter's Youth Club, hanging around the snooker tables, enjoying the view. One of the boys pushed me. Jimmy jumped to my defense. "Leave him alone." My heart fluttered. We became friends after that. Jimmy looked like a thuggy David Cassidy—mousy blond hair, a ski-slope nose, short and lean with a perfectly round bum and the tightest pair of school trousers you've ever seen.

I was infatuated with him, doing ridiculous things like going fishing or to see Charlton Athletic, Jimmy's favorite football team. We used to bunk over the wall—that was my favorite part, watching him climb over.

Our friendship lasted about a year. It was odd, because we had nothing in common. I spent every waking hour with them, staying weekends at their house, having my dinner there, I never knew why they wanted me around. Normally boys like that kept well away from me. They knew I was the school Mary, yet they seemed protective toward me. I used to run around for them, trying to win their approval, maybe for a moment I even wanted to be like them. At that age I was like a neurotic flea, jumping from one new friend to another, desperate to belong. It wasn't long before I was somewhere else, being someone else.

After I left school I stopped seeing Jimmy and Terry, then months later I bumped into Terry on Eltham High Street. My hair was hennaed bright orange. Terry looked at me, "What *do* you look like? Bloody Quentin Crisp." I was most insulted. I could tell it wasn't a compliment. He told me he was getting married. "That's nice," I said. He walked off without inviting me. I was hurt by his rejection. I felt like a freak. I knew there was no turning back.

Terry's friend Dave would do anything to humiliate me. He was a sly boy, always disappearing off to the West End. He always had plenty of money and new clothes. At the time I thought nothing of it. Imagine my surprise when I came face-to-face with him in a rent boy club off Leicester Square. By this time I was a full-fledged drag queen. So much in my life had changed. I still couldn't believe this bastard who'd made my life such a misery was a rent boy. I felt a little sad. Here was I, lipstick, lashes, and high heels, and there was Dave still working that pathetic little butch act, fooling himself that because he did it for money he wasn't a proper queer like me.

I'd always imagined the gay world was one big happy family, but I discovered quickly that gays are just as territorial as the rest. They make divisions. A lot of queers want to think of themselves as "normal," doing everything they can to appear so. Dressing up as lumberjacks and bikers, with their James Dean and Marlon Brando obsessions, white T-shirts and Levi's, looking down their noses at effeminate queens.

It's all part of the guilt trip. We grow up with the feeling that we are inherently bad. Society doesn't have a place for us. It wishes we would just disappear. Even if our parents know we're gay, they normally don't want to discuss it; they shut it out, refusing to share an enormously important part of our lives. This extends the guilt. Many queens will say, "I don't care what my parents think," but it's a delusion. Most of us never get over parental rejection. We want them to love us for what we are.

What makes us gay? I used to think we were born gay and that was it. A hormonal or chemical imbalance that we had no control over. These days I'm not so sure. In anger I'd scream at Mum and Dad, "It's your fault I'm gay. You created me." And it has to be said, queers cannot exist without heterosexual union. It takes two of you to make one of us. Our parents feel responsible. Fathers think it's a reflection on their virility. Mothers wonder where they went wrong.

My father was all man. A gay son would have been his worse nightmare. He would grab my shoulders and say, "These are all yours." Who was he trying to convince? Was I subconsciously trying to be everything he wasn't?

A large percentage of gay men, and I include myself, are attracted to stereotypical authority figures—soldiers, policemen, sailors. Most queens would like nothing more than to live out their fantasies of romping with a member of the armed forces. We all love a man in a uniform.

My ideal sexual fantasy would be a Sean Penn type, aggressive, passionate, jealous, and protective. My subconscious mind telling me that's how a man should be. That's what I grew up with. Furniture flying, tears flowing, suburban psychosis.

CHAPTER 1

The wrath of God, an illegitimate child, and a broken heart brought my mother, Dinah, across the sea from Ireland in 1958, aged eighteen. The birth of her first child out of wedlock, my brother Richard, raised many questions regarding her future, creating emotional barriers that she hoped, but never believed, she would break.

The Irish scorned premarital sex. There were few things worse than an unwed mother. Dinah had already spent the entire nine months of her pregnancy hidden away—she felt she had let her family down. She thought no man would touch her again, and even if they did, she was sure they would not want the responsibility of someone else's child.

The job of raising Richard was taken over by Bridget Glynn, Dinah's headstrong mother, who, having raised six daughters and two sons of her own, was well equipped for the task.

Dinah answered a newspaper advertisement and accepted a position as a live-in barmaid at the Duchess of Wellington in Woolwich, in the suburbs of Southeast London. She planned to work hard and save enough money eventually to take care of Richard by herself.

Woolwich was a garrison town that had a violent reputation during the early fifties. Squaddies and civilians would often brawl over the local females. The streets were more likely to be saturated

9

with blood than paved with gold. Woolwich was suffering from postwar depression and heavy unemployment. Things had changed little by the time Dinah arrived. Franco Glynn, my grandfather, only agreed to her leaving Ireland because he knew she would be working most nights. The Duchess was a family pub that drew a mainly Irish crowd, a long way from the bright lights of London's West End.

Dinah worked from eight in the morning until eleven at night for two pounds and nine shillings a week. She celebrated her nineteenth birthday behind the bar. That evening, January 23, 1958, she met my father, Jeremiah, a handsome ex-soldier, who had stopped by the Duchess to see his sister May, who was also a barmaid. Jeremiah had just been sacked from his job as a laborer for the Metropolitan Water Board. It was his twenty-fourth birthday, Mel introduced them. Dinah's stark black pencil skirt and jumper made her naturally blond hair stand out even more. She had mischief in those green eyes. Jerry asked Dinah to celebrate with him on her night off.

Jerry O'Dowd was a charmer, thick-set with a Romany complexion. He wore handmade shoes and Italian-style suits, paid for weekly on the never-never.

He took her to the local Ritz ballroom, where they danced to May Torme and his big band. They made each other laugh. Jerry asked to see her again.

"Yes, I'd like that," she said. "But there's something I have to tell you. You might not want to." She told him about her child back in Ireland.

"I don't care what you done before," he said. "I like you. I want to see you again."

When Dinah lost her job and board after a row at the pub, May took her home to stay with the O'Dowds in Burrage Road. At first they welcomed Dinah, but took exception when they discovered she already had a child. Suddenly Dinah was not good enough for their Jerry. Jerry reacted strongly to their moral judgment. Who were they to tell him right from wrong?

Jerry and Dinah took a room together at Vicarage Park, in neighboring Plumstead. Dinah found a new job packing sugar at the Tate & Lyle factory. Jerry worked hardening components in the furnaces at Matchless Motors. He tried again and again for a reconciliation with his family, but the fact they were living in sin only compounded the feud.

When Dinah fell pregnant, a wedding day was quickly sought. The local priest, who disapproved of Jerry, told Dinah not to marry him. He was a roughneck, too unsettled to make a marriage last. The priest refused to see Jerry, no doubt fearful of his reputation as a fighter. A compromise was found, and a more sympathetic priest agreed to marry them.

On the wedding day Jerry knocked off early from Matchless. He picked up his suit from the cleaners and went to the public toilets in Woolwich Market where he washed, shaved, and changed. He met Dinah outside the church; with May and her boyfriend as witnesses they were married.

The first year of marriage was spent flitting from one bedsit to another. Jerry worked long hours, which meant they could make ends meet. But a pattern of loneliness was developing for Dinah. The birth of her second child, my brother Kevin, extended that loneliness. She had to stop working, losing what little independence she had. This was the future. Cut off from her family in Ireland, ostracized from Burrage Road, she was deprived of the love and support most young mothers take for granted.

Finally the O'Dowds relented, and invited Jerry and Dinah to move into the family home, to share with his parents, George and Margaret, three sisters, Pauline, May, and Josephine, and brother Davey. Not the most comfortable of conditions. With money scarce and an extra mouth to feed, there was little choice. Burrage Road was a condemned property that had barely managed to survive bombing during the Second World War. It was meant to be temporary accommodation. The family had lost their original home in Southport Road to Hitler.

When Kevin was eighteen months old he became seriously ill with tapeworm. He was administered the last rites. My mother, pregnant with me, was panic-stricken and vowed, "If they take my Kevin away I'm not having this baby." Doctors managed to stabilize Kevin and he was slowly brought back to full health.

With another baby due, Jerry and Dinah realized the cramped conditions at Burrage Road would become intolerable. They needed to get away. This was no easy task. Decent housing was scarce, and the waiting list long. Their dream of having their own home before the birth was not to be.

On June 14, 1961, I was born at Barnhurst Hospital in Bexley. A speedy birth, less than half an hour from the first pains: six pounds thirteen ounces. George Alan O'Dowd. George after my grandfather, Alan my mother's choice.

We were finally given our own home when I was a year old. A three-bedroom red-brick terraced house with a bright yellow door and an outside loo. Twenty-nine Joan Crescent, Eltham. It was like a palace to Mum. The first place she'd ever been able to call home. The estate was erected between the wars, in the days before planning and municipal housing were dirty words, when they believed in a working-class Promised Land.

Joan Crescent was a small road that turned into a pan-shape halfway down. Number 29 was set to the right-hand corner. The street was typical of most streets in that area. The houses were typical too, they all looked the same—like cut-price tombstones. It was a place without face or space, each window displaying the same identical net curtains. Nobody could afford to keep up with the Joneses, nobody knew who they were. An aerial view of Joan Crescent would have looked like the death of creativity.

A good year after settling into Joan Crescent my parents decided to send for Richard, who was still living in Ireland. He was already five years old and had become the emotional property of my grandmother Bridget, who fought to keep him. After many tears Richard was brought to England and became part of the O'Dowd family. Everyone assumed little Richard was too young to understand what was going on.

CHAPTER 2

It's impossible to determine what you are born with and what you absorb. Mum says I was a quiet child, happy to sit alone and amuse myself. Occasionally I get vivid flashbacks, like my Cub Scout days. Akela. We Will Do Our Best. I received all my honors—bronze, silver, gold. We traveled far and wide to the local field and spent the weekend in tents three minutes from home, cooking sausages and tying knots. Going to visit Auntie Phyllis, Auntie Annie, Uncle Frank in Ireland and four hours of vomiting on the ferry. Not being able to read the *News of the World* at Uncle Frank's. "That's not for your eyes."

I remember birthday parties at Auntie Heather's, being pushed into the swimming pool at Danson Park, playing Knock Down Ginger, being terrified of the Hoolihans' dog, helping my friend Moyna Kane clean out a hundred years of dust from her bedroom, falling off my bike, and the day when we thought my little brother Gerald had gone blind. He was flat out on the grass looking up at the clouds. Suddenly he was still, like a corpse. We shook him but he didn't move. Somebody went screaming for Mum. We were terrified. He had a high-temperature convulsion and was rushed to hospital. Mum used to tell us not to look at the clouds when they were moving or pull a face 'cause we'd get stuck. I still think about it now when I see clouds move.

We had cold linoleum floors scrubbed clean with Ajax.

Everything was minimal. We had a bit of carpet, not wall-to-wall, a Put-U-Up bed that doubled as a settee, a couple of spiteful-looking chairs with flowery grannie covers that were impossible to get comfortable on. A black and white TV with alien reception. Dad was always banging that TV. "Poxy piece of crap." We had a coal fire surrounded by a wire mesh guard to keep us from falling in. Once Kevin stoked up the fire with Dad's wage packet. Dad gave him a good hiding.

The television curfew was eight o'clock. I used to sulk like crazy, there was no getting round Dad when he'd sent you to bed. I'd get up and creep onto the top of the stairs. Pointless, really, because you couldn't see the TV from there. It would drive me mad: all the best things were on late.

Life was constantly interrupted by childbirth. By 1967 I had gained two brothers, Gerald, then David, and a sister, Siobhan, who had been a lifelong ambition of Mum's.

Twenty-nine Joan Crescent soon lost its palatial feel. What had once seemed like a fairly large house was now overpopulated with screaming children. Anyone who wanted space was advised to hang out of the nearest window.

Upstairs three small bedrooms were split unequally between eight people. My parents shared the largest, David and Siobhan shared another. The rest of us were crammed in the third; four boys growing up in conditions that could break even the highest of spirits. We lived in each other's pockets and tore at each other's throats, each of us mortified by the lack of privacy.

Dad developed a passion for animals. Our back garden was home to thirty or more chickens and a rather obnoxious cockerel. Then there was Louis, our Alsatian dog, who often pardoned the foe and savaged the friend. This understandably made us very unpopular with the neighbors. The chickens were the last straw. When we first moved there Dad upset everybody by digging up the garden and putting in a potato patch. Our neighbors, the Baldwins, were aghast. Their garden was "perfect," full green lawn surrounded by vivacious flowerbeds. Our paddy-field spoiled their vision of country life.

Our garden looked like the local adventure playground—piles of junk clashed with screeching chickens running amid rusting car parts and various pieces of furniture that Dad had found. Everything was worth keeping. There was even a demolished Bedford van that Dad had written off in a road accident propped up on a pile of bricks in the front garden; he used it as a shed for his tools. Something to upset all the neighbors.

Inside, things were just as colorful. Piles of clothing littered every available corner, the washing machine buzzing twenty-four hours a day. Mum was every bit the cartoon housewife.

She always hangs out her washing
To dry in the hands of the sun.
She always hangs out her washing
If there ain't any she'll find some.

She kept going day in, day out. When she wasn't washing she was cooking, and when she wasn't cooking she was shopping. She played a totally submissive role, never taking a moment for herself. Putting one kid down to pick up another. Mum never questioned Dad's authority around the home. She was "chief cook and bottle washer." When it came to making decisions Dad never actually said a woman's place is in the kitchen. It was generally taken for granted, mum's the word.

Mum tried to find time to read us stories like *Charlie and the Chocolate Factory*, *What Katie Did*, and *Little Women*. It was an impossible task. There wasn't enough time between peeling the potatoes and making the gravy. Practicality always got the upper hand.

Mum came from a poor background. Her father was a box maker and her mother restored furniture as well as keeping house. They lived in two high-ceilinged rooms at the top of a converted Georgian house in Wellington Street, Dublin. The toilet was four flights down in the backyard, the sink on the next landing. When Mum was pregnant with Richard she shared a bed with three sisters. They were unaware of her condition, much too young to understand. When Richard was born they thought they had another brother.

Mum has a romantic picture of home life in Ireland. Certainly my grandfather Franco was a warm man who displayed a drunken charm. When my grandparents came for Christmas he would be the one playing with us kids, making intricate Plasticine figures and telling stories. I have unpleasant memories of him strangling and gutting chickens fresh from the O'Dowd farmyard. On the whole he was a lovable character, tall and wiry with a pickled gherkin for a nose. He was a poet of the people writing about the nurses' strike, and the state of the government.

> A million nurses every day,
> Pick up a tin of beans and say,
> One for you, one for me,
> One for you, one for me.
> The country is going to the dogs,
> They're blaming the Paddies and Wogs.
> But well they know that this won't go,
> It won't fit into the cogs . . .

Nanny Glynn was a burly woman with a tight mop of brown curly hair and a stern expression, folded arms, and squinted eyes. She wore vivid flowery polyester dresses, sensible coats, sensible shoes, and salad-bowl hats. She would slap us with wet flannels if we got under her feet. I was always ducking out of her way. "I'll bloody brain ya."

She was schooled in the worst possible Catholic tradition, a tradition of ignorance and fear. Raised in a convent, she was forced to bathe fully clothed to protect her from her own vile femininity. This was intended to prepare her for the thorns of the outside world. It created a legacy of guilt and pain.

She was full of love but she'd be tough on us kids if we came in crying. "Stop crying, you big gobshite. Get up the yard, there's a smell of hay off ya." Always calling on the Lord. "Jesus, Mary and Joseph, keep me near the cross." I loved her in my own fearful way, she was the first tough woman in my life.

Dad and Nan were never close. Her visits would always end in tears. "Get that woman out of my house." Us kids were expected to be oblivious to all this. But we could piece things together. We could see the way Nan doted on Richard. We could hear what was being said. Dad called Nan "Naggie Maggie." Sometimes he would call Mum "Maggie" as well to rile her.

Mum was always pig in the middle when Nan and Dad went to war. She couldn't please either of them. It was anger fighting anger. Dad had taken Richard as his son, and didn't want Nan sticking her oar in. Nan saw Richard as her son. She interfered in Mum and Dad's rows. She warned Dad to be careful or she would bring her sons over from Ireland to sort him out. Dad said she'd better bring the cousins and uncles as well.

Dad worked night and day foolishly believing that food and warm clothes were an adequate substitute for love and affection. His was the kind of love stored in the medicine cabinet in a bottle marked KEEP OUT OF THE REACH OF CHILDREN. A distant kind of love, impossible to appreciate. We never went hungry, but a hug is often more substantial than a hot meal.

I wanted his attention for so long and never got it. I wanted to make conversation with him but couldn't. I became disillusioned, convinced he hated me, I kept out of his way.

My dad is someone I have loathed and loved, someone I have hated and held in high esteem, someone I have fought with and cried over, someone I have longed to be close to. He was always too tough to admit he was wrong, always too angry to listen; a fighter, throwing emotional punches at the wrong people. I spent my childhood vowing never to be like him. I told myself, "If that's how a man acts I don't want to be one."

I never understood Dad's anger. When I was very young I didn't think about where it came from. Dad never talked much about his childhood. I know little about my grandparents Margaret and George. I've seen photographs, sepia-toned and frayed, Margaret (in the backyard with Pauline, May, and Josephine) wearing an apron, a tinker's grin, her face creased with hardship. Margaret was a tough lady and, unusual in a time when wives were basically handmaidens, she wore the trousers and knocked back the pints. She'd been a beautiful woman when she was younger. That's where Dad and Josie inherited their looks.

Dad felt pushed out by his family. He and his brother Davey were pretty much left to fend for themselves and kicked regularly like stray dogs. Their roles were defined, boys will be boys. Time taught them to clamp up, keep everything inside. It was a crime to show weakness of any kind.

Dad learned to solve all problems with his fists, whether on the streets of Woolwich or in the army. Attack was the best form of defense. He would return home every evening and head for his favorite chair in front of the TV, burying his head in his newspaper. He referred to the evening as "My Time." He would silence us by yelling, "You've had all day to make noise. This is my time." No one can imagine how depressing that was.

"Daddy, I caught a frog today."

"Shh, son, this is my time."

What he didn't realize was "My Time" was the only time we got a chance to be with him. He was always yelling at us to be quiet. He would scream at Mum, "Can't you put these kids to bed?"

"They're your kids too." Mum was always held responsible for the noise level in our house.

"For God's sake, shut those kids up."

"You made your bed, now lie in it."

"I've been working bloody hard today."

"Oh, yeh, and I went shopping at Harrods."

Mum was always ready with a sharp reply. She would goad him on until he went absolutely crazy and grabbed a piece of furniture. *Smash.* Something would go flying across the room, breaking several other things on its way. Dad would curse at the top of his voice. "Sod the lot of ya. You've got no bloody respect."

Mum always ran off to the kitchen or bedroom whenever Dad had one of his outbursts. Then she'd appear red-eyed ten minutes later, as if nothing had happened.

"Want a cup of tea, love?"

"No, I'll get me own tea."

The big green enamel pot was always puffing away on the stove. Dad liked his tea stewed not brewed—Mum called it Indian Firewater. There was a ritual when Dad came in from work. Tea, a cheese and onion sandwich, and then more tea. Too bad if you were watching your favorite TV program. When he walked in the door he expected to be obeyed. "Put the kettle on, son. Fetch us a hankie." We all hated doing it, and would try to get each other elected.

"Can't Kevin do it?"

"Don't worry, son," he'd say. "I'll leave you in me will."

More food was thrown than eaten in our house. Dad liked dramatic gestures, throwing his tray of food up in the air if we cheeked him back, knocking ashtrays over as he went to grab one of us darting out of the room. Half an hour later he'd have his arm round your shoulder. "You're all right, son. You're all right."

I couldn't understand why he hit out so much. That was the way he dealt with everything. I knew it wasn't right. I used to hate Mum for not stopping him. If you'd done something really bad he would march you upstairs. I'd scream the house down.

Dad's ambition was to have a family of boxers. Boxing runs in the O'Dowd blood. Dad's great-uncle Mick O'Dowd was World Middleweight Champion twice between 1918 and 1922. My great-grandfather's brother George was a prizefighter.

Dad wanted us to be able to defend ourselves. "It's tough out there, son." He brought home two pairs of old brown boxing gloves for us to spar with. I kept well out the way. He took us all to the local boxing club at Southend Crescent in Eltham. I did a bit of skipping, jumping, and knocking the punchbag. I was too scared and embarrassed to get into the ring. Gerald was the star boxer. He had the same dark looks as Dad, who saw a part of himself in Gerald. We all thought Gerald loved boxing. He hated it. He lived out the role to please Dad.

Dad was at his worst in the mornings. He exploded out of bed, screaming at Mum for clean socks and underwear.

"It's in the pile of washing by the bed."

"No, it's not."

Mum would whisk up the stairs and pull underpants out of the fresh ironing. "Try looking next time." Like most men he didn't realize that running a home was also hard work. I don't imagine he pictured Mum lazing around on a pile of silk cushions, but he still had no idea how much work she really did. Hers was the hardest job—housewife, mother, and emotional dartboard.

If I came home from school and the milk was still on the doorstep I'd know Mum was in one of her moods. Sometimes her sadness filled the house. You could feel it when you came through the front door. She'd be wearing her dressing gown and slippers, and that look on her face.

Most of the things Mum and Dad argued about were petty and pointless. Dad was quick-tempered, he cooled down fast. Mum held on to things. She said, "They say you hurt the ones you love. But it ain't right."

I resented Mum for not asserting herself. When she got all dressed up for her first driving lesson, Dad was mad with jealousy and chased the instructor out of the pan. Maybe he thought she would drive off and leave him. Sometimes I wondered why she didn't. I used to tell her all the time, "Don't let him treat you like that." Then she'd get angry with me, "You've got too much to say."

A lot of the arguments were about money, or the lack of it. Mum and Dad weren't scaling the social ladder, they were simply trying to fulfill their obligations—feeding and clothing their children, making sure we ate properly, that we never caught lice. Other kids were allowed to stand outside the chip shop, eating out of packets, their parents only too pleased to get them out of the house. We were fed at home. We ate good food, not "rubbish." And God help us if we left anything on the plate.

"Eat your food. There are kids starving in India."

I was always tempted to say, "Okay, Dad, name one of them." More often than not, I just kept my mouth shut and cleaned the plate. I'd heard of other kids going home to plain old bread and butter.

Mum would say, "My kitchen floor is clean enough to eat off." Only the dog ever experienced that pleasure. It was a clean home, cleaned from top to bottom every day. One reason Mum had to work so hard was that Dad brought his work home with him.

Our home was a builder's paradise, shovels and ladders blocking up the hallway, pieces of timber propped against the bedroom walls, fresh tins of paint, bags of cement. Mum hated the mess. She wanted a home that she could be proud of. "No, that's not a work of art, that's my husband's tool kit."

She was always changing the furniture around. It gave the illusion of space. She would do it in our bedroom. With a single bed and two bunks in a room roughly twelve feet square the options were limited.

I tried to help but mostly I got in the way, I had a mania for cleaning. I used to hoover around guests and clean ashtrays before they were finished with. Mum would snap, "Stop that, it's rude."

When Dad started talking shop, that would set Mum off about the mess. Dad would go into great detail about how he had unblocked someone's sewer.

"It stunk to high heaven. It stunk of s——"

"That's enough, Jerry. I'm trying to eat my dinner. And while you're at it you can clear the shit out of my house. It's beginning to look like number forty-five."

That was where the Kanes lived. A scruffy Irish family with a mysteriously bedridden father who slept in the corner of the living room. Their kids, Moyna and her brother Lee, went to the same school as us. Moyna was my friend. We used to sit in her bedroom and listen to the chart rundown on Sundays. When we were thrown out for being too noisy we'd walk the streets with a transistor radio to our ears. Moyna looked real Irish with freckles and bushy hair. She had a hard life at home always picking up for her dad and running errands to the shop. She was a bit sad—that drew me to her. My brothers used to taunt me. "Moyna Kane's your girlfriend, Moyna Kane's your girlfriend." I used to say, "Yeh, so," but Siobhan would scream when we said she was going out with Lee. Name calling was a daily ritual. My brother Gerald was "Paki" or "Back of the Jam Jar" because of his dark skin. David was "Dumbo" or "Flappers": he had big ears. Kevin's glasses earned him the name "Brains" and Richard was "Ginger" or "Spotty." Siobhan was "Poop Arse" and I was "Woman" or whatever other poof name was rife in the playground.

Uncle Jimmy and Auntie Heather Higgins lived next door at number 27; they were Mum and Dad's best friends. We called them Uncle and Auntie, even though we weren't related. We said their kids, Denise, Jimmy, and Sean, were our cousins. We shared our birthday parties, they'd come to family weddings and to Birmingham to stay with Nan. Denise and I were always together, running around the pan holding hands, dancing on the doorstep.

Jimmy was a merchant seaman and brought treasure back from around the world—Beatles wigs and posters from America, funny windup toys from Singapore. Jimmy had a drinks bar; it was his pride and joy, stocked with exotic bottles, jars of bright red cher-ries, silver soda syphons. We never had much drink in our house, the odd bottle of sherry at Christmas, a bottle of Warnink's advocaat for Mum's snowballs.

Heather looked after us on Saturdays while Mum went shopping. She made us Spam fritters with chips, eggs, and beans. I preferred that to the stew we got at home. Mum said, "It all goes down the same hole." I liked shaped food like Bird's Eye fish fingers and Findus burgers.

Dad was a great cook. He made the best roast dinner in Southeast London, though he hardly ever ventured into the kitchen. His bubble and squeak was legendary. He made a great fried breakfast on Sunday mornings. Mum hated him going in the kitchen. She said he would use a hundred pots just to boil an egg. Once, he made a delicious curry. And then announced while we were all scoffing away that we were eating our pet cockerel. It made us all feel sick.

When Heather and Jimmy moved to Charlton, Prossie Pam moved in with her retarded brother, Brain. He used to frighten us kids, we called him Quasimodo. We didn't understand what was wrong with him. Everybody in the pan thought Pam was a prostitute. There were always men going in and out of her house. "Dirty cow." She had two young kids. We'd stare at her bedroom window at night and watch the silhouettes, making up our own stories about what was going on.

One evening Pam's house went up in flames. Dad had just come home from work. He heard the screams and went running to help. He had to kick the door down. Pam and one of her fancy men had been at it in the front room. He was still pulling his trousers up, and he disappeared out of the pan like a greyhound. Pam was half naked, and Dad had to drag her out kicking and screaming. She was trying to go upstairs to get her savings book. She called Dad every name under the sun. Her two children were still in the bedroom. Dad managed to get them out.

Then there was Dracula, she lived at number 31. She was a real horror, waking everybody up at three in the morning, fighting with cabdrivers. "Bunch of fucking thieves. Piss off." Hanging out the window screaming at the police, shaking a stiletto at them. She wore microminis and hooker makeup. From behind she looked like a teenager. Workmen would wolf-whistle, and nearly fall off the scaffolding when she turned round.

Across the pan was Mrs. Scannon. She was la-di-da, with a silver bouffant and glasses dangling round her neck on a gold chain. She had a stripy plastic canopy over her door—she was dead posh. "Who does she think she is?" She blew hot and cold with us kids. She liked Kevin and took him to her chess club, but sometimes she was rotten, refusing to give footballs back if they went in her garden.

CHAPTER 3

I was trussed up in my crisp new uniform, gray flannel shorts with matching jumper, white shirt, school tie, and cap. The other kids had name tags sewn into their clothes. I wondered why I didn't. I thought it was because Mum was going to give my clothes away.

It was my first day at Middle Park Primary School. Everyone was crying. There was a Chinese boy with a runny nose. I couldn't drink my bottle of free milk. I could see him out of the corner of my eye, sniffing and dribbling. He was in most of my classes throughout primary school. He didn't stop dribbling for six years.

The first three years were easy, painting pictures, playing in sandboxes. The teachers were a mumsie lot tending to our tears and grazed knees. "There, there. It's all better now." As we progressed to long trousers, things got gradually worse. The teachers changed from roly-poly matrons into thin-lipped humorless tyrants. Suddenly we were required to grow up, snap out of it. The transition from infant to junior was like being woken up with a bucket of cold water.

Reading, writing, arithmetic. Such a shock to the system of a dizzy growing child. I had no concentration, I couldn't get my brain around geometry. I still don't know what it is, I don't care. I know that Pythagoras was a vegetarian. Lord knows where he got his hypotenuse from.

If I couldn't understand I'd get aggravated, and my mind

would shut off. I was lazy when it came to academics. I'm the same now with technology. I only learned to use my washing machine five years after I bought it. I would rather throw something on the floor than get wrapped up in how it works.

I was creative. I loved art, English (not the grammar part), writing stories, poetry. Of course, there were some subjects I would have been hopeless at whoever taught them. I'd sit in some classes and wonder whose idea it was to put me there. I always thought it was pointless to give us subjects that we hated.

I achieved top swimming honors and was picked for the school team. I bailed out when they wanted me to take it more seriously—I wasn't interested in the survival of the fittest. If you were good at sports, you could be brain dead, and the school would still be proud of you. "On the 'ead, on the 'ead."

Middle Park was only three minutes' walk from home. Still we were always late. Getting us out of bed was the difficult part. We were all hateful in the morning. Bad breath and puffy faces, barking and bickering around the breakfast table. Mum would make us porridge; its consistency changed with her moods. I liked it creamy and smooth with lots of sugar sprinkled on top. There would always be fights over who used the milk first. "Mum, Mum, the milk's run out." One of us would get a slap round the head. "Shut ya bloody noise. Eat ya breakfast and get to school."

I wanted to take a packed lunch to school, in a Tupperware container like the other kids, cheese sandwiches and chocolate digestives. Mum couldn't afford it: school meals were free and "quite sufficient." I plagued her so much she sent me to school with a bag of Pick 'N' Mix broken biscuits. I was so ashamed I peed myself on the way to school and had to go back home.

The O'Dowds had a rogue's reputation, not only with the neighbors but also at school. Teachers had us marked. We were blamed for everything, thanks to my eldest brother, Richard, who crazy-paved the way. Mum was always being called up to the school. One morning Gerald and David were caned in front of assembly. I had to sit and watch. Mum came swinging for the headmaster. He tried to placate her: "Remember the Old Country." She told him, "Don't you give me the Old Country. If I wasn't a lady I'd smack you with this handbag."

I was slapped by Miss Hobbs when I told her "Fuck off" in front of the whole class. She hit me so hard she left a bright red hand mark. Ever since a kid I've had sensitive skin. If someone just taps me I come up in welts—it always looks worse than it is. Miss Hobbs started crying. I felt sorry for her, but I opted for maximum drama and locked myself in the toilet.

The O'Dowds have been described as a large, close-knit Irish family. The only thing that made us close was the lack of space. We never had a proper holiday together. When we went to the seaside, it always rained. I hated the seaside, sand in your clothes and your sandwiches. It seemed stupid to sit on the beach when there was no sun. I'd always get lost and spend hours trying to find everyone.

We went to the Dreamland funfair at Margate and had to take turns on the rides—there wasn't enough money to go round. The rides turned my stomach, and what little pocket money I had dropped out of my pockets on the bumper cars.

Us boys would always bait each other. Someone would go too far. None of us had a great capacity for letting go. I would run off crying. It didn't take much to upset me. I would scream that I hated them, and I was going to run away and never come back. Ever dramatic. I thought about running away all the time. It's what Dad did when he had fights with Mum. You'd hear the door bang, and he'd be gone for hours.

Dad took us fishing in Deal, in the Kent countryside. We would all pile into the van, fighting with each other for the front seat. Otherwise it was in the back with the building rubbish. Dad used to sing sometimes, funny old songs that no one knew. It was nice when he sang. He used to shout out the window, "All right, darling?" Old ladies gardening would look up in horror and we'd all laugh. I hated fishing. It always seemed like a good idea when we started out, but I'd get bored quickly and moan about going home. I would sit in Dad's van slouched in the front seat with my legs up on the dashboard and arms folded, sulking.

When I was six, Kevin and I were sent off to stay with a family in Bath. Greenwich Borough Council set up a scheme to give poor kids the chance of a holiday. Mum dressed us up like evacuees, in shorts and long socks, tie and cap, and navy mackintosh with an address tag tied to the lapel. She was still spit-washing our faces when the train pulled out. She wanted people to know we came from a good home.

We arrived at Bathford, near Bath, in a state of wonderment. The house we were staying in was a mansion, Tudor style with wooden beams, covered in ivy. I could smell fresh-baked bread, cow dung. There were no car noises.

The family were posh, but nice. They had four kids of their own, two boys and two girls. The kids were nice too, they weren't spoiled. They shared everything. I was happy in Bath, even though I didn't want to go. I felt the shame of being poor. I worried they wouldn't like us.

We went on picnics and day trips to ruined castles. They made us honey sandwiches, me and Kevin thought they tasted 'orrible, we ate them slowly to be polite. Even though the kids were our age their parents talked to them like they were adults. It was strange. I wondered why I couldn't have a family like that. We went to stay with them two or three times—I looked forward to going back.

One year we stayed with an elderly couple who had no kids. The husband repaired dartboards. He used to drag us around the countryside, from pub to pub, making us stay in the van while he went about his business and had a few drinks. They shouted at us and made us go to bed early. The only good thing was her maca-roni cheese and late-night snacks. The husband slapped Kevin and he ran away. I was frightened and crying. We both wanted to go home. In the end we got sent to another family.

There were other trips. Kevin, Richard, and I went to a farm in Wiltshire. The couple that looked after us were hippie types. The husband had a beard, played guitar, and wore corduroy trousers, she looked like one of the New Seekers. They lived in the con-verted roof of the farmhouse. There was a big metal spiral staircase that you had to climb to get up to the roof. I was terrified of falling and had to have somebody with me every time I went out-side. They had no children, so we played with the farmer's kids who lived underneath. We'd get up at six to watch the cows being milked, and saw a calf being born. Those holidays were a special time in my life.

CHAPTER 4

We would go and stay with Nan in Birmingham, where she moved after Grandad died. She lived with Mum's youngest sister, Teresa. Teresa was partially disabled in a childhood accident—she's had to wear callipers all her life.

The first time I saw her was in the kitchen at Joan Crescent. Mum said her sister was coming to visit. I rushed home from school, always excited when we had guests. I couldn't believe what I saw. Teresa was four feet tall, with really long hair dyed half black and half white. She was wearing a chessboard dress and John Lennon glasses.

Nan was horrified at the way Teresa dressed. She would say, "Don't look at her, you'll only encourage her." I fell in love, I wrote her letters asking her to marry me.

Teresa would shout at us and wave her crutches if we tried to help her upstairs. "Get away. I'm quite capable." I loved her fighting spirit. Doctors told her she'd never have kids. She had two, Trevor and Vanessa.

Teresa got married in 1970 to Barry Gladwyn, a boy from college. Everyone was proud of her. We all went to Birmingham. Weddings were substitute holidays, full of joy, everyone smiling, like Christmas. We got to see our Irish relatives. Someone would always sing "Danny Boy" or a rebel song. Everyone clapped and sang along.

Mum looked totally glam. Her dress, shoes, and handbag matched perfectly, all edged in daisy trim. She had a beehive and wore spider lashes. We were dressed like ventriloquists' dummies, starched white shirts, elastic velvet bow ties and patent shoes, our hair slicked to our heads. Siobhan was dressed like a toy, a frilly dress covered in ribbons and bows, and a daft kiss-curl hairdo. Mum was always on the sewing machine making new clothes for Siobhan. She was spoiled rotten.

I hated the clothes Mum bought me, sensible "things that will last." I wanted bright colors, rainbow tank tops, red velvet split-knee loons, a sky blue satin jacket. She said I'd get bored with them in five minutes.

I put Mum's makeup on, blue and green eye shadow, salmon lippy, and pranced about singing into a hairbrush, "Metal Guru is it you. Yeh, yeh, yeh." Mum had the minimum of makeup, she never really used it. It was there just in case someone decided to get married. I was only just eleven but I wanted to dress like Marc Bolan and David Bowie.

I wanted girls' shoes, cork platform slingbacks like Bowie wore on his Japanese tour, they sold them at Shellys under the bridge in Deptford High Street. I held constant vigils. All Mum would buy were pathetic ones with half-inch soles. I begged her for proper stacks. She went to the flea market in Brick Lane one Sunday and came back with a pair of three-inch platforms. She thought I wouldn't wear them because they were so outrageous. I put them on straight away. I tried to get away with wearing them for school, but they sent me straight home.

When Dad cleared out houses he would find all sorts of good-ies—antique clothes, knickknacks, old picture frames, photos, rugs, and curtains. Once he brought home four *Sgt. Pepper* jack-ets. I wanted to wear one, he wouldn't let me. He locked them in the shed to rot.

Aunt Josie sent up some old clothes. They were much too loud and skimpy for Mum. I found an all-in-one silver Lurex catsuit and wore it round the house. "That's not for you. Get it off." I edged toward the front door. I wanted to waltz into the street looking like a Lurex legend. Dad wouldn't have it. Strangely, that catsuit disappeared.

Richard was a mad Bowie boy and Bolan fan. I borrowed his records and clothes when he was out. Sometimes he would pass on a pair of battered platforms or a groovy flared-sleeve unisex T-shirt. He kept the best things for himself. He bought his clothes at Paraphernalia in Lee Green or from Chelsea Girl, and wore his girlfriends' clothes, scoop-necked T-shirts with apple and rainbow motifs. I'd try to go off to St. Peter's Youth Club in them, and Richard would have a fit. "I just bought that. Get it off. Mum, George has been touching my stuff."

Richard's girlfriend Sandy wore bubble wigs and hot pants, white frosted eye shadow and stick-on stars around her eyes. Mum would tut when she saw her coming up the path. Sandy was loud and brassy, she used to kiss everybody. "'Allo, Di luv. Aw'right, Jerry." I thought she was the coolest girl in the whole of Southeast London.

If I was the pink sheep, Richard was the black, lying, wheeling, and stealing. Mum and Dad were always being woken in the middle of the night by the police. "Oh no, Jesus Christ, what now?" Richard and his thieving mates broke into Eltham Green School and stole the charity boxes. They got into the gym and played football, leaving fingerprints everywhere. Eventually Richard got sent to a detention center.

Whenever Richard got into trouble Nan would take him on holiday to Birmingham, buy him clothes, and pamper him. It used to upset the rest of us. Here was Richard, breaking the law, being a complete tearaway, and being rewarded.

Richard and his gang—Danny Hoolihan, Barry Foley, Pete Millburn—were glam hooligans, dressing as *Clockwork Orange* droogs for football matches, painting their faces silver to see Alice Cooper. There were lots of pop concerts at Lewisham Odeon, and Richard went to most of them. If he couldn't afford it, one of his gang would buy a ticket and open the side door. I would follow them, Richard told me to "sod off."

I hung around the stage door with my mates, Wendy Foley and Karen Foot. It was mostly girls there. We saw Rod Stewart being carried in waving a bottle of Jack Daniel's. His girlfriend, Bebe Buell, got spat at, she was pushing the fans out of the way. I got into the concert for nothing. He was brilliant.

Richard would jump from one pop star to another, Bowie, T. Rex, Alice Cooper. Somebody told him he looked like Rod Stewart, so he got himself the same haircut. He already had the nose.

He gave me my first Bowie album—*The Man Who Sold the World*. I learned the lyrics by heart. Bowie was something new. I loved the pop music they played on the radio, the Sweet, Slade, Wizzard. But this was different.

He swallowed his pride,
And puckered his lips.
He showed me the leather belt,
Round his hips.

I bought a copy of *Ziggy Stardust and the Spiders from Mars*. It was a huge leap from "Wig-Wam Bam."

A cop knelt and kissed the feet of a priest,
And a queer threw up at the sight of that.

When Ziggy Stardust and the Spiders from Mars came to Lewisham in 1973 I rushed to buy a ticket. Nan, who was staying with us, said Bowie was a "big woman" and that Mum shouldn't let me go. I had a big row with Nan. Dad took my side, just to spite her. He gave me the money for the ticket.

I tried to give myself a Ziggy Stardust haircut. It was a disaster— I looked like Dave Hill from Slade. Richard lent me his Indian patchwork jacket. I wore it with my white cheesecloth shirt and a pair of loons. I spent the whole day hanging around Lewisham, watching the crowd well up. Hundreds of Ziggy and Angie clones. Girls in fox-fur stoles and pillbox hats, boys in glitter jackets.

Bowie was like an alien. It was the most exciting thing I'd ever seen. The crowd were screaming, "David, David, over here, me, me, I love you." I was screaming too. Everyone was singing. I knew all the words, "Suffragette City," "Jean Genie," "Life on Mars," "Five Years."

I walked home singing into an empty Coke can. No concert I have seen since has had the same effect.

*   *   *

Richard sent us on errands, bribing us with sweets or the odd 10p.
It made him feel grown-up having us run round for him. He sent
me off to the chemist to collect some photographs; instead I
jumped on the bus to Beckenham. That was where Bowie lived, at
Haddon Hall. I spent the day standing outside with the rest of the
fans. Angie Bowie opened the window and told us to "fuck off." I
was really happy.

I was the youngest one there. We sat in the local Wimpy Bar.
The other fans talked about how many times they'd seen Bowie.
I'd only seen him once. Of course I lied. When we got bored we
went looking for Brian Eno's house. Eno was everyone's favorite
from Roxy Music, he had the best clothes.

When it got dark I started to feel nervous. My day at Haddon
Hall was going to end with a clip round the ear from Richard. I
got home about nine. Richard and Mum went mad. They couldn't
understand the pleasure of hanging around outside someone's
house. I didn't get to see Bowie. That wasn't important. I met
other people like me. I felt like I was part of something.

CHAPTER 5

Even as a child, I sensed my father's frustration. He was walking on the spot financially, things were just pulling him down. He had six growing children to feed, and rent and bills to pay on top of that. Life owed him more. Dad allowed the pressure to isolate him from the family. He allowed problems at work to enter his personal life until, eventually, there was no such thing.

"Eltham Decorators—We work to a standard, not a price." That's what it said on his business cards, and he meant every word. Dad was honest. He treated his clients like friends. They often returned the compliment by not paying up. He was a tough guy in every way except business.

His workforce was a motley crew of drinkers and tinkers with roll-ups behind their ears and family members down on their luck. When all else fails, go to Jerry, he'll help you out.

They would meet round our house first thing in the morning, and sit in the kitchen puffing and slurping endless cups of tea, driving me crazy with their inane comments, filling the house with the stench of Golden Virginia. It was a total invasion of privacy which Dad was oblivious to. It made us feel uncomfortable, not being able to eat our breakfast in peace. It drove Mum crazy too.

Dad started out decorating newly built houses, undercutting other firms, working evil hours to build up a reputation. After years of grafting he won a contract with the Quadrant Housing

Association converting old properties for the homeless and those on probation. This meant he had to expand his workforce. He had several jobs on the go at one time, and he would drive around all day from site to site in his beaten-up green Bedford van geeing his workers out of their tea breaks, trying to meet deadlines.

Dad started to make decent money. The problem was not how to spend it, but how to stop him giving it away. Mum watched him waste a lot of money on horses and fair-weather friends who were only too willing to help relieve the burden. When anyone cried, Dad would always be there with a builder's bucket to catch the tears. He was terribly compassionate when it came to strangers and relatives.

Mum would complain about not having a decent washing machine, about Dad not decorating the house. "Just because you live with a builder doesn't guarantee you're going to get your house decorated." She was right. It took Dad about ten years to decorate the kitchen.

Dad hated to be on his own. He'd let us kids have days off school so that he would have someone to talk to on his travels. He would break up his day with constant visits to greasy caffs for fry-ups and tea. He'd always end up sitting there for hours talking to people. Like Bubbles the drag queen who ran a caff in Dulwich. Bubbles used to perform at the Valley Club in Charlton and spent his days dishing up sausage, egg, and chips to butch builders. They all loved him, a big roly-poly queen who would cut them down to size if they dared make a snide remark.

Dad was a popular face in Woolwich, Dulwich, Peckham, the Old Kent Road. You couldn't walk down the street with him without someone saying, "Aw'right, Jerry." He would often leave me sitting in the van for hours. "Sorry, son. I haven't seen that bloke for years." Dad loved to be surrounded by characters, buying them cups of tea, listening to their twisted tales. Some of them were quite Dickensian with faces like thousand-year-old trees.

Bill Pooley was a lovable rogue who would talk of being torpedoed in the war. His favorite word was "sub," not as in submarine, but as in subsidy. He would pawn his bicycle for a sub to buy a pint or have a bet. He would put all his money on a horse, and lose it. When Dad gave Bill a job he always left him a spare gallon of emulsion. He knew Bill was going to steal some, he allowed for that so there was always enough to finish. Dad defended him. He said he made his life richer.

Our cousin Terry Coulter was on the workforce. He was six foot with shoulder-length hair and a mouth like five hundred Millwall supporters. He was cute and not quite as geriatric as the rest of them, but it took him just as long to get out of bed.

Then there was Albie Lake. Dad took him on at the request of the probation service. Albie's gambling had put him in jail. He was a magpie—he would steal anything that wasn't nailed down. If he didn't turn up for two or three days Dad knew he had won on the horses. His family rejected him, he was homeless. When Dad was converting a property he would make one room an office, install a camp bed and it would become Albie's temporary home. If anyone asked questions Dad would say Albie was guarding the tools and the property.

Uncle Alan was a criminal type with a Che Guevara beard and shifty eyes. He would work for Dad when he wasn't fencing furniture. Alan was married to cousin Tina, Terry's sister. She ruled him with a rod of iron. She was an ex–go-go dancer with tits like slaters' nail bags, long bleached blond hair, and eyelashes that stroked the sky. She looked like she had stepped out of a Mike Leigh play. I liked Tina. I liked her arrogance, her cockiness. She was so different from Mum, crude and bawdy.

Alan and Tina's flat had every mod. con. He would get her anything she wanted. Unfortunately he forgot to pay for it. I baby-sat for them when they went to parties. It was great fun watching Tina get ready to go out. She would spend at least an hour applying her mascara, layer after layer, and then spend at least another hour fixing her hair. She wore massive hoop earrings and A-line halter-neck dresses and platform boots like you've never seen.

She was insanely jealous. One Saturday she was in Woolworth's with Aunt Josie, Mum, and Alan. There was a promotion going on for Uhu glue. The girl behind the counter shouted to Alan, "Yoo-hoo." Tina started punching her out. Mum hid behind the sweets counter.

Tina would be horrible to Alan, but there was also a soft side. Deep down she was terribly insecure. Once when I was baby-sitting I had to hide with little cousin Billy in a bedroom while she was throwing her platforms at him.

She could be hilarious. She once gave me some money and asked me to get her a record called "Beneath the Knee." "You know the one, 'Beneath the knee, I'm so in love with you.'" She meant "Denis" by Blondie.

She was always generous with her husband's money. Every Friday he would hand over whatever he had and she would carry it around in her fat purse.

Tina and Terry were Aunt Josie's kids, Dad's sister. She was married to an ex–professional boxer and convicted armed robber, Billy Coulter. He spent seven years behind bars, wrecking what little family life they'd had.

Josie was a sad and lovable woman. She was stunningly beautiful, with the same Romany complexion as Dad. She dressed like a teenager when she was in her thirties and forties, skimpy minidresses and seamed stockings. She had an incredible figure even then.

There were always rows in the family over her. Dad really loved her and was always bailing her out. Billy treated her badly, kicking her and the kids out of the pub they ran. She always went back to him. While Billy was in prison, Josie turned to drink. She waited faithfully for him to be released only to be met with rejection.

Josie would often spend Christmas with us, along with Auntie May. She would hide bottles of drink all over the house and try to act sober, but everyone knew what she was up to. One Christmas we were just about to have dinner when Billy turned up ranting and raving outside the front door. "Get her out here." Dad went after him in a rage. Josie was crying, saying how sorry she was for ruining our Christmas. Mum braved on, dishing up the Brussels sprouts while all hell broke loose.

When Mum fell out with Josie, she told us we weren't allowed to visit her. We sneaked round. I liked to visit Josie. She looked after us and fed us up. She made us pub sandwiches and gave us pickled onions. She was one of the few adults I felt comfortable around, I still miss her. Auntie Josie died tragically in 1979 from an overdose of pills and alcohol. Soon after that Dad lost his only brother, Davey—he also died from alcohol abuse—then his sister May died. Dad was distraught, burying three of his family in one year.

Uncle Davey was like Dad's twin. Except for Davey's gammy eye they were almost identical. Davey was hit by a scaffold pole when he was a schoolboy. The injury took away a lot of his confidence. He worked for Dad right up until he died. I baby-sat for his and Aunt Jan's children, Emma and Lisa. I stayed over at their house most weekends. They were like a second family.

Auntie Jan was a hairdresser. She gave me a proper Ziggy Stardust. I cut out a picture of Bowie from a pop magazine. "Make sure you cut it properly. It's got to be exactly like this." It was perfect. Spiky on top, short round the ears, and long at the back. The only thing wrong was that it wasn't orange. I went to school and everyone laughed at me.

When Uncle Davey died I was really sad, I couldn't believe it, both him and Josie were dear to us kids.

Dad was never a drinker. He liked a flutter on the horses or the dogs. I would often go with him to Catford dog track or White City. I could never see the point of it. But Dad used to get a thrill if he got lucky. Sometimes he would win a fortune, but he can't have ever got back what he put in. Mum would nag him about wasting money.

"It's my bloody money and I'll do what I like with it."

"It's our money."

Saturdays, Dad would be out all morning placing bets at the bookies and then spend the rest of the afternoon glued to the TV. "I knew I backed the wrong horse," he'd say. "Story of my life."

He told Mum, "I only bet small amounts, love." She knew it wasn't true.

As with his aggression, Dad has never been able to face up to his gambling. It was never just a bit of relaxation on Saturdays, it was every day. If he was ever missing, Mum would say, "He's at your Uncle Charlie's." For years we never knew who Uncle Charlie was. Eventually we found out. It was Charlie Webb's betting office in the high street.

All my brothers went to work for Dad (I preferred to paint and decorate myself). All of them at one time or another went through the ritual of sitting outside the betting office, waiting in the van. Dad would say, "All right, son. Don't say nothing to your mother."

CHAPTER 6

Eltham Green School was like a backstreet abortion—it happened, I wish to forget it ever did. There were no proud moments, no major victories—just long days, months, and years of complete boredom.

Any signs of self-expression or individuality were crushed immediately. Words like "insubordinate," "cheeky," phrases like "toe the line," "get in step" I heard a million times.

My school reports said, "O'Dowd is bright. He would achieve more if he looked at his books instead of out of the window." I spent most of my time at Eltham Green comprehensive looking out of the window, dreaming, gossiping, scrawling obscenities on the desks.

I had no encouragement at home. We weren't made to sit down and do our homework like in the movies where parents pressure their children, "You've got to become a lawyer. What will happen to you when you leave school?" You didn't need an education to be a builder. Mum and Dad were too busy to show an interest in our schoolwork. They left it to the experts, they thought we were in good hands.

If you arrived late for school you were made to wait outside the assembly hall in the black-and-white-tiled concourse. You had to stand on one of the black tiles with your arms by your side and your shoulders back like a conscript.

At 9:30 A.M. Dawson, the headmaster and resident Hitler lookalike, would ascend the stairs from the assembly hall. Latecomers were his breakfast. He'd circle around you, eyeing you up and down with a crazed glare. If you were late often and your excuses feeble, it was off to his study for a beating.

"O'Dowd. Why are you late?"

"Dunno, sir."

"Don't know? O'Dowd."

"Got up late, sir."

"Wait outside my study."

Before Peter Dawson arrived at Eltham Green it had been a school with a bad reputation. Dawson had a reputation of his own. He was a first-class authoritarian and advocate of corporal punishment. Eltham Green was his big chance. You only had to look at him to see he had an ego the size of a barrage balloon. He was a midget of a man, yet wielded immense power and control. Not only with pupils, but teachers too.

He would parade the school in mortarboard and tassel with matching black pin-pleated cape, peering through the glass partitions in the classroom doors. If he spotted someone not concentrating, or talking, he would fly in like a demented bat. "Outside." It infuriated the teachers, and undermined their authority.

He spread terror over the P.A. system, calling out names during lessons. Momentarily you'd feel like a hero, walking out of class, everyone wondering what you'd done. But as you got closer to the corridor of fear the terror set in. You would be made to wait, sometimes for an hour. That was the worst part.

Dawson had a glass cabinet full of canes, various shapes and sizes. Some hurt more than others. He would point to one and make you fetch it. "Bend over." He would always wait before he hit you. Everything was done methodically. He savored the intimidation. This was meant to teach you respect.

Along the corridor from Dawson was the deputy headmaster, Mr. Deacon. He was unconvincing in his role. He looked like he ought to be carrying a sawed-off shotgun and wearing a stocking over his head. He was physically intimidating, flat-nosed with a vicious crewcut. He would at least listen before he lashed out.

Miss Klein, our library attendant, looked like the victim of a medieval stretching rack. Her vivid pink lipstick clashed ludicrously with her corduroy maxiskirts and ruffle-necked blouses.

She waltzed around the library as if on invisible casters, hushing every whisper and the occasional riot; boys pulling books from the shelves and letting them crash to the floor. "That's enough," she would shriek. "Silence, silence." Children were a ghastly annoyance.

Our English teacher, Miss Tyler, was a class act. She would leave the door open and strut in and out like a pensive hen. She wore pearls and expensive knitted dresses. She rolled her Rs and did a perfect Southern belle when reading *Tom Sawyer;* a frustrated actress. "You're a bit of a freak, aren't you?" she told my friend Tracie Carter. "She should know."

Mr. Riddock, the art teacher, was brilliant too. He educated on a superior level. He would drop plates on the floor and scream, "Class has begun."

"Right," he would say. "I don't want anyone using my class to draw or paint like a spastic nun. Use your imaginations." In his class we were allowed to have one. I would draw pictures of Robert Plant and Marc Bolan with naked women reclining in their hair. Bowie as the Diamond Dog. I did a pencil drawing of my sister Siobhan that was hung up in the school. It was the last thing I saw the day I was expelled.

Drama was fun too. Our teacher, Mrs. Cankitt, was a blond hippie type. She made us roll around the floor or pretend to be trees. Her classes were taken outside the main building in an adjoining hall. You immediately felt a sense of freedom. We took advantage of Mrs. Cankitt's gentle nature, we gave her hell. She wasn't the type to send you to the headmaster. Mr. Cankitt, her husband, was our history teacher. I couldn't believe they were married, he was so camp.

My eyes were always on the clock during class, waiting for lunch break. I loved the taste of the school cabbage and mashed potatoes. I would eat plates and plates of it, going back for more.

I sat with the girls at lunchtime, Tracie Carter, Shelley Hughes, Tina Parmenta. There would always be a teacher somewhere in the dinner hall. You couldn't even eat without their beady eyes on you. McIntyre was the worst. He used to make me move tables.

He couldn't understand why a boy would want to sit with girls. "What could you possibly have to talk about?" I pitied his wife.

Mum was a dinner lady at Eltham Green, and did playground duty, which meant patrolling the girls' toilets, making sure they weren't being defaced. She caught one girl writing our phone number on the toilet wall. "If you're looking for sex call 856—" Mum locked her in the toilet and made her scrub it off.

During a normal school day we would have three recreation periods, one around 11:30 A.M., one at lunchtime, and one in the afternoon. We would be shoved out into the playground, rain or snow. Most of us would hang around the large gray concrete area, the more athletic types would play football. I never understood why anyone would do it voluntarily.

Some pupils were brave and went for a smoke behind the gyms. Fights were started. "What you staring at?" "Dunno. It ain't got a label." Fists would fly and a crowd would gather. "Kill 'im, kill 'im."

A few boys used to pick on me. I warned them, "Touch me and I'll get me brothers on to ya." Mostly it was just name calling. "Bum bandit." "Shirt lifter." I hated fighting. Some boys would wait for me outside the gates. I would escape over the fence or through one of the gardens that backed onto the school.

I had a fight with a ginger-haired boy who kept taunting me. "Your family are all wankers." I was about to get off the bus when he punched me in the face. I grabbed him and started banging his head against the metal stairs. Everyone was cheering. "Go on, O'Dowd. Sort him out." The conductor stopped the bus and threw us off. The fight continued on the pavement. I was punching him and ripping at his clothes. Kicking him with my wooden platforms. Afterward I walked home through the woods in tears. I hated that feeling of anger. I wanted to kill him.

Whenever I looked at my timetable and saw "gym" I'd feel ill. Mum wrote me notes. "Please excuse George . . . " When she refused I'd write them myself. McIntyre, our blood-faced gym teacher, would screw up the notes, "Get ya kit on, O'Dowd. Don't be such a big woman." I hated him, sadistic git. He was a recurring nightmare, head of year and gym teacher. Having him for PE was a joke. How could someone who looked like a bludgeoned haggis teach us fitness?

He would bellow at me across the football pitch, "Pick ya feet up, lassie." I stayed as far away from the ball as I could, shuffling from foot to foot, giving the illusion of participation. There was no chance of me taking a pass.

Ninety minutes of torture. I froze in my regulation shorts. Then the embarrassment of communal showering. Normally I wouldn't take a shower, but if McIntyre was vigilant you had no choice. I tried not to look at the other boys. I kept my eyes to the floor. "Oi, O'Dowd's looking at your dick." "Bender." I would be stripped, dipped, and dressed in seconds.

Once McIntyre made an example of me in front of the class to warn other "shirkers." He gave me a choice. "Hand or backside?" I held out my hand. He hit me so hard I bled. I ran out of school crying.

Mum brought me back and went looking for McIntyre. The teachers had their own floor where they would smoke, swear, and bemoan their fate. Hypocrites. She went along the corridor. "Where is he?" She called him a big coward and told him to keep his hands off me. Mum's rage gave McIntyre more ammunition. He taunted, "Don't upset O'Dowd, he'll bring his mum up the school."

Mum's school visits were legendary. When Gerald was at Middle Park they banned him from going on a school trip. Mum stood in front of the coach. "If he can't go, no one's going." The teacher outsmarted her. "He can go if you go with him." Mum had curlers in and was only wearing a nightgown under her coat. The coach left without them.

CHAPTER 7

Mum had been on the council list for a bigger house for years. She plagued them with letters and phone calls. Dad had tried too. Mum stopped paying the rent as a protest; she put the money into a savings account. The council threatened us with eviction. Mum was defiant. Finally they relented and offered us another house.

When they sent us our new address, Mum suggested we went and had a look. The new house was a couple of miles away near Oxleas Wood, at the top of Shooters Hill. I was moaning about how far I'd have to walk every day.

When we found the right number we both stood there amazed. "Can't be it." I climbed onto the window ledge and gave a detailed description of the inside. We still thought we'd made a mistake. It had a huge stone arch over the doorway and a glass-paneled door with THE CREST written across the top. It was just like the houses I'd admired for years in Blackheath.

I was so happy when we moved, in September 1974, even though I still wouldn't have my own room. There were four bedrooms. One for Mum and Dad, one for Richard, one for Siobhan, and one for David, Gerry, Kevin, and me. It was still cramped. I used a wardrobe to partition off my own area. I painted my corner orange and chocolate brown. I had a mushroom lamp with a silver lightbulb. I covered my wall with pictures of Bowie, T. Rex, and David Cassidy.

*   *   *

I could sense my brother Gerald's animosity toward me. I played up to it. "Yeh, you're hard. Go on, hit me."

We always argued at the dinner table. I would take my food upstairs on a tray and eat on my own.

"Snob. You think you're better than us."

"Fuck off, Paki." I had a choice, to feel insecure or superior. I chose the latter.

I was ironing my clothes, getting ready to go out. Gerald kept pulling the plug out of the wall and knocking the ironing board. I lost my temper, picked up a tin of paint, and threw it at him. It exploded over Mum's brand-new Axminster carpet. I started to scream and cry. Both of us were running around the house grabbing towels to mop up the paint before it dried. I tried to use the Hoover to suck it up. It got blocked. I was making it worse, spreading it everywhere, walking it all over the carpet. I must have ruined about twenty good towels.

In the midst of all the panic I caught sight of Dad's silhouette against the front door. I heard him coughing. I knew he'd kill me. Barefooted I ran for it, out the back door, over the fence, into the freezing cold. I ran about a mile and hid in a phone box. After a couple of hours I made a reverse charge call. "I'm sorry. I'm sorry." Dad was cold. "Get home now. Don't make it worse for yourself." Mum was merciless. The paint did come out, but it left a discolored patch, a permanent reminder to think before you throw.

Kevin was older and thought he could tell me what to do. He would creep up behind me and pull my earphones off when I was listening to music and shout in my ear, "Oi." I was watching telly, enjoying a plate of egg and chips. He came in with his mates. "What you eating that for? It's nearly dinnertime. Did Mum say you could have that?" I told him to stop showing off. "No one's impressed." He pushed me. I lunged my fork at him, catching him in the elbow. It dug right in. He was writhing around on the floor. "He stabbed me, he stabbed me." I ran upstairs and locked myself in the bathroom. I could hear him going on downstairs.

I used to cause trouble by opening my big mouth at the wrong time, poking my nose into other people's conversations. I did it when Mum and Dad were arguing. Not knowing when to shut up was one of my greatest faults.

I spent most of my spare time with Mum, shopping or down at the welfare office. I would make comments about everyone I saw. "State of her. Slag. Ugly bitch." Mum would tell me off. "Why don't you shut up? You've never got anything nice to say about anyone." She was right. I knew I was different. I'd started a one-man battle—myself against the rest of the world.

Dad hated it when I answered him back, especially if what I was saying was true. He expected us to behave in a way he could never behave himself. Explanations were never offered as to why we could not do certain things: "Because I said so."

I would mumble under my breath, "Pig." If he heard me he'd give me a whack. I'd run out of the house screaming, "I hate you. I hate you." I'd be terrified to come home.

The others would tell me to shut up in case Dad took it out on them. It wasn't so much that I minded making Dad a cup of tea, it was the way that he spoke to us. There was always an air of tension when he was around. You could never be sure what would upset him—a bad day at work, a job that hadn't been finished.

I found a porno magazine in a builder's skip and hid it under the cushions on the settee. Dad found it and pulled it open in front of everyone. I thought he was trying to embarrass me. I swore at him. "Fuck off. I hate your guts."

He chased me up the stairs and started banging on the bath-room door. "Get out here."

He punched his fist through the door and pulled it open. I tried to run past him. He caught me with a swipe, I tripped and went flying down the stairs and whacked my head on the radiator.

I was screaming, "Look what you've done." I could feel the blood pouring down my face. Dad was panicking. "I'm sorry, son, I'm sorry." I flew out the door in bare feet and ran to my girl-friend Ruth's. I must have looked like I'd been in a road accident. Ruth's mum was a liberal divorcée. She thought it was disgusting and said I could stay there. I hid out for four days. I didn't ever want to go home. Mum eventually tracked me down. I told her I wasn't coming home unless Dad promised never to touch me again. I was fourteen and too old to be treated like a baby. Dad got on the phone, said he was sorry. I went back to Shooters Hill, terrified. He kept his word and never hit me again. The ranting and roaring carried on. I kept out of Dad's way and out of the house as much as possible, staying round at friends or just wandering around Blackheath looking at the big houses. I went window shopping, staring in furniture-shop windows at the showpiece living rooms, making mental lists of things I'd like to buy. I thought about making loads of money and buying Mum the kind of house she really wanted. Perfect, with no builder's junk.

It was hard to be close to Dad or forgive him because he couldn't stay calm for long. His displays of affection were rigid and usually came after an insane outburst. When he tried to put his arm round me I would flinch like a nervous dog. Because of that I found it hard to let anyone touch me, even in the most innocent way. If a friend was walking too close to me on the pavement I'd get agitated and I was always pulling away. "Don't touch me, don't touch me."

I tried to play the straight boy. I had girlfriends though there was never much to it. Laura McLachlan was my first official girlfriend. She was a wispy blond with a lisp who went to a neighboring school, Eltham Hill. Laura would wait for me outside the school gates. All the "dickheads" fancied her, they couldn't understand what she saw in me. We'd walk off holding hands. She was so pretty I felt like I'd got one up on all those boys who picked on me. Laura looked like one of Charlie's Angels, she had a flicked fringe and carried a purse with a steel comb sticking out. I wore four-button high-waisted flares and a green acrylic polo neck tucked into my trousers. I'd take Laura to cousin Tina's when I was baby-sitting. The perfect setting, nothing really happened. We'd peck and cuddle, and rub up against each other. Laura was as passive as I was. What I needed was a Brenda Ritchie type who would initiate me and be done with it.

There were other girls, Shelley Hughes, who went to Eltham Green. She was small and round-faced with frizzy hair and a posh voice which marked her for persecution. Snobs, poofs, and Pakis were the scum of the earth.

I never went hunting for girlfriends, they always came to me. A smile, a rumor, a bit of school gossip. "Shelley Hughes fancies you." I'd seen Shelley around school. She always smiled at me. God knows how we ever got it together, we were both hopelessly shy. I was all mouth when it came to cheeking teachers or around the playground. When confronted with romance I fell apart.

Shelley lived in Lewisham with her mum and two sisters. Their house was "modern open plan": leather couches, sheepskin rugs, and a paper-moon lamp. It wasn't a home like ours. It was beautiful, but you couldn't relax. Mrs. Hughes didn't like us sitting in the front room. If you stepped on the rug Shelley would quickly shake out the footprints. We stayed up in the bedroom out of the way, a huge poster of David Essex staring down at us. She was mad on him—she dragged me to his concert at Lewisham Odeon.

With Shelley the cuddling led to more, but not much more. I got aroused sliding my fingers into her bra, she wouldn't let me take it off. It was the first time I'd got an erection with a girl. I wanted to go further, I couldn't. The fear was so physical. I held on to her and hoped it would happen by itself.

We had a good laugh when Shelley missed a period. Her mum thought I had made her pregnant—some chance. I swelled with pride that I might even be thought a candidate. Shelley's best friend, Tracie Carter, was amazed to find that after nine months we hadn't got any further than touching each other up. Tracie thought I was a wanker anyway and this confirmed it.

Tracie and Shelley had been friends since they were five. They fell out when Shelley started seeing me. Tracie was a hard case, with a Suzi Quatro feather-cut hairdo, floor-length waisted jean coat, and ripped sneakers. She was one of the school troublemakers, along with Susan Sledge and Tina Parmenta. They were the prime suspects when used Tampaxes were found littered on the concourse roof. Tracie defaced her school clothes, scribbling names of bands on in ink, and had the word BUM strategically placed on her skirt.

Tracie thought Shelley was too "girlie," a monumental crime, and took the piss out of her voice. Shelley was always reading out street and shop signs. "Woolworth's . . . Lee Green Road . . . " Tracie cruelly mimicked her, calling her a "Wimpy" and a "Burger." She made Shelley's life a misery. Tracie was vile to me too. I liked her toughness even though I didn't like being told I had a fat bum.

Things got awkward when Bowie announced his Station to Station tour at the end of 1975. It was six months away but we wanted good seats. Tracie wanted to come to the show but didn't know how to bite her lip. I called a truce by buying her a ticket. She said she'd pay me back, but she never did. After that Tracie and I became best of friends and she became official gooseberry, much to Shelley's distress.

Tracie was my way out of a relationship that was obviously going nowhere. I was fond of Shelley, she'd been a sweet and loyal friend, but she was looking for something I could never give. The voices inside my head were getting louder. "Go forth, my son, and plant your twisted seed." I knew I was gay, I was having technicolor wet dreams about boys. Tracie was the perfect female companion. She was independent, tough, and didn't fancy me one bit. She thought of herself as ugly and hated all things pink and sentimental.

I'd go to Tracie's after school. It was a brown bread and Earl Grey teahouse. They had uncut loaves and real butter, not Stork margarine. We made toast and tea and listened to records. It was peaceful there.

I asked Mum, "Why can't we have brown bread?"

"Fuck off back to Tracie's if you don't like it here."

Tracie had a massive influence on me—she turned me on to Bob Dylan and politics. She played Dylan's song "Hurricane" over and over again and explained the story of Rubin "Hurricane" Carter, the black boxing champion who was jailed for murder.

We'd call the Capital Radio Hitline and vote for Bob Dylan, putting on fake voices to bump up the votes, listening religiously to see if we'd kept him at number one. The Dylan albums belonged to Tracie's mum, Rita, who was in the middle of a divorce from Tracie's dad, who lived like a stranger at the top of the house. Rita was hippie trippie, a nonconformist. She belonged to the Communist Party and did relief work for Vietnam. One Christmas Tracie and I helped out, stuffing and licking down envelopes for the cause.

Rita was an enigma. I hardly ever saw her, and neither did Tracie. I envied Tracie being left alone in the house, I wished I was her. I never knew how lonely she felt. She hid it with her anger.

I was fast discovering other ways of living, different bread, different butter, not content with the four corners of Southeast London. I wanted to travel and see things. When I rode on the train I'd gaze out at the hundreds of thousands of lit-up windows. I'd think about the millions of people living out there. Would I ever know them? Would they ever know me?

I was there to meet Bowie at Victoria station in May 1976 when he came back from his exile in Berlin and gave the shocking fascist salute. I had my head stuck through the barriers, screaming. Bowie had abandoned the drag of Ziggy Stardust for the Thin White Duke: slicked-back hair, white shirt, and pegged trousers. I copied the look, wore one of Dad's white shirts, and greased down my hair. I wore it for the concert too.

Shelley dressed down in an old lumberjack shirt and jeans; her only concession was a smear of lip gloss. Tracie looked like a Greek soldier in her outfit, pilfered from Shelley's mum's wardrobe. She spilled Ribena down the front. Shelley was freaking. "Oh my God, she'll kill me." We managed to clean it and get it back in the cupboard without being found out.

I looked pathetic next to all the brilliant Bowie clones with dyed hair and makeup. I made up for it by singing every word to every song as loud as I could. I made Tracie whistle and scream in between songs. I thought maybe Bowie would look up and see us.

During the heatwave summer of 1976, Tracie disappeared to the grassy plains of Wimbledon to live with her grandmother, who was recently widowed. Life without her was miserable. I kept writing and plaguing her to come back to Eltham Green. She came back for a while and I got expelled soon after. I didn't see her for a good year. We met on the bus in Blackheath. I was a punk with white spiky hair and bondage trousers. Tracie had gone all sixties, cat eyeliner, white lipstick, a beehive, and Dusty Springfield's old wardrobe. She was living in her friend's garden shed and dating a cool-looking guy called Brian with a Louise Brooks bob. They had their own beatnik group singing Andrews Sisters songs with an acoustic guitar and maracas and went busking around Europe. Later Tracie and Brian moved into a council bedsit in Deptford. I used to visit them all the time and listen to Tracie's traveling stories and political doctrines. She hated Margaret Thatcher with a vengeance and convinced me too. Tracie has drifted in and out of my life since school. She took over one of my squats, then we lost contact again.

Fame, drugs, acid house. I ran into Tracie at a rave in 1990. She had a bare midriff and looked like a proper girl. These days she calls herself Miss Carter and is still as brilliant as ever. She is doing a degree in Spanish and Latin American studies. It looks like we both proved the headmaster wrong.

CHAPTER 8

I started seeing Ruth McNeale, a soul girl who hung out at St. Peter's. She dressed like the black girls from Peckham: gold chains, Gabicci jumpers, pencil skirts, and espadrilles. We'd go to soul nights at Greenwich Town Hall and to the Fox-on-the-Hill, dancing to Archie Bell and the Drells' "Soul City Walking" and "Midnight Train to Georgia" by Gladys Knight and the Pips.

I went out with girls for the sake of it. Somehow you felt better if you had a girlfriend—everyone else had one. I kept getting myself entangled in pointless relationships. Unwittingly I targeted insecure girls and made them feel more insecure.

Ruth confided in her friend Tracy Burch. "George never comes near me." The lack of physical contact made her feel ugly. She wondered what was wrong with her. Ruth's frustration came out in many different ways. "You don't care about me." Maybe she couldn't summon up the strength to say, "You don't fancy me." Sex was too much of a taboo. Her fear created a safe environment for me, and plenty of headaches. That's how I managed to avoid the clinches.

Tracy Burch's shrieking style embarrassed Ruth. Tracy was thirteen. Her spaceship hairdo was the most exciting thing in New Eltham, bright red with a butchered green medieval fringe. It looked like she'd cut it herself.

Ruth said Tracy encouraged me to look stupid. "How can you

go round with someone who looks like that?" Tracy wore all black; tight leotards, fifties dirndl skirts with layered petticoats, a black beaded handbag, and winkle-picker stilettos. I wore garish Hawaiian shirts, blue workmen's dungarees, plastic sandals, and odd fluorescent socks.

Tracy and I were both exhibitionists. There was an immediate intimacy between us that infuriated Ruth and made her feel left out. Tracy was Ruth's best friend, and she wished she'd never introduced us. She said Tracy was trying to steal me away. I said there was nothing going on. Ruth wouldn't believe it. She told me I had to make a choice.

I didn't fancy Tracy, even though she was very pretty. I liked her because she had style. She didn't have a small-town mentality. Her sister's boyfriend was *bisexual*! She didn't think there was anything wrong with it. Michelle, her older sister, was an Angie Bowie clone. She had plastic dungarees. I thought she was really amazing.

Tracy got her strange haircuts for free by modeling for students at Vidal Sassoon's and at hairdressing exhibitions. Michelle was a trainee hairdresser, and used to practice on her too. Tracy took me to Vidal Sassoon's training school. I watched them dye her hair pink. I was so jealous—I knew I'd get strangled if I went home with dyed hair.

I knew Tracy suspected I was gay. She used to ask me if I fancied any of the male hairdressers. "He's nice. What do you think of him?" They were all spindly queens with wedge haircuts and jumpers tied round their shoulders. I laughed it off. I didn't dare tell her I preferred builders.

During the summer holidays of 1976, I spent most of my time with Tracy visiting every charity shop you could reach on a Red Bus Rover. We rumbled around jumble sales hunting for forties clothes and shoes. Tracy's mum worked in a fabric shop and brought home exotic fabrics: suedette, rubber, plastic, and industrial nylons in Day-Glo colors. We couldn't afford the clothes that were sold on the Kings Road, in Acme Attractions, and Sex, or the Beaufort Market, so we made our own. A lot of stuff came from Oxfam. Instead of us donating to their charity, they donated to ours. We would go into the changing rooms and put the clothes on under our own.

Mum took secondhand shirts apart at the seams. I dyed the sections different colors and she'd sew them together. We copied the style of Bryan Ferry wearing GI shirts and army Sta-Prest trousers from Laurence Corner government surplus store. I went back to school wearing forties drainpipes and a slim tie.

"Oi, Grandad. Got your dad's clothes on, then?" When I said my clothes were from Oxfam, they couldn't believe it.

"What's the matter? Haven't your parents got any money?"

"You get athlete's foot from secondhand shoes. Ugh, you don't know where they've been."

Everyone at school was still wearing flarcs and feather cuts. The only trendier ones were three black girls; one of them, Michelle, had a pink streak in her hair. I was a fan.

I was full of myself, the height of fashion. But I still had a horrible haircut.

Tracy said they were looking for models at Glemby International in the West End. Mum let me take the day off school. She made me promise not to have anything ridiculous done. I'd already had a run-in with Dad. I colored my fringe blue using the inside of a felt pen.

"What the bleeding hell's that in your hair?"

"Nothing, it washes out."

"Well, wash it out now."

At Glemby they gave me a wedge and took photographs of me for *Hairdresser's Journal*. I'd wanted a wedge ever since I'd seen Bowie on the cover of *Young Americans*. They asked if they could dye my hair. "Just a brownish tint." I was too embarrassed to say my mum won't let me. It was dim in there, it didn't look that different. When I got outside into the daylight I looked in the side mirror of a parked car, it was more orange than brown. I waited till it was dark before going home.

Mum grabbed me as soon as I walked in the door. She pulled me under the light. "What did I tell you? It's bright fucking orange. You won't be able to go to school. Why did you let them dye it?"

Sure enough they sent me home from school. Dawson said it would encourage other pupils to flout regulations. Mum explained to Dawson it would have to grow out. She wasn't going to let me dye it again. Kids shouted at me from the tops of buses.

"State of your fucking hair."

"Oi, Quentin Crisp." Quentin was a regular taunt at school ever since *The Naked Civil Servant* was shown on TV. I watched it openmouthed. A man on TV with dyed hair openly admitting, "I am an effeminate homosexual for all the world to see." Mum and Dad were embarrassed, I was glued to the TV. It was the talk of the school for weeks. Everyone thought he was "disgusting." I thought he was brave and stylish, I wanted to meet him.

Kids at school had always called me a queer, a poof, and a pansy. I stopped caring. "So what if I am? Takes one to know one." I didn't want to be part of their boring little world.

My wedge was a shock sensation. "Why you got a girl's haircut?"

I arrived late for school again. "O'Dowd. Why are you late?"

"Dunno, sir."

"Must have been all the work you did on Friday."

"I wasn't here Friday, sir."

"Correct, O'Dowd. Do you think you can abscond from school with hair that color and not be seen? Get to my study."

My visits to school were becoming more infrequent. I shrugged at careers advice. I just wanted freedom. I longed for that day. I bunked off school, hung around Eltham High Street or Oxleas Wood, or took a bus to the West End.

I knew the only way out was to get expelled. I walked out of the Special Needs Unit at lunchtime, went to the local shops, bought a loaf of bread and scooped it hollow, buttered it, and filled it with chips. On my return I was sent to Dawson for the final showdown. He screamed and ranted.

"O'Dowd! Think about your parents. Think about what you're doing to them." He paced the room, tapping his palm with the cane.

"I don't want to stay here," I told him. "I hate this place."

"You'll never make anything of yourself, O'Dowd. You're a fool."

As I left the school Dawson's voice echoed down the corridor. "Don't worry. You'll be back."

September 29, 1976. "Dear Mr. and Mrs. O'Dowd, I am writing to inform you that I find myself with no option but to officially suspend George from school."

The next day Mum dragged me back. I sat in Dawson's office, my head bowed. Mum asked one simple question.

"Do you want to stay at this school?"

"No."

Mum took me out of school at the risk of being prosecuted by the education authorities. She told them I'd gone to stay with relatives in Ireland.

Years later Dawson and I continued our feuding. He was the head of the Professional Association of Teachers. Newspapers queued up for his wisdom.

George O'Dowd was a classic example of the word 'misfit'. He did not fit in and he did not want to. I went to the school in 1970 and it was a place running under very difficult conditions. Discipline was the only way to bring it under control.

George came there after we had straightened things out. He did not like the fact that you had to behave and work. He did not get on with his teachers and he did not get on with the other boys and girls.

At the time there was no evidence he was in any way confused as to whether he wanted to dress up as a boy or a girl. But there was one thing he was not confused about: he did not want to work. He was a perpetual truant. He would not come to school and would not work when we got him there.

He wasn't a hard case and didn't mix with the difficult boys and girls, but he ended up in our sanctuary unit, run by a master with experience of difficult children.

Even there he had to be watched all the time. If he asked to leave the classroom that would be the last you saw of him.

Dawson's views generated a heated correspondence in the *Times Educational Supplement* in 1984 over whether as a headmaster he should have spoken publicly about my education. It was typical of Dawson to run off his mouth. He couldn't understand how I'd become successful.

CHAPTER 9

When I left school unemployment was the highest it had been since the war, not that I cared, I had no intentions of working. For a couple of months I avoided the subject, rolling out of bed when I felt like it. A wonderful feeling, no panicking running out the door with half my breakfast still in my mouth. The euphoria was short-lived. Mum started nagging. "Don't think you're going to sit around here all day. You wanted to leave school. You'll have to get a job. I ain't gonna keep ya."

Reluctantly I started visiting the local careers office. Hard as they tried they couldn't find a suitable job. I was offered a wonderful future in dishwashing, kitchen jobs, local factories. They asked me what I saw myself doing.

"I wouldn't mind working backstage at a theater company, or training to do makeup, something creative."

They looked at me as if I was crazy. "Mr. O'Dowd, these types of jobs are rarely offered. You must try to be more practical."

I knew I couldn't just walk into a job at the Royal Opera House, or as Lindsay Kemp's personal dresser. But if I was going to work, it would have to be something I'd enjoy. Eventually I had to take a part-time job at Tesco's in Eltham High Street. I had the creative role of shelf-filler. It was the most annoying job. As soon as you'd arranged the tins of peas some housewife would come along and grab one off the bottom. Still, I had my first job, even if it was just one day a week. I was giving Mum a couple of pounds toward the housekeeping. I felt that I could now start doing exactly what I wanted.

I slipped a box of Clairol hair bleach into my pocket at work. I'd decided to go blond and Tesco's were going to foot the bill. I locked myself in the bathroom and applied the contents to my already hennaed hair. I didn't know red was the hardest color to remove. My hair turned out like a Dulux color card: orange, yellow, white. It was great. I managed to avoid Mum until the next morning. She came into the bedroom to get me up. "Come on. Get up. I don't want you in bed all day." She screamed when she saw my hair. "You animal! You're not to go out of this house. D'you hear me?"

She came back from the shops clutching a packet of black hair dye. "Get in that bathroom and get that shit out of yer hair."

I liked my new hair color. I pleaded, "What's wrong with it? It's my hair."

"What's right with it? You look like a scarecrow." Mum's little plan was a total failure. My hair turned blue-black. I was happy, I looked like Patti Smith. Auntie Pauline came round. "Oh, my Gawd. What ya done to yer hair? Makes you look really ill."

Mum said, "Should have seen it half an hour ago. It was canary yella."

Shoppers at Tesco's did a double take when they saw me in my gingham overalls, odd socks, and plastic sandals. They looked at my spiky hair. "'Ere. Put your finger in a socket, did ya? Look, it's Ken Dodd." The supervisors turned a blind eye to my coif. They didn't care what the slave labor looked like. Whenever I could, I would retreat to the stockroom for a catnap behind the dog food. My clubbing made me far too tired for strenuous shelf-filling.

I was always a little late for work, fifteen or twenty minutes. I'd roll in with dog's breath and sleep in my eyes. I didn't care about the job—the eight pounds they gave me hardly kept me in hairspray. My life revolved around the night. I couldn't wait for the day to end, to throw off my overalls and rush home to get ready to go to the Black Prince.

I only did the job because Mum made me, she wouldn't let me go on the dole, not while I was "big and ugly enough to work."

That was remedied, however, when Tesco's gave me the sack for shoddy timekeeping. They expected me to work out my one day's notice. I was livid. For five weeks I'd been a selfless employee. I pushed over several pallets in the stockroom and stormed out.

Mum ordered me to find another job. "Quickly." I browsed through the local paper and found myself a weekend job, collecting glasses at the Tiger's Head pub in Chislehurst. The landlord was unperturbed by my dyed hair and bright clothes. The job required little skill. I topped up my paltry wages by syphoning off the soda syphons from the cellar and returning them to off-licenses. I got 50p a bottle. I was terminated after a fracas with a pissed customer who ordered me to pick up a broken glass. I told him, "You dropped it. You pick it up." I found out the customer is always right in poncy, leafy Chislehurst. My glass-collecting days were over.

Laura McLachlan was my constant companion—we were like "girlfriends." Our relationship had always been platonic and that's why we remained close, even after our hopeless schooldays romance. She lived in a large musty mock-Tudor house over in Eltham Park, a five-minute walk from Shooters Hill through Oxleas Wood. Her house swallowed ours. What furniture there was was Victorian and threadbare, faded elegance, a pale blue chaise longue, a ripped leather sofa, a frayed Chinese carpet.

Home life was unpredictable, if not unstable. The kids, Laura, Andy, and Charlotte, had full run of the house. Olive, their mother, lived close by with her boyfriend. Their dad lived miles away in Catford. Andy and sister Charlotte were twins. They couldn't have been less alike. Charlotte was into the Eagles, Bad Company, and Led Zeppelin. She kept to herself, adopting a parental role, ordering the others around in vain. Andy was a soul boy and reluctant punk. We called him "Splinter," "Twizzle," or a "Streak of Piss," the last only out of earshot. He was gangly and translucent. I'd joke he'd get lost on a zebra crossing.

Laura's parent-free environment was a safe place to experiment with our brave new wardrobe. We spent hours swapping clothes, putting them on back to front, gelling our hair. I played makeup artist on Laura and her schoolfriend Lorraine Price. My makeup skills were yet to be perfected.

Andy was a trainee hairdresser. We marveled at his hairdressing skills, begging for free haircuts. He shaved a huge V out of the back of my hair. "Oh, my Gawd," Mum squawked. "You look like you've 'ad an operation. It looks hideous." I would constantly be looking over my shoulder joyfully registering the looks of horror. Andy used us as guinea pigs, shaving track lines into our hair, giving us lopsided cuts.

You never knew when Olive would appear, flapping and snapping, demanding to know why the freezer was empty, why there was no bread. They lived in constant dread of her visits. Laura was rebellious: "You can't just come here when you like and tell me what to do." She goaded me to be cheeky to Olive. I tinted my hair in their bathroom and wrote KILL OLIVE on the tiles in hair dye as a joke. Olive was not amused and threw me out. Usually she just blew in like a hurricane, issuing orders and chores, going out as fast as she came.

Olive was outside my experience; she fascinated me. She had the look of a retired headmistress, manic and scolding, gray hair, pointy features. She wore tam-o'-shanters and green tartan shawls, long pleated skirts and flat shoes.

I was envious of the McLachlan kids. They had freedom. Olive's visits, however neurotic she was, were scarce. It seemed a heavenly setup. Olive would bark at them to be in at a certain time but they still came and went as they pleased.

Thursday nights Laura, Andy, Lorraine, and I went to the Black Prince in Bexleyheath, a Tudor-style pub stuck on a roundabout in the middle of a dual carriageway on the A2, where they held a freaky disco in the functions hall. No buses went there. You'd have to cadge a lift or pay for a cab. I would often walk the five miles home or get Dad to pick me up. I did anything to get there. The music at the Black Prince was mainly disco and funk with a bit of Roxy Music and Bowie thrown in. Most of the crowd were into the soul look: Smith's American jeans, bright-colored combed-out mohair jumpers, wraparound shades, and winkle-pickers. Some of the more full-on types were starting to wear plastic bags and trousers, feather earrings, safety pins on their clothes and in their ears.

I made lots of new friends at the Black Prince. Jayne Morgan was a leading face, six-foot-two with Jagger lips and a bin-liner dress. She had her own gang, Screaming Siobhan, Horse Face Terry, Quiet Beryl, Sarah, Cara, Andrea Arnold, and Lenny with the badger hairdo.

The local *Kentish Independent* newspaper ran a story: "Way Out in Bexley—It's the Arnolds." It was October 1976, and all the papers were on the lookout for punk rockers following the first shock-horror reports in the Fleet Street tabloids. They mockingly called us the Arnolds after Andrea Arnold told them she was our leader. When the story was printed people shouted at us in the street, "Oi, Arnold." It was my first taste of fame and I loved it. I copied Jayne and made myself a cut-price outfit out of a Tesco carrier bag, and wore it as a vest with a baby's dummy round my neck. Jayne was one of the many girls I looked up to. She was cocky and had a sex life. She encouraged me to go after Lenny the badger, who I'd had my eye on for weeks.

Lenny's hair was cropped tight with a white streak down the middle like Steve Severin from the punk band Siouxsie and the Banshees. I was sure he was queer, but then I thought everyone was. He used to look at me all the time. Finally I snogged [kissed] him at a party. The lunge was sponsored by vast amounts of Pernod sucked desperately through a straw. I was all hands and tongue. It took ages to get his fly undone, I didn't dare look down. His dick was shaped like a banana, but it felt good to be finally holding one in my hand.

Lenny was my first boyfriend and naturally I wanted to tell the world, or at least all at the Black Prince. He wanted to keep it quiet. He was first in a long line of boys who couldn't make up their minds until they'd had a few beers. The sex was groping and infrequent, in a dark corner at a party, up a quiet alley. Despite or because of this I fell madly in love. Love for love's sake. I was cloying and desperate.

Lenny and I were walking through Blackheath Village on our way home from a club. I saw a gang of boys coming and made him hold my hand. They shouted, "Queers." Lenny started to shout back. I told him to shut up, they'd probably kill us. We were lucky they walked away. A few weeks earlier we'd been jumped on by a gang of black boys at Crayford station. Lenny had got hurt. He screamed, "Don't tell me to shut up." I said I didn't want him to get hurt, but he wouldn't listen. He kept shouting, "Don't tell me what to do. You don't own me." I told him to fuck off. He ran off and left me in Blackheath. We never spoke again. I was distraught. Of course, he'd used the situation to get rid of me. There was no reason for him to be so hysterical. He wouldn't answer my calls, his parents kept saying he was out. I went and stood outside his house and stared up at the bedroom window. I wanted him to see me and realize what he'd lost.

Deranged with self-pity I downed a bottle of Christmas whiskey and a half bottle of gin. I ran maddened into the night, and ended up in the middle of the road on Welling High Street, three miles away. The woman who brought me home thought she had knocked me over. I was in a right state. To this day the smell of whiskey or gin makes me retch.

While dancing at the Black Prince I knocked a drink out of a soul boy's hand. He punched me and grabbed me by the throat. "I'm sorry, it was an accident." His animal reflex scared the life out of me. I grabbed my coat and got out of there as quick as I could.

That was the trouble with clubs in suburbia. The thugs always outweighed the trendies. Soul boys were football hooligans with wedges. If you looked at someone the wrong way, or said the wrong thing, you were liable to get hit.

"Spill my drink."

"Look at my bird."

There had been a couple of violent incidents at clubs around the area. The naffer soul boys got upset if they saw you wearing plastic or something that wasn't "normal."

Jayne hired a minibus so that we could go to the Lacy Lady in Ilford, the premier soul club. I wore my Tesco vest and faked a safety pin going through my lip. Our crowd were the most punky there. I hated it and wanted to leave. The aggressive glares from the speeded-out soul boys made me nervous.

At weekends we went up to the Global Village, better known now as Heaven, underneath the arches at Charing Cross. The bouncers would often turn me away, I looked so young. Going to the Global was the highlight of my week, my life. I loved it there, even though it had its fair share of soul boys. I would chat to everyone in the queue, cracking jokes, putting my face about, befriending those who could get me in on their membership.

The queue was as exciting as the club. Everybody killed to dress. The screaming Trotter sisters, Debbie and Jane: they wore loud fluorescent clothes and had mouths to match. They would bound round the corner into Villiers Street shouting, "The Trotters are here. Make way for the Trotters." Outside was one big fashion parade, everybody pointing and nudging. "Look at him." "Look at her." You didn't have to be rich or famous. If you had the "look" you were a star, whether you were boring Brenda from Billericay or skinny George from Woolwich.

Fashion was no longer being dictated by the High Street chains. We joked, "Soon they'll be selling bin-liner dresses in Dorothy Perkins."

However, at home fashion was being dictated.

"You're not going out the house looking like that. Jerry, look at him."

Dad peered up from behind his paper. "It's all right, if he wants to get beaten up."

Mum carried on. "What about the neighbors?"

I laughed. "You don't speak to the neighbors. Who cares what they think?"

She blocked the front door. "I'm not letting you go out like that." She moaned about my wedge when I first had it done. She hated my Hawaiian shirts and builders' dungarees. But rips and safety pins pushed her to the limit. I'd have to put my punk clothes in a carrier bag and throw them out the bedroom window, go out in my soul norm and get ready at Laura's.

One weekend we all wore pyjamas and nightclothes. Jayne brought her teddy and sucked on a dummy. I wore a pair of blue-striped psychiatric pyjamas from Oxfam. People thought it was rag week and tried to give us money. We bundled into the photo booth at Charing Cross and fought over the pictures. "That one's really good, I want that."

All of our crowd would catch the same train—Laura, Andy, Jayne, Andrea, Lorraine, and myself. Everyone would hop on at their stop along the Dartford Line, our freaky heads popping out of the windows. "Up here, quick. Up here."

CHAPTER 10

It must have seemed well dodgy, a fifteen-year-old boy walking around Heathrow airport at three in the morning with no money. I was a real eyesore. My hair was milk white and spiky, my clothes splattered with paint, covered in pins, chains, and padlocks.

The police nabbed me the minute I reached Terminal Three. I couldn't believe my luck. I'd taken tubes, buses, and trains, walked for miles, only to be arrested and dragged off to Heathrow police station. It had seemed like a good idea when I left home the previous night. Mike was coming back from South Africa. I wanted to surprise him. Some surprise.

"Look, son, it'll make things easier if you tell us his name."

"What flight's he coming in on?"

I looked up at the two police officers. The room was violently bright. I was tired and scared.

"Don't you understand? I'm gay. No one's forced me to do anything."

"You're underage, son. This gentleman's committing a serious offense."

I held my head in my hands. I couldn't believe this was happening.

"We're going to need a statement from you."

"Why? What have I done? Why can't you just let me go?"

I carried Mike's letters with me in case Mum found them. He'd sent me two or three from South Africa. "I can't wait to get back and do all the things I've dreamed of" and other perversities. Thank God he hadn't signed them. They were initialed "Love M." There was no address.

The police searched me and found the letters, they promised not to tell my parents, then said they had to due to my age and the seriousness of the offense.

I started to cry. "Why do you have to tell them?" I was terrified of what Dad might do. What if they arrested Mike? What would happen? It would cause so much trouble.

The police kept hounding me. Leaving the room, letting me sleep for half an hour, and then bursting in.

"Come on, son, tell us his name."

"I'm not telling you anything."

Mike was my second homoneurotic experience. Laura spotted him staring at me at the Global Village. "He fancies you. He fancies you." She was excited at the prospect of us having sex. I was too scared to approach him. It went on for weeks. We'd see him every Saturday at the Global. His beady eyes were all over me.

We called him "Bumble Bee" because he always wore a black-and-red-striped mohair jumper. He had a shaved head and wore leather trousers.

Laura spoke to him. She came running back. "He likes you. Go and speak to him." I went over, shaking, sick with nerves.

"Do you wanna meet me tomorrow night? We'll go to a film."

"Okay. That'll be nice." I made plans to meet him at Waterloo Station, 7 P.M. Sunday night. We went to see *The Omen*. Afterward we went back to his flat. I was totally intimidated. My previous experiences had been quick grope sessions in corners at parties. I'd never actually gone to bed with a man. I was frightened, he was a complete stranger with mad eyes, he might kill me, and no one would know where I was.

Mike couldn't wait to get me into bed, he didn't even offer me a cup of tea. He hurried me out of my clothes. I felt like a Sindy Doll. There was nothing romantic about it. The room was cold, the bed was hard, he had ginger pubes and a flabby bum. I had hoped for much more.

I left the next morning with mixed feelings. I felt liberated, and a little disappointed. I couldn't wait to get on the phone to Laura. I went round for tea and told her all the gory details.

"Did he do it to ya?"

"Do what?"

"You know what I mean."

"Oh no." I was horrified. "I wasn't going to let any old bumble bee deflower me."

It was 9 A.M. when Dad finally arrived at the police station. He spoke to the police, then they left us alone. I was crying and crying.

"What's going on, son?"

"I know you already hate me. Now you've got a reason."

"I don't hate you, son. I just want to know what's going on."

"Haven't they told you everything? Haven't they shown you my personal letters? They had no right to read them, they're mine."

Dad took me home in the van. My brother Richard and my cousin Terry Coulter had come along for the ride. I was angry Dad had brought them. I cried all the way home.

The next evening I was taken to Shooters Hill police station for more questioning and a medical examination. They checked to see if I'd been sodomized. It was humiliating. Mum and Dad were convinced I'd been molested. I kept telling them over and over that I was gay. Why couldn't they understand?

Mum said, "Why didn't you tell me? Why didn't you tell me?"

What was I supposed to say? "Pass the sugar, I'm queer."

Dad took my brothers out for a drive. "I want to tell you something about your brother Georgie. He's a bit funny."

David said, "What do you mean? Funny ha-ha or funny peculiar?"

Dad wriggled and mumbled, trying to find the right words. "Well, Georgie's a bit different, yer know."

David teased, "No, we don't know. But if you're trying to tell us George is queer, we know that."

There was a bad atmosphere at home. I felt exposed. Mum didn't speak to me properly for a few days. She wanted me to promise not to see Mike again. I told her I couldn't.

"What kind of man is he, going with a boy your age? I don't want you seeing him, do you hear me?" Dad didn't talk about it.

I fought with Mum every time I wanted to go to the West End.

"I know you're not twiddling your thumbs up there." She was worried. I thought she was trying to control me, stop me having fun. I was bratty and impervious to her feelings.

"You don't care about me." I thought she hated me because I was gay.

"It's because I love you that I won't let you go."

"Do you think I'd just go off with somebody?"

"It's not that, son, there are cleverer people than you."

We stayed at war for weeks. Finally she made a conciliatory gesture.

"I've left something for you in your drawer."

It was a record, "The Killing of Georgie" by Rod Stewart.

Georgie boy was gay I guess,
Nothing more, nothing less.
A victim of these gay days, it seems.

I did see Mike again. I went to his house in the mornings when I was supposed to be doing my paper round. I was always worried about the police following me. Mike was worried too.

At first I thought Mike was dead trendy. He had a £60 Sex jumper. I was impressed. But really he was just mutton dressed as punk. One Monday morning I had the pleasure of seeing him in his work clothes: blue polyester pin-striped suit, white shirt, college tie, and Hush Puppies. Frightening. What really pissed me off was that he wanted me to leave the flat with him when he left for work. It was nice to be trusted.

The following Saturday he let me lie in while he went shopping. I was out of that bed and into the drawers in seconds. I stood on a chair and pulled down some boxes from on top of the wardrobe. My God, pervert. The boxes were full of child pornography, books, pictures, magazines.

When he came back he asked me why I hadn't cleaned up the kitchen. It was my cue to work a drama and leave.

"I'm not your bloody maid. Clean it yourself."

"You could at least help out if you're going to stay here."

"I'm not." I grabbed my coat and slammed the door behind me.

CHAPTER 11

The Filth and the Fury," "Who Are These Punks?" Every day a new shock-horror headline to cut out and safety-pin to the back of your jacket. The soul clubs quickly changed their dress policy, fearful of the punk reputation.

"Sorry, no punks."

We'd slouch away. "Boring gits."

Due to a lack of funds we had to be very artful with our styling. The essential ingredients were clothes "liberated" from Oxfam and Dylon fabric and shoe dyes from Woolworth's. When I couldn't find the right shade of pink to dye my Jesus sandals, I used some of Dad's emulsion. They looked perfect until I started walking. When our experiments failed we'd go back to Oxfam for more pilfering. Even when bought, the shirts were only 10p and 20p. That was before Oxfam became an outpost of Habitat.

We'd pick the sequined collars off twenties dresses and sew them onto a jacket, get Mum to taper baggy old trousers. She laughed. "These look like the trousers your father married me in."

We'd buy old pairs of socks, cut holes in them, and wear them over our own, creating a punk polka-dot effect. We ripped up shirts and trousers and safety-pinned them back together, girls deliberately laddered their tights. The DIY punk look was simple to achieve, though we all longed to shop at Sex and Acme Attractions.

Saturdays, we'd parade the Kings Road in the same clothes we wore to clubs, full of our own superiority. We'd walk slowly from Sloane Square to World's End and hang around outside Malcolm McLaren and Vivienne Westwood's shop Sex, daring each other to step inside. Entering was like testing the water in a freezing pool.

Jordan, the psycho-hived manageress, was every bit as intimidating as the premises, a small dark shop with a sloping wooden floor and blacked-out windows. She dressed like a sadistic Tiller girl, carried a whip, and hissed at customers. Hers was a very modern sales technique.

Sid Vicious worked there before he was a Sex Pistol. He was a sweet boy in those days, goofy in Hawaiian shirts and fifties pegs, congenial to Jordan's sneer.

Sex clothes were so expensive. Skimpy ripped T-shirts £30. Mohair jumpers £60. Anarchy in the U.K.? More like Avarice in the U.K. Still, I would have bought them if I'd had the money. Mum would never have given me £30 to buy a T-shirt, especially one displaying naked prepubescent boys.

We'd try the clothes on in Acme Attractions, fluffy fake-fur jumpers with plastic see-through breast panels, rubber tops, and trousers. I wanted plastic dungarees, but they looked horrible on me. I got Mum to copy the clothes, tight black T-shirts with zips across the nipples. "I should open me own shop. This stuff takes five minutes to make." Mum didn't understand the importance of a Sex original.

My DIY home-painted purple winkle-pickers came in handy for my first court appearance. I went forth remembering Quentin Crisp's triumphant trial where he dazzled the authorities with his style and wit. Mum told me to "keep it shut," so I kept my head bowed and hoped for the best.

My thieving technique had never failed me before. I unfurled a wire coat hanger, leaving the hook intact, and pushed it through shop letterboxes pulling out whatever I could from the window display. Most of what I got was useless, a nylon shirt, a fake snakeskin plastic belt. Nothing that I'd ever wear. It was just the thrill of getting something for nothing.

I dragged Tracy Burch with me on one of my pilfering escapades in New Eltham. Someone spotted us and alerted the police. I saw the police car coming down the road, pushed the hanger through the letterbox, and pretended to be snogging Tracy. The car stopped and a policeman came walking toward us. He beckoned to me. "Can I have a word, son?" I panicked and ran like hell.

He caught me, I grabbed him and spun him round, pushing him to the floor, ripping his shoes and the knees of his trousers. I tried to run again, but was headed off by the car. Two other policemen grabbed me and threw me into the backseat. My heart was pounding. The officer I sent flying jumped in beside me and punched me in the face. I became hysterical. "Fuck off. You can't touch me. You won't get away with it."

They were laughing. The policeman in the front shouted at me, "We can take you round one of these back alleys and give you a good hiding and no one would know anything." I covered my face and cried. An innocent childish prank had suddenly become very ugly.

At Eltham police station I was punched again, strip-searched, and thrown into a cell. I kept screaming that I wanted to see my parents. They ignored me and left me in the cell. My eyes, nose, and lips were swollen. They tried to swab me with cold water, I pushed them away. They could see how bad I looked and were worried.

When Mum and Dad arrived they went mad. Mum was crying. "Who hit you, son, who hit you?" I pointed at the ginger-haired copper behind the desk. Dad went for him. "You want to hit someone your own size? You fucking coward." The other officers held him back. Dad went out and phoned A10, the internal investigations department at Scotland Yard. He said he wanted them to take pictorial evidence of my battered face. They came and photographed me and I gave a statement.

I was charged with attempted theft, resisting arrest, and assaulting an officer. The police didn't know I was only fifteen years old and that they'd committed an offense by strip-searching me and keeping me in the cell for so long without informing my parents.

I was given a conditional discharge and advised to drop my complaint against the police. Dad and Mum were angry, but we all decided it was for the best.

Most of my days were spent riding around in Dad's Bedford van, keeping him company. He'd give me a few pounds here and there and keep my stomach full. Nothing could compensate for the boredom of sitting outside Charlie Webb's.

"Won't be a minute, son."

I hoped he'd have a big win and be done with it. Maybe Mum would get a new washing machine and I'd get one of those Sex mohair jumpers I'd had my eye on for God knows how long. I broached the subject with him several times.

"Not now, son."

It was all about moods with Dad. You had to wait for the right moment. It was best to swoop when he was smiling, telling bad jokes, or if he had a glint in his eye coming out of the betting office.

"Dad, I've seen this really nice jumper."

"How much is it?"

"Sixty quid."

"Gawd strewth."

I nearly fainted when he gave me the money.

"Don't tell your mother."

I was terrified traveling on buses and trains. Everyone was a potential enemy once punk had gone national. The *Sun* newspaper printed a picture of a teddy boy, brick in hand, announcing war between punks and teds. The Sex Pistols appeared on late-night TV and then on *Thames Today* effing and blinding at Bill Grundy. Suddenly the whole thing exploded.

Before that people smiled at us benignly, thinking we were going to fancy-dress parties. Their tolerance soon turned to intolerance. Now we had a name. We were spitting, snarling punk rockers.

By the end of 1976, anyone who was anyone was punk. Soul boys splashed paint on their Smith's jeans and wore ripped T-shirts. They tried to make themselves look scruffy. You could spot those with sensible jobs.

Hundreds of teddy boys appeared on the streets with gum-chewing bobby girls on their arms. The girls were worse than the boys, cocky bitches, sneering at us in disgust. "You're all bent. Go 'ome and 'ave a bath."

There were many varieties of ted. Greasy Gene Vincent clones in leather jackets, black Levi's, straddling Nortons and Triumphs. They were my favorites. They made me weak at the knees. One, because they were tasty; two, because they wanted to wring my scraggy punk neck.

There were traditional spiv teds in drapes and bootlace ties, brothel creepers and fluorescent socks. I drew caricatures on toilet walls of teds giving each other blow jobs with the slogans "Rock Around the Cock" and "Rockabilly Willie."

The rivalry between punks and teds attracted idiots spoiling for a fight. The Kings Road was divided. Teds one side, punks the other, police in the middle.

Punks bastardized drapes with safety pins and wore paint-splashed brothel creepers to annoy the teds. I was punched in the face and booted several times for wearing brothel creepers. Every time I saw a quiff in the distance I would run. "Teds, teds, quick, run." They filled me with terror.

Punks wanted to destroy the past, they jeered at nostalgia and called Elvis a fat pig. I loved Elvis, he was the world's most beautiful rock and roll hero. I had a collection of Elvis records and other fifties classics, Eddie Cochran, Buddy Holly, the Platters.

I dressed down for my first proper job interview: army greens, black T-shirt, leather jacket. I flattened my dyed hair. I still looked like a freak. Mum was sure no one was going to employ me looking like that.

She was wrong. I was taken on as office boy and messenger at Red Tape Printers in Hanover Street, in the heart of the West End. My £24 weekly wage seemed a fortune. Most of my time was spent on tubes and buses. I whizzed around town delivering parcels. In the office I made tea and stuffed envelopes.

I slowly broke in my new employers, a bondage strap here, a zip there. My hair rose slowly over the first few weeks. My office colleagues suppressed their sniggers in true British fashion. There were no memos from the boss.

Mornings, to save time, I'd take the 192 bus to Lewisham and catch the fast train. I was always nodding off, falling on some innocent commuter seated beside me. "Do you mind." I'd straighten up, apologize, only to slump to the other side. One morning, as I struggled to stay awake, my bleary eyes fixed upon a large pair of brothel creepers glaring up at me from Platform 4. A massive ugly ted worked as a guard at Lewisham station. He was harmless while on duty, though he did his best to make me feel uneasy.

"Oi, punker. Tell your mates to meet us down at Margate."

"What mates?" I inquired.

"Yer know, the rest of your lot."

"Oh, go away." I twitched nervously. Where's the bloody train?

"You're all a bunch of fucking wankers, you lot."

A barking granny jumped to my defense. "Young man, mind your language. Kindly go where decent people are not. I shall report you to British Rail."

He skulked off. "I'll see you later."

All trains to Charing Cross stopped at Lewisham. The brain-dead ted would be on the lookout for us punks. We'd shout insults as the train pulled out. "Oi, Jaffa legs."

Once he blew his whistle and stopped the train. "Off. Come on, the lot of ya." Me, Jayne Morgan, and Terry sat there giggling. We knew he couldn't do a thing.

CHAPTER 12

Laura and I tried to get into the Monday soul night at the Lyceum Ballroom, off the Strand. The penguins on the door were merciless. "Sorry. No ripped clothes." We rolled our eyes and hung around on the pavement, wondering where we could take our dancing feet.

A swishy boy in rubber trousers threw us a lifeline. "Why don't you come to Bangs? You can wear what you like there." We followed him eagerly.

"By the way, it's a gay club. You don't mind, do you?"

I caught my breath. What luck. "Will we definitely get in?"

"She might have a problem. But they're normally okay. They let girls in if they look right."

Laura was wearing her fake snakeskin PVC coat and matching mini, I sighed with relief.

I arrived at Bangs in Charing Cross Road, quivering with anticipation. My first gay club. What would it be like?

The queue went round the corner into Oxford Street. I'd never seen so many queers. Fat ones, thin ones, butch ones, camp ones. They greeted each other with hugs and kisses.

"Hi, girl."

"Ooh, look at her."

"Varda the lallies."

"Look, Sue Catwoman," Laura squealed, squeezing my hand. I glared at her to keep cool.

Sue Catwoman was a punk legend. We'd seen pictures of her with Johnny Rotten and the Bromley Contingent in the *NME* [*New Musical Express*]. Her hair was bleached white, shaved down the middle with two black cat's ears sticking up at the sides. They whisked her to the front of the queue.

Some queens tutted. "Who the fuck's that?"

I couldn't believe they let us into Bangs, I was shaking as I went through the door. Inside it was much like any disco, mirror balls, glass, chrome, plastic plants, and overpriced drinks.

The dance floor was dotted with shirtless queens in white shorts, jiving, high-kicking, and flicking their wedges. Older men in leather jackets with Zapata 'staches swung their sweat-drenched T-shirts above their heads. The DJ was playing "Cherchez la Femme."

We gazed wide-eyed at the shuffling bodies. Men kissed and fondled, others sniffed from small bottles. "Wooh." They threw their heads back and lifted their arms into the air, spinning and screaming. There was a strange heady smell.

A leather-clad stranger shoved something into my face. I reeled back and grimaced. "It's only poppers, love."

I smiled, "No thanks," pulling Laura away with me.

"What was that?"

"I don't know. It smelled like dirty socks."

Laura pointed. "Look. That bloke's wearing a skirt."

We were transfixed by the demonic horned vision dancing gaily before us. "My God, he's brilliant." A man in a long black velvet skirt, pit boots, fingerless black leather gloves. His torso was bare, a black Egyptian collar covered his shoulders. He wore black lipstick and masklike eye shadow. His hair was shaved at the sides and lacquered up into devil's horns.

When he disappeared into the ladies' toilet I made Laura go in after him.

"Go and talk to him."

Laura came out smiling. "He's really friendly. He lent me his lipstick."

He came out of the loo and walked straight up to us. "Hello, dear, what's your name?"

"George."

"Laura."

"How d'ya do. I'm Philip. Where you from, then?"

"Woolwich."

"Ooh. Right out in the sticks."

Philip caught sight of someone more important over our shoulders and disappeared. We were glad we'd spoken to him. I was desperate to make new friends. Other queers, to be precise, and Philip seemed very queer.

We stayed at Bangs till it closed at 3 A.M. Philip was outside in the street chatting to everyone.

"Hello, dears. What other clubs do you go to, then?"

"We don't know any other good clubs, really."

"You should go to Louise's on Fridays. It's in Poland Street. Byeee."

We headed off to Waterloo station and slept in one of the stationary trains. We caught the 5:30 A.M. back to Blackheath. I got Laura to phone work and say I was sick.

That Friday Laura and I made plans to go to Louise's. We didn't invite anyone else, a crowd would have ruined our chances. Louise's was a tiny Soho drinks club down on its luck that the punk elite had discovered and taken over. Its regular clientele were hard-core dykes, upmarket hookers, and the odd overweight horny businessman. Entry was gained by banging on the door. They gave you the once-over through a peephole. There was no queue, which added to the mystique.

The door opened. Laura and I grinned nervously. We were both wearing black lipstick. We tried to look as though we belonged.

"Come in." A glamorous old dame in a fur coat and pearls ushered us in with a smile. The doorman blocked our way.

"Are you members?"

"Er, no. We didn't know you had to be."

"They look a bit young, Louise."

She smiled again. "Go in, dahlin', go in."

I turned, thanked her, and rushed in before they changed their minds.

The club was virtually empty. A few unfashionable people were seated at tables. There was a small bar to the right-hand side. We edged toward the spiral staircase leading down to the dance floor, carefully surveying the room. There didn't seem to be anyone interesting. We reassured each other. "It's still early. The pubs ain't shut yet."

A snarling dyke in a leather biker's cap manned the DJ booth. She seemed happy playing for herself. She pulled on a cigarette and gave us a cod look as we came downstairs. We quickly sat in one of the booths by the side of the dance floor and waited for the crowd.

"I wonder whether Philip will come?"

"Well, he said he comes here."

The music was pure disco and Philly.

"I hope they're not going to play this all night." We hoped they'd play the Sex Pistols or some Bowie.

The club slowly began to fill. We were disappointed by the distinct lack of style. Maybe we'd come to the wrong place.

There was a commotion. Philip skipped down the stairs.

He kissed the DJ. "Hi, Caroline dear." She seemed pleased to see him. Certainly more pleased than she was to see us.

Philip was wearing a dull gray overcoat. His lips, eyes, and hair were styled as before. He was clutching several carrier bags. His eyes darted round the room. We quickly turned away. Maybe the black lipstick wasn't such a good idea. He spotted us.

"Hi, they let you in. It's the best time to come."

We gave coy smiles. He didn't mention the lipstick.

Some people had taken to the dance floor, clumsily moving around to "Love Hangover" by Diana Ross.

"Watch my bags, dears."

Philip waltzed into the middle of the dance floor, kicked off his boots, tore off his coat, and threw them to us. We tried not to laugh. He was wearing a pink surgical corset, Y-fronts, white socks, and white gloves. He threw himself around like a deranged flapper, admiring himself in the mirrored walls.

"Do you like the outfit?"

Laura and I both thought Philip was fantastic. If he'd been wearing nothing but a car aerial it would have been okay by us.

"Do you like the Sex Pistols? They come here, you know."

Philip talked nonstop, nervous chatter, pausing only to catch his breath or wave at someone across the dance floor. More and more freaky types arrived. Philip knew them all.

"This is Berlin." My God, two celebrities in one week. I'd seen him in a magazine with Catwoman. I told him we'd seen Catwoman at Bangs. He glared at me hatefully. I felt like a silly little fool. Philip sympathized. "They're all pretentious queens here."

There were lots of tough punky boys in tight plastic trousers. I eyed them longingly. Laura and I caught our breath at the sight of a baby-faced blond standing by the bar. I don't think I'd ever seen anyone so beautiful. All eyes were on him. I turned to Philip.

"That's Billy Idol. He sings in Chelsea. Do you want to meet him?"

"No, it's okay. I don't want to be scraped off the floor. Philip, can I ask you a personal question?"

"What?"

I hesitated. "Are you gay?"

"Why, you interested?"

I was thrown by his reply and giggled. "Er, n-n-no."

"What's wrong with me?" he snapped.

"Nothing."

"It's okay, dear. I understand." Philip's face lit up. "You're one of us, then. I must give you my phone number."

When I phoned, his mother screamed. "He's not here." She wouldn't even take a message. I tried again and again. When I spoke to Philip he was ever friendly.

"Don't mind my mother, she puts the phone down on everybody. It's nothing personal." Over the years I learned that screaming was like drawing breath for the Sallons.

All the Sallon family are eccentrics. Of course, the rest of them considered themselves quite normal compared to Philip. His mother, Anna, constantly raged, "He's not normal. He's not normal." A fiery woman with electric-shock hair, larger and louder than life, her Welsh boom would rattle the chandelier. She despaired of Philip, but brought him tea and lightly buttered toast every morning. Philip spoke fondly of his mother.

His father, Ralph, was equally dynamic, a distinguished cartoonist for the *Daily Mirror*. He was over eighty when I first met him. Still he rode every day from Cricklewood to Fleet Street on a bicycle. Philip, though at war with him, was always eager to show off his work. "Look, that's my dad's drawing." Philip inherited Ralph's talent and is a brilliant artist himself.

Any one of Philip's sisters, Judith, Ruth, or Sarah, could tie you in knots with their tongues. Ruth once had an audience with a renowned yogi. She so incensed him he told her calmly, "Every word that comes out of your mouth is shit."

Philip never called himself a punk. "Labels, dear, labels. Clothes don't make people interesting. It's what's in your head that matters."

He was, after all, "the first boy in London to have green hair." Prepunk, he was thrown out of gay clubs for letting the side down.

"I want attention. It's those that are petrified of attention that are abnormal. Those who try desperately to conform have the real hang-ups."

He'd appeared alongside Johnny Rotten and the Bromley Contingent in the *Anarchy in the UK* fanzine. The story was, Philip turned up uninvited to the photo shoot and edged himself into the frame.

He was fond of dropping names—Johnny Rotten, Billy Idol, Siouxsie Sioux—while insisting, "I'm no social climber." He was the ultimate social climber, but one with a conscience. He loved to fawn around the in-crowd, yet was just as eager to take a green teen under his wing. He didn't care where people came from, as long as they were nice.

Philip became my touchstone. I wasn't the first wide-eyed boy from the sticks to fall under his spell. I was one of many moths around his flame, intoxicated by his bent logic; intellectual, deranged, rational, and ridiculous.

Friday nights there would be a fleet of cars outside his parents' home in Dollis Hill, eagerly awaiting the night's itinerary. He told everyone to get there early, only to keep them waiting, appearing on the doorstep in different outfits.

"What do you think?"

If one of his entourage didn't quite have their look together, he would pull something out of his wardrobe. "I want it back at the end of the night." He wasn't joking. No one went home in a Sallon original. "I'm sorry, dear, I've had stuff nicked."

He was generous and mean. He wouldn't lend you 5p, but played the Yiddisher mamma, making smoked-salmon bagels and cups of tea. "Are you hungry, dear? There's plenty of food in the fridge."

During the Art Deco revival of the early seventies Philip hung around the big Biba store in Kensington. Biba revolutionized fashion and makeup, reintroducing twenties vamp—the Jean Harlow chalk white face, etched ebony brows, blood-red and black lips. A glamour renaissance. Philip shimmied around town in top hat and tails. He would talk of the "thieves and mad drag queens" that worked at Biba. What they didn't steal themselves they allowed friends to, forcing the store into liquidation.

There was Biba, a ferocious Scottish drag queen who named herself after the store. She was midway through a sex change, and popped hormone pills during tea breaks. She inquired of customers, "Och aye, dear, fancy being a lesbian tonight?"

When I met her I couldn't believe she'd ever been a man. She told me, "Och, don't worry, dear, I can't believe it either."

Biba was one of many transsexuals and transvestites I got to meet through Philip. She was high-class and convincing. But there were others you wouldn't want to meet in a dark alley.

Petal was a knife-wielding transvestite pimp who controlled the Piccadilly rent boys. She wore a dirty floor-length Afghan coat and a curly blond nylon wig, which she pulled on and off like a hat. Wigless she looked the spitting image of David Soul from *Starsky and Hutch*, though I never dared tell her.

Queenie, Maz, and Pearl ran a torture chamber in Old Compton Street, Soho. Philip took me round for tea and a free floor show; we viewed activities through a peephole. Naked men in shackles cried out as they were whipped viciously across the buttocks. There were stocks, vices, and nipple clamps. The walls and floors were covered in black plastic in case a trick wanted "a golden shower" or a "scat job." A lot of their customers wanted to be peed or crapped on. At fifteen I was learning a lot about human nature.

Maz, like Biba, feigned sophistication. Queenie, however, was a twisted variety act with a mouth like a rat-filled sewer. "I'm not a slag, I'm just a good sport."

Queenie was an ex–coal miner. She spent two years down the

pit after leaving school. Watching her dance around the brothel with an empty Coke bottle shoved up her vagina, it was hard to imagine her digging for coal.

"Black men are a delicacy," she told us. "I never charge a black man. If you know any cute ones, send them round."

Pearl, at sixteen stone, was an arresting sight, but it was her whoring activities that put her behind bars. The courts refused to acknowledge her dual sexuality and sent her to a male prison, where she was again rejected: "It's not staying here." She eventually served out her time at Holloway women's prison.

Philip gave me a whirlwind tour of London's whorehouses with a difference. He dragged me to seedy rent-boy clubs and on sightseeing tours to the darkest parts of Hampstead Heath. He took me to the annual drag ball at Porchester Hall where I saw women dressed as John Travolta and bearded men dressed as Bonnie Langford. All my preconceptions of the gay world disappeared in a puff of pink smoke.

Philip was known at every club. "I never pay to get in anywhere. They can pay me." We tiptoed in behind him grateful that we could hold on to the train fare home.

If there was a problem, he always knew somewhere else to go, an opening, a party, he didn't care that he wasn't invited.

Gay clubs were the only safe havens, Rod's, Louise's, Chagerama's in Neal Street which became the Roxy, the Sombrero in High Street, Kensington. The haughty gay clientele were put out by the arrival of us punks. Caroline, the dyke DJ at Louise's, would holler, "Fuck off, you straights. You've got your own clubs to go to."

The Roxy was the first proper punk venue, opened in December 1976 by Andy Czezowski, then manager of Generation X. A dark and unglamorous hovel. Blood-drained gobbing students pushed, shoved, and pogoed. Bruiser punk girls in ripped fishnets and dog collars did their best to look mean.

"Dump." Philip hated the Roxy. He would pass through "just to be seen," his outfit carefully chosen, black plastic hot pants, a tailed jacket covered in Maltesers wrappers, horns, and black lips. "What's the point of being here? They're all straight." He was always trying to drag us off to the Sombrero.

Philip covered his ears to punk music. "Noise, dear, noise." I joyfully foamed at the mouth. The Pistols, the Clash, the Ramones, the Slits, the Buzzcocks, later groups like Penetration, X-Ray Spex, Talking Heads. My favorite song was "Bored Teenager" by the Adverts. I had the record, the badge, and the T-shirt. I was desperate to be part of the punk army, dressed in my ripped and torn. I'd always considered myself an outcast, now I had the wardrobe, safety pins and a pained expression. I adopted the sulky attitude, dragging my feet, scoffing at the civilized world.

I'd proudly tell of the time I saw Siouxsie Sioux fixing her makeup in the ladies' loo at Louise's. She was haughty, irritated by those attempting to brush with greatness.

The new punk stars were every bit as pretentious and puffed up as the seventies rock dinosaurs they despised. It was street-level elitism. They may not have wanted to live isolated in mansions, but they certainly didn't want to talk to the likes of us.

Like Philip, I had little in common with the punk mass. But I rarely saw anyone I fancied at gay clubs. If I ever did they were butch types that wouldn't spit on a freak like me. I wanted a boyfriend with ripped jeans, a leather-studded belt, and blue hair. Gay fashion consciousness amounted to check shirts, white vests, and jeans. Predatory fashions to show off the balls and the biceps.

Gays were as straight as the straights. We were bad-news queers, refusing to abide by their unspoken code of discretion. Philip always made a beeline for those prissy affluent types, professional homosexuals, he called them. They gave false smiles and tried to avoid long conversation. Philip was a gay leper. I was happy to join his colony.

"You'll love her, dear, she's a scream." Philip dragged us down to Brighton for the weekend to visit his friend Stephanie Suspense. I didn't know what to expect—Philip was always full of surprises. He didn't say that Stephanie was really Steven. Stephanie had kaleidoscopic hair of orange, yellow, and white with black roots; her mad eyes were framed by a pair of Buddy Holly glasses; her clothes a mixture of the old and new, a tight baby blue fifties jumper worn over bondage trousers, topped off with a flasher's mac.

She picked us up at the station and we took a taxi to her flat in

Dyke Road. Philip joked, "They named the street after her, you know." After much innuendo I realized that if something was amiss it certainly wasn't Stephanie.

I felt like I'd infiltrated a secret world. I wanted to ask a million questions, but didn't dare. I watched Stephanie in awe. I wondered if I would ever be tempted.

Stephanie lived alone, but there was always an influx of visitors. Strange girls with deep voices. Paul Frecker couldn't leave his parents' home as Paula, so he came round to Stephanie's with drag in a bag and swiftly stripped out of the civvies. Paul's father owned one of the big hotels on the Brighton seafront. His dad was none too happy when Paul made the headlines by getting through to the finals of Miss Brighton. He was a beautiful girl, though these days he looks like a right geezer.

Mandy, another one of Stephanie's mysterious sisters, was the most incredible transvestite I'd ever seen, a complete girl. It made me chuckle to hear builders wolf-whistle her as she walked down the promenade in cutoff denims and halter neck. We'd walk behind singing at the top of our voices, "Oh, I do like to be beside the seaside. Oh, I do like to be beside the sea . . . "

On one of our many visits to Brighton we were attacked by two drunken Scottish football hooligans who took offense at us wearing kilts. I was punched in the nose and kicked to the floor. Philip's shirt was ripped, which hurt him more than the physicals. Luckily, a police car was passing and the thugs were caught. We gave statements and said we definitely wanted to press charges. Philip lied about how much his ripped shirt cost. He said he would buy himself something nice with the compensation.

By the time it came to trial a few months later, Philip and I had fallen out. I'd called him "Big Nose" one too many times. We traveled down to Brighton separately for the court case. I tried to talk to Philip, but he was being childish, turning away whenever I spoke. The police gave evidence, neither of us was called. I sat outside the courtroom; Philip sat in the court, giggling.

The thugs were fined and ordered to pay damages. Afterward one of their fat girlfriends screamed at Philip, "You dirty queer." He screamed back at her, "Fuck off, fat bitch. At least I'm not eating my way through society."

CHAPTER 13

I was late for work yet again. Panic. I jumped on the first bus that came along. There were three main stations where I could catch the London train—Welling, Blackheath, or Lewisham. I headed for Blackheath on the 178. Office workers eyed me with disgust, schoolchildren pointed and sniggered. I stared moronically out of the window wishing I was still in bed.

A cheery elfin-faced schoolboy snapped me out of my daze. "Like yer hair. Nice color." It was yellow like straw.

I smiled. "Nice shoes." His boat-sized blue brothel creepers swam on his feet.

"I'm Jeremy."

"George."

"See yer around." He clomped down the stairs.

Weeks later I saw him on Charing Cross station. He was with two very cute boys, we didn't speak. He was being cool like his outfit, leather jacket, black jeans, winkle-picker boots, and quiffed hair.

Then I saw him again outside the Marquee Club in Wardour Street, slurring drunk, wearing red Wellington boots decorated with spider's webs and a navy blue school mac. His hair was messy and punked out. We spoke briefly, then he disappeared ranting. It was inevitable that we would meet again, either at a punk gig or on the train.

Jeremy Healy lived in Kidbrooke, at the bottom of Shooters Hill, and attended St. Joseph's Academy in Blackheath, where the Christian Brothers called him "Satan's Imp" after he appeared at school with green hair.

He was often mistaken for Phil Rowland, the fourteen-year-old drummer with the punk band Eater—even Johnny Rotten mistook him. Jeremy cashed in, using his vicarious fame to enter clubs free. He wore a leather jacket with DID YOUR MUMMY AND DADDY LOVE YOU WHEN YOU WERE LITTLE? daubed on the back.

I thought Woolwich was the back end of nowhere, but I was beginning to see I was not its only ambassador of style. First Jeremy and now Steven. I'd seen Steven at Bangs, dancing like a dizzy marmot, bulging eyes, pursed lips, geometric hair, shaved eyebrows. I was drawn to him.

"Where you from?"

"Woolwich."

"Woolwich!" I didn't know whether to choke or smile. Steven was by far the most advanced queer I'd ever met. He and his boyfriend lived with his parents, a concept far beyond my comprehension.

"What's it like?"

"Normal."

"Normal!" I couldn't imagine Mum and Dad being able to deal with that. I wasn't sure I'd like the idea, anyway. Sex was never mentioned in our house. We blushed at *Carry On* films.

I was so excited when Steven invited me to a party at his house. On the way to the party I bumped into Jeremy and his school-friend John Keogh outside Woolwich station. They were about to jump on the train to London. I brought them with me, I hoped Steven wouldn't mind.

We all got very drunk. I grabbed Jeremy and snogged him briefly over the punch bowl. No stars collided or comets fell. Jeremy forgave my indiscretion. We both liked Bowie and Lou Reed, that was excuse enough. We exchanged numbers.

I was horrified to discover Jeremy's association with Sheila, a snooty punk girl I'd spied in the Crisis charity shop in Blackheath Village. I smiled at her, and she sneered back. I couldn't believe it, a fellow freak snubbing me on home territory.

The next time I saw her was at the bus stop outside Charing Cross station, I was on my way to work. She acted like she'd known me all her life.

"Hi." I was surprised by her painted-face charm.

"Where you going?" I asked.

"Up the Kings Road, to be photographed by tourists."

A curious phenomenon of the time. Tourists would pay up to a pound for a photo of a real live punk. Sheila had turned herself into a living work of art. Her scatter-cushion lips were vermilion, her face ghost white, her eyes painted a thousand colors. She must have been up for hours.

Jeremy took me round to Sheila's bedsit in Blackheath. She instantly excused the decor. "The landlord's got great taste." It certainly wasn't as colorful as her cartoon face. Pictures of her idols, Bette Davis and Marlene Dietrich, sat unframed on the mantelpiece propped up by burned-out candles and bottles of garish nail polish. Vintage clothes hung from wire hangers along the wall, fifties cocktail dresses, mohair cardigans, a pillbox hat with a dotted veil, a flamenco fan, and a manky fox stole. More colorful clothes littered the floor; she trampled them indiscriminately while searching for a lost lipstick. Her favorite soundtrack was Patti Smith's *Horses*. "Jesus died for somebody's sins, but not mine . . . "

Sheila wouldn't even take the milk in without her makeup on. It wasn't unknown for her to paint herself twice a day. She preferred, when she had time, to do it while taking a bath. She said the steam helped set her foundation.

She loved cats but she was an undomesticated feline herself. She never had any food, milk, or teabags, just plenty of Kit-E-Kat. We used her flat as wardrobe base. She lived close to Blackheath station. We could walk to the trains, reducing the chances of abuse and attack.

When Philip met Sheila he instantly renamed her Myra. Her blond beehive and secondhand gear made her look like the sixties murderess Myra Hindley. Philip said she should carry an ax in her handbag. The name stuck. She's known as Myra to this day.

CHAPTER 14

"Punk Jayne" was the snakebite queen of Northwest London. Snakebite (lager and cider) and blackcurrant and lager were her favorite drinks. She was the archetypal punk tomboy—fluoropink spiky hair, leather jacket, bondage trousers, and DMs; stumbling round the West End drunk as a punk skunk.

She turned her parents' home into a punk dosshouse. Their three-bedroom council flat in Swiss Cottage, off the Finchley Road, was perfectly situated, only a 20p bus ride from the West End.

Her mum and dad worked long hours. When they were around they didn't seem to mind the stench of Elnett hairspray or us boys dolling ourselves up in the bathroom. The neighbors complained, "If I had a daughter like that, I'd chain her up." Mrs. Mitchell defended Jayne, though she paid her to stay away from family weddings.

Mrs. Mitchell never batted an eyelid at all the freaks, deviants, and crossdressers that came bobbing along the landing and in through her front door. She just carried on frying her sausages. "If you want tea you know where the kettle is." Still, we were all glad she wasn't around the night Marilyn appeared.

"This is Marilyn," squealed Philip. "As in Monroe. Don't you think he looks like her?"

There was an expectant silence. Everyone turned to look at the quivering mass of effeminacy Philip was referring to—Marilyn, a pretty pig-faced creature that talked with a wiggle and walked with a lisp.

Philip was always seducing innocent people off the street, dragging them to meet his dangerously weird circle of friends. To us Marilyn was just another pleb who'd come to stare, unstylish and very queer-looking, a common or garden homosexual.

Philip and Marilyn were not alone. In tow was their personal chauffeur, "Gay Robert," a pointy-nosed queen, dressed for a day out at Henley Regatta. He didn't like me one bit. Bitchy George, back-combing his raven hair, hissing and vitriolic, staking out his territory.

Philip was always gregarious to a fault, but this night he was behaving like an overanxious game show host. "Doesn't he look like Marilyn Monroe?"

"Looks more like a pig," I snapped.

Marilyn flushed, Robert glared. Philip reacted for them by pushing his well-proportioned nose into the air. It was unusual for Philip to say nothing, but he was educating his new sidekicks, and lesson number one was always—never show weakness.

I had my own reasons for being hateful. Philip and I had fallen out. Marilyn was my replacement. He was no gargoyle either, naff but perfectly pretty, and knew it. A beautiful full mouth, long lashes, slanted half-closed almond eyes, and an angel's complexion. His unnaturally blond hair cascaded over one eye. He flicked it intermittently like a disco tart. His clothes were of the drabbest kind, blue jeans, loafers, and a houndstooth jacket.

If Robert and Marilyn thought I was like Bette Davis, they were about to meet the skinhead version. The kitchen window suddenly exploded, glass splattering everywhere in the wake of a large red house-brick. Several venomous skinheads had popped round to sort out our sexual disorders. "Queers . . . Scum."

Philip grabbed a startled Marilyn and took refuge in the toilet. "Oh dear, what's going on? Call the police, do something." The rest of us were equally hysterical. There were no men around to protect us.

Oh, God, what was going through Marilyn's head? Visions of

playground persecution? Marilyn was definitely the type you picked on at school. (Yes, I do mean YOU picked on, because Marilyn and I were sisters under the skin.)

The skinheads soon disappeared, their retreat hastened by the number of lights flicking on in the tiny block of flats. There were voices as neighbor upon neighbor searched for the guilty party. Someone grumbled, "Must be those bloody weirdos upstairs." Just like the British to kick a freak when it's down.

Philip got a severe ear bashing when he finally emerged from the toilet. We all agreed he'd been the biggest coward. He didn't excuse himself, darling. He wasn't into any kind of masculinity trip.

The room started to reverberate with every last coward spinning his or her own version of the story.

"I picked up the bread knife."

"I was going to jump out the window."

"It would have been difficult from under the bed, wouldn't it, dear?"

Easter Monday 1977 we all went to Margate, Punk Jayne, her brother Steve, Jayne Morgan, Andrea Arnold, and others from our gang. Punks and teds followed the tradition of the mods and rockers of the sixties, invading seaside resorts on bank holidays for futile wars.

Punk had become of public concern, and we were barred from most pubs, clubs, and cafés. We'd wander listlessly from one place to another. "Sorry, don't want none of you lot in here." I found it very boring, not being a big fan of seasides. There was always the big pretense that being barred gave us a dangerous edge. All it did was give us blisters.

One place that welcomed us in Margate was the Galleon pub, next to the Dreamland funfair. It was the favorite punk trough, packed from 11 A.M. to 3 P.M. Why anyone needed to go all the way to Margate just to get tanked up was beyond me. Still, a wise punk stayed with the crowd. The threat of marauding teds was always imminent. They loved nothing more than to corner two or three punks and give them a good kicking.

"Tarts." I envied the ropy punk girls with their tattooed car-mechanic boyfriends parading along the promenade arm in arm. I joked that all that stood in the way of bliss was a quick nip and tuck and a plastic miniskirt. I made myself look like a punk girl, frilly-collared shirt, a kilt over bondage trousers, panstick, and glossy red lips. I fluttered and flirted in vain, dreaming of my blue-haired punk boy.

Those trips to Margate and Bournemouth were one big hetero nob-in. I felt like a gay gooseberry. Punk, despite its abandon-all-rules pretensions, had little room for poofters. It made me laugh to see boys wearing Seditionaries T-shirts depicting fist-fucking leather queens or drawings of well-hung cowboys by Tom of Finland. They saw it as an anti-Establishment gesture, I was the reality. My obvious leanings and my big mouth made me a target for queer jokes and threats. The girls played bodyguard. "Leave him alone." I often pushed my luck, making camp gestures to everyone I met. I measured their reactions on my naff-o-meter. Of course I loved rough boys, especially those who would have punched me. Some of them loved girlie boys like me, they liked being adored, and we always had the most fun. Punks, poofs, skins, Jayne knew them all. Often she had to play referee, convincing some National Front skinhead that her mates George and Philip weren't "dirty queers" and were all right really.

Andy Keeves and Paul Douglas were two straight boys who joined our throng. Jayne and Steve met them in the Galleon. I yawned as they bragged of their battles with the teds. One of Andy's friends had lost the top half of his ear. "Oh, really, that was clever." Andy and Paul had real trouble adjusting to us. Philip and I were the first poofs they'd ever met. We weren't black-market queens either, loud, proud, and probing.

Andy was the prettier of the two, a bandy-legged Narcissus, who loved the fact that I couldn't take my eyes off him. Paul was podgy and miserable; he was Andy's stooge. Their lives revolved around three things: pints, pussy, and posing. Andy fared better than Paul. Philip called them "social-climbing suburban wankers." He couldn't understand why I would want to associate with them. The fact that they lived near me was reason enough. We could catch the London train together. It was always wise to travel in numbers, and they were quite tough-looking.

Dad pointed out two boys walking hand in hand along Eltham High Street. "'Ere. Isn't that your mate Jeremy?"

"Er, er, no," I replied, red-faced, knowing full well it was Jeremy and John Keogh. Jeremy was the only boy in South London with peacock blue Doc Martens.

I was sure Jeremy was gay. There had been rumors of a romance between him and gorgeous sleepy-eyed John. Jeremy did little to dispel them, but then we all did our best to appear sexually ambiguous.

We were all surprised by the perverse union of Jeremy and Punk Jayne. Philip joked, "Which one's the woman, dear?" Jayne said she only started dating Jeremy because he'd been rude to her. She wanted to get her own back. Hate the one you're with.

Jayne and Jeremy were physical and cultural opposites. He wanted to watch Warhol and Yoko Ono movies and listen to the Velvet Underground. Jayne preferred a pint at her local and a good Walt Disney cartoon. "Who wants to watch a grapefruit going up and down on an escalator?" She was profoundly insulted when Jeremy suggested she have her back teeth removed to heighten her cheekbones. That, along with him constantly calling her stupid, ended their alliance. She fittingly left him for a skinhead called Ron.

My Vivienne Westwood red tartan bondage trousers were my pride and joy. I couldn't believe I finally had a pair. I'd made several trips to Seditionaries, formerly Sex, in the Kings Road, gazing at them longingly. "£60. I'll never be able to afford them." I saved £30 from my wages and creeped around Dad for the rest. "They'll have to take a check." I rang the shop and they told me to make the check out to Sex. Dad refused.

"I can't have Sex on my check stubs. What will my accountant think?"

Frantic, I phoned back. They laughed and gave me a company name. Dad was disgusted when he saw what he had forked out for. I definitely got my money's worth. I wore them until they could pogo on their own.

My punk attire proved too much for the powers that be at Red

Tape, where I was working. My boss ordered me to remove the strap from my bondage trousers, worried that I'd get caught in the machinery. The trousers were a mass of zips and buckles with a strap joining the legs together. Concerned commuters tapped me on the shoulder, "Excuse me, your belt's dropped." Others would ask, "How do you run in them?"

I kept makeup to the minimum for work, a smidgen of mascara and a smudge of kohl. The hair was most important. At night I back-combed and lacquered it and tied a piece of ripped T-shirt around my forehead to hold it up and minimize early-morning styling. Mum rolled her eyes as I bounded out the house. My porcupine hair, Dennis the Menace mohair jumper, and bondage trousers sent ripples of mirth down the train platform. I relished the attention but protested in true punk fashion, "What you staring at?"

I paraded around on the buses and tubes delivering parcels, convinced that I should be awarded an Arts Council grant for merely existing. Japanese and American tourists stood next to me for photographs. I never charged.

One afternoon while riding the Central Line I was accosted by an Italian businessman.

"'Allo, what izza yorr name?" I snootily turned away.

"If you want a photograph, just ask."

He moved round in front of me. "Do you avva girlfriend?"

I was startled by both his question and good looks.

"Er, er, I don't have girlfriends."

He smiled. "Where are you going now?"

"I'm delivering a parcel. I'm a messenger. What do you want?"

"Can I walk wid you?"

I shrugged. It seemed a ridiculous request. "If you want to."

The handsome stranger in an expensive Burberry mac stepped off the tube with me at Chancery Lane. I was miffed and flattered by the attention.

"My name is Danny. You are?"

"George."

"You are very beautiful, George."

"Thanks, but really . . . "

He walked with me and waited in the street while I dropped off my parcel. When I returned he took hold of my hand. A weighty gold ring sparkled on his wedding finger. His blue-green eyes were piercing. I began to tingle all over.

"You will meet me tonight?"

"Okay," I mumbled. "But I have to get back to work."

He scribbled an address on a piece of paper. Orme Court, Bayswater Road. I quickly took it and walked away. He shouted after me, "Eight o'clock. Is okay?" I didn't look back. I wondered whether I should go.

After work I hung around the West End. It was pointless going home. I rifled through the secondhand records at Cheapo Cheapo's in Soho and treated myself to a McDonald's milk shake. Time seemed to drag. I was full of anticipation and fear. I called Mum and told her I was going to spend the night at Jayne's in Swiss Cottage.

I walked from Oxford Circus to Marble Arch and along the Bayswater Road. I found the address easily. It was seven-thirty, still too early. I hung around outside the red-brick Edwardian mansion block. Shortly before eight I rang the bell. A posh camp voice came over the intercom. "Hillo."

I said I was a friend of Danny's and was buzzed in.

The hallway was dripping with style: a glistening chandelier hung above a gilt-framed mirror, classical oil paintings lined the walls. As I climbed the stairs I could hear chinking glasses and the subtle commotion of a dinner party. Danny greeted me at the door. He kissed me on the mouth, took my hand, and walked me inside.

Several theatrical types were seated around a candlelit dinner table. They gave knowing smiles as I entered the room. I felt cheap and out of place.

A silver-haired gentleman in a velvet smoking jacket held out his frail hand. "Anton Dolin. How do you do? I'm your host."

I smiled. "Thank you."

A laughing Buddha in an orange kaftan, bald and wide-mouthed with heavily kohled saucer eyes, pulled me toward him. He lifted my hand and kissed my knuckles one by one. A mischievous grin erupted across his face.

"Lindsay Kemp. The pleasure's all mine."

"Lindsay Kemp? I can't believe it." My voice rose several octaves. I quickly contained myself. "You worked with David Bowie."

He laughed. "Yes, and he worked with me."

I sat down at the table, nodding politely to the rest of the guests. I had no idea what an esteemed gathering it was. Anton Dolin, John Gilpin, Alicia Markova and her one-eyed shih tzu. The cream of the ballet world, except for the dog.

After dinner Danny took me to the bedroom. A poky white-walled room with a single bed. He closed the curtains and stripped me. That night I lost my virginity. I had expected to scream, cry, and beg, but I experienced only pleasure. I woke the next morning in his arms. I wanted to stay there all day. I arranged to meet him again after work.

Danny was a sophisticated older man, late thirties, tanned with white teeth, dreamy eyes, and warm skin. That night we sat in Trafalgar Square. He played acoustic guitar and sang romantic Italian songs. He revealed little about himself. When I questioned him he laughed, stroked my face, and called me *bambino*.

He took me to an expensive Italian restaurant where again he took out his guitar and sang. They fussed over him like he was someone special.

I saw him constantly for five days. Mum was alarmed when he phoned Shooters Hill. "A strange foreign man called here today. He sounded very old. Where did you meet him?"

Our romance ended abruptly. Danny disappeared without so much as a goodbye. When I phoned Orme Court they were curt. "He's gone back to Italy, dear." I cried, but somehow it seemed the perfect way for it to end.

CHAPTER 15

Only Philip would have the audacity to ask someone outright, "Are you queer? Have you dabbled?" He'd call them a liar whatever their reply and concluded, "Those who get upset have something to hide." If you told Philip you fancied someone he would rush over, "My friend fancies you, you interested?" Often he made you look a fool, sometimes it was fruitful.

We were at Lazers, a poky gay club in North London where, of course, Philip knew everyone.

"He's nice."

"What—Les? Oh, you can have him."

Philip dragged him over. "Les, meet my evil friend George. He wants to have you in the long grass." I was so embarrassed. Les was even cuter up close. Small, boyish, conservative, in blue jeans and a white T-shirt. We stared at each other for a while. He wrote down his number. It was pointless trying to have a conversation over the wails of Donna Summer, "Ooh, I feel love, I feel love, I feel love, I feel l-o-o-ve."

I called him the next day during my lunch break, half expecting a wrong number. It rang forever. When he finally answered he was friendly. I met him after work at his office close by in Newman Street. I wondered what he'd think of me in daylight.

Les was editor of a teeny magazine called *My Guy*. His office walls were plastered with pictures of dishy boy models and pop stars. I laughed. "Must be a hard job." He showed me the latest edition. The pinup of the month was Jon Moss, drummer with an unknown punk band called London.

"Isn't he cute?"

I had to agree.

We went back to his flat in Queen's Mansions, West Hampstead. It was like an old lady's place, pristine and flowery. He kept calling me dear, which I didn't like. We drank tea and chatted for ages. I was praying he'd jump on me because I could never have made the first move. He was shy, too, and asked, "Can I kiss you?" He had a comfortable bed and a soft body. In the morning he brought me tea and toast and we listened to "Chelsea Girls" by Nico.

I started seeing him regularly after that. We never went club- bing or out to eat, we just had sex. I think Les found my spiky hair and bondage trousers embarrassing. I didn't care, it suited me to come and go like a cat. Sometimes I would ring him from a club and go round at three in the morning. He was always easy, cook- ing me beans on toast and being filthy. The only trauma came from an ex-lover, John, who had a key to the flat and would walk in on us. I'd hide under the duvet while Les fought him off.

I loved Les but didn't realize how much till he died of AIDS in 1993. In those early days there wasn't enough drama to keep me in the relationship. I chased after those boys with trouble in their eyes. After about six months we drifted apart, but we remained friends right up to his death. Whenever we saw each other we would always embrace and I proudly told everyone he was the only boyfriend I still talked to.

Having a sensible job seriously cramped my style. Leaving a club or gig to catch the last train home was deeply unstylish. My attempts to juggle clubbing and career were faltering. I received my first warning at Red Tape.

"How do you expect to get on in life?"

I promised to improve my timekeeping while remaining realistic about my future. I was still making tea and licking envelopes eight months after I joined. I didn't see myself behind the executive desk. In truth, I hated work and had a problem with authority figures. The idea of slogging my guts out for the rest of my life for a paltry wage, free weekends, and a lousy pension brought tears to my eyes. It all seemed so pointless.

The following month I was finally given my P45. How I managed nine months I'll never know. It was my longest service record. Getting the sack made me instantly eligible for the dole. I signed on for a few weeks, until the shadow of Mum loomed over me.

"Get a job."

I tried to explain my new philosophy to her.

"I didn't raise ya to be a layabout." She despaired for my future.

I decided working with friends was my only hope of achieving job satisfaction. Jeremy, Myra, and I went to the Labour Exchange in search of triple employment. We found a job at Chingford Fruit Packers on the Woolwich Industrial Estate, working from 8 A.M. until 5 P.M. for £14 a week. It was only £2 more than the dole. I took the job to appease Mum. Jeremy and Myra followed me blindly.

It was Jeremy's first experience of full-time employment. "If this is work, I'm never going to work again."

The Chingford slave force were mostly Indian women, villager types, and old wheezing biddies who sat by conveyor belts weeding out bad apples. I loaded the full crates onto another conveyor belt. Jeremy and Myra performed some other unfruitful task. That place was like a labor camp. "No eating the apples." It wasn't as if there was a shortage. When they refused to let us leave early to see Patti Smith at the Roundhouse we all stormed out. We only lasted three weeks.

Mum wasn't happy but she stayed calm. "You'll be up at eight tomorrow and down the Job Centre." I was too. I couldn't believe my luck when I landed an interview at a hat shop in Poland Street, Soho, just up from Louise's club. I was tempted to wear a hat to the interview, but Mum thought otherwise. Barnett and Co. was a wholesale hat and knitwear shop. The owner was a friendly old Jewish man who said, "I think you'll do." His manageress was a stern old dragon. She didn't like the look of me at all. I did my best to look normal, but I couldn't hide the fact that I had no eyebrows and my hair was obviously dyed. What did it matter anyway? I spent most of my time downstairs in the stockroom, well out of view. It was my job to organize incoming stock and supply orders. I was good at it, I loved organizing and keeping things tidy. It also meant I could decide how many jumpers and feather boas could go missing. I used to stuff goodies in the rubbish boxes and come back for them at night.

Early one morning the police raided Shooters Hill. One of Dad's disgruntled ex-employees had tipped them off that Dad was selling illegal car documents. It was a total lie. I thought they were on to me and lobbed my booty out the window into the grounds of the water tower next door.

I loved working in Soho. I used to visit Punk Jayne, who worked at Joe Coral's betting shop round the corner, at lunchtimes or go and see Philip at the London College of Fashion. The food was tasty and subsidized and Philip always put on a show. He would bring a change of clothes just to wear for lunch. When the Sex Pistols released *Never Mind the Bollocks* he made a dress out of the offending album covers and danced on the table.

I made a new friend, Betty Valentino, an older girl who worked above Barnett's for Mike Mansfield's TV production company. I was most impressed, having been an avid viewer of *Supersonic*. Had she ever met Marc Bolan? Could she introduce me to David Bowie? Betty was the kind of person you meet and fall in love with straightaway, a beautiful Italian with high cheekbones and a curvaceous figure. She loved gay boys and talked in Palare, a secret gayspeak that we used when we were eyeing up boys. "Varda the dish, girl. Nada in the larder." "Lovely bum, nothing in between the legs." Betty lived near me off Shooters Hill Road. We rode the train together and went drinking and clubbing after work. We'd visit her friend Shane Fenton, who worked at London Weekend Television. I loved hanging in the bar mingling with the celebrities.

Stargazing and disco hopping made me late for work too often. Barnett and Co. employed a new manageress, a Sloaney type in a Burberry skirt. She hated my clothes and stirred it with the boss at every opportunity. It was Christmas 1978 and we were about to break for the holidays. Friday night I picked up my money as usual and headed off home. I hadn't bothered to read the letter which they placed in with my wage packet telling me not to come back.

Imagine my shame when in January I waltzed back into Barnett's expecting to start work. "What are you doing here?" said the dragon. "You were fired." I couldn't believe it, how could they just sack me like that and not have the decency to tell me to my face after all I'd done for them. They were really embarrassed, I was really angry. I went back a week later in the nighttime and poured black paint through the letterbox and over the windows and superglued the door lock, returning the next day to gleefully watch them cleaning up.

After that I secured a part-time job working in Chelsea Antiques Market up the Kings Road for a cool black guy called Troy who sold retro chic. I did everything, running for coffees and sandwiches, collecting stock, and cleaning hundreds of pairs of fifties stilettos. I didn't care, I loved working on the Kings Road.

In my lunch break I would make a vigil to the Beaufort Market and browse around Polystyrene's punk boutique. Polystyrene was the singer with X-Ray Spex, my favorite punk group.

Mum made accidental history by dyeing six white boilersuits khaki for Bob Marley and the Wailers for their Rainbow Theatre show. Troy was friends with Bob Marley. I delivered the boilersuits to a house in Cheyne Walk. When the door opened I almost suffocated in a fog of marijuana.

CHAPTER 16

Philip Sallon hated closets. He had the view that all boys were queer or at least bendable. TBH: "To Be Had." He would hound people if he thought they might be gay and hiding it. It was his mission in life. "I smell perverts." For instance, if someone was called Ben, he would taunt, "What's your second name, Dover?" or "Is it Ben with a silent T?" He would have everyone in stitches except the person at the end of his tongue. It was a big mistake to tell Philip your personal business, because he would wait until you were with a crowd and announce it in every detail. He loved to spread gossip, especially if you asked him not to. It was funny most of the time, but not always.

Most of us had a thing about straight boys. Philip called them "conversion jobs." There was something much more appealing about getting off with a hetero—maybe it's just that old cliché of only wanting what you can't have. I always used to say, "If I wanted to have sex with a queen I'd buy a mirror."

Gary had blue hair and a pug nose. I used to blow kisses behind his back and pretend to grope his bum. He was another mate of Jayne Mitchell's. She told me, "You're wasting your time. He's as straight as a die." I said, "He won't know the difference once the lights are out."

When I first met Gary he was in hospital after a car crash. His legs were in plaster. He looked so cute and helpless. His girlfriend

Joan used to draw the screen around the bed and give him blow jobs. I wouldn't have minded sorting him out myself. I was quite sure I could have him if I could only get rid of his sidekick Jeff. Gary knew I fancied him, he played on it, I was so obvious, I fussed around him at every opportunity. I bought him clothes and dyed his hair for him. He'd call me "My Georgie."

One night we were at a party. I was pissed and had to lie down in an empty room to sleep off the effects of too much blackcurrant and lager. I was just dozing when the light came on. I heard Gary's voice. "Get up. Don't sleep, don't be boring." He started shaking me and held on to my arm. I pulled myself round on the bed, he was standing over me with a stupid grin on his face. His leather trousers were undone and I could see his white underwear. I slid my hand in and grabbed hold of his cock. It was hard, I'd never felt anything so big.

Gary wouldn't look at me or talk during the train ride home. There was an embarrassing silence. Him staring at the floor, me looking out the window, and Jeff wondering what was going on. For a few days we didn't speak. When we did it was as if nothing had happened.

A few weeks passed and Gary was drunk again. I blew him on the couch at Shooters Hill while everyone was asleep. He never kissed me or showed the slightest bit of affection. He just lay there while I did all the work. Afterward he was fraught and guilt-ridden. He obviously enjoyed it, but it disgusted him. That made it all the more exciting.

I couldn't keep it to myself, I was dying to tell Philip, or someone. That was all part of it. It was a major conquest to have a straight boy. Affirmation of your gorgeousness. Telling people was almost as exciting as having a cock in your mouth.

Philip used to say, "People only tell me things because they want them spread," which was true in most cases, but I begged him to keep this to himself. Philip loved spending hours on the phone spreading rumors, telling girls that their boyfriends were "obviously queer." Hating this person, hating that person.

We were at Billy's club in Dean Street. Everyone went there, London's disco royalty, shoulder pads and panstick, eager photographers from *Paris Match* magazine clicking away, Philip jumping into every photo.

Philip always arrived late. This ensured maximum impact. Dressed head to toe in bin-bags, painted gold, followed by an array of hangers-on, pretty punk boys, girls with cars who could taxi him from club to club. Beer boys in bondage suits. "I dressed him up, dear, he looked so normal." Cursing because one of his entourage had been asked to pay. Giving showbiz kisses to everyone. Bitch, bitch, bitch. "I was wearing that when it was in fashion."

I was always nervous when I was with Gary. Philip had a knack of saying the wrong thing at the wrong time. "Hi, dear! I hear you got George pregnant." Running off around the club. "Ooh, I think I've upset someone." Gary went to punch him. Philip screamed, "You touch me and you're dead." He was nelliefied, running behind tables, cowering in the corner. Gary knew it would be a mistake to hit Philip, so I gave him a shove. He'd betrayed me and I was never going to forgive him.

My friendship with Gary was making me miserable and very unpopular. Everyone took Philip's side. He screamed at me down the phone, "I'm gonna get the St. Albans boys to kick you in." They were a gang of mad punks, Psycho Steve, Pru and Frank Kelly, that Philip got into parties.

It was the first time I'd fallen out with Philip and the first time I got the chance to find out what he was really like—a bitter, twisted, shit-stirring old queen, with nothing better to do than cause trouble.

Things went from bad to begging with Gary. He went off with girls all the time, acting like I didn't exist. I would be distraught, crying on Punk Jayne's shoulder, wanting the impossible. The more he rejected me, the more I clung. He would say, "You know I'm straight." Of course I didn't want to hear it. I did everything I could to scare away hunting females. I made him miss his train after clubs, so he would be forced to stay with me. Even when I had him cornered he wasn't always obliging.

I turned all my frustration and hatred on Philip. I had to get my own back. I devised an evil plan. It was Valentine's Day 1979. I sent him a homemade voodoo doll complete with pins, made by using one of my sister's dolls. I spiked its hair, painted its lips black, then I spent hours decorating an old shoe box with shiny silver wrapping paper and flowers. "To Philip with love on Valentine's Day." Afterward we set up a Ouija board and cursed him.

When Philip received the doll he freaked out and called in the local rabbi to exorcize the demons. He claims he woke up in the night sweating and was thrown about on his bed by some unknown force. He lost control of his mouth (for once) and went into a trance. It was all very Linda Blair.

Philip's sister and her boyfriend came to Shooters Hill to tell Mum, who found it ridiculous.

"How old is your brother?" Mum asked.

"Well, I don't think that's got anything to do with it."

"How old is he?" He was at least thirty. "Don't you think he's a little old for you to be coming round to this house?" She shut the door on them. I got a good slap round the face and a letter from Philip's solicitor warning me not to intimidate or harass him.

CHAPTER 17

Ooh competition, Martin?" Martin gave a little smile, but I could tell he didn't like the doorman's remark as we went into Barbarella's. I was wearing my mauve tartan clown suit. I was prettier than him, it has to be said, I looked more girlie.

Martin was scary, white-white face, no eyebrows. He used to darken round his eyes and cheeks to create a skull-like effect. Some people said he copied Pete Burns from Liverpool, another disco celebrity, like Philip Sallon in London. I'd never met Pete Burns but I knew of his legend and reputation for being evil.

I first met Martin Degville in Bournemouth one bank holiday in 1977. I spotted him from miles away in the street. He wasn't like the other punks, he was wearing stiletto heels and had a massive bleached quiff and huge padded shoulders. He looked brilliant, I had to talk to him. He was a bit snotty at first, until I recognized his accent and told him I had relatives in Brum. He gave me his number.

Some weeks later I arranged to visit Aunt Teresa's in Lady-wood. I caught the coach, clutching a few specially chosen outfits and my bag of Leichner. I had the most brilliant weekend hanging out with Martin and his friends. The freaks up there were much friendlier than in London. There was no elitism, they all wanted to know your name. Everyone mingled together—punks, queers, dykes, straights, all under the same roof, whether at the Crown pub, Barbarella's club, or the Ramulus, a trendy wine bar where we went for a preclub dance. Barbarella's was a huge club split into different levels. They had a reggae room, a disco room, and a room where live bands played. Toyah played there to about fifty people just before she had all her hits and hairdos. The Tourists played too—that was the first time I met Annie Lennox. I tried to get backstage but security threw me out, so I climbed back in through the dressing-room window. Annie was really friendly, considering I behaved like a psycho fan.

There were loads of great characters in Brum, Patrick Black in his dominatrix drag, Beehive Marie, Patrick Lilley, who we called Beelzebub. Patty Bell and Jane Kahn, who ran a freaky clothes shop. They had Mohican hairdos, stuck diamanté all over their faces, and wore leopard-skin dresses and bits of animal fur in their hair. I became addicted to Birmingham, going up every other week. I traveled north with my old schoolfriend Tracie Carter and her boyfriend, Brian, new friends like Jeremy and Myra, Andy Keeves, Shane Chapman, Gary, Jeff, and deadly Daisy. Daisy was a pretty punk girl who I stupidly allowed to get too close to Gary. I thought she was my friend and shared all my deepest secrets.

"Do you like the outfit?" Daisy whooped, twirled, and cat-walked toward us ruffling the petticoats on her multicolored tutu. Her impromptu fashion show disturbed the Saturday-morning calm on Charing Cross station. She was radiant, bubbling, and loud. "I'm really looking forward to our holiday." She hugged and gave us kisses. "Don't get too excited," I told her. "You might have to sleep on Martin's floor." She flung her arms around Gary and Jeff's shoulders as we walked toward the tube. I trailed behind, wondering if I'd made a big mistake inviting her to Birmingham. On the coach I fought the urge to open the emergency door. Daisy didn't shut up for one minute, screeching, running up and down the aisle. Gary and Jeff were hanging on her every word. Jeff was in love with her, but he had no chance.

That evening Martin took us to see UB40 play at a college in Edgbaston. It was long before they had a hit record, but they were already popular in Birmingham—you could tell they were going to make it. Afterward we went to the Crown to buy speed. The

Crown was a punk pub and preclub hangout near New Street station. Hard-core groups like Discharge used to play and drink there. I had a hard-on for Colin, the singer. I was a sucker for spots and spiky hair. We ended up at Barbarella's rushing off our trolleys. Everybody took speed in those days; it was cheap and effective. Martin and I used to chew people's ears off.

I was happily speeding around Barbarella's when I bumped into Jeff. His eyes were red—he'd been crying.

"What's wrong?"

"That cunt Gary. He's getting off with Daisy."

I felt sick. "That bitch. She's been flirting with Gary all day, and God knows how long before that. I should have known."

I rushed back to where they were sitting, draped around each other with a look of innocence on their faces. I took my beer and threw it over Daisy.

"I hate you."

Gary jumped up and knocked me flying.

"Mr. Fucking Macho."

I ran off to find Martin, I was hysterical. "Oh my God, I can't believe it. Don't let them stay at the flat, please don't let them stay." Martin and I took a taxi back to Walsall. He was really sweet that night.

When Gary, Jeff, and Daisy came back there were more scenes. I threw hot coffee over Daisy. Gary tried to hit me, Martin stood in the way and told them, "I want you out of here first thing in the morning." I locked myself in the bathroom and scraped a broken lightbulb across my wrist. It was pathetic, I knew Gary wasn't worth piss. Let alone blood. I didn't sleep, I sat in the kitchen. I could hear them upstairs in the bedroom fucking away. She sounded like a seal at feeding time.

I left early the next morning to catch the coach back to London. I destroyed their tickets by chewing them into tiny pieces and spat them onto the pavement.

I had to wait three hours at the coach station. I hid in a doorway. I cried so much my jaw was shaking, I couldn't control myself, I was so sad. I felt like a right fool. Philip had been right all along—Gary was a suburban wanker.

By the time the coach was ready to leave, Jeff and the lovebirds had arrived. I could hear Gary's hateful voice, "Where the fuck is he? I'm gonna kill him." I was resigned to my fate.

Jeff's fat face came leering toward me. "Oi, where's my ticket? I've got no money. Are you gonna pay my fare?" I pushed past them and boarded the coach, they followed shouting, "He's got our tickets, he's got our tickets." I sat at the back and pretended I didn't know them. Gary tried to pull my bag off the coach. Daisy stood there like a cold killer. The driver told them to get off if they didn't have tickets. I got off instead, I had nothing to go back to London for. I caught the bus back to Walsall and stayed there for two weeks.

While recovering from my heartache I had a surprise visit from Gary, Jeff, and another soon to be ex-friend, Andy McLachlan. Egged on by Gary they had come to sort me out. They waited outside the flat until Martin came home, and forced their way in. Luckily I heard Martin scream. I ran up to the top of the house and locked myself in Rhonda's room. They were banging on Rhonda's door and shouting, "Open it, open the fucking door or we'll kick it down." I pushed my weight against the door. I could hear Andy McLachlan. "Where's my fucking records, thief? You started this." I shouted to Gary, "I'll phone your dad and tell him if you don't go away. I mean it, I'll tell him everything." They started mumbling and disappeared down the stairs. I heard the sound of a car. I thought it was a trick, I laid low in Rhonda's room for ages and cried to myself. I couldn't believe how vicious Gary had been. He'd driven all the way from London with the sole purpose of hurting me. That was how important it was to him. "Kill" rather than face up to what he is.

I never saw Gary again. Last I heard he was married with kids. I'm sure he brags about our friendship now, leaving out all the important details. I hear Jeff just got uglier and more boring. Years later when I was touring America with Culture Club, Andy McLachlan turned up at my hotel in New York trying to make peace. I wasn't ready for it.

I knew I had to leave London right away. Philip hated me, which meant I had no social life, and I didn't want to run into any of my enemies. It was spring 1979, I was seventeen.

Martin offered me a room at the flat and a job working on his clothes stall. All I had to do was break the news to Mum and Dad. I had very little money, I couldn't afford the luxury of the coach or a removal van. My new friend Beehive Marie said she would help me move, so we headed for the motorway and stuck out our thumbs. It was the first of a million hitches up the M1, listening to lorry drivers oozing about football and birds.

Back at Shooters Hill, I had an emotional scene with Mum. I told her I needed to go away for a while to forget about things. We both cried and hugged each other. It was the first time I'd ever felt really close to her. I told her all about Gary and she said that she'd never liked him, he was a "snidey-looking git," and if she ever saw him she'd slap him round the mouth. That made me laugh.

Hitching back to Walsall was a nightmare. I kept having second thoughts and rows with Marie. She was wearing stilettos and a pencil skirt, and kept dropping things, it was cold and pouring with rain and no one wanted to stop.

Leaving home was so liberating, I felt grown-up. I had my own room with a door I could lock. I was free, gay, and independent. I painted the door and the window frames black, nailed a bamboo pole across one of the corners to hang clothes on, and decorated the walls with pictures of naked men.

Martin's flat and my new home was on the corner of Goodall Street at the top of Walsall Market. It was lively by day and lonely at night. Most of the other houses were used for warehouse space. There was a gun shop, a sports shop, a Salvation Army hostel down the road, an art college, and a derelict courthouse dead opposite. Our most interesting neighbor was Ket, a white witch who ran an occult store called the Eye of Horus. I bought one of her witch puppets to hang in my window and called it Philip.

Seventy-nine Goodall Street was an old disused dental studio above a bathroom-fittings shop. As you came through the front door there was a horrible freezing-cold bathroom with chipped walls and no hot water. We had to run a rubber hose down from the kitchen if we wanted a bath. Martin had the biggest and best room on the first floor. I was between him and the kitchen in the old dining room. There was a frosted-glass serving hatch in the wall. Whenever the light went on in the kitchen it would illuminate the room and wake me up. Above us on the second floor there were two more bedrooms, occupied by Rhonda Freeman and Janet Pitt. Rhonda and I became friends as quickly as Janet and I became enemies. I was always fighting with Janet about the state of the flat. She used to hide curry-stained plates in the washing machine and leave her dirty clothes everywhere. I was a bit of a cleanliness freak and I wanted to prove myself. I took on the role of Cinderella, scrubbing the flat from top to bottom, behind the cooker and inside the cupboards. I drove them mad, moaning about the mess. My cleaning fetish nearly got me arrested. I was standing in the middle of the street, hosing down the brickwork and windows, when a stroppy young policeman came along and said it was a traffic hazard and if I didn't stop he would arrest me for obstruction.

Janet used to Krazy Kolor her pubic hair green and blue. She'd lift up her skirt and cackle like an old witch. Martin called her "cabbage cunt." I loved winding her up, pulling the hose off the kitchen tap while she was having a bath. You could hear her for miles, "Who's arsing around in that kitchen? Fuck off, ya bastard." Once I Super Glued her door and she had to call out the fire brigade. We all used to taunt Rhonda, "You're a lesbian, you're a lesbian." When I first met her she had a hideous feather-cut hairdo and looked like Kevin Keegan. She wore a horrible tweed jacket with nasty leather elbow patches and creased catalogue-style jeans. We dragged her kicking and screaming from the closet. It was a case of "Come out or we're coming in." In a matter of weeks Rhonda was a new woman. Spiky, short black hair, black plastic trousers, and a silver stud in her nose. We called her Rhonda Honda, the biker dyke.

Our flat became a target for local yobbos and queer haters. The police kept watch because some guys kept coming round in a van shouting, "Queers, we're gonna kill you." One local copper would pop in all the time for tea. I think he admired us. We were the first poofs he'd ever met, or at least the first to admit it.

Looking extreme was no act for Martin, it was his natural state. He couldn't have looked normal if he tried, with his shaved eyebrows and gaunt cheeks. He looked like an Alsatian from outer space. I loved watching him paint his face, crouched down in front of the mirror like a kabuki star, clothes strewn everywhere, the strains of northern soul wafting through the air.

We were both mental about music. Martin loved northern soul and dub reggae groups like the Scientists and early Aswad. I preferred postpunk electro like Cabaret Voltaire and Fad Gadget. We both loved Bowie, Lou Reed, Roxy Music—music, music, music. Marc Bolan, Patti Smith, Sly Stone, Nico, Tammy Wynette, and the soundtrack to *Cabaret*. Jumping on chairs pretending to be Liza Minnelli. "Willkommen, bienvenue, welcome . . . "

I had aspirations but I wasn't thinking beyond the next day. I knew I didn't ever want to have a proper job. Both Martin and I wanted to sing but it seemed so far out of reach. I wrote poetry, normally limericks about friends or people I hated. I would sing at every opportunity. People told me I had a good voice, some told me to shut up. They got so sick of me doing my endless Bowie impersonations. I must have learned every lyric. I joked that my only qualifications were A-level Bowie. For a laugh Martin and I thought we would record a version of the sixties classic "My Boyfriend's Back." Martin knew some record producer, but nothing came of it.

We thought we were stars anyway, both of us lived to be noticed, but Martin and I had very different personalities. Martin was cool and alien, already a legend on the Birmingham club scene. He could be a bit rude and snotty. I was bitchy but I would talk to everyone. I made friends quickly. Both of us had a mad crush on Roger Taylor, the drummer in Duran Duran, who were just forming around that time. He was a sweet guy—he used to come to clubs with us and often spent the night at Goodall Street in Martin's bed. Martin assured me nothing happened. I wouldn't have let him just lie there.

Martin and I entered a competition at a glitzy new club called the Holy City Zoo, owned by Andy Gray, a footballer with Aston Villa. I was voted weirdest person in the north. Much to Martin's annoyance. He thought I was his clone. He influenced me, it's true, but I had plenty of my own colorful ideas and a personality to match.

My winning outfit was a medieval coned hat with chiffon veil, a padded black Lurex jacket, baggy pleated trousers, and Ali Baba shoes. They gave me a magnum of champagne and I appeared in the local paper next to Andy Gray. Jeremy Healy was up from London, wearing a Vivienne Westwood bondage top as a dress with stockings and suspenders. He was much camper in those days.

The star treatment didn't last very long. We had to catch the night bus back to Walsall and got into a fight at the bus stop with these casuals. Rhonda fended them off with my champagne, threatening to break the bottle over their heads. Riding the bus back to Walsall was always a nerve-racking experience: we regularly got spat at and jostled. The night buses only ran halfway to Great Barr, we had to leg it and hide in the cab office. I thought Martin was brave living in the Black Country—I suppose I was too. That's what I admired about him most, his courage, and he could work stilettos better than a hardened hooker. Martin was less cautious than me: he expected a whack in the face at least every month. He would kick off his heels and run at the first sign of trouble. I'd be ahead of him.

Martin was chased through the center of Brum by teddy boys for wearing an electric blue drape coat. The police hassled him too. He got strip-searched in the snow. They made him take off his boots, they didn't find his dope. He was lucky that night.

A safe haven after the clubs was Patty Bell's house in Edgbaston. Patty was a punk mum and designer. She had a clothes shop in Hurst Street with her friend Jane Kahn. We would sit round Patty's talking till seven in the morning. I often slept there. Patty was an adorable warm person, a curious mixture of youthfulness and wisdom. I loved listening to her tell stories. When she was fourteen she'd appeared as the half lady in a water tank at a fairground, some trick done with mirrors. As a teenager she went out with Tom Jones and Engelbert Humperdinck. She was married to rock 'n' roller Steve Gibbons, a gorgeous gypsy heartthrob. I once sat for days studding a leather jacket for him. Patty used to say to me, "You're famous you are, you're famous." She would run round the clubs screaming drunk, checking to see how many dresses she'd sold. "Oh, look, there's a Kahn and Bell."

Martin's stall, Degville's Dispensary, was in the basement of Oasis, an indoor market in the Bull Ring Centre. It was full of jean shops and hippie stalls selling patchouli oil and incense. They were trying to jazz the place up by renting out to young designers. There were loads of other freaks, like Angela, who had the stall next to us. She had purple hair, purple clothes, and purple makeup and moped around like a psychedelic sloth, always sleepy and in a bad mood. "Go and get us a tea, wi' ya." Working on the stall was a right laugh, even though Martin only paid me £3.50 a day. I called him Ebenezer Scrooge. We rowed all the time about money. I always added a little extra onto the price of the clothes and pocketed the difference. A quid here, a quid there.

Martin knew I was pilfering, but I was better at pulling in customers. He scared people away. I would say, "Everyone's wearing them in London. I suppose they're a bit loud for Birmingham." It always worked. They would come back ten minutes later and buy. Martin's creations were brilliant, considering he knew more about northern soul than pattern cutting. He would spend hours attacking rolls of gaudy Lycra which somehow ended up as dresses. Pink with green sleeves, yellow slashes across the front, trimmed with marabou feathers or curtain fringe. He was the Salvador Dali of fashion.

Every Saturday, religiously, Martin would hunt through the rag market for loud new fabrics. The women who worked on the stalls were brilliant, massive beehives and Mr. Spock eyebrows. They thought we were weird. We'd say, "Did you look in the mirror this morning, Peggy Lee?" There was a lot of affectionate catcalling— we loved those women. We used to go there especially to see them. They would scream at Martin, "Eh oop, luv, what yow coom as?"

I thought my sex life would boom in Walsall, especially having my own room and being the new boy in town. It was no more fruitful than London. Typically I always fell for the straight boys. I thought I was going to grow cobwebs until one quiet night there was a loud bang at 79. I heard Martin shouting, "Ket doesn't live here. She didn't pay the rent so we kicked her out, ha, ha, ha." I stuck my head out to see who was there. My eyes dilated when I caught sight of the hunky soldier in full camouflage and black beret.

"Do you wanna cup of tea?"

He smiled. "That'd be nice. I've come a long way."

Martin kicked me. "Fuck off, George, you don't know who he is."

I laughed. "Yeah, but I want to."

I made him tea and we sat in the kitchen chatting. Martin was milling around like a jealous queen. "Oh! Don't I get a cup then? I only live here." By this point, our guest must have realized he wasn't with two center forwards from Aston Villa. He didn't seem fazed. He was a queen's dream with a skinny little mustache that moved like clock hands whenever he smiled—he had a nice smile. His eyes looked glazed, like he was stoned, and he would laugh for no apparent reason, which made me uncomfortable. We talked for hours—it was obvious he had nowhere to go. I said he could sleep on my floor. When we went into my room he just stripped off to his pants, jumped into bed, and lay back with his arms behind his head. I couldn't believe my luck. His body was perfectly taut and he had cheap tattoos on his arm. I left my T-shirt on and slipped in beside him.

I was so paranoid, I never let anyone see me without my clothes or face on. I would jump out of bed in the morning and make myself look human. I wasn't a pretty sight first thing, I always slept with my makeup on and woke up with panda rings round my eyes.

Paul the soldier stayed for about three months and we had warm, cuddly sex every night. Typically he left without saying goodbye. He stole some clothes and a ring from my room, it was a small price to pay—the ring was a piece of junk. I definitely had the better deal.

My next dysfunctional romance was with Colin, a skinhead car thief. Martin and I met him on the train and he ended up living in my room for months. Colin was dead bony and nothing much to look at. He had trouble in his eyes and that was enough. Sex was whatever I wanted it to be and Colin's favorite position was rigor mortis. When he ended up in prison I became even more passionate, writing every week and waiting for my man to be free. I loved being a prison wife, telling people, "My boyfriend is in the nick, you know." It made Colin sound like a bit of criminal rough.

One weekend I decided to visit him at Devizes prison, Wiltshire. For some reason I thought it was near Birmingham. I talked my friend Hilda into hitching there with me. I was wearing huge drawstring pants made from vivid curtain fabric, my hair was shooting straight up, and my face was painted like a psychotic clown. Hilda looked like a refugee in her forties Oxfam coat and white pointy stilettos.

Arriving at the prison we caused a riot. The boys working in the gardens came running up to the fence shouting and pointing at us. "Oi, Sinbad." "State of that." It was already way past visiting time but the guards let us in. They were desperate to know who we were visiting. Colin was cold, ungrateful, and embarrassed. Our visit brought him nothing but grief. I received a brief letter from him saying the other boys had tried to pull him behind the fridges and have sex with him. He probably loved it, lying bastard. When he was released he came straight back to Goodall Street. I stupidly gave him a key to the flat, and the bastard robbed Martin's and Janet's rooms. Martin went to the police, but they just laughed at him. I never saw Colin again.

In the autumn of 1979 Degville's Dispensary opened at Kensington Market in London. The new shop was more successful than Oasis. Martin cornered the market for people who wanted to look like Joan Collins crossed with Daffy Duck. I admired his commitment. He sat on the sewing machine from Monday to Friday, then dragged sacks down to London and worked in the shop all day Saturday. He always made himself something ridiculous to wear, a pink PVC catsuit that displayed the groceries and pulled up the crack of his arse, red ankle boots, and a fuchsia feather boa wrapped around his head. Only Martin could carry off the look. His customers looked like extras from *Dr. Who*.

We both started to spend more time in London and drifted apart. Martin was tired of my ever-expanding persona and obsessed with his booming fashion empire. I was back in with Philip and over the northern experience. I wanted to move home.

I didn't want to go back to Mum and Dad, so I wrote to my friend Hilda and her flatmate Sophie asking if I could stay with them in London till I found a squat. I met Hilda at Billy's in 1978. She was dressed as a twenties flapper. Her real name was

Jackie but I nicknamed her Hilda because she looked like one. She hated being called Hilda and at first told me to piss off. I bought her a little diamanté H to wear which sealed our friendship. Hilda was real skinny with pretty eyes and a kind heart that she tried desperately to conceal. She was tough and could shoo you away with one of her cod looks. We went everywhere together and when I moved to Walsall we wrote to each other constantly.

This time I couldn't wait for Hilda's reply. Some punky friends were delivering furniture to London and offered me a ride. It was an overnight decision. I loaded up my bags and boxes of clothes and a big carved-wood mirror liberated from the courthouse, stole £50 from the stash under Martin's floorboards, and left my witch puppet swinging in the window. Bye!

Years later when I was Boy George the pop star Martin let me know how he really felt. We were at my friend Stephen Linard's birthday party in Camden Town. Martin was bitter. "Oh, you're slumming it tonight." I was feeling uncomfortable anyway. Stephen's tiny council flat was packed with faces I'd known for years. They didn't seem able to adjust to my celebrity and I had no idea how to behave. Martin cornered me, telling me Culture Club was "pop shite." He was forming a group himself and it wouldn't be a crass sellout. His comments stayed with me. So I had to laugh when he finally got his band Sigue Sigue Sputnik together in 1986. Martin virtually fornicated with the media. He was the biggest pop tart of them all.

Shoot it up.

Shoot it up.

Hilda was already sharing her tiny room with Myra, it looked like a halfway hostel. A big mattress swallowed most of the floor, surrounded by a sea of clothes and girlie bits. I found a corner and slept on the carpet, leaving my clothes in their bags, pulling them out as they were needed. Some nights if it was cold—it was always uncomfortable—I'd jump in with the girls and grab all the blankets. Even with the discomfort, it was brilliant living there. We all played Mum with Sophie's nine-month-old baby Athlynne, taking her round the shops and off to the park. Sophie was a punk designer, she made Athlynne loads of freaky outfits. Punky romper suits covered in zips with padded spikes on the shoulders. Housewives and grannies would eye us in disgust thinking Hilda and I were the twisted parents. We thought Athlynne was the best-dressed baby in North London.

Hilda had a crush on me. I must have encouraged it in my own stupid way. I was always touching her up, grabbing her tits—I did it with loads of girls. Myra said I was a closet straight. I loved Hilda as a friend. I thought we were like sisters. She knew I was queer. I always told her the lurid details of my sex life. She'd cackle, "You dirty cunt."

One weekend she invited me to Stevenage for a family wedding. I'd been there loads of times and stayed at her mum's. The wedding was a right laugh, even though we were the joke with all her straitlaced relatives. We got totally pissed and stuffed our faces. Hilda wanted to share a bed. I sensed her desire for the first time and maneuvered my way out of it.

On the train home we were bickering at each other. She snapped, "You don't care about anyone." I was embarrassed and knew what was coming. "Of course I do." She started sobbing. "You don't care about me and I love you." I wanted to jump off the moving train. I didn't know what to do or say.

I tried pretending it hadn't happened, but after that day things were never the same. Hilda had exposed herself. It was easier for her to hate me and that's what she did.

Myra and I decided to look for a squat. I couldn't stand the silence and Myra needed her space. We scoured the streets after dark like cat burglars and found an empty flat in one of the council blocks over the road. Number 64 Kenbrook House was padlocked like a fortress so I went to Shooters Hill and borrowed a couple of screwdrivers and a crowbar from Dad's tool kit. We were laughing so much we were sure we'd get caught. Once the lock was loose I cracked it back and threw myself at the door. The bang echoed round the empty courtyard. We cowered in the hallway, listening for angry neighbors. Myra protected the flat while I ran back and forth with our belongings and we spent the night in our new home. There was no electricity but the radiators had been left on for months. We woke with hideous headaches.

Myra and I pooled our pennies for a new lock and keys, candles, bacon sandwiches, and tea, then spent the day trying to make the place homey. The decorations were nasty, orange brown walls and a dusty and worn chocolate carpet. We chose our rooms. Myra took the small dark one at the end of the hallway, a perfect cocoon. The other rooms were just as poky so I moved into the living room, which joined onto the kitchen. Even with all our scrubbing the place stank—the heat and dust had created its own special odor. I put my mattress in the corner and plastered the ceiling and walls with gay porn and cutup headlines. Myra painted her room black and hung her clothes and hats around the walls like a jumble sale. She had no domestic aspirations. "Whatever. I don't mind." She was a girl without reason or routine. Suddenly she would start doing odd things you hadn't noticed before, like putting her makeup on in the wrong order, lips first, eyes last, and she was always soaking in the bath.

Before not long there were three of us. Myra's old flatmate Andy Polaris moved in with his record boxes and soul-boy threads. He'd been living in a rented flat in Manor Park, but it was much more trendy to squat. Andy was quiet and never around. I'm sure he just used the flat for storage. We used to root through his belongings. However hard we tried, we could never work him out. Was he gay? Was he straight? He wouldn't tell. There were no clues, except for a few pictures pinned on the wall, Montgomery Clift, James Dean, Marlon Brando, jazz-age ladies, and an old snap of Bowie. He had hundreds of records—it was a pity we couldn't play them, Kraftwerk, everything by Bowie and Roxy Music, Stax, Motown, and weird electro-pop. Andy wrote brilliant poetry. My favorite was Love.

Love is like a glittering pool,
Its opaque beauty invites the fool
To look more closely,
To dive right in,
Which he does forgetting he cannot swim.

While we were out clubbing, Mum and Dad came by with food supplies. Dad tricked the lock. They filled the cupboards and left a note. "Nice wallpaper. Love you, son." I couldn't stop laughing, thinking of Mum's face and all those dicks. She hated me living rough and kept asking me to come home. I could never have gone back to Woolwich and risked missing all those wonderful adventures. Our squat had hot water, which was a real luxury. Having no lights was the biggest problem. I had to put my makeup on before dark or I looked like a battered housewife.

Tuesday night we went to the Blitz club in Covent Garden hosted by Rusty Egan and Steve Strange. There were always queues outside. Steve Strange lorded it on the door, making us wait while he turned away some poor freak from the sticks. I felt sorry for some of them, they'd spent so long putting on their makeup and lampshade hats. Steve was so superior: one week he was your best friend, the next he'd stare right through you. The success of the Blitz led him to believe he had created the New Romantic scene. There really was no scene. At capacity the Blitz held three hundred; it wasn't a national phenomenon like punk. Most of the crowd had been around as long, if not longer than Steve Strange and we all resented his self-appointment as king of the weird. His nicknames were Wally Weird or Nobby Normal.

Steve Strange was a punk like the rest of us. I knew him from the early days up the Kings Road, at the Roxy and the Vortex. Even then he carried a collapsible ladder in his back pocket. Hanging around Billy Idol and the punk elite, decked head to toe in Sex clothes, borrowed from the stockroom.

Rusty Egan was drummer with the Rich Kids, formed by Glen Matlock after he left the Sex Pistols. I never saw them play but I knew they were crap. Rusty was friendlier than Steve but just as patronizing. He would always stop and talk and never needed a platform. His clothes were very dapper, jodhpurs, tweed forties jackets, crisp white shirts, silk scarves, and slicked-back hair. Rusty tried to be so refined but his slickness was easily rattled. Marilyn and I bitched at him so much he grabbed me by the throat and blew his cover.

Steve and Rusty's clubbing legend began in June 1978 when they took over Billy's at Gossips club. They were the first of a new breed of club entrepreneurs, quick to see the potential for making money and creating a safe place for us freaks to dance the night away. Steve was the doorman, Rusty deejayed, playing Bowie,

Roxy, film scores, and electro-pop like Kraftwerk. The emphasis was on style, the invitation read "Bowie Night. A Club for Heroes." It had more to do with decadent prewar Berlin than reflecting life on a South London council estate. Punk had become a parody of itself, an anti-Establishment uniform, attracting hordes of dickheads who wanted to gob, punch, and stamp on flowers. I got beer thrown over me at punk gigs and called a poser because I wore makeup and frills. It was sad because I loved the energy and music of punk. In the beginning it was screaming at us to reject conformity but it had become a joke, right down to the £80 Anarchy T-shirts on sale at Seditionaries.

Punk was safe, we were spinning forward in a whirl of eyeliner and ruffles. Getting a reaction was the ultimate goal. I would sit in the front room at Shooters Hill painting my face and teasing my hair into gravity-defying shapes, ignoring Mum's pleas and Dad's smirks. I followed in Philip's footsteps, styling every public appearance, making sure to stand out. Our crowd were all competing for the prize. Friends like Clare with the Hair, who had a crown of twelve-inch lacquered spikes shooting up from her head and wore squiggles on her face, or Pinkietessa, who, like Clare, threaded her own clothes and looked like Scarlett O'Hara mixed with Little Bo Peep.

CHAPTER 18

Jeremy and I heard weirdos and punks were needed for a new movie called *Breaking Glass*. Perfect, cash and cameras. Extra hours were spent preparing for the auditions, held early morning at the Production Village in Cricklewood. We were a sight at 8:30 A.M. on the Bakerloo Line. My face was green, I wore a quilted plastic jacket with shoulders that sprang out like wings. Jeremy was in a biker's jacket with bondage trousers and kabuki makeup. We lacquered and crimped our hair into clumps.

Phil Daniels, who was one of the actors, took one look at us and burst out laughing. Jeremy got a bit part, I was rejected. I joined the crowd scenes with every punk, skinhead, and freak in London, which were filmed at the Rainbow Theatre, Finsbury Park.

I was determined to be seen, and so was everyone, Myra, Andy, Jeremy, Philip, Gay Robert, Marilyn, Slag Sue, Pinkietessa, Punk Jayne. Finsbury Park looked like a futuristic punk city.

The skinheads and other troublemakers were kept in the balcony—it didn't stop them jeering, spitting, and throwing food. Philip and Marilyn got the most stick, Philip prancing down the aisle in an Egyptian tube dress, platforms, and green hair, Marilyn as Norma Jean incognito, headscarf, dark glasses, donkey jacket. The chanting was deafening: "Queer, fucking queer." He loved it, stripping down to an off-the-shoulder leotard, corset, and black

PVC mini. Marilyn had certainly changed since we first met at Punk Jayne's mum's. The transformation from pig to butterfly was remarkable.

During lunch we ended up at the pub together. Marilyn put on a gala performance, pulling out an electric razor, pretending to shave his made-up face, bending over in front of straight boys, "Oops, I've dropped something." He stuck one of Slag Sue's Tampaxes in his leotard with the string hanging out. Everyone in the pub was transfixed, including me. Despite a million reservations Marilyn became part of my life, hanging out at the squat, getting ready for soirees and nights at the Blitz. He flattered me, "Oh, you look good in everything." It was true, I was dead skinny then and could make net curtains look stylish. I made the best of what I had, cleverly disguising myself, painting my eyes like Liz Taylor. Marilyn looked good without makeup and clothes, his body was fit and muscular, his self-confidence even more obnoxious.

Myra and Andy didn't like having Marilyn around the squat when they weren't home, he was always poking through Andy's boxes, trying on Myra's fox stoles and hats, tossing them to the floor. "Uch, fleas." He kept hinting that living in Borehamwood was a nightmare. The thought of living with Marilyn made Myra and Andy dog-sick, but I fancied a live-in sister and vetoed them.

Marilyn arrived like a dawn police raid, shouting, kicking at the door. "Is my room ready? Where's the maid?" Myra slid under her duvet, Andy started packing his things. I strolled down the high street with my new sister to check out the boys. There was a cute rockabilly who worked in a retro record store by the tube station. Marilyn stopped in front of the window and fixed his hair. We both got evil looks. The rockabilly was Jess Birdsall, later to star in the movie *Wish You Were Here* and the BBC soap *Eldorado*. Even then he was just like his bastard character, eager to punch anyone and everyone, especially queer cunts like us. He tried to throttle me at Billy's because I was wearing a teddy-boy drape coat with seamed stockings and stilettos. A big black bouncer saved me. I lived in fear of bumping into Birdsall and wouldn't go back to Billy's or near the high street.

Marilyn and I spent our days doing loads of nothing, we often wandered down Oxford Street and cadged free makeup and perfume samples at Selfridges and D. H. Evans. The salesgirls were sarcastic and patronizing, especially the old ones. Marilyn wouldn't take their shit. He made them show him every lipstick and eye shadow in the range. One old dear at the Clinique counter was particularly pissy, especially as she looked like she was ready for Christmas panto. Marilyn asked, "What's that soap for?" She said it was antiaging and very expensive, meaning we couldn't afford it.

"Do you use it?"

"I use all Clinique products."

"Well, it didn't do much for you. Aren't you supposed to retire at sixty-five?"

We had a laugh walking behind housewives talking loudly about our boyfriends' big dicks, sniggering childishly. We were evil most of the time. We loved picking on the out-of-town freaks at the Blitz, acting no better than beer boys. Jeremy and I were the worst. We demanded the right to be individual, yet condemned others for getting it wrong. So much energy was wasted on who wore what first. We were all thieving magpies anyway. Jeremy had his own clone called Ricky with the same conehead hairdo and eyebrows. He treated it as a joke until Ricky's picture appeared in a national newspaper. Jeremy vowed to chop off his hair. We went hunting at Studio 21, a New Romantic club on Oxford Street, armed with large scissors. We didn't get our trophy. I collared Ricky at another club. He pushed me and I fell on to a table, cutting my finger. I had to go to Middlesex Hospital to have stitches—I still have the tribal scar. We especially loathed the fashion-student types that went to the Blitz, Kim Bowen and the rest of her stuck-up clique who attended St. Martin's College. They lived in a big squat in Warren Street and looked down on everyone.

Before Marilyn arrived in Kentish Town our relationship with the neighbors had been mediocre. They ignored us, we ignored them. My only problem was a ginger skinhead across the courtyard who was always staring. Our next-door neighbor was an ordinary fat slob with two noisy kids and a miserable wife. He'd smile or grunt depending on his alcohol levels. He thought Marilyn was a blond tart and embarrassed himself by trying to chat him up. After that he couldn't look us in the eye and his kids started calling us "poofs." It didn't help when Marilyn told his wife to go fuck herself.

We were chatting round a candle when a loud thud hit the front door, "Turn that fucking music down, turn it down." I ran into the hallway half amused and shouted, "You're mad, we don't have electricity, there's no noise." He carried on, "You've no right being here." I let out a scream as the glass came crashing through. Our lunatic neighbor was trying to hack the door down with an ax. Myra was crying, "Leave us alone, leave us alone." Marilyn threw open the back window. We were only one floor up, but in the panic it seemed like a long drop. Myra wouldn't jump. I shook her hard. "Do you want to get killed?" Marilyn went out first. I threw myself out and landed in a heap, twisting my ankle. I hobbled down the road behind Marilyn. I had visions of Myra with an ax through her bald head.

We found a phone box, dialed 999, and waited for the police to come. They were unsympathetic when they did, taking the side of the residents who were out in force, gawping and gossiping on the balconies. The police said they couldn't guarantee our safety if we stayed. I was disgusted by their attitude. They didn't seem concerned that someone had axed our door down and tried to kill us or that we had nowhere to go. Luckily we only had clothes to move. We grabbed armfuls and threw them into carrier bags. The police stood watch till we cleared out. I felt like one of those Frenchwomen who'd slept with the Nazis during the Second World War.

Luckily I knew of an empty property in a neighboring block in Islip Street, five minutes away. We were so angry and frustrated we managed to rip through the padlocks. The windows were all boarded so we couldn't see a thing. The smell of fresh paint and wallpaper meant it was clean and probably about to be inhabited. We laid our clothes out and slept on the cold hard floorboards.

In the morning I was ratty and insecure, I hated everyone. It was the miserable side of squatting I didn't want to deal with. We had to buy a new lock but no one had any money. I said I'd bunk the train back to Woolwich and get some off my dad. Even though

I'd declared my independence I was always going back for alms. It would be an excuse for an I-told-you-so lecture and a home-cooked meal. Dad gave me a lock from his van and thirty quid. I nicked half a loaf of bread and a slab of cheese.

Once the lock was secured we were confident. It would take six months for the council to get us out. We tore down a couple of boards to let in the light. Our new squat was in a block called the Forties, it should have been called the Eighties, that was the average age of most tenants. I grimly recall the aroma of boiled mince-meat and cabbage. None of the old folk spoke to us, but I was sure they were busy writing letters to the council. The old ones were always the worst. My instincts were right. Three weeks after moving in we were issued with an eviction order and a date for a court hearing we were not obliged to attend. I didn't care, I had my eye on the West End, one of those big houses in Warren Street near the fashion students. Myra and I wandered the area night after night, house shopping. Marilyn went one better, jumping the Monopoly board from Kentish Town to Knightsbridge. He met a blond Hooray called John Cochran-Patrick and was gone.

The day of our court hearing in January 1980 we trudged down to the High Court in Fleet Street dressed to distress. Myra's head was freshly shaved, my face was green; our idea of a protest. The usher warned us we'd be done for contempt if we entered the courtroom. I was laughing. "I sentence you to ten years for drag." We were given eight weeks to vacate the property.

From court we took the tube to Warren Street to check out a four-story house we'd been stalking in Great Titchfield Street, deliberately passing by the fashion squat. Someone shouted from the window and I spun round. It was Kim Bowen, smiling! "Fancy a cuppa?" I was half expecting to be drowned. She threw down the key and we let ourselves in. We sat in the kitchen, chatting and drinking tea like a true pair of creeps. I was surprised at how nice and common Kim was, just like us. Even in daylight she was glamorous, her flame hair spun up on top of her head, bare feet and a silky white shift dress that clung to her nipples. Like all students she existed on a shoestring, but that didn't stop her. Her room was like a Grecian boudoir, white from floor to ceiling with ruched draping and gold cherubs everywhere. Her voice was as varnished as her toenails. All the Warren Street lot had this put-on voice, stretching their vowels like Kenneth Williams. Kim's motives were soon revealed, she was after my friend Jeremy. I told her, "He'll have sex with anyone."

Myra and I moved to a five-story Edwardian house in Great Titchfield Street. Dad moved us in his pickup truck. Mum was mortified. "You can't live here, it's filthy." She brought us food and candles. The house was filthy and it stank. The basement was stuffed with broken furniture and rotting mattresses. We cleared it out and scrubbed the house until it smelled of pine and damp.

As soon as all the hard work was done we had a full house. You couldn't keep a good squat quiet. Andy Polaris was back. My clubbing friend Julia Fodor, who worked at PX with Steve Strange and did the door at the Blitz, took a room. At first sight Julia was classy and beautiful with her beehive, Cleopatra eyes, and fake gold jewelry—till she opened her mouth, that was. Our next guest was Patrick Lilley, "Beelzebub" from Birmingham, who took the attic room, and Hilda moved in with Myra, ending our six-month cold war.

My room was cozy and tidy. I needed to create a homey atmosphere. I covered the walls in pictures of heroes and hunks, Bowie, Bette Davis, Little Richard, drop-dead models out of fashion magazines, Chinese umbrellas and Japanese fans. I made a dressing table out of a door on bricks and stuck a broken mirror on top. Bed was a mattress on the floor with ten blankets pilfered from home along with a big Deco wardrobe with bow doors. I nailed a broomstick between the wardrobe and the wall for extra clothes space. I was so organized. Everyone gathered in my room for gossip sessions. The only time doors were closed was when someone was at it or in a stinking mood. Mostly we came crying to each other.

I fell willfully in love with a boy called Wilf Rogers who lived in the basement of Warren Street and helped us fix up the electricity. He wasn't one of the fifties pinup types I normally fancied. There was nothing trendy about him. He was small with a beaky nose and freckles and wore home-knit jumpers and scruffy jeans. He made me laugh. I used to crimp his hair and dress him in my clothes. At first we did nothing but shag [screw]. I thought I'd found the perfect boyfriend who would never leave me. Wilf said he was straight. I knew he was lying when he let me fuck him. I ran round telling everyone. It was the first time I'd been the man.

It wasn't long before Jeremy and Kim were locked together like dogs. Jeremy left his mum's and moved into Warren Street. We all became friends. Kim was queen whether anyone liked it or not. Her room was the largest, situated next to the kitchen, the central meeting place that doubled as a studio and bedroom for milliner Stephen Jones. The house was full of latent and blatant creativity. Above the kitchen lived lovers David Holah and John Maybury. David was a fashion student, John was studying film. They were both unnervingly beautiful and reminded you of how unfair Mother Nature can be. They kept to themselves, except when one needed refuge after a stonking row. There was always plenty to row about, David was the ex-lover of Lee Sheldrick, two floors down, a tall pretty boy who had briefly dated Kim. It couldn't have been more incestuous. Lee would have made a good Avenger in his polo necks, tight slacks, and winkle-pickers. I couldn't see him as a ladies' man even though Kim insisted they'd gone all the way.

The aunt of the house was Melissa Caplan, a loud aberration, with purple hair and a pierced nose. She lived in between the squat and her mother's in Hendon, like any sensible Jewish girl would. Melissa was a designer and gained early notoriety dressing Toyah Wilcox and later Spandau Ballet, who were hovering around the Blitz scene on the fringe of stardom.

Sisters Lesley and Jane Chilkes were closest to the front door, the worst position in any house. Lesley was official door slammer, small with scraped-back hair, booming red lips, and a voice you'd never forget. "All right, I can fucking hear you." Jane was older and wispy. She claimed to receive psychic messages from Oscar Wilde and scribbled them all over his books.

Under the house was a huge basement stretching over to Euston Road into the shell of an old boarded-up shop. Hunky and tattooed Barry Brien lived there with his white rat. Entering the basement was like crossing a dangerous border: it was damp and claustrophobic, perfect for all the nefarious activities. Barry looked like a beat-up Bruce Weber model, and everyone talked about his huge dick. He was tough for sure, but always sweet to us queers, the mark of a true gentleman.

My boyfriend Wilf and Stephen Linard lived in the rooms above Barry. Linard was the odd one out—he was a fashion student. He says he only took the room because it was first to have electricity and running water but we knew he was desperate to run up a jock-strap for Barry. Stephen was a real *Carry On* character, thin with milky white skin and bulging eyes. Kim called him "the pessimist." He was always whining, "Forget it, it'll never work." Stephen loved to drink Pernod. He once peed over the balcony onto the dance floor at the Blitz, showering among others Rusty Egan. He was so ashamed he disappeared to his parents in Canvey Island. We all thought it was hilarious and quite justifiable.

Lots of other creatures moved through Warren Street. Club faces like Steve Butler, Barry O.D., who later sold an evil picture of me to the *Sun,* Chris Sullivan, Christos, budding writer Robert Elms, Steve Dagger, and the various members of Spandau Ballet were always having their photographs taken in Kim's bedroom. Everyone wanted to hang out there, or at least claim they did.

Our squat was second in rank and less exclusive. I threw out a trawler net. I envisaged Great Titchfield Street like a wartime community with everyone popping in and out, borrowing eyeliner and sugar. For all my freakishness I still craved normality. I wanted a family of friends around me and a regular boyfriend, preferably with a job, who wouldn't be round my feet while I was cleaning. When I met boys I fell in love instantly and became too obsessive, driving them away. I was always testing them to see how much they cared. That coupled with my extreme selfishness made for a tempestuous brew.

Wilf pretended to be one of the Waltons, all hammer and heart, but he was shifty. We started squabbling and having fistfights. I wrenched his hair out and battered him, he tried to hit back, it was like a Pekingese fighting a Rottweiler. He started refusing sex and avoiding me for days on end. It was torture for a girl who likes a reaction. Then I found out he'd brought Hilda home from the Blitz. I knew it was her revenge. Before I could throw her out they'd shacked up at Warren Street. I was deranged and kept going round, asking questions, driving everyone mad.

Our love affair ended painfully at one of the legendary Warren Street parties. The theme was cowboys and Indians and I was ready with my arrows, my body painted yellow like a cosmic squaw, feathers in my hair. I got drunker than I needed to and downed twenty tabs of speed, running around in bare feet kicking the doors and walls, screaming for Wilf's blood. I ended up at University College Hospital. The nurses didn't know what to do with me. They had to send me home even though I was halluci- nating, going out of my mind. I thought someone was trying to kill me. I sat on my bed for days, crying, floating my arms around in the air. I saw Rastafarian gunmen in the garden and faces in the walls. Myra and Hilda kept vigil, holding my hand, I was too mad- dened to know who was there. They were both convinced I would never return. When I came down I carried on pretending to be mad. I enjoyed the fuss, turning up at the Scala Cinema dressed as Marc Bolan in a curly black wig and deathly panstick, talking in tongues.

I'd been taking speed since I lived in Walsall. After being so sick I never wanted to touch drugs again, I became self-righteous. Sex was something else—there were no risks in those days. No straight boy was that uptight if you got them in the right mood. I was eager for a one-night stand or a quick grope behind the toilet door.

I picked up this bawdy northern bloke in a phone box in Kings Cross. He wanted directions and called me "luv." I was in full makeup and terrified to open my mouth in case he punched me. He grabbed my jacket, "'Ere, are you a bloke? You're really pretty, you are." He wanted me to go round the back of the flats with him. I took him back to Great Titchfield Street even though he looked like he might murder me. We had great sex. Typically he wanted to be the lady—so many "straight" boys were like that. My friend Christos arrived as he was leaving. He couldn't believe he was queer. I laughed, "Conversion. My dad was a builder, you know."

Christos Tolera was wet-lipped, dark, and especially handsome, dressed in berets, smocky shirts, and leather jodhpurs. All the queens fancied him, and he was too nice for his own good. I always hoped I could bring him round. He was Greek, after all.

Linard and I used to jump on top of him and stick our hands down his trousers. He went mad but he still hung around with us.

Linard and I became really close, bothering boys at the Blitz and the Northumberland Arms, our local pub. I went to his parents' house for weekends and they took us out to posh restaurants in Knightsbridge. Stephen's dad owned a handbag shop in Beauchamp Place, which was poetic I suppose. Stephen was always trusting and too kind, and was abused because of it. He moaned about people stealing his belongings and constantly having to step over drunken stoned bodies outside his bedroom. One night Stephen brought some trade home. Jeremy had poured itching powder in his bed and on his towels. He lost it, he was sick of "Warren Street station," I let him move into our squat.

Stephen and his friend Christine Binnie borrowed a British Rail luggage trolley and began carting his stuff round. They were on their last haul, skipping and singing "She'll Be Coming Round the Mountain . . . ," when Jennifer Justice swooped. Suddenly there were four squad cars, a lot of fuss for one measly trolley. Myra and I were hanging out the window screaming, "Leave him alone, go catch a criminal." Stephen was dragged off to Tottenham Court Road police station, charged with theft, and locked up for the night. He appeared before the magistrate in a crumpled red tartan bondage suit with wilted spiky hair and was duly fined.

We felt so sorry for him we made up his bed, placed his sewing machine on a box, and laid out his things. He was proud and tearful. Having Stephen at the house was brilliant. He was down-to-earth, clean, and congenial, except in the mornings if he didn't have his cup of tea. The house had no water so we had to get supplies from Jack's café round the corner. Stephen was a living contradiction. By day he attended St. Martin's College, and he was studious, unlike the others, who were always skiving. He came home and did all his homework, but at night he went mad. Even a quiet drink at the Northumberland Arms turned into a shindig. There were rumors that Stephen shagged the landlord for an after-hours drink.

Slinky Mitsu was one of Stephen's best friends. She worked as a receptionist at Vidal Sassoon's, but that didn't explain her Thierry Mugler wardrobe. She treated Stephen to a champagne bed-in at the Albemarle Hotel in Mayfair using a stolen credit card. He had no idea. They were rollicking naked, chomping on a smoked-salmon platter, when the Fraud Squad burst in. Stephen was lucky that time, but Mitsu got done. She had a drug habit and avoided serious charges by agreeing to go for treatment.

On the surface Mitsu had it all. She was half Norwegian and half Thai, leggy and gorgeous, and managed to look expensive even if she wasn't. She spread it around that she and Iggy Pop were once lovers and that "China Girl" was written about her. I believed it. Whenever I hear that song I think of Mitsu, "Shh, just you shut your mouth." Everyone said Mitsu bought her drugs from Wilf. I didn't want to believe it.

I bumped into Wilf at the Blitz and he was all over me. I fell for it and went back to Warren Street for a reunion shag. Hilda was away so it was a chance to get my own back. We had a little grope and roll around, then Wilf said he had to do something. I waited half an hour, then went looking and found Wilf and Mitsu in bed in Barry's room. I felt so stupid. I wanted to kill Mitsu and went home cursing and wishing her the worst. I didn't sleep much. I got up at nine and walked round to the café facing Warren Street. The squat door was wide open. Kim, David, and Lee were sitting in the café looking gray. I knew Mitsu was dead before Kim said anything. Wilf had woken and found her cold beside him. I couldn't believe it was true. Stephen took it worst. He was meant to meet Mitsu for lunch. He thought the others were playing a sick joke.

Drugs weren't an issue for any of us: it was fashion, free drink, sex, and nightclubs. We all knew about the heroin dealing in the basement. It was more ignored than condoned. Most of us took speed occasionally, a hangover from the punk days. Heroin was for dirty hippies and heinous junkies. After Mitsu's death the basement was cleaned out. Wilf and Barry disappeared for a while. Mitsu's heartbroken mother came banging on the door night after night, weeping in the street, "You killed my baby." It was so painful for everyone.

CHAPTER 19

My old stomping ground the Global Village was turned into London's biggest gay club, Heaven, in December 1979. We were there most nights checking out the trade. It was a waste of time really—we didn't belong in that scene of body-conscious queers and leather boys who arrived on motorbikes or bus carrying their helmets. Occasionally I would dress down so that I could pick up. I went home with some tasties and monsters. I brought this huge muscle man back to the squat, he was gorgeous to look at but his body felt like plastic. In the morning I discovered he'd stolen my Seditionaries plastic tie. I was livid. Philip, Marilyn, and I would go to the gay pubs in Earls Court dragging whoever with us. The Coleherne was the most popular, full of Tom of Finland real lifes. I really fancied some of those leather boys, but didn't like the idea of being tortured and spanked too hard. We heard all sorts of horror stories about fists and bike chains. There was an S&M shop next to the Coleherne that had some scary accouterments.

Weekends were one big club crawl. Philip insisted on going everywhere just in case he missed some fresh young thing. An hour at Heaven, then on to the Sombrero, ending up at a seedy rent-boy club for a laugh—at least that was Philip's excuse. We went through so many people; Ashley, a small, skinny queen with a Phil Oakey hairdo, shrink-wrapped in PVC and rubber, tottering around on Cuban heels. He wanted people to think he was kinky, but I reckon it was all show. We all talked about being rent boys. It was thrilling and dangerous but we could never have gone through with it. Ashley set up pervy photo sessions in his flat with himself dressed as a rubber Nazi and Marilyn stroking a whip. I often stayed at Ashley's. One night we had awkward sex—his flat-mate Frank was ten feet away in the other bed. Sometimes I had sex with people just because I couldn't be bothered to go home. Like the time I ended up in Pinner with a male nurse whose ailing charge was in the next room.

Through Ashley I met Dave Baby, a psycho tattooed builder from Stoke Newington. I had sex with him a few times, so did Marilyn. Neither of us got jealous about it. Dave liked draggy boys with soft skin but he wasn't boyfriend material. Marilyn and I were after something permanent. Though sometimes Marilyn went for the impossible. He slid onto David Bowie's lap at Legends and kissed his ear. Bowie was stone-faced and ignored Marilyn's pleas to fuck him now.

Marilyn's relationship with Hooray John ruined my first chance for fame. Before they met we'd been rehearsing as part of a cabaret and were promised a season on the French Riviera. I was so excited, I'd never been out of England. The cabaret was the creation of two theatrical queens we met at Heaven. Marilyn was playing himself, emerging from a coffin singing "Diamonds Are a Girl's Best Friend." He was brilliant. I played several roles: Boadicea, a black widow spider, and an alien rock star. We spent every afternoon rehearsing. I couldn't believe Marilyn's attitude. He got what he wanted and damn everyone else. The show's creators were devastated, especially when I ran off with all the costumes. It was an awful thing to do, but I'd worked so hard and reasoned it was my due. They came to the squat looking for me and the clothes. I pleaded innocence. A week later I was dressed as Boadicea down at the Blitz.

My Boadicea helmet was made by Stephen Jones. It was silver lamé with a mane of white plumage, too amazing to give back. I wore it to the changing of the guard at Buckingham Palace with a white toga and stilettos, carrying a Union Jack shield and trident. The Japanese tourists had a field day. Everyone was taking my picture and I felt important even if I wasn't. Some old monarchist poked me and moaned that I was blocking her view. I sneered at her with all the contempt she deserved.

I scoured the press to see if Miss Boadicea made the news. I was disappointed. Still, I was getting my face in more and more magazines. It was like a drug. I kept a scrapbook and showed it to Mum and Dad—they didn't understand what I did. I was claiming dole and eating when the hunger got too much, washing now and then. If I got invited to a party at someone's house I'd quickly take a bath. All of us used to do it. Kim was renowned for leaving her signature tide mark.

Steve Strange gave me a job working the cloakroom at the Blitz. It wasn't ideal being stuck in a dark corner, but I needed the pennies. I was sure Steve was trying to demean me and when I became famous he couldn't resist telling the world, "Boy George was my cloakroom attendant." He forgot to say how much he paid me. I was always rifling through pockets and handbags. Mostly people were too pissed to notice. A couple of times I was challenged, but was convincingly innocent. A certain amount of thieving was essential—everyone did it. A bunch of us would go into the local Indian grocer's all dressed up and cause a commotion while Kim shoved bread and cheese up her bustle skirt.

There was a gracious side to Steve Strange, but it was often buried underneath the thick panstick. He drew you in with a mix of charm and ruthlessness. He did some vile things. Philip and I turned up at a big party he was throwing at a rich friend's house in Notting Hill. It was a summer evening, the crowd spilled out on to the street, all our friends were there. Steve ran down the staircase, past the oil paintings, and yelled, "O'Dowd. Sallon. Get out, we don't want you here." Steve only wanted to be friendly with you if you could make him look good. I always thought he was ashamed of being Welsh and working class. He loved to hang out the arse of the aristocracy, favoring the likes of Francesca von Thyssen to Mick Jagger, who he turned away from the Blitz for wearing sneakers and a baseball jacket. It made Steve special in a lot of people's eyes, not in mine.

I was always making up wicked jokes about Steve, knowing they'd get back to him. My mouth was my power over him and everyone. I could get the whole of London to laugh with me. What I hated most about Steve was his inconsistency. He would use you and drop you when he felt like it. Often his charm was disarming. He could be genuinely nice, and that was even more scary.

He arrived unexpectedly at Great Titchfield Street, showing off his new look, the latest Seditionaries boots, leather bondage trousers, a walnut quiff, and black contact lenses that covered his whole eye. Some local kids were laughing and pointing, "Oi, space creature, can you see?" He looked brilliant, and we went for a drink at the local pub.

On the way we met Steve's friend Jenny and her boyfriend, Kirk Brandon. Jenny and I needed no introduction, "Uch, it's Bet Lynch," she sneered. We'd had a run-in when I was bartending at a Swanky Modes fashion show. I showered her with peanuts and wine because she got lippy. We had a good laugh about it and they joined us for a beer. I couldn't take my eyes off Kirk: he looked like Billy Fury in his heyday and was so cool and cheeky. It was his birthday and I was dying to give him a kiss. Steve invited us to the Blitz to watch Biddy and Eve in cabaret. I ran home to do my face and crimp my hair. When I reappeared in full makeup Kirk couldn't stop staring. At the Blitz we got into deep conversation. I didn't know he was a revered punk singer and I'd never heard of his band Theatre of Hate. I was impressed. It made him all the more attractive. Jenny kept nudging me. "Don't bother, he's straight." She was obviously worried. I invited Kirk to the Blitz the following Tuesday. He said, "What is it, one of those poser's clubs?" I didn't think he'd come.

I was so happy when Kirk strolled in saying he was passing by. He sat by the cloakroom all evening, chatting, fetching drinks, tearing apart the "sad clowns." The Blitz was Sodom and Gomorrah to him. Kirk was a true punk with slept-on hair, a combat jacket, jeans, and monkey boots. He talked socialism while I sucked beer through a straw to protect my lipstick. Most of his talk went over my head, but the sincerity was riveting. Kirk's visits became a regular event and something I lived for. I never saw him outside the club but every Tuesday after rehearsing with Theatre of Hate he would come and hang out with me. I could tell he looked forward to seeing me. It was all unspoken, eyes and sighs.

My theatrical efforts amused Kirk no end. One week I was dressed up as a nun in one of the costumes I'd stolen from the cabaret. Someone took a Polaroid snap of us. We looked so perfect together. When Kirk left that night he kissed my cheek and said, "You know, I've got a soft spot for nuns." Had I been less holy I would have seized the moment.

Steve, Rusty, and fellow entrepreneur Chris Sullivan started a new night called Hell at Mandy's club in Henrietta Street, Covent Garden, on Thursdays. I got more work, which was great, and Kirk had another excuse to visit me. A couple of times he brought his band, Luke, Stan, and Steve. Steve was the friendliest; he was Kirk's flatmate and chauffeured him around on a big Kawasaki. Luke and Stan didn't know how to take me at first. Kirk was always edgy when they were around.

After a gig he brought the band, the roadies, and some rowdy hangers-on to Hell. They all dumped their coats for free and spent the night ogling birds from the bar. Kirk was behaving like a right jack and ignoring me. When his friends left I acted like a hurt girlfriend. He made up to me like he really cared. He asked if he could spend the night at the squat rather than go back to Staines. I said I didn't have a spare bed. He grinned, "I'll be safe, won't I?"

I got into bed trying not to brush against him and lay there for a while in awkward silence. When Kirk pulled me to him I felt like crying. I don't think I've ever wanted anyone so much for so long. I'd been falling in love from the moment we met. Sleeping with Kirk wasn't sex, it was absolute love. In the morning I jumped out of bed and threw on some more makeup.

When Kirk left that day I felt so insecure and wondered if it was a one-off caused by too many beers. I ran from room to room screaming jubilation. Kirk came back with his toothbrush and stayed the rest of the week. I followed him round like I had no life of my own. No one could believe I was going out with Kirk, and neither could I. He even held my hand in the street.

However loving Kirk could be, he was quick to switch off around the band and friends from the business, like his manager, Terry Rasor, or the boys from the Clash, who shared the same office in Bayswater. Rasor saw me as an embarrassment and was puzzled like everyone by this strange friendship. Kirk shrugged off the jibes but I knew it bothered him. He denied being gay, preferring to think of me as a girl. I tried to live up to the role, telling everyone I was having a sex change. Kirk blindly told Philip, "I'm a hundred percent heterosexual." Philip thought it was disgusting, like denying my existence. I defended Kirk's every word, whether it made sense or not, warning Philip to keep his mouth shut. Marilyn acted like my mother, telling Kirk, "You'd better take care of George or you'll know about it."

Within a matter of weeks all the houses in Great Titchfield Street were squatted, spreading round the corner to Carburton Street. Friends of friends, some faces we didn't know. Once word got out they were "safe" council properties, everyone was homing in. Stephen's friend Christine Binnie moved into the corner house above the old Lewis Leathers shop with the two Roberts, Durrant and Laws, and Loud Mouth Tracy. Binnie opened a beatnik café in the disused shop and called it the Coffee Spoon. There was no running water, so she organized a water patrol, which consisted of filling empty cider bottles next door and carrying them back. The limited menu was poetic, tea was a "T. S. Eliot," toast a "Robbie Burns," and coffee a "Cavafy." Miss Binnie, as she was known, truly had her lid off and everyone loved her. She held poetry readings where her film student friends John Maybury and Cerith Wyn Evans would project their latest works over her naked body. We were all encouraged to express ourselves through poetry or song. I made use of her old Remington typewriter for evil purposes.

Hark, hark, I hear a sound,
Philip Sallon is in the playground.
He likes them young, he likes them thick,
Philip loves a juvenile prick.

Somewhere in a corner Steve Strange paints his face,
Squiggled lines and polka dots, he looks a real disgrace.
Trying so hard to be "in,"
Sucking in his double chin.

Soon he'll be a lonely clone,
Being exclusive on his own.

The two Roberts were a music-hall double act, loved for their dry wit, loathed for their poncing way. They would swig your drink while you weren't looking or pour it into their empty glasses. "Ooh, what's that you're drinking? Gissa sip. Gissa fag for later. Lend us a fiver." I wrote a Coffee Spoon classic about them.

See the beggar in the sand,
Holding out his crusty hand,
As he talks his pockets sway,
All your cigarettes walk away.
Drinks your coffee,
Swigs your tea,
Eats your hospitality.
Robert, Robert, on the run,
Owes a pound to everyone.

The Roberts were an essential addition to the street and to every social situation. Loud Mouth Tracy was their best friend and had once been the girlfriend of Robert Laws, a lesbian marriage made in hell. The three of them together was a noise to behold. Tracy was small with bow lips, fifties hairstyles, dirndl skirts, and mohair cardigans. A bit of a latter-day Judy Garland, and she could certainly drink her under the table. We taunted her, "Bulldyke. Lesley." Years later she lived out our prophecy after she'd shagged every available man.

The funniest moments were when we were leaving for a club or party, the noise, the camp, the color—we moved as a crowd for safety. Crossing the road was dangerous enough: the local lads would give us gyp, throwing stuff and catcalling. Riding the tube was another assault course. You never knew who would have a go. If there was trouble it was always the girls who put their fists up. Life was exciting because anything did happen.

I met a French boy called Philippe on the tube. He was sweet and needed somewhere to live. When I realized he didn't fancy me I decided to charge him £10 a week. He stayed in the room adjacent to mine. Everyone thought it was outrageous, but it was fair exchange—I got him into clubs free.

No matter how many locks I had on my door I never felt safe squatting. I came home from a club and found my room trashed. I sat down in the mess and cried. My clothes had been ripped up and my padded Mugler jacket swiped. I vowed to draw blood if I caught anyone in it. It must have been someone I knew.

I decided to move round the corner to one of the cleaner houses in Carburton Street and threw a huge party to kiss the old house goodbye. I told everyone at the last minute. They were all furious but it was hardly worth protesting when I'd invited half of London. Myra, Julia, and Andy stored their stuff in Patrick's room on the top floor. Patrick was away visiting his family in Birmingham. Stephen had already moved to a legal tiny bedsit because he needed his PG Tips.

The party was more like a riot—the house and the street were rammed with people. Marilyn walked in and right out. "Ugh, punks." He went off to the Embassy club in his zebra dress and fox stole. I was larger than life in my Boadicea helmet, toga, and stilettos, all you could see were white plumes bobbing above the crowd. When the police arrived Kirk and I took refuge in Patrick's room and watched the drunken masses from the window. The police cordoned off the street, shouting at them to go home. Their presence only encouraged people to show off, smashing windows and demolishing the house. Even when almost everyone had gone the police hovered outside. Kirk went home, I changed into my tartan bondage suit and Myra and I headed down to the Scala Cinema in Tottenham Street. The police stopped us and dragged me into a van because I was feisty. They asked me to drop my trousers. I said, "If you want them off, you do it." I was thrown onto the street. A woman copper stuck her hand down Myra's bra looking for drugs. Myra pulled away. "Don't touch me." The WPC assured her, "We're not all lesbians like you, luv."

Myra, Andy, and I soon settled into our new home in Carburton Street. I took the ground floor with the sink, Myra was above, then Andy. We had a sitting tenant at the top, Paranoid Pete, a photographer's assistant with a James Dean fixation. I don't know where he came from, he was just there. His paranoia tag came from taking too many blues—he was always looking over his shoulder. Paranoid Pete made a big show of being straight like all boys, but rumors abounded that he tied up Robert Laws and fucked him. The rumors were, of course, spread by Robert.

Roaring drunk after a night at the Blitz, Stephen Linard and I went back to Pete's studio in Poland Street. I did some topless poses. Stephen stripped off and stuck a Hoover handle up his bum, I still have the photos though Stephen remembers nothing, just like the night he was too drunk to walk home from Heaven. He climbed into a cardboard box with a tramp.

Most of us were no cleaner than tramps due to the lack of sanitation facilities. I never washed that much, it was too much of a hassle. Philip told everyone I smelled, but no one else complained. Myra and the two Roberts washed in the toilets at the Regent Crest Hotel over the road. Our toilet was outside with no door or roof. If it was raining you had to take an umbrella. We nailed together a makeshift roof, but Nick the Skinhead, another straight friend of Robert Laws, chucked an old TV out the window and demolished it. We had lots of fun watching people cowering on the bog.

Warlock, an old punk friend, and his girlfriend, Alison, found a house in Great Titchfield Street with hot running water. We were furious we didn't find it ourselves. Warlock let us take baths, but in the end it drove him mad. The Roberts solved the problem by moving round there. They liked their comforts and were none too happy about the impending arrival of Marilyn.

I hadn't seen Marilyn for ages when he turned up behind the wheel of a Gold GTI with his hair in two cutesy plaits. His boyfriend, John Cochran-Patrick, had taught him to drive while visiting the ancestral stately home in Scotland. There were stories that Marilyn had sweet-talked John into selling off some heirlooms, hence the car. It may have been another fabulous Marilyn story, but when I went to visit them in Knightsbridge, I was cornered by John's angry mother. "You know that Peter, don't you? I'll have him arrested." I assumed a society wedding was out of the question.

Marilyn and John needed somewhere to live. Marilyn had his eye on the basement but it was blocked up with rubbish. We'd blocked the stairs with a couple of old doors to hide the mess and smell. John did all the work, single-handedly scouring the depths. It was like one of those old movies where a man constructs his dream. He was so sexy, hammering and fixing—everyone dreams of a man like that. He fitted a new window and Marilyn smashed it an hour later. John cried and stormed off in his bare feet to the pub.

John and Kirk were reluctant husbands. They never spoke for fear of confronting their sexual dilemma, but they had much in common. John thought he was straight too and living in a squat was hardly like living in the shadow of Harrods. I loved to hear him swearing at Marilyn in that fuck-orf voice. John had the schooling and the mannerisms but he never lorded it, he was a nice boy. Marilyn was the local snob. He had important friends who he kept to himself, like designer Rifat Ozbek, photographer Johnny Rozsa, and Stevie Hughes, who was a brilliant well-known makeup artist. They would call round and take him for dinner and go off to the Embassy club. Marilyn never once invited me—he couldn't stand the competition.

I devoted myself to Kirk, following him around to gigs, standing in the wings with love pouring from my eyes. I knew every lyric and guitar riff. The hard-core punks eyed me suspiciously: they didn't want to believe Kirk was bent. The band knew about me and Kirk. Stan Stammers the bass player asked, "Are you and Kirk . . . you know?" I laughed. "What do you think?" He said Kirk had written a new song, "The Original Sin." He knew it was about me.

Since you came in my life,
I've had to rearrange my whole mentality, my sexuality.

"The Original Sin" was a double A-side of the first Theatre of Hate single. My life was fulfilled: I had a song written in my honor. When Kirk sang it onstage it felt like he really loved me. I wanted him to express that love openly, but there was too much fear. He was the one who couldn't handle it. One time he kissed me in the back of the tour van. It was as if he was trying to prove something.

Kirk wanted to be famous but was reluctant to admit it even to himself. I encouraged him to work on his image and scored a major victory by persuading him to bleach his hair and cultivate a quiff. He even asked me what he should wear onstage. Terry Rasor hated my interfering, he wanted to control Kirk's every breath. I felt Rasor was keeping him down by encouraging his punk martyrdom. Kirk cited Adam Ant as the worst kind of sellout but he went to the other extreme and festered in his own credibility. I appointed myself official PR for Theatre of Hate, taking photos to the music press, making sure his gigs were listed, trying to convince journalists to do reviews and interviews. I created posters for the gigs, and hand-pasted them up around the West End, and designed an official T-shirt with Bette Davis sneering from behind an eyepatch. I got one of our new neighbors, photographer Mark Lebon, to do a free session with Kirk and Luke, I styled them as cowboys. Sadly the pictures were never used because Kirk or Terry thought they were too posy.

Mark Lebon lived at the other end of Carburton Street with his girlfriend, Ruth, and friend Peter Fried. I met him on my way to the launderette. "Wow, you look amazing." He was surprised to see me painted so early in the morning. Normally I despised flattery, hissing, "I know how I look." But I took to Mark straight away, he was a lovable giant and he had cameras.

Mark's cute brother James lived next door to us. He was a hairdresser, budding filmmaker, and looked like John Travolta in *Grease*. He was so tactile and style-proud I presumed he was gay. One day I grabbed his crotch and he turned on me. We didn't speak for ages. I got my revenge when a Japanese photographer took our picture outside the squat. I was wearing stilettos with pedal pushers. We appeared in a Japanese fashion mag, captioned "James Lebon and his girlfriend go out on the town." James lived with his official girlfriend, Elise, Kevin Petrie, Nick Watson, and Toby Mott, a nervous dish who later formed the Grey Organization, arty types who didn't do that much. Toby wouldn't go near me and Marilyn—we were always threatening to tie him up and have his arse. We thrived on terrorizing vulnerable straight boys. Mark Lebon was cooler than James about us queer things. Openly describing himself as a "closet queen or healthy heterosexual," calling me darling and letting me sit on his lap. He was the first person to take glamorous pictures of me. I loved the flashbulbs—I couldn't stop once I saw how amazing I looked in photos. Hours were spent in front of the mirror playing with the possibilities: wigs, flowers, bells, and bows. The secondhand stores and charity shops were still my lifeline. A big event was the closing-down sale at Charles Fox, theatrical costumiers in Covent Garden. Everyone from the squats and clubs was there loading up bin-liners. I couldn't afford much, even at the knockdown prices. I bought a couple of gladiator belts and a Chinese hat. Kim bought an Elizabeth I costume complete with a neck ruff and bustle skirt. She wore it to the Blitz with her tits out and her nipples painted gold. That was nothing unusual for Kim. She often wore white muslin chemise dresses that displayed everything. She looked brilliant all the time.

There was so much fuss when David Bowie came to the Blitz looking for extras for his *Ashes to Ashes* video. I was excited but refused to be a crawler. Steve Strange and a chosen few got to sit at his table while everyone else lingered trying to look nonchalant. Fashion designer Judith Franklin was sent round the club to hand-pick potential people. She whispered in my ear, "DB wants to see you." I followed her but couldn't get near enough to be seen. I badly wanted to meet Bowie but it just wasn't the right moment. It was odd being so close after all the years of trying. I wondered if Bowie liked people sucking up to him. A week later he came to Hell. I said hello, and he told me I looked like Klaus Nomi, the freaky operatic singer from New York. I was insulted. I was an original. I decided Bowie was better as a concept than a reality, an ordinary bloke with crooked teeth and a funny eye who happened to change my life.

I could have kicked myself when "Ashes to Ashes" got to number one and Steve Strange was on *Top of the Pops*. Steve was ever more conceited and I was ever more jealous. I called him Bowie's sidekick. He must have been worried because he slagged Bowie off in a newspaper: "I was wearing that pierrot costume last Christmas." It was true that Bowie swept into the Blitz scene and soaked up all the ideas, but he was the reason that most of us were dressing up in the first place.

*　　　*　　　*

I couldn't stop stealing. I dreamed of robbing banks but had to make do with piddly change from the cloakroom. I'd go shoplifting from the makeup counters at Woolworth's and Boots, bagging bottles of perfume. I pilfered from parties and friends' rooms, silly things like hairspray. Maybe I'd watched too many Divine movies at the Scala. "I can steal ten dollars faster than you can earn it. I don't know why anyone works, it bothers my imagination." No one else found it kitsch. Steve sacked me from the Blitz for thieving. Convinced of my innocence I stormed out of the club.

When I made an appearance at Hell and found Judith Franklin doing my job, I got sloshed, crawled under the counter, and snatched her handbag full of the night's takings. I ran back to Carburton Street panting and hid the bag in a water tank over the toilet in the backyard. At 3:30 A.M. a vigilante crowd led by Jeremy Healy appeared on the doorstep. I was so barefaced I could have won an Oscar. They demanded to search the house. I warned them, "Step one foot in here and my brothers will kill you." Jeremy was shouting, "You know you did it." I slammed the door on them.

In the morning I felt guilty and took the two Roberts and Tracy for a fry-up at Sam's café. I gave some money to tramps on the street, bought twenty eyebrow pencils and two huge tubs of translucent face powder. Everyone wanted me to own up. Marilyn was the only one who found it funny—he was just as bad. Binnie bought some red biker boots from Johnson and Johnson with a stolen check book. Marilyn broke into her room and stole them saying they weren't hers in the first place. A baying crowd came round from Warren Street and Marilyn chucked them out the window.

My karma came a week or so later when I popped round to Warren Street for a cup of tea. Kim shouted out the window, "Go away, thief." Stephen Jones had lost £10, and I was the only suspect. I went home tearful and dejected, promising I would never steal again. Stephen came to Carburton Street and apologized after he found the money at work. I decided I would only steal from shops in future.

*   *   *

Mum didn't understand the disco celebrity concept. "You can't wander round clubs forever." Forever was the last thing on my mind. I told her I was working at the Blitz, and she said, "That's not real work." I didn't want to think about packing apples and hats, ugh, and being told what to do. I wanted to live in a big house and have lots of clothes and money. I had no idea how I might achieve it. Always a dreamer, like it said in my school reports. As long as I was being photographed and noticed I had a purpose, a reason to get up and dress up. Of course it was superficial, but it made me feel important.

Everything else in life was so unreliable. My romance with Kirk was up and down, as opposed to in and out. He didn't know what he wanted to be. Bliss then bullshit. I didn't know what I was doing wrong, but I always blamed myself. Kirk wasn't any old boyfriend, he was talented and special. When we were alone it was always perfect. I couldn't bear the thought of losing him, though in my heart I knew it wouldn't last.

Things deteriorated when Kirk's prissy sister Jane and her friend came up from Devon for his gig at the Music Machine. They were a pair of Victorian dolls in cream lace with personalities to match. I was dressed as Boadicea, Marilyn was dragged up, and Binnie was wearing only a bra and knickers under her coat. They'd never seen anything quite like it. We made it worse by talking like farmers. They made it clear they didn't approve. We attempted to go for a drink at the Southampton Arms in Mornington Crescent but were ordered straight out. "No, thank you!" While Kirk was onstage Binnie ran on and shook her tits. Jane asked Kirk, "Why are you hanging out with people like this?" She threatened to tell his dad.

When she left we did nothing but argue. Kirk said he needed some space. He took his clothes and disappeared on the back of Steve's bike. I broke down, screaming and crying. I trashed my room, threw a tin of paint through the window, and daubed "I love Kirk" on the wall. I walked twenty miles to Staines in the rain, determined to confront Kirk and make him change his mind. Kirk was unmoved; he gave me a bed but refused to talk about it.

In the morning we took the tube together. I was crying again. Kirk told me to stop showing myself up. I didn't care who was looking. When he got off at Paddington I followed him down the platform. It was as if Kirk had never felt a thing for me. I went back to Carburton Street to face the mess—my room was like a bombsite. I curled up on the bed and cried myself to sleep. I knew it was time to move again. There were too many memories to stay there without Kirk.

I went to see my friend Jean Sell round the corner in Goodge Street. Jean was a casual friend from the clubs, an older woman with bleached hair who made leather designer jackets. She came to the Blitz with a Japanese photographer, Herbie Yamaguchi, who was snapping the freaks. We became friends. As soon as you met her you felt like you'd known her forever—she spilled out all her personal dramas. I sat and listened while she did her cutting and sewing. Jean was sympathetic: she said if I was ever desperate she had an old workroom downstairs. Her face dropped when I said, "Well, actually . . . " I talked her into letting me stay for a while.

The room was perfect, with a dusty full-length mirror, an old clothes rail, and a couple of dress mannequins. I made good use of her old worktops too. Jean kept shaking her head, "I can't believe I'm doing this." She lived on the top floor of a three-story house above Ryness electrics shop. The house belonged to her ex-boyfriend Johnny Gems's family. Johnny's mother, Pam, wrote the West End hit *Piaf*. It seemed Jean and Johnny were planning to get married, and Johnny passed at the last minute so the family let her live there rent free. She didn't know how long we could get away with it.

You couldn't get away with much in that house. On the first floor lived the sprightly Mrs. Marks, a small Jewish lady with horn-rimmed glasses and Day-Glo lipstick. She could hear a pubic hair drop. Next to me lived a big fat blond woman who didn't seem to have a name. She avoided eye contact on the stairs and came and went at odd hours, bringing black men back for squealing sex sessions. I could hear her through the partition wall and had to ask Jean if all women made those noises.

I tried to keep on Jean's good side, cleaning her flat and washing up. It drove her mad, she was comfortable with her chaos. There were dramas with the telephone too. She accused me of doubling her bill and locked the phone in the cupboard when she went to work. Jean was lovely when she wanted me to run errands, make coffee, or lie to her boyfriends on the phone. But when she had one of her hangovers, she was e-vile. After living with Martin I was used to flat-share hell, but this was the fastest turnaround in history. I nicknamed her Mad Jean when she started storm-trooping my door demanding rent.

When things got really bad I'd exit across the rooftops and visit my friend Tim Buerke two doors down. Tim was a friend of Toby Mott and a Grey Organization member. He looked just like one of those 1940s newsmen you see in the movies, baggy gray peg trousers, knitted tank tops, and old men's jackets. A sweeter boy you couldn't meet. We became friends as soon as I moved to Goodge Street. He invited me for tea and I became part of the family. Tim lived with his brother Tom and bohemian parents, Gill and Terry. Mum was a teacher, Dad an artist. Despite their liberalism they didn't know how to take me. They thought Tim was turning queer. I was like a human cat clambering across the roof for tea and whatever free food was going, and I often came in via the fire exit when I forgot my keys. It was dangerous and peaceful up there, especially at night, when I sat watching the city, thinking about my life. I was nineteen years old and doing nothing except going to clubs and showing off. Tim was at college studying photography—he was always taking pictures of me. I put them on my wall with my other glamour shots, stuck up with Blu-tack. I wished they were in gold frames.

Quietly I was starting to panic about my future. As much as I enjoyed the freedom and benefits of unemployment, I knew I couldn't be a professional poser forever. I occasionally joined the early-morning queues outside the Job Centre in Mortimer Street and secured a few days' work washing up in restaurants.

So many of my friends were making careers, names for themselves, and time was ticking away. I decided to look for an interesting job. I created my own résumé, though my main asset was the gift of tongue. Morticia, a punky friend described perfectly by her name, introduced me to her boss, Peter Small, who owned the Rock Art shop in Old Compton Street. They sold pop T-shirts and studded accessories. Peter liked my style and gave me a job window dressing one day a week at Street Theatre, another shop he opened in Newburgh Street, behind Carnaby Street. "If you can dress like that you can do my windows." I was buzzing after my first day, telling everyone, "I'm a window dresser." I never believed work could be so much fun.

Peter was middle-aged, slightly trendy, with an overactive mind and a passion for nicotine. He'd made his money manufacturing and selling badges. He was a gambler like Dad, only he bet on ideas rather than horses. He was cool if you turned up late or came on the wrong day. He wanted expression not subservience. I quickly became an expert at window display, checking the windows on Carnaby Street, appalled at their lack of style. When I wasn't doing the windows I hung out at the shop keeping Charlotte, the assistant, company. Charlotte was a striking punk beauty, even with all the pancake slap and kohl round her eyes. I wasn't surprised when she became an international model. We had a right giggle together. I would swoop on all the nervous boys and offer to take their leg measurements.

Kirk was the only boy on my mind. I kept calling his house in Staines, but the phone just rang and rang. I got all dolled up and hung around rock venues like the Marquee and the Music Machine, hoping to see him. When I caught him snogging some ugly tart, I ran over and slammed him against the wall. "You cunt." He was so arrogant, and carried on kissing her. I punched him again. He went to hit me back. Steve stepped in. "What are you doing? You don't have to treat him like that." The bouncers rushed Kirk. "Right. Out." They thought he was trying to beat up a girl. I knew they would have battered him, so I calmed them down and left. I walked back to Goodge Street with my adrenaline pumping. I knew Kirk still fancied me whatever he did. I went back to the Music Machine that night and sprayed "Kirk is a cunt" on the wall. It was soon scrubbed off, but the faded message stayed there for years.

It was a month before I saw Kirk again. A crowd of us went to see Malcolm McLaren's new protégés Bow Wow Wow at the Roller Disco in Hammersmith. It was a big trendy night, I was all dressed up, I didn't know Kirk would be there. I caught him staring at me in the bar. I wouldn't speak to him. The following night he phoned Mad Jean's and said, "Hi, it's Kirk. I love you," then he rang off. I was jumping up and down. "Where is he if he loves me?" It was so frustrating. An hour later he called back and I went to meet him at the Golden Egg in Tottenham Court Road. He was sorry. That was good enough for the woman who loved too much.

Kirk moved into a flat in White City with his friend Vaughn Toulouse, singer with the punk band Department S. We started seeing each other again. Kirk wanted to keep it relaxed, I wanted to be with him every minute. The nights I didn't see him I was sure he was shagging girls. We played phone tag with Vaughn as the middle man. I was always screaming at Kirk, "Do you wanna go out with me or not?" He would say, "No, not if it's like this." I went to the flat and virtually kicked the door down, pushing my way past Vaughn. Kirk was in his T-shirt and pants ready to have a bath. We had a mad scuffle on the bed, I pushed the wardrobe over and smashed the telephone. It was the end of communication for good. I kept going to Theatre of Hate gigs, it was hard to keep away.

When the Blitz and Hell shut down in autumn 1980 Steve Strange took on a night at the Venue, an old dance hall that was far too big to fill. We all went the first night and bitched when it died a death. Chris Sullivan and his new partner, Graham Ball, opened Le Kilt in Greek Street where the music was funk and Latin, apparently ahead of the next craze. Like sheep we rushed to gigs to check out the next big thing, bands like Spandau Ballet, Blue Rondo à la Turk, Funkapolitan. They hired out boats and disused cinemas to turn their gigs into happenings.

The fashions were nostalgic and theatrical: showgirls, Dior girls, top hats and tails, kilts and cassocks. Malcolm McLaren and Vivienne Westwood unveiled their new pirate collection, although pirates were first seen at St. Martin's College in student designer Rifat Ozbek's end-of-year show. I could only afford a hat, scarf, and a squiggly T-shirt, which never came off my back. Everyone had their own idea where fashion was going. Spandau Ballet were sporting a romantic Highlands look designed by Simon Withers. Blue Rondo à la Turk were decked out like Latin gangsters with zoot suits and goatee beards. The real stars of the scene took notes but always added their own touch. People like Clare with the Hair, who was wearing crinolines with dreadlocked ringlets and African jewelry, and, of course, Philip who was always guaranteed to wear something no one else would.

I created a new look every night. My room was like backstage at *The Mikado*. I loved the eastern flavor: kimonos and geisha makeup, straw hats decorated with fruit, flowers, and birds, twisted up with platform shoes and a big mandarin umbrella. Putting on my face was a time-consuming ritual. Foundation and powder first, then a cup of tea while it settled. My eyebrows were shaved so I could wing them in any direction. Eye shadow was applied with fingers, I couldn't afford brushes. It was all instinctive. Last was always the hairpiece, hat, and earrings. Then I twirled in front of the mirror for an age.

It was hard (literally) to drag myself up for work. I never saw daylight without some kind of grooming. You had to look good with all those trendies coming into Street Theatre eyeing you up and down. Peter Small put me on a £50 retainer, I was window dresser cum style consultant. He called me his eyes and ears on the street. I liaised with the designers at Street Theatre and scouted the competition up the Kings Road and Kensington Market, looking for new designs and designers. I got Clare with the Hair a job with Peter. Her clothes didn't sell, they were too ahead of their time, but they looked great in the shop. Peter paid all his designers £25 for each design, whether it was used or not. He was so fair. Some of them just wanted the cash. Peter wanted to create a cooperative, with everyone swapping ideas. It was often chaotic. Lizzie Joyce, Peter's in-house designer, didn't always agree with Peter's methods or my ideas, though we were very fond of each other. Business meetings were held in the local Italian café, Peter chain-talking and puffing, his pretty wife, Dali, taking notes and rolling her eyes.

Peter Small was the first person to show any confidence in my ability or creativity. When I talked constantly of starting a band, he was sure I could make it. Everyone else thought I would end up as a Sunday turn at the Vauxhall Tavern. I thought, if Johnny Rotten's a singer, so am I. I used to hang around at Theatre of Hate rehearsals and mess around singing with the band when Kirk was late. Luke said I was better than Kirk.

My friend Gabriella Palmano was living with and loving Matthew Ashman from Bow Wow Wow. Philip and I used to go over to their flat in Whitechapel on Sunday afternoons armed with bagels from Brick Lane. Philip would instigate singsongs, forcing Matthew to play Hebrew spirituals and songs from *The Sound of Music*. Matthew told me I had a brilliant voice and said he'd rather have me in Bow Wow Wow than Annabella Lu Win. "She ain't got an ounce of rock and roll in her." Everyone knew Malcolm was finding it hard to manipulate the nubile Annabella. Having been plucked from a launderette at fourteen she wasn't accustomed to lesbian photo shoots and having her nipples painted gold. I thought, This is my big chance for fame. I approached Malcolm in a club and asked if he was looking for a new singer for Bow Wow Wow. He laughed and said, "No, no. We're happy with Annabella." He told Matthew I was too Jayne Countyish, the punk sex change who sang "If You Don't Wanna Fuck Me, Fuck Off." Matthew didn't give up. When Bow Wow Wow started rehearsals for a big London show at the Rainbow Theatre, he invited me for a tryout. I sang a few of their songs nervously but well. The other members, Lee Gorman and Dave Barbarossa, hated me, both on sight and from a distance. They didn't want to back up a poofter. Matthew kept on at Malcolm, who came round to the idea, relishing the friction it would cause. He decided to use me as part of the Rainbow show, planned as a big carnival extravaganza with fairground rides and sideshows. He chose a silly redneck classic, "Cast Iron Arm" by Peanuts Wilson, for my debut. I didn't care about the song, I knew everyone in London would be there.

February 28, 1981, I made my stage debut with Bow Wow Wow. It was a strange baptism and typical of Malcolm's perversity. When Bow Wow Wow went back on for their first encore I skipped on instead of Annabella. The crowd were confused and barely raised a cheer. I was too elated to consider their reaction. Going onstage in front of thousands of people was a big thrill for me. Philip said he was too jealous to watch, others were impressed by my confidence. Dave Fishell, Bow Wow Wow's tour manager, wasn't, calling it an obnoxious performance. Vivienne Westwood gave me a free T-shirt for being the best thing all night. She couldn't stand Annabella. I scoured the music press hoping for a picture. The bastards barely mentioned me. Matthew said I'd work with Bow Wow Wow again but I didn't believe it.

A month or so later Matthew and Malcolm surprised me by turning up at Goodge Street. We took a cab to Malcolm's flat in Lancaster Gate. I didn't ask any questions. Secretly I was hoping Malcolm would ask me to join the group, but he was still playing games and hadn't finished toying with me yet. We arrived to a commotion. Vivienne Westwood had just sped off on her bicycle after bricking a window. A Lebanese waiter was pointing at the damage. "Crazy lady, crazy lady." Vivienne was upset about Malcolm's seventeen-year-old German girlfriend, Andrea.

Malcolm cooked me a steak sandwich and talked weird business. He said he was going to put me on a retainer and wanted me to record a new song, "The Mile High Club." He spun out the story about children getting gang-banged by animals on an airplane and a pilot called Lieutenant Lush. Which would be my stage name. It was hard to take Malcolm seriously, the only thing I wanted to believe was that he was going to make me a star. I left that night thinking I would be part of Bow Wow Wow. Dad told me, "Don't you sign anything with that man." He'd read about McLaren in the *Sun*.

I started rehearsing with Bow Wow Wow, new songs especially scripted for me. "The Mile High Club" and "The Biological Phenomenon of the Yellow Retina," which was rapped in the style of a racing commentary. All the horses were named after well-known or closet homosexuals, MPs, pop stars, the lot. I can only mention the dead ones. "First away it's Oscar into the lead from Michelangelo, Benny Hill and Plato . . . On the straight a few furlongs to go it's Nureyev . . . " It was impossible to sing, most of the time I was cracking up. Lee and Dave still hated me, but I got my own back by being as camp as possible. I called Lee "Uglee Gormless" and went on about his fat bum and giving him blow jobs. I ignored Dave because I knew he'd hit me.

My moment with Bow Wow Wow was the blink of an eye. I performed one more gig with them at Manchester University. This time I came on in the middle of the set and sang "The Mile High Club." The punky crowd didn't know how to take this pretty apparition and spat their appreciation. I swung the mike stand at them, shouting obscenities.

No one told me I was sacked. A picture of Annabella and me appeared in the *NME*, "Bow Wow Wow to Quit EMI and Tour." Malcolm said of me, "One thing in his favour was that he was a good friend of the guitarist ... We expanded the show with another singer and dancer so that the band could express themselves on the instrumentals. If George had a band of his own that would be a lot better." The *NME* added, "Poor old George, he seems to have offered his ample services at a particularly inconvenient moment." However inconvenient, I was addicted to the idea of becoming a pop star and exacting my revenge on the ginger Svengali.

CHAPTER 20

In February 1981 Philip opened his first club night at Planets in Piccadilly. The opening was a triumph. Vivienne Westwood set up a stall in one of the fire exits, which was great credibility for the club and Philip, but she only sold two T-shirts all night. Jeremy Healy, Dick Breslaw, and myself were hired as DJs. We were all clueless, but had great taste in music. The Cure, Pigbag, Bow Wow Wow, Lynx. I played lots of seventies stuff, T. Rex, Gary Glitter, LaBelle, reggae, like "Uptown Top Ranking," chucking in "Cabaret" and a Hare Krishna record I bought on Oxford Street. It didn't matter that we kept jumping and scratching the records, or that Philip only paid us £20. I loved being up in the DJ box where everyone could see me. People were constantly asking for dull requests. "'Scuse me, can you play Flock of Seagulls?" I'd snap their heads off. One Saturday I had a brawl with a catty Australian girl who called me a fairy and threw wine in my face. I pushed her onto the crowded dance floor and showered her with beer. Tony, the Italian manager, dragged me off. "I want you out of my club now." I stopped the music and started packing my records. Philip came screaming, "You can't sack the DJ. Are you insane?" I was quickly reinstated and celebrated with Heaven 17's "Fascist Groove Thang."

While deejaying at Planets I met Mikey Craig, the first member of my rock and roll supergroup. Mikey had seen my picture in the

NME: he thought I looked interesting and came to ask me to start a band with him. His friend Michael who worked at World's End brought him to the club. Mikey was so out of place in his slick suit. He said he played bass. I didn't know if he was any good, but he was black, and that was a good start. I arranged to go to his house and hear him play. I asked Clare with the Hair along because she was into reggae.

Mikey met us at the tube. It was Saturday; Hammersmith was full of housewives. Clare and I looked like we'd crept from our tombs. I could tell Mikey was embarrassed—he kept seeing people he knew and crossing the street. The audition was held in his bedroom at his mum's house in Studland Street. Mikey played "Exodus" and "Boogie Oogie Oogie," it sounded like a load of old rumbling to me. I kept making faces at Clare. It was hilarious. Normally a bass player would jam with other musicians, but there weren't any. We chatted about the music we liked, reggae, funk, and soul. Mikey like rock too. I told him the band was going to be tribal and ethnic, like Bow Wow Wow but different. Mikey knew some "great musicians" and said he would put a rehearsal together. The idea terrified me but it had to happen sooner or later.

While we were talking at Mikey's the bedroom door flew open and a white Rastafarian kid burst in on roller skates. Mikey jumped up and shooed him out. The kid, who was only thirteen, sucked his teeth. "Easy Rasta. Seen." I laughed, I'd never heard a white boy talk so black. He looked brilliant too, all spindly in a yellow tracksuit with spidery blond locks and blue eyes. I wanted to know what he did. Mikey was dismissive—it was just his girlfriend's little brother Amos. When we left I was straight in Clare's ear. "What do you think, what do you think?" She thought Mikey sounded funky like Grandmaster Flash. We both loved Amos. I wanted him in the band, even if he played triangle. I didn't want an ugly bunch of musos. Mikey was good-looking but a bit normal. He claimed to have worn it all, from rubber to zoot suits, but that didn't account for his pressed jeans and Arran jumper.

I had the name of a guitarist called Suede who I'd met through Kirk. I set about looking him up. Again I didn't know much about his playing, but he was available and enthusiastic. Mikey and I went to Suede's place in Shepherd's Bush and he strummed his guitar for us; he seemed competent and had a really nice manner. Suede dressed American fifties style, baggy Levi's and bowling shirts, with scruffy blond hair. I couldn't see him in pirate gear, but he passed. We met up several times. None of us knew what we were meant to be doing, it was all talk. I came up with pretentious names for the band, In Praise of Lemmings, the Sex Gang Children, a line stolen from a Bow Wow Wow song. We drowned our ideas in tea and went home full of stars.

After a few weeks and no progress I started to worry. Mikey hadn't found any musicians despite his promises. He had no excuse as he worked part-time in a rehearsal room beneath the Townhouse recording studios in Shepherd's Bush. I thought he was too embarrassed to introduce me to his cool musician friends and put his reputation on the line. They were mainly black guys from the reggae sound systems, not known for their liberal attitudes to queers. Mikey had some gay friends but it was all very secretive and up the West End.

I was drifting up the Kings Road with Kirk Brandon when I first laid eyes on Jon Moss. Kirk the reluctant muso was always pointing out other musicians and barbing them. "That's that Jon Moss from the Damned." I didn't much care for the Damned but I always wanted to know who was who. Jon was one of those rock types that had crossed over to punk, a New Waver. He wore the uniform, pointy black boots, tight black Levi's, black T-shirt, and biker's jacket. His hairdo was still stuck somewhere in the mid-seventies, feathery, spiked on top. I remembered Jon because he was cute and the first famous-ish drummer I'd ever come across. I didn't connect him as the drop-dead pinup my old boyfriend Les Daly had been cooing over in *My Guy* magazine.

With a bit of nifty detective work and access to Mad Jean's phone I tracked Jon Moss to his parents' house in Hampstead. "Hello, my name's George. I used to be in Bow Wow Wow. I got thrown out for being too effeminate. I'm starting my own group, and I'm looking for a drummer. You interested? We're having a rehearsal soon."

Jon was cool. "Yeh, sounds all right."

"Have you got a drum kit?"

He laughed. "I might have."

I was worried when I put down the phone. Have you got a drum kit? What a stupid question.

At the Beat Route I told everyone about my new drummer, Jon Moss. "He used to be in the Damned, y'know."

I was so happy that Jon turned up for our first proper rehearsal at the School Rooms down in Elephant and Castle. He looked dead normal, jeans, white T-shirt, and leather bomber jacket. His face was heavily scarred, he had a gold earring and stank of after-shave. I noticed he had a nice bum as he pulled his drum kit out the back of a shiny white Golf GTI convertible. He was bossy. "Right," said Jon. "Let's hear ya." I had to explain quickly that we'd never rehearsed before. If he wanted to be in the band this was where it started. I was so nervous. "Why don't you just play something and I'll sing along?" Before long Jon was telling Suede and Mikey what to play. It wasn't the sound I had in my head, but it sounded like real music. I improvised over the top, bits of Myra's poetry and anything that came out. Mostly we talked and drank tea. I didn't think Jon liked us. He seemed far too profes-sional to be wasting his time.

After rehearsal Jon gave me a lift home. He said the band was primitive, he liked my voice and would come to the next rehearsal. I was pleased. He quite liked the name Sex Gang Children, but didn't think it was very commercial. He thought it was good to have a sexy name. Right away there was a powerful connection between us, I fancied Jon and he liked it. He told me he'd audi-tioned for Adam and the Ants and played on their single "Car Trouble." He called Adam "anally retentive and pretentious," though he liked some of his musical ideas, especially the Burundi beat. He said the band should be colorful and positive. He was sick of droning suicide music. I nodded, it all seemed fantastic to me.

Our next rehearsal was even fun. We warmed to Jon's Napoleonic charm. I couldn't deny the shift in energy. For a drummer, he seemed to know a lot about everything. He and Mikey jammed, trying out different rhythms and bass lines. Jon insisted there were only two ingredients to any good song. "Look at Motown. Rolling bass lines, great melodies." By the end of that rehearsal we had the makings of our first song, "The Eyes of Medusa," which was more droll than soul.

The Eyes of Medusa, control and compel,
To love I surrender, I'm under the spell.
He loves me, he hates me,
He knows me too well.

Medusa was a bitter camp ditty I'd written about Kirk, the music was a real mishmash, Bow Wow Wow meets soca on the road to Cairo. I didn't know what to make of it—it was such a big thing to be putting my words to music. I walked round for days telling myself and everyone else I'd actually written a song. We started rehearsing twice a week as the Sex Gang Children. Jon asked everyone to contribute whatever they could afford to rehearsals, but he ended up paying most of it. The songwriting process was slow and laborious. I was brimming with words and melodies and couldn't wait to hear them materialize. Mikey and Jon seemed to understand each other and worked well as a rhythm section, but Suede took forever to pick out the chords. My huffing didn't help either.

I started seeing Jon all the time, even when we weren't rehearsing. He took me for dinner at the local Italian trattorias around Goodge Street. It was a thrill to eat in restaurants—the closest I got was the chippie in Whitfield Street. I'd never met a man like Jon. He was so polite and considerate. We'd discuss our plans over cappuccino and profiteroles. I assumed he was straight, though he was very flirtatious. He talked a lot about his girlfriend, Caroline. I talked about Kirk, who I was still madly in love with. Jon called him an Aryan and asked why I liked meatheads. He was critical of everything and everyone, we had loads in common.

CHAPTER 21

Ashley Goodall, an eager A&R man from EMI, was always sniffing around the clubs and gigs for the next Spandau Ballet. I told him so many lies. "I'm being managed by Malcolm McLaren now." When I said I had a band with Jon Moss from the Damned, he got very interested. He invited the band into EMI for a meeting. Jon convinced us he should go alone and do the talking. I didn't like the idea and wondered what he was up to. Whatever my fears, Jon persuaded Ashley to put us in EMI's demo studio without even hearing a note. We were all impressed. I skipped, jumped, and screamed. The EMI building in Manchester Square was where the Beatles shot the cover for the red-and-blue hits albums. We recorded the two songs we had, "The Eyes of Medusa" and "I'm an Animal," an inane Bow Wow Wow rip-off I thought was a definite number one. The engineer stopped me singing "Medusa" all concerned. "Excuse me. You're singing 'he' instead of 'she.'" I was agitated and assured him it was deliberate. I'd never considered the gender realities of a pop song. Jon said the engineer had a point. It was better to be ambiguous and not alienate people.

We were disappointed when Ashley told us EMI were interested but wanted to hear more songs. I was sure they didn't like my lyrics. "Straight cunts." Jon agreed that we should write more and even if nothing happened with EMI we'd been given a chance to work in a studio for free. It was a learning experience we couldn't afford on our own wages.

Jon wanted to take the EMI demos to other record companies and get some publicity shots to hype them up. I called my friend Mark Lebon and he gave us a free session. Jon thought the photos were too camp. I was perched on a table dressed in virgin white wearing a gun holster, surrounded by my topless band. It was Mark's idea for the boys to strip. I didn't mind getting a preview of Jon. He looked down the back of my shirt and said, "Oh, you've got a hairy back." I snapped at him to fuck off.

Soon after that photo session Jon suggested we replace Suede, saying he was "dead wood." I thought it was disloyal—we'd just done photos and everything. I got really confused. I didn't know a good guitarist from a duck-billed platypus. Mikey said Jon was right. I told Jon he'd have to tell Suede himself, I could never have done it. I realized how serious Jon was about career opportunities. For months I worried if we'd done the right thing.

When Jon went on holiday to California to visit his cousins he took our demo tapes and said he'd visit a few record companies. I knew that was all talk. I received a postcard. "Dear George, I don't think America's ready for the Sex Gang Children. Missing you, Jon." I was thrilled to get the card and to hear he was missing me. I innocently went to see Jon's girlfriend, Caroline, who worked for an art dealer in Endell Street, Covent Garden. I mentioned Jon's card. She was furious. "That's bloody nice. He hasn't sent me one."

Jon returned from America and came straight to Goodge Street from the airport, suntanned and smiling. We went for a meal and talked about his adventures. He was more enthusiastic than ever. I was pleased. His holiday had left a void in my life. Over dinner he looked at me and said, "You're really pretty, you know." Cupid could have scraped me off the floor. It was the first time any boy had told me I was pretty without my makeup on.

Jon invited me round to his flat while Caroline was away skiing. He drank too much red wine and started pouring out his heart. He'd been fighting with Caroline, she said he was selfish because he wanted to stay in London and work with the band. He said I could stay the night. I could see there was only one bed and panicked. "Er, er, no. I'll go home." I didn't know if he was coming on to me or just being thoughtful.

Friday night we went to the Beat Route. I got dressed up like a dragon's dinner in a torn sack skirt, red Crimplene flowered blouse, and matching tights that Mum made out of a chair cover with a black twenties tabard and a big wooden crucifix. My hair was plaited, covered in ribbons and rags, topped off with a big black fedora.

"Blimey," said Jon. "You look great." I loved turning up at clubs with him. I let people think what they liked—they always did anyway. When Jon dropped me home he kissed my cheek and said, "I won't be able to sleep." I ran inside and sat down on the stairs in the dark, I could have strangled myself for not grabbing hold of him. We spoke the next morning. Jon had to go to a party with Caroline, but he said he'd see me Sunday and joked, "How will we live without each other for one day?" That evening he turned up on the doorstep with cat scratches all over his face. Caroline had attacked him. He said she was screaming at him, in front of all their friends, "You fancy George, don't you? You spend enough time with him." I asked him what he said. He looked at me dead straight. "I told her it was true." We sat in my room, Jon on the chair, me on the bed, staring at each other, not knowing what to say. Jon made the first move and we snogged and hugged on the bed. His mouth tasted so sexy. I didn't want to ever let him go. He said he was going to tell Caroline their engagement was off. I felt guilty, even though he claimed it was nothing to do with me.

Sunday night Marilyn and I went to see Kirk's new band Spear of Destiny at the Lyceum. Jon was there with Caroline. I was upset and thought Jon had gone back to her. I kept out of their way. Someone in the crowd shouted at Kirk, "Oi, where's Georgie?" I didn't hear Kirk's reply but he didn't look happy.

Jon split with Caroline and moved back to his parents' place in Hampstead and we got on with the business of falling in love and finding a new guitarist. It was such a perfect moment in my life—everything was coming together. With Jon there was more affection than I'd ever known. Sex was tender and adventurous. My other boyfriends were all planks of wood who were happy to get blown off and roll over. It was like learning to love from scratch. I couldn't believe Jon had never been with another man, though he swore blind. Eventually he admitted to once kissing his friend, but I always suspected he was hiding something.

I don't know what it is about me. I always seem to attract so-called straight boys on their first outing to queerdom. I loved the challenge, it made me feel like I had something special. They all loved my eyes. I knew the makeup eased the self-deception. Somehow they weren't really queer if they could think of me as a girl. Of course, massive insecurity went with the territory. You never knew how long any romance would last before they ran back to the comfort of a warm rug. I didn't hate women, but I envied them.

Keith Giddens was a regular at Street Theatre, one of the many cute straight boys I spent hours flirting with. He worked in a local office and hung out in his lunch break. I told him I was looking for a guitarist. He said his friend Roy Hay played keyboards and guitar in an electro band called Russian Bouquet. I was immediately put off. "Ugh. I don't want any naff New Romantics." Keith brought Roy and his girlfriend, Alison, to the shop. Thankfully he looked nothing like Gary Numan: Roy was handsomish and blond with a tearful expression and loads of charm. I could tell he was nice even though Alison did all the talking. She was a peroxide blond with glasses and an ambitious glint in her eye. She asked if there were any jobs going. I said I'd ask Peter Small, and it wasn't long before she was behind the counter.

We auditioned Roy to Jon's favorite song, "Private Number" by William Clay and Judy Bell. He wasn't the best guitarist we tried out. There were some real ax gods, like Jon's old punk mate Riff Regan, and a couple of real tasties. We wanted someone who connected with us. I said we should go for Roy. He had a quiff and wore a zoot suit—at least he had style. For once Jon didn't argue.

Roy and I started writing together in my tiny room in Goodge Street with a guitar and a miniamp. It was his first experience of my impatience. I expected him to come up with chords instantly and use ESP. I kept going out to get tea and ringing Jon at work.

"I can't stand him. He's too slow."

"Give the guy a bloody chance."

We managed to get the outline for one song, "Kissing to Be

Clever." I was sure I'd frightened Roy away forever but he came back again and again. Roy was a trainee hairdresser, and he could just about afford his train fare from Billericay on his hair clippings. I spent all my money on makeup, beer, and fish and chips. Mikey was still bumming cigarettes. Jon had two jobs, van driving and duplicating soft-porn videos, and he wore gold, so naturally he had to cough up.

Right from the start we agreed that all band earnings would be split four ways, including the songs. We tried to create a perfect pop democracy, thinking if everyone felt equal it would keep the band together. The music was haphazard, with everyone throwing in a groove or a chord. The best songs grew out of my melodies and lyrics, which the others would expand on, Mikey's reggae bass, Roy's blue-eyed funk guitar, and Jon's rhythms from Tamla to tribal. I knew what I wanted but I could never quite explain myself. I found rehearsals frustrating because I couldn't play an instrument and felt left out. If the others got bored they would start jamming. I would scream through the mike, "Very interesting, I know you can play." Musicians seemed happy to masturbate.

Jon loved strategy meetings. For one we had to bring our favorite records. I brought "Mule Skinner Blues" by Jimmie Rodgers, "Rebel Rebel" by Bowie, and "Being Boiled" by the Human League. Jon went for Iron Butterfly and old soul, Mikey obscure rub-a-dub and Roy Steely Dan. The one thing we had in common was an eclectic taste. I always started with the title of a song; "Kissing to Be Clever," "I'm Afraid of Me," "White Boy." Only I knew what I was singing about. "Kissing to Be Clever" was about those so-called straight boys who hung around the flower garden; "I'm Afraid of Me" was about my self-destructiveness. White boys were colorless ignorant people, it had nothing to do with inverted racism or color. Sometimes the others would laugh at my lyrics. I didn't want to write moon-in-June crap. The general themes were sexuality and prejudice. I was writing a lot of songs about Kirk, the biggest white boy of them all. I wrote without structure. I didn't know about bridges and middle eights. Jon talked a lot about simplicity. "Look at Motown." Through trial and error I soon learned to simplify my ramblings.

We all agreed Sex Gang Children was the wrong name. We

toyed with new ones, Caravan Club, Can't Wait Club. Jon said, "Look at us. An Irish transvestite, a Jew, a black man, an Anglo-Saxon." That's how I came up with the name Culture Club. Nightclubbing, roots, and culture. The name Boy George went with the reggae vibe too—lots of DJs had titles like King Tubby, Prince Jammy, Jah Whoosh. I also liked the idea of playing with sexual ambiguity. Is it a bird? Is it a plane? No, it's Boy George.

Despite the early eighties recession, business was booming at Street Theatre. My boss, Peter Small, opened a new shop, the Foundry, round the corner in Ganton Street, specializing in menswear, which he asked me to manage. Our first venture into men's couture was the zoot suit. We were trying to cash in on an apparent trend that didn't go beyond a few nightclubs. It was an ugly design with nasty padded shoulders: Elvis meets Linda Evans. We might have sold two. Thankfully our other designs were more successful. Peter put me together with a young designer, Sue Clowes, who he'd found in Kensington Market. Sue designed clothes and was a textile printer. It was perfect for executing my ideas. I wanted to create clothes that would give Culture Club an identity, like Bow Wow Wow or the Sex Pistols. Sue created brilliant fabric designs based on cultural concepts and a one-nation ideal. We used the Star of David as a symbol which was tied in with Rastafarianism, the lost tribe of Judah. Sue went to the library and looked up Culture Club in Hebrew script and made the first official Culture Club T-shirt, a huge black Star of David surrounded by roses and a golden aura with the words *tarabat agadar,* meaning "movement of all cultures." Both Sue and I were fascinated by Catholic camp, religious taboos, and ancient symbolism. We worked well together because we were so different. I would blabber incessantly, and Sue was studious, a real thinker. She wouldn't throw anything together; it was a painstaking intellectual process. She worked most of the day and night, making the screens, printing and airbrushing everything herself. I loved going down to her studio and watching the first print appear on the T-shirt. My favorites were a picture of a fifties muscle man with the words "Sex in Heaven" and Sue's hobo designs, which were symbols used by travelers and tramps to indicate danger or where food and shelter might be found.

Soon the Foundry was filled with Sue's multicultural designs; the shop sign depicted a Hasidic Jew. It caused a real stir: lots of Jewish housewives would come in and ask, "What is this shop? Is it political?" Our biggest seller were Y-fronts with the Star of David on them. One old lady said they were for her grandson's bar mitzvah. Jon made a spiritual boo-boo by asking Sue to put Adonaï, meaning My Lord, on a T-shirt. We had to destroy them all, though I kept one for myself.

Months on, our EMI demos still hadn't secured us a recording contract. Jon said it was because all A&R men were idiots. When he went to see Island Records they didn't even have a cassette player. Jon would play everything personally or not at all. He said we had to act special. It was all to do with his est training, positive thinking. At one point he was convinced he could change traffic lights.

We decided we should do some gigs outside London to gain confidence. The idea of playing in London in front of friends and archenemies terrified me—I was notorious for slagging every other band. When Sade and Pride did an impromptu performance on the back of a lorry outside the Beat Route, I dismissed them bitterly. "They're shit." I said Sade couldn't sing, and I knew I was wrong as I said it. I loathed ultratrendy Blue Rondo à la Turk, even though my friend Christos was in the band. I said Spandau Ballet were poseurs and would never make it.

Steve Strange was the flavor of café society since his minor hit "Fade to Grey." I told everyone it was an appropriate title and I wished he would. He and Rusty started a new nightclub, Club for Heroes, at the Barracuda in Baker Street. Not only were they attracting the trendies, but stars too. Steve could often be found sharing a toilet with Phil Lynott and Pete Townshend, who later mysteriously collapsed at the club. After the opening night I was noted in *Ritz* magazine. "Among the guests was George O'Dowd of Planets, checking out the opposition no doubt, dressed in a much better version of the clothes Steve Strange used to wear." I screwed the paper up and spat on it. Jealousy was rampant. We all wanted to be stars and couldn't stand it if someone beat us to it.

Jeremy Healy and I influenced each other so much. There had

always been childish rivalry, but when he started his group Haysi Fantayzee with Kate Garner it reached pathetic contortions. I proudly played him and Kim Bowen my EMI demos; they were more interested in drinking their tea. I left feeling so dejected. Had I known then how destructive jealousy could be I would have saved myself a lot of time and heartache. Jeremy and I fell out over a bleedin' hairdo and didn't speak for five years. Everyone was claiming they had dreadlocks first, as if it really mattered. I was so bitter when Kate Garner walked into Club for Heroes looking like a ragamuffin in her natty dread hat and arse-length dreadlocks. I couldn't afford to go to a hairdresser. I bought the fake hair from Shepherd's Bush Market and my friend Sista Jeni weaved it at her flat in Woolwich. When Jeremy saw my locks he was livid. Both he and Kim stopped speaking to me. They thought I had stolen their look. It wasn't their look to steal. Cultural pilfering was the rage. We were all embracing black culture through music and style. Because of our freaky clothes and subversive lifestyle we had become a minority ourselves. I was the independent state of George O'Dowd, connecting with anything or anyone that wasn't part of the norm.

CHAPTER 22

At Goodge Street the run-ins with Mad Jean were becoming tiresome. She kept bursting in on me and Jon in bed. "I want my rent." She had a solicitor friend send me a fake eviction order. I wanted to sit it out and annoy her but Jon said it was bad for my health. I ran around looking at squalid, expensive bedsits. I was desperate. I knew Philip had a flat in St. John's Wood that his parents had bought in the hope he would move. He was already renting one room to Niamh Fahey, sister of Siobhan from Bananarama. He didn't think shy Niamh could cope with me as a flatmate. I begged and begged.

Philip's flat was poky: two small bedrooms, a lopsided living room with a tiny kitchenette, reached by cliffhanger stairs. I didn't relish the idea of having Philip as a landlord, but it was a relief to be away from Mad Jean and the smell of leather. My room wasn't big enough to swing a hat and Philip was popping round every ten minutes. Still it was nice to have a secure home. Niamh and I barely saw each other, which suited us both. She was so quiet it made me nervous. Attracting noisy people must have been her karma. Her boyfriend was up-and-coming Capital radio DJ Gary Crowley, who was all mouth and Bow Bells. Jon felt uncomfortable with Gary around and acted like a lad to cover his tracks. It was a bit of a giveaway when Gary caught us groping on the stairs.

October 24, 1981, Culture Club played our first live show at

Crocs nightclub in Rayleigh, close to Roy's home turf in Essex. The poster read, "Culture Club, featuring Lieutenant Lush, ex–Bow Wow Wow." I was so proud I kept the poster as proof that we were a real band. Jon even managed to get a £60 fee. Our star dressing room was Alison's mum's house nearby in Grays where we were plied with tea and lots of encouragement. Roy's hairdressing skills were put to good use. We all wore Foundry clothes. I wanted us to look like we had a real identity. Sue made me a special outfit, a smock top with matching trousers and shoes all printed with the Star of David. I finished it off with a white Rasta hat made by Stephen Jones.

Crocs was Southend's premier freak club, made famous by local chart stars Depeche Mode. It drew a mixed crowd, office boys and secretaries, white-faced futurists in rubber and dog collars, trendier types in Westwood pirate hats, rockabillies with high-tops and flat-tops. That first gig was exciting and haphazard. I shouted my way through the set, spitting out one-liners between songs. "This is Roy. He's straight, I think." Still, we looked good and the small crowd reacted well. We were relieved to have done our first gig, and in front of a celebrity audience—Dave Gahan from Depeche Mode was there.

Jon set about finding us a manager. He insisted he had to be Jewish. He recruited Melvin Dubell, a lawyer friend of his father's, to help in the search. Jon was so business-minded. I thought it was pointless as we had no business to mind. He was paranoid about being ripped off.

A potential Jewish manager was found: Tony Gordon. Jon and I went to meet him at his Mayfair office. I was scruffy, camp, and cocky, my spiky hair pulled up into a pineapple, heavy makeup, and dirty unironed clothes. Tony was chubby, paternal, and straight-talking. I didn't trust him, but that was standard for me. I eyed the gold discs around the walls. My woodpecker chatter and Jon's pseudo business patter seemed to amuse him. Our songs amused him too. I laughed when he told us he used to manage Sham 69 and the Angelic Upstarts. It seemed so out of character and swung things in his favor. Jon and I had tea and chewed over the meeting. I liked Tony but I wanted Jon to take full responsibility.

Ashley Goodall and EMI were still dithering. I'd given up hope,

"We'll never get signed." Jon was ever confident and sure things would work out. Shortly after meeting Tony Gordon I had a surprise visitor at the Foundry.

"Hi, Danny Goodwin, Virgin Music. I really enjoyed your show."

I was surprised. "What show?"

"The one in Southend."

He said he loved what he saw and would like to talk more.

I ran to call Jon.

I didn't realize Danny was a publisher. I was disappointed. Still, we met up with him and he promised us some more studio time. Jon was beaming. He wanted us to learn as much as we could and this was another perfect opportunity.

I was falling deeper and deeper in love with Jon. Life couldn't have been more perfect. We were like Fred and Ginger (Beer). Keeping a high profile at all the clubs, Le Kilt, the Beat Route, Dial M for Dolphins, gigs at the Venue where we saw the Stray Cats and Paul Young with the Q-Tips. I felt that I had met my Mr. Perfect. He kissed me voluntarily, occasionally held my hand in public, and treated me like I had a heart.

Jon always insisted he was straight. And while we were lying in bed together naked it really didn't seem to matter. But when a man says he's straight, while humping another man, it means one of two things: you're unique, or he can't deal with his sexuality. I always liked the idea of being unique. But even in my most effeminate moments I was never very female. There are some things makeup cannot disguise. At first Jon seemed different. He was so loving to me I lost all those old insecurities about girls. I felt safe, until . . .

We were at the opening of a new club, Dial M for Dolphins. It wasn't that busy. A few people were toe-tapping impatiently around the edge of the dance floor to Spandau's "Chant No. 1." Jon bought me a Pernod and blackcurrant and disappeared to talk pop maneuvers with Steve Dagger and club host Perry Haines. I sat talking to friends. I was suspicious when I noticed Jon's attention had turned to a petite blond. Later and drunker he pulled me to one side. "Listen, I'm just going to give my friend Sam a lift home. I'll be straight back."

"What, her? Can't she get a cab?" The anger welled up inside. "You can't just leave me here." I was threatened and hysterical. My instincts told me she was about to get a ride, not a lift. Jon left despite my tears. I ran out of the club and back to St. John's Wood. I threw myself down on the bed in the dark. Bastard.

At 7 A.M. I was woken by Jon. He was guilty and sheepish.

"You slept with her, didn't you?"

He didn't even lie. "Yes." He said it was nothing.

A black cloud followed me to work. I didn't dare tell anyone. I'd bored them all with lovey-dovey stories about Jon and tales of Culture Club's imminent rise. Everything had been too perfect. We had record-company interest, maybe a manager, the music was shaping up. I felt like such an idiot. That same day Tony Gordon appeared unannounced at the Foundry. He was embarrassed. "Hope you don't mind me popping in." We went for a cup of tea round the corner at Cranks. He said he was really interested in managing us. That made me feel worse. I said I'd have to speak to Jon but I didn't want to. Jon kept phoning to say he was sorry. It was too late. I said I wanted the band to continue, but there would be nothing further between us. He turned up on the doorstep buzzing persistently. I left him outside.

I went to the Beat Route on the arm of an old fling, Mohican Dave. I wanted to wind up Jon. I knew he'd appear. He called Dave a brainless piece of meat. I said, "You should know all about that." Band rehearsals were strained. Nothing sounded or felt the same. Roy and Mikey were oblivious. They knew nothing about our relationship. I wanted to leave the band, but I was hooked, heart and spirit.

It wasn't long before Jon smooched his way back into my bed. Accepting his betrayal was the biggest mistake I ever made. As dear Myra once wisely wrote,

Forked tongued serpents don't regret,
Snakes in the grass make dangerous pets.

By forgiving Jon I opened myself up to six years of sheer misery and heartache. I never trusted him again, though my obsession and desire knew no limits. Our relationship was built on power tripping and masochism. My deep-rooted insecurity gave Jon incredible power over me. Sex was always filthy and wonderful. When the lights went out the pain disappeared, but it was always there the morning after. Our love, however diseased, was the creative force behind Culture Club. I wanted fame badly but without Jon Culture Club would have meant very little to me. My love for him made it all worthwhile. Love has always been more important than success. Love is success. There are those who suggested Jon's interest in me was purely mercenary. That I was a meal ticket. Jon could be callous and manipulative, but not so that I couldn't recognize real passion. I do believe Jon loved me. So much that he often hated me. I was hateful to any remotely attractive female. I was twitched out. My eyes were everywhere.

Danny Goodwin kept his promise. He persuaded Richard Griffiths, head of Virgin Music, to give us £500 to make some more demos. We recorded on the Virgin studio barge, next to Richard Branson's houseboat in Little Venice. Three new songs, "Put It Down," "Kissing to Be Clever," and "You Know I'm Not Crazy." My pain was starting to seep into the songwriting. Simple pop songs with blatant messages to the boy I loved. My heart-bearing failed to impress Virgin Publishing. No deal was forthcoming. Danny stuck with us all the way: "Keep the songs coming."

Jon set up another gig at Crocs. Harry the manager liked us and was willing to pay more money, which we needed for rehearsals. We talked about putting our record out independently. Jon said that was small-time. We were going to make it no problem. I was frustrated, I wanted nothing more than to see our name on a seven-inch piece of plastic.

I was gaining notoriety as a pop wannabe. My picture appeared in the *NME* gossip column with the rumor that I was dating Billy Duffy, ex–Theatre of Hate, then guitarist with the Southern Death Cult. It was rubbish. I knew Billy from the punk days—I got him the job with Theatre of Hate. That was the sum total of our relationship. He was cute, though, and it made me look good.

The Foundry shop became official Culture Club headquarters. Slowly we were beginning to attract a handful of followers, exhibitionist punks and New Romantics. They bought the clothes and took my picture. Letters arrived at the shop for Boy George and Culture Club, asking when our record was out. The Trendy magazine *New Sounds, New Styles* ran a feature on Sue Clowes and the Foundry. Mikey and his kids, Kita and Amber, Amos, Jon, and myself modeled the clothes.

The snippets of press helped swell our audience. Our second appearance at Crocs on Boxing Day 1981 drew a full house. We played better than ever, though I still hadn't lost my habits of singing with my back to the audience and swearing. Sista Jeni and Clare with the Hair danced onstage. Clare looked like Nancy Cunard gone Rasta. We used Roy's parents' house in Billericay to get ready. His father, Bill, was amused. "That George comes in looking like a man, goes out looking like a woman."

Mark Lebon did another photo session, the first with our permanent lineup, and made me look like a beautiful girl. He cleverly projected a Star of David into my eyes. I scraped back my locks and wore a Sue Clowes turban. The band wore Sue's new Rasta camouflage gear. The photos were so professional, we looked like a proper pop group. Jon touted our demos and pictures round the record companies. They all thought the girl singer was very pretty, but there were still no offers. We decided on Tony Gordon as a manager. Jon said no record company would take us seriously without one. Tony offered to work free of charge for six months so we could assess his ability before signing a contract.

After we finished the second demo it was clear we needed a producer. Jon said we should find someone sympathetic and objective, who could mold our sound. Through Tony's connection at EMI we went back into the studios with Steve Levine, EMI's new in-house demo producer. Steve's credits included the Angelic Upstarts and Honey Bane, ex-singer with the Fatal Microbes, who made one of my all-time favorite records, "Violence Grows." We recorded our favorite new song, "White Boy," and another, "I'm Afraid of Me." I had problems pitching "I'm Afraid of Me." But after two days in the studio we were sure we had our first single. Tony Gordon was sure too. We were bitterly disappointed when EMI gave us the thumbs down again, despite Ashley championing us. We knew they were the wrong company.

Jon decided a London gig would be a good idea. I wanted to

make a night of it, find a club, hire our own DJs, fill it with our crowd. "Make it really exciting." Peter Small put up the money and found a club, Fouberts, just off Carnaby Street—he helped without having any stake in the band. In preparation we played a warm-up gig at the Regency Suite in Chadwell Heath, Essex, on January 19, 1982. Danny Goodwin managed to drag Richard Griffiths to see us. The night was a disaster. We arrived for the sound check to discover there was no P.A., Jon had to arrange one. Our dressing room was a disused bar. There were more hecklers than admirers. "Poofter. Get off." I told them to scream all they liked. I had their money now, and I was going to spend it on eyeshadow. It must have looked very amateurish to the head of Virgin Publishing. I played Danny the new EMI demos in his car. He thought the songs were great and promised to play them to Richard at a more opportune moment. We called the Fouberts night "The Can't Wait Club" and it was a big success. Roy invited his DJ friend Gary Turner from Crocs to spin records and Amos chatted live. "Brrr comes, a bran nu mullical style wicked and wile. Buss it." Every trendy and quite a few A&R men were there, Muff Winwood from CBS, Chris Briggs from Phonogram, David Betteridge from RCA. None of them rushed forward with a contract. They thought I was too gay to be a pop commodity. David Betteridge signed Haysi Fantayzee. I was riddled with jealousy.

I never considered toning down. Having been a T. Rex and Bowie fan, I knew style and content went hand in hand. I was niggled that Jeremy and Kate were smart enough to think of doing a home video to promote their music. I was sure that was why they got signed.

I made my TV debut appearing on a Tyne Tees youth program, *Check It Out,* to talk about Peter Small's budding alternative fashion empire. Peter chose me over the designers—he thought they'd be too boring. I flew up to Newcastle with Peter's wife, Dali. It was my first flight too, and I thought I needed a passport. During the interview I was shaking with fear and staring at my feet. They asked me whether London was the capital of fashion. I said, "Fashion is everywhere. If you want it, you'll find it." I wore my Stephen Jones Rasta hat, a brown jacket made from post sacks, my notoriously smelly and frayed mauve Ali Baba trousers, and a pair of Vivienne Westwood blue spider boots. My face was painted to perfection. I'd been up since 6 A.M. Two models showed off our clothes. They were stiff, uncomfortable, and made the clothes look tacky. I said my inspirations were Margaret Thatcher and London Transport.

I sent our new demos to a new BBC-TV arts magazine program, *Riverside*. Assistant producer David Croft wrote back saying we were unsuitable for the show and sent tickets to be in the audience. They tried to create a club atmosphere. All the desperadoes were there, Jeremy, Kate swishing her locks, Philip, Andy Polaris, all desperate to get on TV, like me. I went back every week until they asked me not to.

Dali sent off for tickets for *Top of the Pops*. I'd always wanted to go. I couldn't believe how small the studio was. It was stuffy and formal. They made it look much more exciting on TV. We danced around to Shakin' Stevens. Dali said, "You'll be on here one day."

Niamh moved out of St. John's Wood, leaving me in blissful solitude. Philip very kindly waived half the rent, but said he would have to look for someone else. I was worried—I didn't want Philip choosing some scabby rent boy or noisy drag queen. I couldn't believe it when Philip said my flatmate was going to be some cute boy he'd met at Heaven.

"Look, Philip. I'll move out."

Philip brought Richard Habberley and his supposed girlfriend to the flat. I was hostile: I didn't like him before I'd met him and now he was sitting in front of me thrusting his tongue down a girl's throat, I liked him even less.

I called Philip the next morning. "Forget it. I'm not living with a closet."

Philip sniggered. "He is tasty, though."

Due to Philip's lust, my weak nature, and a lack of cash, Richard moved in. He was pretty once he stopped pretending to be straight. Sulky-lipped with Araby features and quiffy hair. Over the coming weeks his presence grew on me. He had an MG Midget that could taxi me to clubs, and didn't mind popping out for a pint of milk.

*   *   *

The new EMI demos produced by Steve Levine created the biggest buzz so far. Richard Griffiths at Virgin Publishing offered us a contract, and Jon handled the deal behind Tony Gordon's back. Jon thought he was being clever cutting out the middle man, but Tony was furious. It turned out to be a lousy deal after all, and Tony eventually had to renegotiate it.

Our demos were played at a Virgin Records A&R meeting where Danny described us to much laughter. They decided to have a look for themselves. Simon Draper, head of Virgin Records, Jeremy Lascelles, and Jumbo from Virgin A&R were invited to Hollywood Studios in Stoke Newington to see us play. To our embarrassment, Tony hired a chauffeur-driven car to bring them to the grotty run-down rehearsal rooms. I was so nervous I stopped singing and snapped, "Would you please stop staring at me and stand over in that corner." Their blank expressions unnerved me.

We went to Virgin for a meeting. The atmosphere at their rambling offices in Vernon Yard, off the Portobello Road, was warm and chaotic: people and paper spilling from cluttered desks, music blaring, phones ringing. It was far from the corporate monster it has become. Virgin put us into Maison Rouge Studios in Fulham with Steve Levine to record three songs, "White Boy," "I'm Afraid of Me," and "I'll Tumble 4 Ya." All of us felt Virgin was the right choice.

Steve Levine gave us a bigger sound, adding brass and keyboards played by Phil Pickett, a member of the seventies pop group Sailor. I was excited, I'd bought Sailor records when I was a teenager. It seemed mad that he was playing for us. Steve also used the Linn drum, the first programmable drum machine. It was the first in the country. Jon wasn't averse to using a drum machine—it was revolutionary, the way forward.

The additional musicians made a real difference. We sounded polished and professional. Steve was easy to work with but I hated the studio straightaway; everything took too long. I went shopping when I got bored. Jon and Roy were the most active and attentive in the studio. Mikey arrived when he felt like it, setting a pattern.

I wrote a song called "Love Twist" as a B-side for "White Boy" and got Amos in to toast. Mikey was against it. I insisted that we use Amos. Everything about him, his look, his toasting, was perfect for Culture Club. I wanted him in the group permanently. Mikey didn't want his girlfriend's little brother checking up on him and he was jealous.

I was struck by a strange dark mood the day we signed to Virgin. Like I'd lost my liberty. I avoided the celebrations and sat outside on the stairs, refusing the champagne. I had so much to think about. My relationship with Jon was the biggest worry, and I didn't understand the contract or how I would get my money. Would I get any money? I put my trust in four virtual strangers, Jon, Roy, Mikey, and Tony.

I'd signed a six-year contract with options. From the outset we insisted on complete artistic control. We knew exactly what we wanted. I didn't want any interference from Virgin. Jon's friend Jik helped me come up with a Culture Club logo. He worked for an advertising agency and had access to the office after hours. Jik and I designed the first Culture Club sleeve using Mark Lebon's Star of David pictures and Sue's tramp designs. My face was on the front because it looked strongest. The band were on the back along with another picture of me. No one objected; their jealousy was stored for later.

"White Boy" was chosen as the single and released on April 30, 1982. I rushed to Shooters Hill with some promo copies. "Look, Mum, look, Dad." They were so proud. I don't think the music was their cup of tea. I took a copy into the Camden Palace and asked the DJ to play it. The club wasn't that full anyway. Those on the dance floor swayed around politely and seemed to like it.

The Camden Palace, formerly the Music Machine, was the place to be. Steve Strange and Rusty Egan were running Thursday nights. They'd refurbished the old punk dump and turned it into a tacky Deco-style posers parlor. All the so-called important people hung out in the balcony VIP star bar. Steve fussed over celebrities. "More champagne, please." Grace Jones, Kid Creole and his Coconuts, Jack Nicholson, another photo of Steve with someone famous to hang up on the various picture boards. Flashlights,

flashlights. The club hired photographers to make everyone feel important.

The reviews of "White Boy" were surprisingly good. The *NME* said, "There's a word for this, and that's impeccable." I was described as a geisha with dreadlocks. Other reviews centered around my sexuality, which was discussed more than the music. I rattled our new press officer, Ronnie Gurr, by taking over his office. I wanted the band to appear in fashion magazines, which went against his rock and roll education. Ronnie phoned Jackie Modlinger, fashion editor of the *Daily Express*. She wasn't interested, and neither was anyone else in Fleet Street.

Virgin wanted any old press. They sent us off to agency photographers who made us look naff and ugly. We were duped into believing it would be good for us. Those photos haunted us for years: ugly pictures appeared on mugs, mirrors, and cheap T-shirts. It wasn't about money—I would have been happy for my face to appear on a toilet seat, as long as it was a good picture and the right toilet seat. I appeared on the cover of the *New Musical Express*. I was so proud. All my heroes had enjoyed this honor, Marc Bolan, Bowie, the Pistols, Siouxsie Sioux. Paul Morley wrote an affectionate piece, the sayings of Chairman Meow. "George on Steve Strange: 'People look at Steve Strange and the general opinion is that he's a prat. They look at me, see I wear make-up and think I'm a prat as well. I think he could have been a lot more successful and respected if he'd just been a bit human about it all.' George on money: 'I just want money so I can be really irresponsible.'" I rambled and ricocheted through interviews, tricking and slipping, making sense, making no sense. I was contradictory and evasive about my sexuality, uttering ridiculously: "I'm not gay or anything like that." When asked what type of person I was likely to fall in love with, I replied, "The lorry driver's mate." One lie tripped up the other. Jon said it wasn't a good idea to discuss our personal business. Keep 'em guessing. He worried that if the press discovered our secret they would plague us or, worse still, ignore us. There were other people to consider—Jon's family, the rest of the band. Just when I thought our love was destined to remain in the closet it slipped out for a quick game of confusion. Jon and I appeared in *Flexipop* magazine wrapped around each other in sensuous embrace. Hardly the stuff teenage dreams are made of. The photos were taken on the roof of Philip's flat in a moment of gay abandon.

Of all the cartoon heroes,
You remain so fit
A challenge to my self-respect
But no challenge to my wit.
I met you at a moment
When you could take a risk.
Shine on, I said shine on.

I was protecting something sacred and twisted, my love for Jon. It was never about housewives. I wanted people to know I was gay. It went against every corpuscle in my body to deny it. Certainly those around me, management, record company, were worried about sales potential. I don't know whether being open would have made me any less popular. In private and around the clubs I was known as the queen supreme. My wardrobe wasn't exactly boy-next-door. There are a million ways to say something.

Jimmy Somerville and others of the new gay wave targeted me as a hypocrite for not flying the gay flag. Somerville's own father was reluctant to watch his first *Top of the Pops* appearance, fearful he would appear dressed like Boy George in ribbons, bows, and makeup. In many people's eyes, I was the premier poof, the benchmark by which others would be measured.

Gay News wrote, "It's not often that a male pop singer admits that he likes going to bed with men, particularly when the band they are with is very near the big time. But Boy George—as he likes to be called—does so readily."

"White Boy" received instant support from Gary Crowley on Capital and a handful of selective plays, but failed to make the Capital Radio or Radio One playlists. It sold just over eight thousand copies, reaching 114 in the charts. I was happy that anyone had bought it. I wanted to write and thank them all personally. There were those around the clubs who bitched about "White Boy" not making it. Still, I'd done something they hadn't. I'd made a record, and people I didn't know had bought it. It was the most wonderful, brilliant, fantastic thing that had ever happened to me.

"I'm Afraid of Me" was chosen as the second single. Jon said we should capitalize on the momentum and bring it out quickly. We did another photo session with Mark, dressed as cowboys. I wore a big frayed straw hat and yellow foundation. Jon looked like the cute one out of *Bonanza*. I kept my drag on and went posing down at the Palace where I was confronted by snarling Liverpool legend Pete Burns. "You ripped me off, you cunt." His Scouse roar tore through me. Burns was another freak staking claim to the invention of dreadlocks and androgyny. He was flanked by a gaunt red-haired boy and a bruiser female, who turned out to be his wife, Lynne. She was ready to punch me out. I warned them, "You touch me in this club and you're dead." I walked away, shaken. I'd always had a distant respect for Pete Burns. I couldn't believe he'd been so hideous. So what he had a straw hat and dreadlocks? So did Kate Garner. It wasn't who did it first, it was who was seen in it first. That was the law of the powder-puff jungle.

"Fuck him, dear." Philip wasn't going to jewelry designer Andrew Logan's benefit that Heaven was hosting to pay for his Alternative Miss World overheads. Richard and I weren't wearing our charity hats; we just wanted a night out. We bumped into Marilyn and Miss Binnie outside. "Oh, you've missed the best part, our cabaret and Helen's singing. It was really good."

"Helen?" Who was this Helen?

Binnie had a knack of making even distant planets seem familiar. "This is Helen. You should use her in your pop group." Marilyn joined in. "Listen to her sing." I smiled, hoping Helen wasn't another of Binnie's neonaturist howlers. She was a big girl. I could just imagine her onstage covered in mud, wearing a twig head-dress.

"Give us a song, then."

"I'm not a performing poodle."

"Oh, go on," I insisted.

Helen let out a black-mama wail that almost lifted me off my feet. "Will that do?"

"Yeh it will. Give us your number?"

*   *   *

Culture Club's second single, "I'm Afraid of Me," was released on June 25. It sold better than "White Boy," but again it failed to grab the attention of the masses, reaching 100. I was disappointed and wanted to give up. Jon remained steadfast. "It's early days." To add to the depression, Haysi Fantayzee's debut single, "John Wayne Is Big Leggy," was being played on Radio One. It became the soundtrack to my despair, slowly climbing the charts and staying there for ten weeks, niggling at my psyche. I knew it was a good record too. Clever, original, and very annoying. I wanted to retire when I saw the video on Saturday-morning kids' TV. I couldn't believe they had a video and we didn't.

It was beginning to look as though we were guilty as accused. So many trendy bands had gone by the wayside after being trumpeted as the Next Big Thing. Virgin wrung their hands and wondered whether they should let us continue recording the album. They felt they'd done everything they could, but Tony persuaded Virgin to stick with us. We continued recording our first album, *Kissing to Be Clever*, at Red Bus Studios off Church Street Market near Edgware Road. Most of the songs had been written prior to signing the Virgin deal. We were short of one or two, but we had time. The early songs were very fashion conscious. Instead of following my instincts I followed trends: I wanted a record that would impress the in-crowd. I was envious of Haysi Fantayzee's tongues-out bums-out irreverence. But no matter how much I berated Roy to play like Matthew Ashman, or Jon to pound like Dave Barbarossa, it never sounded the same.

Kissing to Be Clever started out in my eyes to be the album that Bow Wow Wow had never made. During the recording it turned into something unique, confused, and eclectic. It was an early "world music" album and we didn't even know it. All of us secretly had our own vision, and the conflict of ideas pushed us forward. As things progressed I became very proud and confident of what we were creating.

Phil Pickett's keyboards added a worldly sophistication, the brass added pizzazz. I wanted to bring in more people to play on the tracks and to appear with us onstage. I thought bands like Rip Rig and Panic, and Kid Creole and the Coconuts, were doing it right—kick off your shoes and throw down. "Who wants to look at four people chugging away onstage?" I wanted exotic dancers, percussion, and fireworks.

The music scene was healthier than it had been in a long time, perhaps overhealthy. Haircut 100 sanitized the charts with their cutesy, fresh-faced smiles. ABC's collaborations with Trevor Horn brought production and schmaltz to a new high. The champagne-swilling, yacht-sailing Duran Duran touted playboyeurism and a new pop superficiality. Suddenly it was okay to be rich, famous, and feel no shame. Some saw it as the natural consequence of Thatcherism. Jon was a staunch Tory. "Thatcher, bloody brilliant." It was hard to know whether he meant it.

Long before any chart success I was attracting female admirers, mostly tubby little schoolgirls and teenage Goths. A handful of boys, too, with painted faces and Foundry clothes. They all attempted to capture part of the image—black hat, eyebrows, mirrored specs, and plaited hair. More and more were coming into the shop to buy outfits, some even asked for autographs. I was flattered by their adoration. One or two brought copies of Haysi's record "John Wayne" for me to sign. Of course I refused. They were unaware of the division between the two groups, they didn't care, and why should they?

We were fighting about nothing important while dreaming of the same things. It seemed silly to shun each other over a few strands of nylon hair. Jeremy and Kate were like Dickensian Rastas, with the emphasis on dick. Theirs was an altogether more sexual stance, midriffs exposed, flies undone. I was a doll, covered from head to toe in frocks and bows. I was unwittingly safe. I'm sure I thought about and enjoyed sex as much as Kate and Jeremy, but it wasn't woven into my act. I was insecure about my body, the kind of boy that avoided beaches, gyms, and communal toilets. I had short arms, short legs, and a fat bum. I dressed to disguise my bulk. I never considered myself sexy. But with makeup I could certainly look exotic.

Jon and I spent a lot of time hanging out at Jik and Jem's flat off Fitzroy Square, drinking tea and listening to Jem's wicked new reggae tunes. He was another one of those culturally confused white boys, lost in a world of Rizla and reggae. I was very wary of drugs after my speed delirium at Warren Street. I didn't understand that different drugs had different effects. As far as I was concerned all drugs made you lose control, and that was it. I used to nag at Jon for smoking dope round at Jem's. I'd leave the room in a huff saying it was boring and hippie-ish. Once I tried it, I almost choked, it did absolutely nothing for me. I consigned it to the bored bucket.

One May Sunday, we were all hanging out at the flat. Me, Jon, Jem, Jik, and Sista Jeni. An obscure Studio One classic was spinning on the deck. I grabbed a pen and started scribbling: "Do you really want to hurt me? Do you really want to make me cry?" Sista Jeni rocked in appreciation. I sang my new song at the next rehearsal. Everyone liked it. It was home territory for Mikey, sweet lovers' reggae. His seductive bass line brought the song together.

We debuted "Do You Really" for our first Radio One session on *The Peter Powell Show*. I was excited that we were going to be heard on national radio. We recorded four songs, "White Boy," "I'm Afraid of Me," "I'll Tumble 4 Ya," and "Do You Really." "Do You Really" was played live. I got Amos to chat. He made a prediction, "Peter Powell a play it, and it reach to Number One. Virgin dem a cut it, and it sell a million." He must have known something we didn't. Despite his cheering prophecy, I ticked him and Mikey off when I caught them smoking a spliff in the dressing room. Mikey was lethargic at the best of times, spliff made him worse. I didn't want him messing up our session.

When we recorded "Do You Really" for the album, it was again played live, without the aid of Steve's newfound gadgetry. It sounded a lot better than everything else. My vocal was done in one take. Steve panicked when he discovered the tape machine was running slow, and worried that it might be less than perfect. I refused to sing it again. The technical doctors were called and the problem was solved. Steve and I agreed that Jon, Roy, and Mikey's terrace chants would be unsuitable for "Do You Really." What we needed was soulful backing vocals. I remembered Helen, and called her.

"Have you done backing vocals before?"

"Yeh."

"Can you do harmonies and things?"

"Yes! I'm a professional."

I'd never heard Helen sing apart from that brief wail outside the Heaven. Screaming and singing were two different things, as Jon pointed out. I hoped Helen wouldn't let me down.

There were rumors going round (probably started by Helen) that she'd sung the do-da-doos on Lou Reed's "Walk on the Wild Side." I didn't care whether it was true or not. Her performance on "Do You Really" gave her enough credibility. Her vocal arrangements added magic and real soul; Helen became a very important part of our sound.

Jon said touring was the only way to prove we weren't just fashion plates. A minitour was arranged for June 1982, taking in the north of England, Nottingham, Manchester, Derby, finishing in Southend and Brighton, before facing London. We played the newly opened Hacienda in Manchester to a bored and anorexic crowd. They raved at the Derby Bluenote, and we received our first live review, in the *NME*. "Not for one minute did I expect to be confronted with a hot Tamla beat soul goddess, or should that be god?" The review was ridiculous, but I was pleased. It felt like we were being taken seriously.

Phil Pickett played keyboards on the tour along with Terry the Trumpet and Nick Payne, our sax player who I nicknamed "John Denver." We used backing tapes to strengthen our sound; the Linn drum patterns were lifted from studio recordings. This meant the band had to keep perfect time. It didn't always work. There was a power cut on the first night at Nottingham University. The tape stopped during "I'll Tumble 4 Ya." Luckily it stopped right on the beat. The crowd thought it was part of the show. Jon, Roy, and Mikey were worried about the credibility of using a tape. I didn't care. One of my favorite bands, the Human League, played with nothing but tapes. They had them right out onstage for everyone to see. Our Revox was hidden away.

Our London gig at Heaven was a big risk. We didn't know if we could pull the twelve hundred capacity, especially during a transport strike. It would be embarrassing to play to a half-empty club. They offered us a paltry fee or a cut of the door. Jon said we'd take the door money. He was confident he made the right choice. By the afternoon there were already people hanging around. There was an incredible buzz. I knew it would go well.

Musical Youth, our support group, built up the atmosphere with their nappy dread reggae. I skipped onstage and I told the audience, "This is 'I'm Afraid of Me.' It wasn't a hit because you bastards didn't buy enough copies." I was effing and blinding like a fishwife. All my brothers were there. They were surprised at how professional we were. Philip didn't bother watching us. He paraded around the club instead. "You know me, dear, I hate to see other people do well." Neil Tennant, then features editor for *Smash Hits,* thought we were dire. "The worst thing about Culture Club is that they use tapes." I was angry and wanted to kill him—the whole piece had been bitter. Mikey said he'd slap him down. We were invited to appear at the Capital Radio Junior Best Disco in Town. It was full of screaming prepubescent girls, reaching out to touch us, clamoring for autographs. We felt famous before our time. I noticed a sheepish character in the backstage bar clutching a notepad. Every time I looked in his direction he tried to avoid eye contact.

"'Ere. Aren't you Neil Tennant?"

He was flustered. "Er, yes."

"Why d'ya write that shit about us?"

"Oh, er . . . "

Mikey, muscles rippling in a Sue Clowes vest, came over. One stare was enough to make Neil run. He wrote of our meeting in the next issue of *Smash Hits,* don't mess with Culture Club. Funny, when Neil started the Pet Shop Boys there were no musicians onstage.

A meeting was called at Virgin to discuss the next single. Tony, Jon, myself, Simon Draper, and an independent radio plugger, Howard Marks. They played "Do You Really Want to Hurt Me?" Simon asked Marks, "Do you think this is a hit?" I protested, "This is really boring." Jon shouted at me, "Shut up a minute. Listen to what the guy's got to say." I was against "Do You Really" being released as a single. I loved the song, but it was too personal, and it wasn't a dancey record. Marks said the track was a hit and we should cut twenty seconds out of the middle. I continued my tirade, "Don't blame me if it flops."

Mikey brought in a gruff-voiced Rastaman called Papa Weasel to chat on the B-side. He had a different style from Amos. I didn't like it that much, but it added the Jamaican flavor. When he finished the session I asked him how he wanted to be credited. He said, "Leave me off, I don't want no credit." He was ashamed to be chatting with a "batty man." I put his name on the record anyway, "featuring Papa Weasel." We were surprised to hear from him when "Do You Really" topped the charts. He phoned Tony Gordon's office from a phone-box, demanding publishing and royalties, claiming he helped write the song, that we stole his lyrics and forged his signature on the release form. I was hurt by his accusations. I never wanted to screw anybody. I was very conscious of that. I always gave people credits and made sure they were paid. Weasel took us to court and lost. But it didn't stop him harassing us. He tried to attack me on the Kings Road and picked an argument with Mikey at a friend's funeral.

"Do You Really" was released on September 3, 1982. Howard Marks warned Virgin that the reaction from Radio One was lukewarm, one of their reporters had told him, "We don't interview transvestites." It was the same at TV. Cathy Gilbey from BBC's *Swapshop* was adamant. "We don't want that kind of person on our show." Strangely Radio Two's "Diddy" David Hamilton made us Record of the Week; I was unaware of how important it would be. "Radio Two? Who listens to Radio Two?" It was ironic because when I was eleven I spent a cold day outside Broadcasting House hoping to meet someone famous. I met "Diddy" David and handed him a drawing I'd done of Bowie.

The reviews of the single were mostly mocking. "It's plain the group's only asset is the ludicrously unphotogenic (ignore the airbrushed sleeve) Boy George. God help 'em."—Robbi Miller, *Sounds*. "Boy's performance here is hilariously thespian."—Allan Jones, *Melody Maker*. "This is weak, watered-down fourth-division reggae. Awful."—Dave Henderson, *Smash Hits*. In support, the *NME*'s Danny Baker wrote, "Whilst slop like the pea-brained Haysi Fantayzee are rolling in it, this group reach their third fine record without a sniff of a hit."

I couldn't believe it charted ten days after release at 85. The second week it jumped to 38. Then due to a fluke we were offered a slot on *Top of the Pops* because someone pulled out—the normal criterion was Top 30. I was so nervous. Everything happened so quickly. I didn't have time to think or decide what to wear.

Mum and Dad sat at home, watching nervously. Mum was worried I would trip over on TV and make a fool of myself. She didn't know it was prerecorded. Most of the eight million people watching *Top of the Pops* thought I was a girl. The following day the phones rang off the wall. Radio One producer David Tate pulled Howard Marks into his office. "I can't play this record again. I don't think it's right for *The Breakfast Show*. What on earth was that last night? Was it a boy? Was it a girl? What was it?" The press reaction was the same. Nina Myskow in the *News of the World* branded me Wally of the Week. I was the happiest wally on earth.

We got to make our first video with Julien Temple. My head was bursting with ideas. The band said no to everything. No mermaids, no sailors, and no drag queens, apart from myself. The video was shot in three locations: a courtroom, a fifties health club, and a thirties nightspot. They re-created the old Gargoyle club in Dean Street, Soho, and filled it with all my nightclubbing friends. Stephen Jones was dressed as a well-heeled Moroccan in linen suit and fez. Dykes with monocles pulled on cigarette holders. The band were dressed forties style. Jon looked like a pint-sized Clark Gable. I appeared as if from another place and time dressed in my Sue Clowes gear, and the bouncers dragged me kicking and screaming from the club. I was chased and shunned like a modern-day Quentin Crisp. Mum and Auntie Heather appeared in the courtroom scene where I was convicted and sent to jail. I always joked that I started my career in court and ended it the same way.

The morning of the shoot we all laughed. It was typical of Mikey to be late. The crew were flapping. My laughter turned to rage when I discovered Mikey was not going to turn up at all. His brother Greg had to stand in for him, while he stayed at home recovering from a ganja binge. I couldn't believe Mikey ruining one of the most important days of our lives. I never understood his lack of commitment.

After *Top of the Pops,* "Do You Really" jumped to number three, then to number two. Musical Youth were at number one with "Pass the Dutchie." We canceled a live show to appear on *The Late, Late Breakfast Show* with Noel Edmonds. At the end of our performance he walked over and talked to me. "I understand that you're a great fan of Liberace's?" "Not anymore." I just said the first thing that came into my head. I was so nervous.

Noel said, "Next to you I feel so horrifically conventional in my jacket and tie."

I said, "I thought you were trying to look outrageous." The next week we were at number one.

CHAPTER 23

"Sorry if I sound like Joe Cocker. Thank God I don't look like him." I struggled through three numbers and ran from the stage. Jon followed.

"What the fuck's wrong?"

"I sound like shit."

"Let's just do it."

"I can't. Go and tell them we'll come back."

He glared. "Do it yourself."

Roy and Mikey came backstage. "What's going on?"

I told them I couldn't sing, in case they hadn't noticed. I asked them to make an announcement. They were adamant. "You do it yourself." I went back out.

"I'm sorry. My throat's fucked. I'm sure you can hear. We'll have to come back another time."

The crowd at the Rooftops club in Glasgow erupted.

"Boo . . . get off . . . fuck off . . . you're crap."

I cried all the way back to the hotel. Shame, they were probably thinking I couldn't sing. Jon, Roy, and Mikey had been really vile—they never understood what it was like out front trying to hold the whole thing together. No one would have expected Jon to play with a broken finger or Roy with his arm in a sling. I was beginning to think I had nothing in common with them.

I barged past the handful of fans already waiting outside the hotel and disappeared into the lift. The puke-colored room with its orange curtains and matching candlewick bedspread did little to soothe my state. These were the days of low-budget hotels and room-sharing, Mikey and Roy, me and Jon. It was never me and Roy, or me and Mikey, for obvious reasons.

Jon came in slamming the door behind him. He threw down his stage clothes.

"Pull yourself together. What's the big deal?"

I was crouched on the bed, crying, feeling sorry for myself.

I screamed out, "You're a cunt."

He was right. What was the big deal? We could come back in a couple of weeks and do the gig again. But it wasn't about the gig. Jon hadn't supported me when I needed him.

"You could have gone out and told them. You could have helped me out."

"Why should I? You're big and ugly enough to do it yourself."

My alarm bells rang. "Who you calling ugly?" I lashed out, pushing him against the door.

He grabbed my throat. "Don't fucking hit me."

I started kicking and punching. We fell around the room tearing at each other.

Jon threw me onto the bed and held me down, grabbed a wine glass from the bedside cabinet, smashed it, and held the spiked remains to my face.

"I'll fucking kill you."

I'd never seen him so angry or ugly.

He stormed off to the bar and left me to my tears.

In the morning we were woken by a bubbly Tony Gordon. "Whoopee. We're number one. Congratulations, boys." I couldn't hide my joy, or sadness, some irony. "Do You Really Want to Hurt Me?" number one in the charts. Roy and Mikey were ecstatic. I felt guilty for not jumping around. I forced a smile. It was typical of my luck to be miserable on a day like this. The *Daily Star* had dispatched photographer Joe Bangay to take pictures of the joyful new pop sensation. He shot me in bed sipping champagne. It would have been a different story appearing in the *Daily Star* had he known what had happened the night before. Jon put his arms around me and kissed my face. "I'm sorry. Don't carry it on."

Our next stop was Edinburgh. Roy hurried us into the van. "I want to hear the chart rundown. I want to hear them say we're number one." It was as if he didn't believe it. There were cheers when Tommy Vance read out the chart. My sad mood put a damper on things. I had the ability to lift and kill an atmosphere. I always felt sorry for the rest of the band, having to suffer our fighting. No one was meant to know about me and Jon. It was a big joke. Our arguments went far beyond the professional. Jon would always write me off as a drama queen, I played my part so well. I always felt everyone was on his side, Roy and Mikey because they couldn't deal with the "gay thing," the sessions because they wanted to keep their jobs.

That afternoon Phil Pickett and I went out for a walk along Princes Street in Edinburgh. We ventured into a department store. Within seconds I was surrounded by housewives and shop assistants. "Och, it's him off the telly. Give us your autograph." They shoved scraps of paper under my nose and kissed me. I signed what I could, and ran outside to the refuge of a black cab. Phil smiled. "This is it. Your life is going to change." Even the taxi driver wanted an autograph. I loved it, it was what I always wanted.

My success hit my family like a bombshell. They ceased to be individuals. They were Boy George's mum, Boy George's brother, extensions of my stage persona. My boxer brother, Gerald, was embarrassed at fights: "Ladies and gentlemen, in the red corner . . . Boy George's brother." This made Gerald resent me, even though he knew it wasn't my fault. People constantly ribbed them. Bet you got a few bob. Buy us a drink then. 'Ere, is he really a poof?

The press homed in on my family, following my sister to work and printing her picture. Calling up Mum and Dad, tricking them into giving quotes, which always turned out to be misquotes. It affected our friends too. People said we'd changed, but that was only because we were being treated differently. Some friends kept away, fearful of being seen as crawlers. There seemed to be no middle ground. They fawned or fled. If you didn't return a friend's call, it wasn't because you forgot, it was because you were Boy George and you didn't care anymore.

*   *   *

The crowd were going wild before we even hit the stage. "We want Culture Club, Culture Club, Culture Club." Hundreds of Boy George clones, mostly girls, screaming and crying. Flowers, dolls, and teddy bears rained down on the stage. I looked back at Jon. He shook his head in disbelief. Every movement and sound I made was greeted with shrieks: "We love you, George." I was excited and uncomfortable. They weren't listening to the music, they were staring at me, scrutinizing every detail, looking up my nose. I felt my body expand at least a stone as I skipped awkwardly around the stage. We were at the end of an eleven-date slapdash tour of Britain. The tour was planned some weeks in advance to push the single. We had no idea we would get to number one. The show at Raquel's in Basildon, Essex, was mad. We'd become teen idols in a matter of two weeks. I never pictured myself as the *My Guy* pinup.

After the show we were mobbed and mauled. I shouted at the fans, "Shut up. Don't scream at me. Clam down if you want autographs. Stop pushing each other." They were startled by my schoolteacher aggression. I signed their books and pictures and answered their questions. They would probably have been happier if we'd just bundled into the van and driven off so they could chase us. They wanted to push and scream. They shoved roses into my arms and letters into my pockets. "Make sure you read it. Promise. Did you get my other letters?"

Certain faces became familiar to me over the coming weeks and months. They waited outside Virgin Records, Broadcasting House, wherever. They seemed to know more about our schedule than we did. Their names became familiar too—Andria, Patsy, Laura, Debbie, Fleur, Shirley, Josie, Tracy, Irene, Melanie, and Margo. Hard-core fans were a new experience for me. I was flattered but couldn't understand anyone waiting in the rain and cold for me.

CHAPTER 24

I overexposed myself in the first fifteen minutes of my career. I went mouth-first into a whirlwind of interviews and loved it. I know I could never have built my career on mystery like Prince or Michael Jackson, though now I wish I'd held back a little. I rattled away, naive and trusting. Jon and I did most of the interviews; his presence was a counterweight. Naturally they'd ask him about the music. I'd be asked about clothes and interesting things like how long it took to do my makeup. The music press were disturbed that I didn't mind housewives and grannies buying our records. I don't believe in the generation gap. I learned at school that youth does not bestow moral superiority. People are people regardless of age, race, or class. Ignorance is not exclusive.

Part of me wanted to be out on the artistic fringe, the kind of pop star your granny hated and your parents warned you about, but I was such a polite, friendly boy and I wanted everyone to love me. I tried in my way to appear intelligent because I knew that people would look at me and dismiss me as an exhibitionist fool. To most I was a pop clown charming the pants off the Establishment. I had to laugh out loud at the situations I found myself in, discussing boxing with talk-show host Terry Wogan; the only thing I ever boxed were tins of tomatoes at Tesco's. Fame was ridiculous and wonderful. I talked a lot, though the extent of my unworldliness was breathtaking. I'd never been outside England. I'd never had a bank account or a passport.

Our first trip abroad was to Belgium, one of the first European countries to pick up on "Do You Really." We flew over to Brussels in a turboprop plane, had lunch in an Indonesian restaurant, the record company picked up the bill, we did a quick TV show, and then flew home. It really was the life.

In Amsterdam things went less smoothly. The set for our TV performance was an operating theater complete with respirator and throbbing organs in jars. "Do You Really Want to Hurt Me?" Ha, ha. I lost my temper. "I'm not performing in front of that." Jon, Roy, and Mikey backed me up. I told them it was a love song, not some joke. The set was replaced with a plain brick wall.

American funker Rick James was on the show. Mikey was desperate to meet him. I watched, amazed, as he strutted arrogantly past our dressing room followed by a fawning entourage, one carrying makeup, one clutching a hairbrush, another a hair dryer. Rick James was a real star.

The two reps from Virgin Holland were stoned out of their minds. I asked for a towel so I could shave and get ready for the show. It came back an hour later. I snapped, "No wonder nothing gets done when you're all on drugs." They didn't like us, we weren't rock and roll. Culture Club opened up the European territories for Virgin. "Do You Really" was number one in twenty-three countries. We did the rounds of TV shows and restaurants, pepper steaks and sauerkraut in Munich, *omelette aux fines herbes* and croissants in Paris. It was a fantastic adventure, Jon and I screwing and strangling our way across the map. We found out that instant success didn't mean instant luxury. Roy screamed when he found pubic hairs in his bed at a crusty Parisian hotel. The maids were summoned to change the sheets. We all moaned, "Why can't we have decent rooms, the record's selling, isn't it?" Our Welsh tour manager, Dai, would console us at every hotel, "Best one yet, lads. Best one yet."

Our debut album, *Kissing to Be Clever,* was released on October 5, 1982, and reached number five. Virgin hurried us to choose the next single. We all felt sure there was nothing strong enough to follow "Do You Really." We'd already released three tracks from the album and wanted to record something new. Virgin said it was bad business but when we played them our new song, "Time (Clock of the Heart)," they were convinced.

> Don't put your head on my shoulder,
> Sink me in a river of tears.
> This could be the best place yet,
> But you must overcome your fears.

The song was a blatant plea to Jon but as always he was oblivious. The woeful violins and rumbling cellos understood perfectly. Steve hired a twenty-four-piece string section. It was his most lavish production to date. Helen worked some more of her magic, even sneaking in a little bit of a lead vocal. The end result was a dream. I had the predictable idea of a clock theme for the video as it was inappropriate to stick to the real story line. Sista Jeni, her friend Annie, and Black Pat Fernandez were extras dressed like druids. Helen was cruelly dressed as Molly Mop and was silently pissed off. I didn't like the video when it was finished. I looked ugly, it was superficial and made light of the song. I cringed when they showed it on TV, but it didn't seem to matter. "Time" reached number two. We were on a ruffle and a roll.

Soon the fat green finger of America was beckoning. When Tony told us we were going to New York I danced around Philip's flat, "Start spreading your legs, I'm leaving today. I wanna be, a part of it, New York, New York." It was the second most fabulous moment of my life after being number one.

It was a late Indian summer in New York. Wide-eyed, I trotted around Manhattan in my thick black woolly overcoat and hat oblivious to the heat. We stayed at the Waldorf-Astoria. Jon was excited when he saw David Hockney in the lobby. I joked, "You might meet Andy Warhol in a minute."

"Do You Really" was slowly moving up the U.S. charts. We went to meet our American record company, Epic. It was so different from Vernon Yard, a gigantic impersonal skyscraper with armed security guards who looked at us like we were thieves.

"Can I help you?"

"I doubt it very much."

"Excuse me, sir?"

"You're excused."

We giggled into the lift and sailed up into the Epic corporate tower. "Oh, my God. You guys are so beautiful." Susan Blond, our press agent, was as subtle as the building. She was no average jeans-and-sweatshirt press officer. Susan wore classic Chanel couture. Various pieces of expensive jewelry fought for pride of place around her neck. She looked like she existed on a diet of truffles and birdseed. When I heard Susan had thrown a baby from a window in an Andy Warhol movie I saw her in a different light. I asked her questions, hundreds of questions. Had she met Joe Dallessandro? Did she sleep with him? Would I be able to meet him or have tea with Michael Jackson?

We met the big guys at Epic, who came down several floors especially to meet us. They were like Thunderbirds puppets with personalities to match. They shook our hands and left quickly. We were a funny little English investment. One of the more colorful characters was Frank Dileo, senior vice president of Promotions, a showbiz mogul, complete with the obligatory Havana cigar. He thumped the leather-topped desk with his fist and vowed, "I'm gonna take this band all the way." Dileo was confident "Do You Really" would "do the business," even though reggae had a negligible history in America. As part of his tactics he decided to "play down" our image and issued "Do You Really" to DJs in a plain white sleeve.

Susan Blond took us to lunch at the Russian Tea Room. I'd never been anywhere so glamorous and expensive. The rest of the band were refused entry because of their common dress. After much fuss from Susan the maître d' supplied them with ill-fitting tuxedo jackets, which made them look scruffier than before. I was allowed to sit down in my Vivienne Westwood sack pirate suit. They couldn't classify me as male or female. There was more fuss because Susan wasn't happy with the table offered. She demanded a prestigious booth. Sly Stallone was lunching next to us in a disgusting sky blue suit. He left after we sat down. Jon pointed at his built-up heels and was pleased that he was so small.

I'd always been scared of visiting America, especially New York. I'd heard stories of people being shot and robbed in broad daylight. America spelled violence. It was so different from how I'd imagined. The aggression was definitely there, but there was also something magical and exciting. The first day, I wrote lyrics for two new songs, "It's America" and "Mr. Man."

> On the street they're preaching violence,
> Mr. Man it's in your head.
> On the street the midnight cowboy
> Needs no gun to shoot you dead.

"Hi, any queers in the audience?" My camp repartee was met with awkward silence. It was December 3, our live debut at New York's Ritz Theatre. It was a much older crowd than we'd been used to, no little girls. A few on-the-button queens but mostly rock-and-roll types, press, and record company. It was a total comedown after the adulation at home. I wanted America to love us but I wasn't getting the vibe. There was no screaming or grabbing when we left the venue. A handful of people were waiting; they clapped politely. "You guys were great." A beaming hippie-type handed me a bunch of lavender roses.

"Hi, I'm Bonnie. These are for you."

"Oh, thanks."

"How long you in New York?"

"Two more days."

"I took some pictures tonight. Would you like to see them?" Bonnie had a kind face, and the camera hanging around her neck looked kind of professional. I invited her to the hotel the following morning. I clambered into the van, wondering if I'd done the right thing, inviting some complete stranger from gun-crazy New York to my hotel. I hoped she didn't think it was a come-on. "Oh, well, it's too late now."

The next morning we did a bleary-eyed photo call in Central Park and a couple of interviews over breakfast. I couldn't believe the food combinations, syrup, cinnamon, hash browns, ham and eggs, sunny-side-up, sunny-side-down, and ten styles of toast. I settled for eggs Benedict and rye.

My new friend Bonnie arrived soon after breakfast, which I thought was rather eager. We had tea in the lobby. Her pictures were good. Not many double chins. She told me to mark the ones I liked and she'd send me prints. I liked her straightaway and felt a common bond. Roy said she was creepy-looking. If she'd been blond and protruding he would have loved her. But then I wouldn't. Bonnie was definitely my kind of lunatic. She looked more suited to the Grateful Dead than Culture Club, dark, lank, center-parted hair, and a tattooed bracelet on her wrist. She said she'd been to Woodstock and on the road photographing Linda Ronstadt and Dolly Parton. I wanted to know all about Dolly Parton. Bonnie said she was as sweet as cherry pie.

Roy had planned to marry his own blond when Culture Club had their first number one. It happened sooner than he expected. Roy and Alison were married on Christmas Eve 1982 at Fulham Register Office. I avoided the ceremony, not wanting to steal the show from Alison. I joined the reception at their tiny flat in North End Road, Fulham. I joked with Jon, "When you gonna make a decent woman of me?" It was a joyful day for us all. We ended the year with two hits, a trip to the States, and our first Christmas *Top of the Pops,* which we were all going to watch over dinner the following day. Christmas at home was as chaotic as touring. Going home to Shooters Hill was a sure way of coming down to earth. Kids, relatives, and Irish rebel songs. Mum constantly reminded me, "You're just Georgie here. Don't forget it." Though everybody expected luxurious presents now I had money. I balanced it by wrapping them in newspaper.

Tony gave us regular reports of our progress in the States. He said things were looking better than good. I didn't believe him. America was so far away, and it didn't feel like anything was happening. Then I bumped into Steve Dagger, Spandau Ballet's manager, at the Camden Palace—he'd just returned from New York. "They're playing your record to death out there." The word on the street was much more important than Tony's statistics.

"Do You Really Want to Hurt Me?" reached the U.S. Top 40 in January 1983. Our first American tour was planned for the following month, starting at the Malibu Club in Long Island. Bonnie and two English fans, Patsy Payne and Debbie Hoare, were already there waiting when we arrived for the sound check. I couldn't believe it. Patsy and Debbie were acting like they'd just popped next door to borrow a cup of sugar. They already knew the tour itinerary and were going to follow us around on the Greyhound bus. The tour was low-budget, absolutely no production, the band, the back line, and our mouthy-toothy tour manager Gary Lee. I had my own impersonal assistant, Dennis May, a miserable creep who had previously worked for Status Quo, "a real band." He hated me and his job, especially ironing my poofy stage clothes, which he burned more than once. "Bloody pop star." Our tour bus was a seventies Dralon tomb, musty from the stench of dried beer and tobacco. Pictures of cartoon babes, breasts thrust and legs akimbo, looked down on us knowingly. Sorry, wrong band. Tony told us traveling by road was a great way to see America, but the tinted windows made it difficult to see anything.

We attracted a confused audience. A lot of people came expecting to see a black reggae group having only heard "Do You Really" on the radio. My appearance onstage was a shock to most. Only the local queens and hipsters knew what to expect. We had heavy local radio support and were being broadcast live in most cities. My voice gave out several times, and always on the night of a broadcast. I wanted to be perfect all the time but my voice wasn't used to touring. I let it get to me and it made me miserable. Bonnie, Patsy, and Debbie were a constant source of encouragement, and worry. I felt responsible for their well-being. I had to lend a tearful Bonnie fifty dollars when her car was impounded. As the tour went on Patsy and Debbie were beginning to look more and more bedraggled. I couldn't see the sense in it. We all thought they must be loonies.

Our schedule was suicidal, late nights, early mornings, and endless travel. We had to drive from Boston to New York the day of a show to do our first TV performance on *Live with Regis Philbin*. It was incredible. The studio audience were in a seventies time warp, dressed in waisted wide-lapel jackets, acrylic tank tops, and polyester flares. We looked like we were from another planet, Planet England.

A handful of paparazzi and excited fans were there to greet us at LAX airport in Los Angeles. I was pissed off: the last thing I wanted after a long sweaty flight was to be photographed. I berated our American travel agent, Jim Rodman. "How do they know what flight we're on?" He said they wait out there for days, all week if they have to. I never liked people turning up at airports or hanging around the hotels. It felt like we were being spied on. I was thrilled by our success and grateful for the support of fans but I hated the feeling of having no freedom. I wanted to be able to relax, go shopping, visit the sights without being jumped on. I tried to explain to the fans that I didn't like being screamed at and trailed. They followed regardless. It was a funny little game to them—some actually wanted to annoy you.

Rod Stewart came to see us before we went onstage at the Hollywood Palladium. I told him I had all his records. I had to laugh, thinking about the time I bunked into his gig at Lewisham Odeon. Here he was coming to see me play. Bet he never had any trouble getting in.

San Francisco filled me with anticipation. I was sure they'd love us there. Tony and I went out for a walk as soon as we arrived. He'd never seen anything like it. The bars and cafés brimmed with gay life. Tony blushed as bearded leather queens walked hand in hand down Castro Street and male couples kissed openly. Every queer necessity was catered for. One shop sold gay wedding cakes with two plastic grooms on top. I bought one of the figurines to show Mum. I made regular calls home—talking to Mum and Dad was my only sanity, describing my luxurious hotel rooms, "Ten dollars for a pot of tea?" San Francisco was our worst show and the reviews were evil.

Everything had changed now that we were number two in America with "Do You Really." We had armed security outside our rooms. Mum and Dad were worried. So many stories filtered back: Boy George this, Boy George that. They never knew what was true. Dad had always been very anti-America: "'Orrible place."

I told him, "One day I'll fly you over. You'll love it."

CHAPTER 25

Success brought new pressures. I became more and more self-conscious. The pretty face adorning bedroom walls and projected onto a million TV screens was carefully constructed. It took time to make myself look like the Boy George people wanted to see. I thought they would be disappointed if they saw plain George. I quickly became trapped in my image. On tour I wouldn't even let the room-service waiters see me. I hid in the bathroom while Jon dealt with them.

At home Philip's tiny flat was a prison and the only place I could let it all go. I curled up on the sofa in my kimono dressing gown, gorging cheese and ham rolls in front of the TV. I was hemmed in by a moat of fans who lived on my doorstep. Richard would pop out to the corner shop for more junk food. Chocolate digestives, Mr. Kipling cakes, cheese, and onion crisps. I was fast becoming the Elvis of St. John's Wood. Philip called me "Boy Gorge" and went around the clubs singing, "Do you really want to eat me?"

While my star was in full spin Marilyn arrived back from Los Angeles. I'd sent him Culture Club's first single and a bunch of cuttings and he started saving for a ticket. Philip was straight on the phone. "She's only come back to feed off your success." I laughed nervously. Marilyn's return signaled a real threat in my mind. His beauty had always made me feel dumpy and insignificant. He was the boy with everything, and now he was going to try and wiggle his way onto my throne. He wasn't wasting any time either. I heard from various people that Marilyn was already in with Kate, Jeremy, and Paul Caplin, and Paul was planning to launch Marilyn's pop career, all in under a week. Paul actually said, "George is the goody-goody Beatles, Marilyn will be the Rolling Stones." I was foolishly threatened by the idea of Marilyn as a rival and worried that he might have a better voice than me.

I knew I'd probably brought it on myself by bitching Marilyn in *The Face* magazine. "I don't know where he is. I don't want to talk about him." Marilyn read it in L.A. and was stalking the room. "Fucking bitch. Why did he say that about me?" He was determined that if I could make it, he could too.

When Marilyn called I slammed down the phone. He turned up at Alma Square and kept his finger on the buzzer for ten minutes. He gained entry by ringing the neighbors' bells and sat outside my room.

"Go away."

"Don't be so childish."

"Go away."

Richard and I climbed out the window into our neighbor Gary's flat and drove off in the MG. Marilyn was left talking to the door. I let my ego run riot and turned Marilyn into enemy number one. Once I started the drama I couldn't stop. It was silly because I really wanted to be friends.

I was packing my suitcases for Amsterdam when "Church of the Poisoned Mind" got its first play on Radio One. I loved hearing our music on the radio. It reminded me of wandering round Eltham High Street with Moyna Kane. Simon Bates thought it was a strange title: "Aleister Crowley eat your heart out." No one knew it was about Jon.

Who would be the fool to take you
Be more than just kind
Step into a life of maybe
Love is hard to find
In the church of the poisoned mind.

I looked forward to going away because it meant I could be with Jon every day. Outside of work we rarely saw each other. Even though he lived a mile away in Regent's Park, I could never visit without first making an appointment. I spent many lonely evenings worrying that he was with someone else. He had girls he would go and shag. He wanted his freedom and sex with me when he felt like it. He would lie about having dinner with his parents. I'd make Richard drive me to Jem and Jik's in Fitzroy Square and look for his white Golf. I drove myself to distraction.

We zipped through Europe, seven gigs, seven cities in seven days. Interviews were slotted into every spare second. Roy, Jon, and Mikey were happy to let me do all the talking if it meant an extra hour in bed. Occasionally they whined, "Why aren't we being interviewed?" They couldn't have it all ways. In anger I would shout, "It's not my fault you're boring." The press targeted me from the beginning. They never wanted to talk to the others, no matter how much I tried to force it. Roy, Jon, and Mikey didn't want people to think they were just a backing band. They didn't miss much. Always the same dull questions. "How did you start? Why do you dress like that? How long does it take to do your makeup?" By the time we went onstage I was sick from talking too much. The cruel schedule and constant bickering with Jon made me especially spiteful. I took all my frustration out on him. He worked my nerves, making some jibe instead of leaving me to cool down. He never wanted to appear weak. Our tour manager, Gary Lee, was always jumping between us to stop a black eye or a fat lip. The songs, however jolly they seemed, were a testament to my pain. Singing about it was my only release, other than screaming or putting a gun to Jon's head. No song said it better than "Victims":

Pull the strings of emotion
Take a ride into unknown pleasure
Feel like a child on a dark night
I wish that we could spend it together.

Our second solo album, *Colour by Numbers,* was full of ambiguous messages to Jon, right down to the chirpy "Karma Chameleon," which caused fits of laughter when I sang it at Roy's flat. Roy and Jon banged kitchen pots and slapped their butts, "Yeehah, Cowboy." Roy said the band would lose all credibility.

In anger I took the song to Phil Pickett and he helped me work it out. He wrote a great middle eight. Phil's enthusiasm brought the others round: Jon tapped out a rockabilly beat and Roy boosted his cred by adding an insipid guitar line, which to this day makes my stomach churn. It was probably Roy's way of reminding us how much he hated the song. He didn't refuse the royalty checks. Phil Pickett's involvement in the songwriting was always resented by Jon and Roy: they objected to sharing the publishing. To me Phil was invaluable—he had pop sensibility and could improvise at the drop of a Hasidic hat. The important thing was the end result, not who got what. Roy and Mikey wanted to write lyrics and melodies. I hated their ideas. It wasn't out of jealousy, I knew my lyrics were better. We presented a democratic front, though it was Jon or myself who had the final say on most things.

Success soon made everyone more confident of their ability. Roy, with a little help from Alison, started to flex his muscles. She had her own ideas about how he should dress. He had ideas about how we should sound. Though initially a guitar player, Roy dedicated himself to the new keyboard technology. He hovered around the control desk, painstakingly watching Steve's every move. Both Roy and Jon had visions of being studio supremos. "That was my idea, you know."

Steve Levine was a technoboffin supreme. He led the band up Silicon Alley. Roy was most willing to follow, craving the polished sound of Donald Fagan and Quincy Jones, who had produced *Thriller* for Michael Jackson. Mikey was a great bass player, but made himself into the weak link through laziness and indifference. He argued for more say, then wouldn't take the initiative. Jon said, "Every band needs a silent member."

I was a lazy singer. I never wanted to do my own harmonies. "Get Helen to do them." Everything had to be immediate for me. I couldn't sing for hours the way that Helen could. My moods affected my ability. I was very tetchy in the studio, I couldn't take criticism: "What do you mean I'm flat?" I would make everyone leave the studio while I was singing—sometimes even the engineer.

I was always insecure about my voice, even though I was compared to Smokey Robinson. There are very few Culture Club tracks I can listen to without cringing. Most of the vocals are slightly under the note. Jon called it bluesy. The studio bored me—I couldn't stand waiting around for drums to be programmed and keyboards sequenced. I went shopping or to Virgin to pry on activities. The fact that I couldn't play an instrument and was technophobic made me an outsider. In arguments Roy would say, "Shut up, you don't even know what key the song's in."

Culture Club became like a bad marriage, one where you lose your personal identity. I'm sure Jon, Roy, and Mikey felt equally frustrated. My mouth and image pushed them into the background, so they had to find ways to make me feel insecure and dependent on them. Jon often told me I'd be nothing without Culture Club and I was always sacking them. It took me years to acknowledge my own abilities. I foolishly believed that because I didn't actually pick out the chords myself, I wasn't a proper songwriter. I was the one who spent 95 percent of my life humming melodies and writing lyrics, jotting them down on pads or just holding them in my brain space. Roy is the only one who can claim his fair share of the writing credits.

I manipulated the band and made them wear things they felt uncomfortable in. I thought if all four of us tried to make decisions we'd end up looking like a flock of Duran Durans. The Foundry designs were perfect and suited everyone but things went downhill after Sue Clowes disappeared. My image got camper and camper, more makeup, more glitter and excess. I persuaded Roy to have blond dreadlocks and he became the Marilyn of Culture Club. Roy and Jon would poke fun at Mikey because I made him wear big Rasta hats and colorful ethnic clothes. Eventually he turned into a real pop star dressed in Antony Price suits. I wouldn't let him wear them in our videos or on TV.

Videos were always an expensive risk. Normally we went along with the director's ideas and chucked in a few of our own. They never lived up to my vision or the director's promise. The worst was Godley and Creme's £60,000 extravaganza for *Victims*. I was lit from underneath and wobbled around on a crane like a prize prat. "I'll Tumble 4 Ya" was better, directed by Zelda Barron: it was a satire on the TV series *Fame,* featuring fourteen-year-old Naomi Campbell dancing with other stage-school pupils from the Barbara Speake Agency. Jon, Roy, and Mikey took brief dancing lessons. It was hilarious. Mikey proved to be the only black man with no rhythm.

Traveling was always the biggest luxury of being famous, better than the money, though most of the time we only saw the hotel lobbies. Jon and I busted up some of the most expensive hotel rooms and shagged on some of the biggest beds. Hong Kong was brief but it was an amazing culture shock—Tony arranged a two-day stop-off and a warm-up concert to prepare us for Japan. I landed barefaced at Kai Tak airport. I was sure no one had heard of us there. Scores of camera-wielding Chinese fans were waiting to snap my natural beauty. I ran to the bus and covered my head with a coat. Hong Kong was no place for panstick. I couldn't leave the air-conditioned hotel for fear of melting like the wicked witch. The day of the gig I badly cut my lip shaving and couldn't stop it bleeding. I went onstage with a bright red mustache.

Tokyo was like New York. I had expected pagodas, temples, and chalk-faced women in kimonos carrying paper parasols. The city was awash with neon signs, Coca-Cola, Kodak, like Times Square. The record company worked us like dogs. We were expected to do press and pictures the minute we arrived. They hurried us from one interview to another. When I suggested a brief tea break I was told, "Not possible. Not possible." The Japanese press took to my pseudokabuki drag, calling me the rock and roll Tamasaburo, a famous Japanese Onnagata performer. Onnagata are men who play women's roles in the kabuki theater. They nodded attentively at every camp quip and reviewed our shows in a factual manner, simply describing what we wore and what we sang. I preferred it to the English seek-and-destroy method.

"Sorry I'm late. I'm English, you know." They didn't dare tell me I was being rude when I arrived late for my interviews still powdering my nose. Their expressions said it all. I found Japanese overpoliteness quite stifling. The fans poked us to see if we were real, giggling at the floor. They followed us around like English fans, but kept a distance. If I stopped, they stopped, it was like a

Monty Python sketch. They gave us beautiful presents and innocent notes: "You are the river that runs to my sea." Quotations
copied from English books. Our security guy Tak taught me an
important phrase, "A-bu-nai-e," meaning "watch out." Very useful for those shopping trips around Tokyo. Sometimes up to four
hundred girls would follow us through the arcades and department stores, taking photos as we shopped. For a laugh Jon, Roy,
and I legged it, top speed, through Nagoya followed by hordes of
squealing schoolgirls, "Boy-ee, Boy-ee," and three panic-stricken
security guards who had orders not to let us out of their sight.

I refused to be photographed anywhere near Mikey because of
his new hairdo. Our squabbling started at Gatwick airport. Mikey
turned up late (as usual) with a squashed bird's nest on his head. I
laughed out loud. "What have you done?" Jon and Roy were sniggering too. Mikey was indignant. "Get lost." His new pop-star
friend Jermaine Stewart had tried to straighten his hair. It hadn't
quite worked. A week into the tour I eventually got him to comb
it out and it looked brilliant.

The doctor had to be called out for Roy, who had a miniemo-
tional breakdown due to excessive drinking and the strain of trying
to conceal Alison and her friend Angie, who were hiding from me
in the hotel. I'd banned all girlfriends and wives from our tours so
Jon wouldn't have any encouragement. Alison and Angie were
creeping fearfully around the hotel. Security were told to alert Roy
of my every movement. I was shocked when our tour van drew up
alongside a taxi carrying two familiar figures. "I've just seen Alison
in that taxi." Roy bluffed, "You're mad. She's in London." After
the gig I surprised everyone by going to the hotel bar for a drink.
I caught Alison red-faced, sheepishly sipping a cocktail. We both
laughed. It took me years to forgive myself for the way I treated
Alison, or to notice. I tried to deny her the pleasure of sharing
Roy's success because of my own insecurity. I built a misogynistic
wall around myself. I didn't want them canoodling in postmarital
bliss around Jon. Mikey already had his beautiful sixteen-year-old
German girlfriend, Natalie, wafting around like hot food under a
beggar's nose. My behavior was doubly cruel because I knew
Alison was as insecure as I was, worried that Roy might pick up his
own Yoko Ono.

I was growing ever more possessive and insecure by the day. The adoration of screaming fans and the flicker of flashguns could not console me. I could think of only one thing. Jon-ee, Jon-ee, Jon-ee. I was a screaming fan myself. Jon was so worried about his straight image, especially around Mikey, Roy, and the road crew, that he turned into a caricature of Jack the Lad. He was sure the crew were making snide remarks behind his back. They were probably wondering which of us was the woman. Jon's frustration spilled into the bedroom: sex was angry and often abusive, especially after a good fight. Jon had no problem saying he loved me; it was just showing it in front of other people. When I first met him he was Mr. Charming, but it didn't last. The longer I knew him, the less I knew him. That's the strange thing about love. One minute you can have your tongue up someone's arse, and the next you can't even communicate. I was selfish too. I never stopped to think about how anyone else felt, especially Jon. I, I, I, I. Me, me, me, me. This inherent selfishness, on top of the pressures of fame, turned me into a petulant peacock. I blamed Jon for everything, never stopping to question my own role in any unnecessary situation. I got off on the drama. It made me feel important and alive. I associated love with aggression and turmoil, having seen little else in my life. I couldn't distinguish between love and sex either. If he fucks me, he loves me. My desire was insatiable. Jon was rampant, but he didn't have quite the same drive. I know he wanted the freedom to screw groupies on the road like Mikey, but there were plenty of cute boys I passed up. Sometimes I wonder whether it was worth the sacrifice or the headaches.

Those rich record-company dinners and all-night room service do little for a girl's figure. I was ballooning under the weight of it all. Food became a reliable friend, a love substitute. I didn't have to resort to trickery to get it down my throat, and it was always there when I needed it. By the time we finished the tour I looked like Rotunda Belle. My dear friend Marilyn was always quick to remind me I was his fat friend, poking me in the gut. "What's that, girl?" Marilyn tried to get me to join a gym. I claimed I was happy as I was. The idea of jumping around in skimpy shorts and a T-shirt surrounded by flexing beefcake was hell to me. Marilyn kept hassling me to leave my St. John's Wood cocoon and enjoy my fame. He persuaded me to buy a bicycle and I rode round London in hat, plaits, and makeup. Shoppers on Oxford Street would point and shout, "Look, it's that Boy George." I was threatened in Regent's Park by black boys on roller skates wielding baseball bats. "Fucking batty boy." One kicked me but I managed to escape.

Marilyn suggested a holiday. Somewhere exotic.

"What about Egypt?"

Of course, he had no money, but promised to pay me back. I resisted the idea at first.

"Egypt. What's it like?"

Marilyn said, "No one will know you there."

Buying those plane tickets was a big step for me. I'd become so dependent on others planning and arranging my life that I was losing the will to do even the most basic things. I envied Marilyn's freedom. I knew he was taking advantage, but I was grateful he made me take that trip. It was a giant step toward independence.

Cairo was like stepping back a thousand years into one of those history books I fingered through at school. Toothless Arab hustlers grabbed at our hair as we walked out of the airport. "Pretty ladies, pretty ladies. You want taxi?" It was a different kind of adoration. One without strings. I liked it. Marilyn's pale beauty and blond locks received the bulk of the attention.

I hung out of the taxi all the way to the Holiday Inn. "Look, Marilyn. Look." He could see how much pleasure it was giving me, and it tickled him.

We were up at first light and rushed outside to see the pyramids. All I could say was, "Wow." I'd never seen anything like it. Marilyn was more interested in the hotel because it was full of American soldiers, and he wasn't going to be taking his breakfast in his room. He wiggled around the self-service counter in Union Jack boxer shorts and cutoff sweatshirt revealing his flat stomach and nipped waist. He was sure the GIs were giving him the eye. I knew they were just laughing.

After breakfast and a swim we took a taxi to Cairo center. Our driver looked like Andrew Ridgeley, and we bounced about in the backseat singing "Wham! Rap." We bought every bit of rubbish going in the bazaars—peacock fans, earrings, mottled plates, and pungent perfumes. "Chanel No. 5 iz zame, iz zame." They saw us coming, we were happy to play tourist.

I traipsed around Cairo dressed head to toe in black, heavy cotton jacket and black sweatpants. My concession to being casual. The heat was murderous, I suffered with a smile. Even in a Third World country I was adamant that no one would see my coat-hanger shoulders and pear-shaped bum. Marilyn constantly moaned at me. "Just wear a T-shirt. Relax."

"Shut up," I told him. "I don't tell you what to wear."

A few days into our trip I was approached by a young Arab. "Ezcuse me, are you priest?"

I had to laugh. "No, I'm a pop star."

He shrugged. "You want guide?"

Marilyn, who'd been bartering at a nearby stall, looked up with a hungry glint in his eye. "Yes." He very much wanted him to be our guide. Our new friend, Ahmed, took us to the zoo and to see the jewels of Tutankhamen. We bought him lunch, he seemed more than happy in our company.

Ahmed was a rose among hairy thorns. Cute. It was just my luck to meet him when Marilyn was around. I knew there was no sense competing. I stayed back while Marilyn showered him with his personality. I don't know whether Marilyn had his wicked way, but that evening they disappeared behind the pyramids, leaving me to gaze at the moon.

Never satisfied, Marilyn continued to flirt with the GIs. One of them asked me if he was David Lee Roth. He looked miffed when I said, "No, it's his sister."

I couldn't resist inviting a couple of photographers out to Egypt to capture the moment. I'd built up a trusting relationship with both Didi Zill from *Bravo* magazine in Germany and freelancer Andre Csillag from London. All I needed to do now was find some suitable costumes for my pyramid poses. Marilyn and I went back into the bazaars with a mission. I found myself a long black silk kaftan with a gold-and-blue jeweled collar. Marilyn bought a skimpy gold chainmail waistcoat.

I painted my face like Liz Taylor in *Cleopatra* and used one of the hotel's plastic wastepaper baskets as a headdress, cutting out the bottom, sticking it on my head, and wrapping a long silk scarf around it. I walked barefoot through the lobby to loud applause and catcalls from America's best. I rode around the pyramids on the back of a camel followed by a gaggle of Arab children. "Nefertiti. Nefertiti." Marilyn sped off into the desert on the back of a horse.

Egypt was a wonderful experience. I forgot all about Jon and hardly fought with Marilyn. For those two weeks he was like the best friend I ever had. We sat by the pool and wrote childish post-cards to Philip: "Dear Philip, Having a fantastic time. Glad you're not here."

We arrived back at Heathrow to the flash of paparazzi, we were expecting them and dressed accordingly. I fluttered my Cleopatra eyes and Marilyn showed off his tan. The following day we appeared together in all the tabloids, "Boy George and Boy Marilyn." The suggestion was that we were lovers. Marilyn was angry. "How dare they call me Boy Marilyn?" Things hadn't turned out quite as he expected.

Marilyn had phoned Patrick Lilley at Haysi's office and arranged for the photographers to be alerted of our arrival. He, of course, twisted the story, saying Tony Gordon arranged it, as if I needed to be photographed with him. Marilyn wanted his picture in the papers. He just didn't expect to be described as my sidekick.

Talks had been proceeding between Paul Caplin and Phonogram Records on securing a record deal for Marilyn. Marilyn had talked of little else during our holiday, though he refused to play me his demos. The press exposure, however embarrassing for Marilyn, helped clinch the deal. Marilyn disappeared into negotiations and I got on with making the video for the new single, "Karma Chameleon."

The video for "Karma Chameleon" was shot on a miserable gray day along the banks of the Thames. We tried to create a Southern America feel with a paddle steamer and a hundred extras. The band hated being dressed up like slave traders, especially as I was dressed as myself. We all loathed the finished video, but wherever we traveled in the world people said, "Ooh, that *Karma Chameleon* video, you all look so happy."

*   *   *

We were pounced on by photographers at Heathrow. It was 7:30 A.M. I was tired, I only had time to pencil in my eyebrows before the car arrived to take me to the airport.

I held my bag in front of my face. "Fuck off." They snapped away regardless. It would have been easier for me to smile like a professional. But I was never one for controlling my moods. It was the first time I'd seen the malicious side of the paparazzi. They got real pleasure upsetting me. "Smile, George, smile."

I was seething as I went through passport control. My outburst made the papers the following day: "Boy George in Four Letter Fury."

"Pretty pop star Boy George hid himself behind his handbag yesterday and compared his problems with those of the next Queen of England. 'I'm sick of you lot. Now I know how Princess Diana must feel.'" They quoted airport staff, "He looked like he needed a good sheep dip," which was exactly why I didn't want to be photographed.

We flew into New York on Concorde and the madness continued. It was only our second tour and we were playing arena gigs to 15,000 people. The tour started with two small club dates in Washington and Philadelphia, we were warming up for New York, our first big date at the Pier. The clones were out in full force: "Boy mania" had hit the States in a big way. Dreadlocked fans filled the front rows of every gig and the lobbies of every hotel.

We'd achieved three Top 10 hits from our debut album, *Kissing to Be Clever*—"Do You Really," "Time," and "I'll Tumble 4 Ya"— the first band since the Beatles to do so.

I could no longer casually walk the streets of America. The stretch limo (my twentieth-century sedan chair) carried me everywhere. In public I was surrounded by security: "Make way. Make way." There was an irony to this protected existence. The limo with its tinted windows drew much attention, as did the pushing, shoving guards. I used to joke, "No chance of arriving unnoticed." Part of me loved the pretentious glamour of it all. But I worried about appearing full of myself.

I kept having to remember, "You're from Woolwich." Sometimes amid all the mayhem I had visions of myself standing on one of the black squares at Eltham Green. I heard Dawson telling me, "You'll never be anything." When I thought about those boys at school who tripped me up and called me queer, I felt really proud and cocky.

There was a conflict from the beginning. In all my interviews I made a point of stressing my normality. But my normality was slowly being stretched beyond recognition. I was living inside the Boy George bubble. Yes, Boy, no, Boy, three bags full, Boy. I was surrounded by yes-men and gofers.

Jon was already accustomed to the fancy lifestyle, however much he tried to play it down. He was a millionaire's son from Hampstead. He knew how to use a soup spoon. Roy was hiring Porsches, and Mikey's West Indian accent had all but disappeared. I wasn't as affected by the trappings, but I became demanding and arrogant. Culture Club were on a success treadmill. We lost control of our lives. We never questioned our success, we just danced madly in its trail. Obviously there were those who knew the band had a limited lifespan and were milking us accordingly. This is all clear now, but at the time we did what was expected of us.

We were out of our depth playing such big gigs. I couldn't hold the crowd, and the band made lots of mistakes. Our show hadn't changed much since the early days—we'd added a few songs, but it was poorly thought out, relying on my kissability and costumes. One New York reviewer described me as "a dadaist calendar tipped on its head." My long white shirt, matching tie and trousers covered in giant numbers, stole the show. Another reviewer called me a bag lady.

It seemed my costumes and sexual ambiguity were far more socially significant than Culture Club's music. There was also the snobbery that a band with such a strong image was not credible. In my case it would have been pointless trying to separate the style from the content. I was asked in a concerned manner, "Do you not think the way you dress distracts from the music?" I had to be honest and say, "No. One really couldn't exist without the other." I told them, "Look at Jimi Hendrix. When you think of him you get a definite image. He was more than just a guitar player. Even groups like Status Quo, their nonimage is just as contrived as David Bowie's. They've made a conscious effort to be boring."

In Los Angeles we stayed at the chi-chi Bel Air Hotel in Beverly

Hills, a measure of our new status and Tony's snobbery. Tony went on about how he got us a great deal and how we were the first rock band allowed to stay there. It was a beautiful place: the rooms were like little villas set in tropical greenery. Inside, the decorations were flowery and frilly. You were almost afraid to sit on the chairs.

I invited my friends Gay Robert and Pinkietessa to the show at the Greek Theatre and for an 8 A.M. breakfast. Pinkie's *Gone With the Wind* breakfast drag drew gasps, as did Robert's tattooed rough Mexican boyfriend. He didn't speak much English, but he kept Robert happy.

There was a commotion at the *Solid Gold* TV studio because I refused to have their dancers onstage with us. Their sequined headbands, Lycra catsuits, and seventies dance routines were out of step with our image. The dancers took it personally and sneered at me. After the show we flew by glass-bottomed helicopter to Costa Mesa. I didn't look down the whole way. We clicked and put on a great show for 13,000 people.

Jon celebrated his twenty-sixth birthday the night of our gig at the Mesa amphitheater in Phoenix. I had a fit because his parents wanted to send a glamorous kissagram popping out of a cake. Jon's mother had liaised with Tony's wife, Avi, who told her, without revealing too much, that it was a bad idea. It was so bloody childish of me to be threatened. I made out that it was too rock-and-roll, but I was just jealous. In the end they sent a singing page boy. I thought that was much more appropriate. Jon stood there red-faced while he sang "Happy Birthday."

My mind was taken off the dramas by the presence of Alice Cooper. He was hanging out backstage with his kid, who was a Culture Club fan. Rod Stewart, Alice Cooper—it was a ridiculous thrill having them come to our gigs. I remembered running up Eltham High Street after school to buy *Billion Dollar Babies,* jumping around at St. Peter's Youth Club to "School's Out."

"Karma Chameleon" was released on September 5, 1983, entering the chart at number three, then hopping to number one and staying there for nine weeks. It sold 1.3 million copies in the U.K., becoming the eleventh best-selling single ever. The joy quickly turned to embarrassment. I got sick of hearing it on the radio and miming to it on TV. "Karma" was the kind of song everyone bought and no one liked. It had a niggling quality that provoked renditions everywhere I went, "Awright, Georgie. Karma, karma, karma, karma chameleon . . . " It went to number one almost everywhere in the world, catapulting us to megastardom. I had a great sense of pride, but however successful we became, there was always the fear that it would end at any moment. I worried so much about failure I often forgot to enjoy what was happening.

We released our official biography, *When Cameras Go Crazy*, and did a signing at Brent Cross shopping center. Five thousand screamers stampeded through W. H. Smith. It was now impossible to go anywhere without ensuing chaos. My doorstep looked like a rag doll's picnic. Teenage girls with plaits and hats and ghetto blasters blocked up the street. They sang along to their favorite Culture Club songs and waited eagerly for me to leave the house.

Some mornings there would be up to thirty girls ringing the doorbell, driving me mad. I hated it. Every time I went out to get a loaf of bread I'd have to wade through them and sign autographs. If I gave one more attention than the other there'd be scenes. One girl threatened to slash her wrists on my doorstep for attention. Even when I screamed at them to go away they wouldn't. They hid round the corner, cameras at the ready. They stole bills from my letterbox to try and get my phone number.

To escape their clutches I found myself a new way of leaving the house. I climbed out of the first-floor window at the back of the house, onto a shed and down over the wall. This was not easy in the clothes I wore, but it gave me some moments of peace.

I lived under a magnifying glass; my image made sure that I could never go anywhere unnoticed. Even without makeup my hair gave me away, and if not my hair, then my voice. Fame gave me a wonderful sense of purpose, but I wanted to be able to turn it on and off when I felt like it. I liked the fans screaming at gigs, but not outside my house. I wanted the glory without the responsibility.

I wanted to tell the fans to fuck off, but I felt guilty because they bought our records, so I smiled and put up with their constant nagging for photographs and kisses. I soon learned that the more you give the more they want and the less they respect you. When I tried to make conversation with them it was hopeless. I did all the talking; they just giggled and took more pictures. The overnight campers were the worst—I worried about their safety out there in the dark.

It became obvious that I was irrelevant. It was fame that excited them. They wanted the association, a picture to show their friends at school. They'd ask me, "Do you know where John Taylor lives? Have you got Nick Heyward's phone number?" I told them, "If I knew it I wouldn't give it to you."

Most of the fans were nice. But I always had to question their logic. They followed us around the country, attending every gig, sleeping rough in cars, hanging outside TV and radio stations and outside the recording studio in all kinds of weather as a show of dedication. I told them they didn't have to come every day. What was the purpose? They formed their own little camps, "cool fans" and "grabbers." The cool ones rolled their eyes at the grabbers and they bitched among themselves.

I tried to treat them like friends, but the very nature of the relationship made it difficult if not impossible. I made the mistake of replying to their mail. I took bags of letters on tour and sent postcards and signed pictures. One letter was never enough. They conferred with each other. Woe betide if I sent a longer letter to one than the other. It caused me endless headaches. They quibbled about silly inconsequential things like the amount of kisses at the end of a page or who you talked to first when you opened the front door.

Our English tour started the day "Karma Chameleon" reached number one. We jumped up and down, Virgin broke open the champagne. Karma, karma, karma . . . Things couldn't have been more perfect.

Three days into the tour Jon broke his finger while trying to pummel me. We were on our way to Sheffield for another sellout date. A fight broke out on the coach. The tension was always there and could be sparked at any moment. Our rows started in the bedroom and carried on smoldering the next day.

I knocked a cup of coffee out of Jon's hand in a temper over a smug comment. He pushed me back into my seat. I kicked him. "Piss off, dwarf." Jon went crazy. He threw a hard punch and hit the window, then yelped, "Look what you've done, I've broken my fucking finger." Gary Lee stopped the coach and took Jon outside to calm down. I sat at the back grinding my teeth.

The coach driver was paid £400 to keep mum. Ronnie issued a press release saying Jon fell over. It quoted Roy, "It was horrible, really horrible. The bus jolted and he fell." I told *Smash Hits,* "It was my fault he broke his finger. I'm not going to add to that, but it was my fault." The tour was postponed until later that year.

Monroe mania was about to hit the U.K. Marilyn was gearing up for the release of his debut single. He gave a press conference from a bed at the Ritz Hotel. The press wanted to know about our relationship. Marilyn, still angry about the airport incident, said, "I rang George and told him that if he really thought I was using him we haven't got a friendship at all. A boy dressing up as Marilyn Monroe is quite a newsy item in itself, so I really don't think anyone else helped me get publicity."

The advance orders for his single "Calling Your Name" were sixty thousand. Culture Club fans rushed out to buy it, assuming we were good friends. We were, in a twisted Bette Davis–Joan Crawford kind of way. A pair of stupid, childish, jealous queens, with a competitive streak running from our heels to our self-bestowed halos.

There was certainly nothing sexual between us. At least nothing I was aware of. I didn't fancy Marilyn, though I could see his beauty. I was addicted to him, as he was to me. Our friendship proved that love and hate are two sides of the same coin.

"Calling Your Name" entered the Top 10 with great ease. I was begrudgingly happy for him. I bitched about his video. Vain cow. He was pampered by a maid and took photos of himself using a remote. Fame instantly went to Marilyn's head. Instead of satisfying a lifelong craving, it turned him into a glittering monster. He flashed his £150,000 advance, splashed out on a Golf GT convertible, and rented a trendy pad in Chelsea. Marilyn was never a mean queen—if he had money he would happily take you out for a slap-up meal at San Lorenzo. He had little or no regard for the green devil. Live fast, eat fast, spend fast.

He had talent too. "Calling Your Name" was a well-constructed pop song, though he was no Janis Joplin. It was his bad mouth and bad attitude that let him down. One hit and he was a legend. Even his friend Stevie Hughes said, "She should have kept her mouth shut. The worst thing she ever did was speak." Marilyn started to bitch about me in the press. I wasn't blameless, I bitched too. Only I was more popular.

By the time he released his second single, "Cry and Be Free," most of the goodwill toward him had drained away. His appearance on *Top of the Pops* did little to help. He wore a sinister black hooded cape which he peeled off provocatively to reveal a luscious pout. The next week the single dropped. Marilyn's girlie performance was too much for the British public.

I continued to ham myself. "I'm a poof with muscles. I've slept with girls and blokes, but I'm with nobody at the moment. I can't be bothered, I don't have time to look." Certainly it was true in some respects, I wasn't with anybody in the real sense. Sex with Jon remained fantastically rampant, especially after a good fight, but screwing, even regularly, does not constitute a proper relationship.

When I told *Woman* magazine, "Sex? I'd rather have a cup of tea," I was lying through my lipstick-stained teeth. It was true that I enjoyed a good cuppa, and tea was certainly more reliable than Jon. But I wasn't the moral paragon I made myself out to be.

The press became more and more interested in what went on behind my closed doors. I continued my ridiculous charade, avoiding the issue. "I'm a very moral person. I believe if you sleep with someone you have to love them."

I was down on normal rock and roll activities. After shows I went straight to my room, not to the hotel bar or local nightclub. I made it clear that if the crew or anyone connected with the band slept with fans, they'd be fired. Of course it went on behind my back. Gary Lee would sneak girls into Mikey's room. There was little I could do from the security of my ivory suite.

If Tony Gordon was on tour with us, Jon and I went to his room after a show for tea and a late-night snack. I liked having

Tony around. I often felt I had more in common with him than the band. Sometimes Jon went for a drink with Roy and Mikey, and I normally threw a wobbly. I couldn't bear the thought of Jon ladding it in the bar, flirting with tarts and groupies.

It worked the other way too. Jon didn't like people getting close to me. He was jealous of Helen and Marilyn. There was no love lost—neither of them liked him. Helen called him "a short-arsed bastard." Jon didn't want anyone interfering, taking away his power. He'd try and plant seeds of distrust in my mind about certain people. I did the same to him, calling people wankers and then going right up and talking to them.

Jon told the press, "The worst thing is, George can get into any restaurant he likes, they'll build him a table if necessary. Whereas if I go and it's fully booked, they'll say who the hell are you?" I can't deny that was true. Though I wasn't always treated like one of the Royal Family. When I went to meet comedian Joan Rivers for tea at Claridges I was ordered out of the restaurant for not being suitably dressed. They made us move, even though we protested.

I took Joan to see Wham! at the Lyceum. She said her daughter, Melissa, was mad about George Michael and Andrew Ridgeley. When they bounced onstage in their shorts she joked, "My daughter likes these pigs. They eat while they sing."

Promoter Harvey Goldsmith brought us champagne in our private box. It had all been different the previous year when Steve Strange took me to Hammersmith Odeon to see Elton John. Elton was sweet and accommodating. He got his security to radio Harvey to make sure we had good seats. I heard Harvey reply, "Who the fuck's Boy Bloody George?" I sipped his champagne with a smile.

Two weeks later I went to Los Angeles to appear as Joan's guest on *The Tonight Show*. I caused another stir at Heathrow. The papers blazed, "Boy George swore at me." Mr. Best, an overzealous security guard, was horrified when I told him, "Fuck off." He wanted me to remove my hat because my hairpin set off the metal detector.

"What do you think I've got under my hat? A bomb?" I didn't think swearing was such a scandal. Four-letter words were commonplace in the O'Dowd household.

"Fuck off."

"No, you fuck off."

Above: **On Mum's knee, Christmas 1961, at Burrage Road, aged six months.**

Above right: **My Dad Jerry, the handsome rock and roller.**

Right: **Aged two, already pulling one of Mum's faces.**

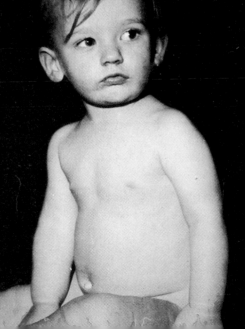

Above: **Me and punk Jayne, the Snakebite Queen of North London, 1977.**

Left: **A-level Bowie, with no eyebrows. Photo booth, Charing Cross Station, early 1976.**

Above: **Philip Sallon, my punk guru.**

Left: **Clare with the gravity-defying hair**

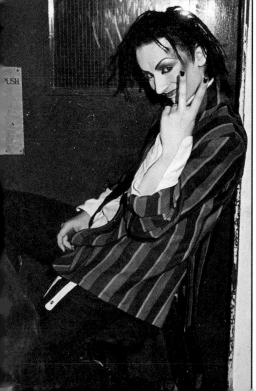

Above: **A subtle little number for travelling on the train from Woolwich.**

Above left: **Frankenstein with his monster. 'You can fuck right off, dear'.**

Left: **Hatcheck girl and thief at the Blitz.**

Top: **Camping up Heaven**. Left to right: **Slag Sue, Myra, me, John Cochran-Patrick, Marilyn and Philip.**

Above: **Borehamwood's Marilyn Monroe and chiselled alien from Eltham.**

Top: **Holding hands with Steve Strange during a truce at the Blitz.**

Above: **Red Stripe and speed at a punk party.**

Right: **Go Boadicea, go. In full plume, 1979.**

Above: **Geisha George, with punk god Kirk Brandon, on the way to Margate.**

Left: **'Miss Carter'** – Tracie and **Brian busking in Amsterdam, 1980.**

Main picture: **Culture Club Mark 1 with guitarist Suede.**

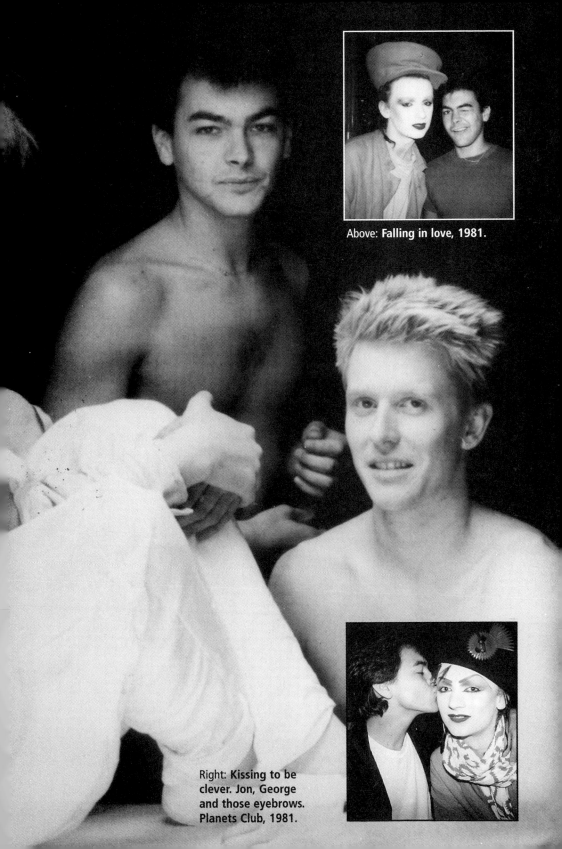

Above: **Falling in love, 1981.**

Right: **Kissing to be clever. Jon, George and those eyebrows. Planets Club, 1981.**

My first glamour session with Mark Lebon, Carburton Street.

Above left: **Live at the Can't Wait Club in Carnaby Street, wearing Sue Clowes' smock top.**
Above right: **The doll next door. Paris, 1983.** (*Jean-Claude Lagréze*)

The family O'Dowd under the spotlight. (Left to right:) Dad, David, Siobhan, Gerald and Mum

Above: **Cairo, 1983. A different kind of adoration.** (*Andre Csillag*)

Main picture: **Nefertiti and the Pyramids.** (*Andre Csillag/Retna*)

Above: 'You pay us'. Posing with Marilyn in Cairo. (*Andre Csillag*)

Right: Gold discs and tired eyes. Culture Club, Toronto, 1983. (*Patrick Harbrom Photography*)

Top left: **Safe as the Queen Mother. Hammersmith Odeon, Christmas 1983.** (*Andre Csillag*)

Top right: **Big Top, the Culture Club circus with Helen Terry, Italy, 1984.** (*Andre Csillag*)

Top Left: **Geisha George and manager Tony Gordon.** *TV Times* **Awards, 1984.**

Top right: **'Billy, where's my powder puff?' Billy Button escorts the diva to the stage.**
(*Andre Csillag*)

Settling into fame and glitter. BPI Awards, 1983. (*Rex Features*)

It's a Boy. Me with Mum and Dad. (*Rex Features*)

Couri, Cornelia, me and Marilyn. Up goes the Chanel skirt. Palladium Club, New York.
(*Vinnie Zuffante/Star File*)

Above: **A Judy Garland from Shirley Temple. Nayana and me, cocktail party, New York, 1986.**

Left: **Couri Hay, me and Marilyn. Aids benefit, New York, 1986.** (*Vinnie Zuffante/Star File*)

Above: **My snap of Madonna and the handsome boy backstage at Radio City, New York!**

Above right: **Miss Ross and Mr Monroe, Atlantic City, 1986; snapped by me and sold to the** *New York Post*.

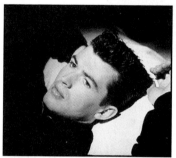

Right: **Michael Dunne. Lost eyes and sweet lips.**

Below: **Pinkietessa and Clark Bent at the Grammy Awards, Los Angeles, 1986. (***Sipa Press***)**

Above left: **Hippie Richard and the ghost of Boy George, 1986.**

Above right: **Having fun on drugs, 1986.**

Below: **Bonnie on guard with me at Hampstead.**

The other guests on *The Tonight Show* were Joan Collins and Victoria Principal. It was such a glamorous evening. Joan Collins invited me into her dressing room before the show to say hello. Andre Csillag took my photo in between the two Joans. It has remained one of my favorite pictures, me with the two queen bitches of Hollywood.

Fearful of Joan Rivers's reputation I spent the whole day geeing myself up in case she decided to tear me to pieces. My press agent, Susan Blond, was surprised by how kind she was. "My God, I can't believe it. She really likes you."

Joan did have a handful of jokes about me, but she saved them for her live shows.

"I met Boy George's mother the other day, Man George."

"Of course he's gay. Michael Jackson lost his other white glove down Boy George's trousers."

We appeared on *Solid Gold* performing "Karma Chameleon" and "Victims" and recorded for *The Dick Clark Rockin' New Year Show*. Mikey finally got to meet Rick James, who was also appearing. The whole band was rallied round for a photo with Mikey's hero. As Andre was about to click the shutter Rick opened his mouth. It was full of New Year's cake. Mikey lost his sense of humor. "C'mon on, man. Don't be so childish." I was in fits.

As a measure of my newfound status I was interviewed by Leslie Stahl on the prestigious CBS *Face the Nation*. Tony fussed and flapped. "This one's really important." But he did that with every interview. The media seemed to marvel at my ability to hold a conversation.

The glamour of L.A. contrasted with our previous excursion to Manchester. We prerecorded a Christmas TV special at Granada Studios and met the cast of *Coronation Street*. A photo of myself and actress Liz Dawn, who plays Vera Duckworth, appeared on the cover of the *Daily Star*. I was disappointed that I didn't get to meet Hilda Ogden. Meeting the stars of *Coronation Street* was like meeting old friends. As a kid I loathed *Coronation Street*. As soon as I heard the theme tune I would leave the room. I grew into it over the years and would get friends to video episodes so that I could watch them when I came back from a tour. Philip and I would discuss Hilda's one-liners. "Ooh, some folk get in where castor oil can't."

CHAPTER 26

That December I was invited to sit for Madame Tussaud's and become a wax legend. I was worried they might want to strip me down to my bare assets and cover me from head to toe in goo. "Can't they just do it from photographs?" They barely managed to get my shirt round my shoulders to cast a mold of my neck and face. I asked them not to pay too much attention to detail and give me a nice strong jawline. They were familiar with such requests. Photographs were taken from all the worst angles, back shots, profiles, up my nose. I felt more like a criminal than a pop star. I couldn't wait to get out of there. I was disappointed to learn I might be boiled down as soon as I went out of favor. Madame Tussaud's had a recycling policy long before it was fashionable. I was told I could end up as the next big thing. When my likeness was finally unveiled at Madame Tussaud's, I looked like Penelope Keith in drag. I made a tape to be played to visitors. "Hi, this is Boy George. I prefer a cup of tea to sex. And if you believe that, you'll believe anything."

Sculptress Judith Craig commented to the press that my nose was too big for my face and that without makeup even my fans wouldn't recognize me. I would have insulted her back but she was so insignificant I can't remember what she looked like. I would joke to friends as we drove by Madame Tussaud's, "Oh, look, there's my shrine." I was twenty-three and as famous as David Bowie.

Inevitably my new accolade caused friction within the band. Roy, Jon, and Mikey hoped they would be immortalized too. We had a Jon and George, but were short of a Ringo and Paul. Jon moaned to *Smash Hits*, "I'd hate Culture Club to go down in history as just being George, which it will unfortunately."

The next day at rehearsals, Jon joked, "Did they have enough wax for your ego?" I had the perfect comeback, "Yeh, there was even enough left for a spare dwarf." We were preparing for three Christmas shows at Hammersmith Odeon, which would be filmed for our live concert video, *A Kiss Across the Ocean*. Designer Dexter Wong had been working all week on stage costumes for the band. Typical of me, I'd only given Dexter a minute's notice to get sewing. I had three changes—a black smock coat sprinkled with diamanté and another in white organza for the finale, worn with a sparkling Egyptian collar made by jeweler Monty Don. Most prized was my *Colour by Numbers* costume, made out of a children's duvet cover I picked up in Barcelona. Jon, Roy, and Mikey were always worried about looking "too poofy." It was a hard life for them. I said, "You didn't have any style when I met you, so shut up."

The cameras followed us from the tour bus into the Odeon. Jon smirked into the lens, "Greetings, poor people." I was furious and berated him in the dressing room. I took issue with every whisper. "What?" I was like Nanny Glynn in the kitchen with her sleeves rolled up, ready with a wet flannel. "I'll brain ya, I'll bloody brain ya."

Tessa Watts, head of Virgin Video, played reporter, interviewing fans. All the little girls fancied Jon, and most of the boys. I knew exactly how they felt. We had a surprise fan in golfer Nick Faldo, who seemed mortally embarrassed to be caught on camera at a Culture Club gig.

The show started with me entering the stage through the head of a giant sphinx, inspired by my trip to Egypt. The first night the sphinx wouldn't open. I was standing behind, screaming, "Fucking open it. The song's starting." The crew pulled it open manually and I skipped through with a smile on my face. The screams were deafening. Hundreds of clones rushed the stage. The place was so full of joy and expectation.

*   *   *

Culture Club were asked to write songs for a new Virgin movie *Electric Dreams,* about a home computer that falls in love with its owner's girlfriend. I felt sophisticated lunching with a film producer. Roy and I wrote two songs, "Love Is Love" and "The Dream" but still split the royalties four ways. I was resentful because Mikey and Jon had done sod all. I collaborated on another song, "Electric Dreams," with Phil Pickett and split it fifty-fifty. "Electric Dreams" was sung by P.P. Arnold, famous for her sixties hit "The First Cut." While recording with P.P. at Sarm West Studios I received a threatening phone call from the members of the new band Frankie Goes to Hollywood. They were in a neighboring studio obviously bored. "You dirty bent cunt. You're dead." At first I laughed it off but when the calls continued I started to worry. I got on the phone to my bodyguard Stuart Page, an ex-policeman, and asked him to come to the studio. Stuart turned up with three mean-looking guys. They went to see Frankie and told them it would be hard to play their instruments with broken fingers. There were no more calls. I never understood the Frankies' homophobia when Paul Rutherford and Holly Johnson were bent cunts, too.

Jon and I visited the set of *Electric Dreams* and Jon met one of his favorite actors, Bud Cort, star of the cult film *Harold and Maude.* Bud was playing the voice of the computer. He invited me out for dinner. I didn't bring Jon—he never invited me anywhere—I brought my flatmate Richard. He was so excited, especially when we arrived at the Athenaeum Hotel to discover the other guests were Ringo Starr and his Bond girl–wife Barbara Bach. As famous as he was, Ringo was extremely gracious and normal. I managed to get through dinner without mentioning the Beatles, though I did discuss James Bond with Babs.

"What eez thiz?" A sour-faced French official took one look at my passport, another at my geisha drag, and ordered me into a room to strip. I lost my sense of humor. "No way. I'd rather go back to London, thank you." Tony tried to intervene in his pidgin French, which only annoyed them more. I was traveling to the San Remo pop festival in Italy with my journalist friend Miko. Miko was interviewing me for a Japanese pop magazine. I made her dress up for a bit of fun—she went all the way, full-on geisha. I was geisha-goes-Hollywood: full face, lashes, hair curled into ringlets, and a torturous corset under my kimono to give me a waistline. After two hours and a phone call from the British consul I was finally allowed to leave the airport, kimono intact. A large press contingent had gathered in the arrivals hall. I hurried into the car like a hassled starlet. "No comment, no comment."

The British press had a field day. "Allez Ooops. French Give Boy George Le Sex Test." They said that Miko was my new girlfriend, and used a picture of us kissing to prove it. They quoted me, "I love Miko very much. She's been very special to me since we met two years ago in Tokyo." It was all fabrication, I never said a word of it. I was very fond of Miko; I trusted her too. She was a journalist and a friend. Miko worked with the record company and promoters in Japan, translating and helping coordinate. She got me backstage at the Kabuki Theatre in Tokyo on my twenty-second birthday, a rare honor for anyone, let alone a Westerner. I sat quietly in the bamboo dressing room and watched one of the stars transform himself. It was fascinating to see how quickly and flawlessly the makeup was done.

While driving across the French Riviera to San Remo, Miko read Alison Hay's palm and told her she would have a child within two years. Alison laughed it off—she'd always hated children and wasn't the least bit maternal. Miko also predicted that Alison would have an affair in her late thirties and leave Roy. Alison didn't like that bit. I remembered Miko's prediction when Alison became pregnant the following year. No one was more surprised than Alison. She had a beautiful baby girl and called her Sunny.

Thirteen Alma Square soon become more of a tourist attraction than a home. I had to get out of there. I moved in the middle of the night with the help of Dad's transit van. My new hideaway was in Charles Street, Mayfair. One room with a bed, a pay phone, and dark brown velvet curtains. Only Jon, Tony, and my new driver, Billy Button, knew where I was. The chauffeur was Tony's idea. He said it would be safer. I thought it was a bit poncy, but I soon got used to it. Jon nicknamed Billy "the porn king"—he said he looked like the type you saw in a *News of the World* exposé. Billy was an ex–minicab driver, round and balding with glasses.

I felt like a fugitive in Mayfair, sneaking in and out. I kept the curtains drawn most of the time. I didn't want anyone to spot me. I was so tired of the constant hassle from fans and sick to death of having to put my makeup on. I didn't want to live like Michael Jackson.

"Quick, George. You've got a phone call." Lolly, the receptionist at Virgin, came running out into the yard. I was in the middle of a photo shoot with Didi Zill from *Bravo* magazine.

"Who is it?" I asked.

Lolly almost squealed, "It's Michael bloody Jackson."

I hesitantly picked up the phone. "Hello."

"Hi, is that George? This is Michael." The helium-pitched voice sounded authentic, so much so that I was lost for words. It didn't help that there were twenty people standing around the phone.

I asked, "How do I know it's you?"

He giggled. "Of course it's me."

A few bland pleasantries peppered the long silences. I gave him my phone number and said call me there. A wave of hysteria swept through the Virgin offices. Inevitably it was leaked to the press and a silly story appeared saying I had turned down a duet with Michael Jackson. Michael called again, at Tony Gordon's office. He said, "I couldn't have talked to you until you got this famous." I said, "That's ridiculous. Anyone can talk to anyone whenever they feel like it. That's why telephones were invented." He giggled. I mentioned that the British press had called us both transvestites. That brought the conversation to an abrupt end.

To add to the twist, Tony received an irate phone call from Frank Dileo, who was managing Michael Jackson. Michael was upset because I'd called him gay in an American newspaper. I couldn't remember saying it; they must have read my mind. Frank Dileo was able to confirm that my caller was a hoaxer. Our secretary, Jean Reynolds, had always said it was a loony fan. That became clear when he switched from being Michael Jackson to Stevie Wonder. I didn't fall for that one. It was always my dream to meet Michael Jackson. I was sure all he needed was some down-to-earth company and a cup of Rosie Lee.

Jon lit a cigarette and stared out of the hotel window. Neither of us said a word at first but the bomb was ticking. We were in Munich to appear on Germany's biggest national pop show, *Musicladen*. The record company had booked Jon and me into separate rooms. They were always doing it. I snatched my key, Jon followed, trying to calm me.

"Look, it doesn't matter. I'll just move my stuff into your room."

"You didn't say that in front of the record company." Jon never wanted to promote the fact that we were a couple.

"You make me sick."

"Why does everything have to be a bloody drama?"

I stormed out of the room, slamming the door behind me. Jon chased me and a fight ensued. I tried to escape into the lift. Jon threw a punch and hit the metal door. There was a familiar yelp. "Shit, my hand."

Jon was rushed to hospital. He'd broken his finger—again. He flew back to London, and we performed using the drummer from the German pop group Nena. Luckily it was snowing in Munich and Ronnie Gurr had the perfect lie. Jon slipped on the ice.

I had no idea how much money Culture Club were making. I knew we were rich, very rich, but I never looked in my bank account or spent that much. I was aware that fame might not last forever and knew all the clichéd stories about pop stars blowing their millions and coming round in the bankruptcy court. My only real luxury was buying my first home, a small mews house directly behind Philip's flat in Alma Square. I watched the row of tiny houses being built and dreamed of owning one. I didn't have the money to buy the house outright so I took out a mortgage. The idea of being in hock to the bank worried me. Dad had fought long, hard battles with the boys at Barclays, and I didn't ever want to be in debt.

Culture Club set up Sharpgrade, a company to channel our ever-increasing funds. Jon was elected as the main signatory.

Everybody trusted him. All checks and bills were paid out under the supervision of our accountants. Jon wanted to make sure we avoided the disasters that had befallen other bands. He always made jokes about managers: "'Ere, boys, buy yourself a nice motor and 'ere's a bit of pocket money." We paid Tony rather than him paying us. This meant the finger of suspicion could never be pointed. I was such a business airhead, it would have been easy for anyone to swindle me. I rolled my eyes and chewed my nails at our accountants, I couldn't wait to leave. I was glad Jon was so astute and money-minded: I knew that by looking after his own interests he would look after mine. I could just about get it together to draw cash from the bank. I had to ask Jon how to write a check. I still acted like I was on the dole and carried little cash with me. Friends would joke, "You think you're the Queen." I'd always lived on my wits before Culture Club. My cheek and painted face got me into most places free, I never went hungry or thirsty, I dived straight for the canapés at the gallery openings. It was the same for all us club kids. We went to clubs penniless and left plastered. As the famous Boy George I had even less reason to open my purse. All doors swung open. I was treated with a whole new level of respect. I'd made it, you see. As soon as "Do You Really" was on the charts people assumed I was loaded. "Get the drinks in, then." They didn't realize how long it took for royalty checks to come through. It was the same for Mum. People would say, "Ooh, I bet he's bought you a nice house."

I was working and traveling most of the time. The only thing I had to remember was my case, my makeup, and to move my feet and lips. It was an unnatural existence. Hotel rooms, room service, dinner with the record company, lunch with a journalist. If I wanted to buy something when we were on tour I borrowed the money from the tour budget or used someone else's credit card. Living that cosseted lifestyle you quickly forget how much things cost, not that I was ever an expert. During the squatting days my shopping list was minimal, fish and chips, pasties, crisps, Mother's Pride, and Mars bars.

My life totally revolved around Culture Club and I expected everyone else's to. I was furious when Helen did backing vocals for the new pop group Jimmy the Hoover. As far as I was concerned, she was our property. Helen was integral to our sound, despite Roy, Mikey, and Jon's views to the contrary. I didn't want anyone stealing her away. I made Tony put her on a retainer. Helen never really got her dues in Culture Club. She was paid the minimum going rate for adding her heart and soul to our records. I tried my best to pull her to the front and get her more money but the others always objected. I really wanted to help her.

When Helen signed a solo deal with Virgin, Roy and I wrote songs for her. It was the first time we'd done anything without Jon and Mikey getting a cut. We penned Helen's first single "Love Lies Lost," which reached number 34 in the charts. I was pleased that Roy and I had managed to do something independently. It wasn't a hit by our normal standards, but it proved a point. Helen didn't feel cut out to be a pop star: she loathed the dishonesty of the business and hated the invasion of privacy by fans and media. She just wanted to sing. When she was on form she could raise the roof and the emotions. I looked up to her as a singer. When we performed "That's the Way" onstage I always felt like crying.

Culture Club won Best Band at the *TV Times* Awards and I got to shake hands with Robert Mitchum, who told the press, "He may be a fag, but I'd like to adopt him." I was insulted by his arrogant backhanded compliment. It was unreal meeting legends and having personal encounters with them. They tried to match my camp at the British Phonographic Industry Awards by having Frankie Howerd present our award for Best Single and Best Band. "Ooh no, missus." I couldn't stop laughing.

I picked up the *Daily Mirror* Pop Personality of the Year Award for the second year running, and in the U.S.A., Culture Club received a prestigious Grammy for Best Newcomer. "Karma Chameleon" had topped the American charts and stayed there for three weeks, selling 1.2 million. *Colour by Numbers* went platinum six times, selling six million. In Canada we were the first group ever to sell more than a million albums. We accepted our Grammy Award by satellite in the company of comedian Joan Rivers. The band were understandably distressed when they discovered only two chairs had been placed for the broadcast. The producers decided it would look better. This time I sympathized, it was such an important occasion for us all. I refused to accept the Grammy without the band.

I was buzzing all day, trying to decide what to wear. Helen suggested I check out her designer mate Chris Barnes, an old club freak who was making a new name for himself as an avant-garde jeweler and stylist. Chris worked under the name Judy Blame. He was nicknamed after Judy Garland, but he didn't look much like her with his Mohican hairdo. It was more his liking for pills and champagne, which often took him somewhere over the rainbow.

I went over to Judy's workshop in Old Street and picked out several pieces of garish gold neck jewelery and a pair of razzle-dazzle earrings. Five minutes before we went on air I still couldn't decide which necklace to wear, so I wore them all. Judy roared when he saw my picture in the newspapers the next day. My acceptance speech caused a few roars too. Though brief, it did not endear me to Middle America or, for that matter, Tony, Jon, Roy, and Mikey. "Thank you, America, you have taste, style, and you know a good drag queen when you see one." For added camp I blew a kiss. I was only having a laugh. I didn't think about it. I just opened my mouth and I came out. Maybe secret demons were working in my subconscious. Up to that point, my sexuality had been hovering in a puff of question marks. By saying I was a drag queen, I'd unwittingly told America I was absolutely queer.

Reports came back that Susan Blond had burst into tears, Frank Dileo dropped his cigar, country singers gagged, R&B artists shook their heads. From then on the American press referred to me as "self-acclaimed drag queen. . . ."

Meanwhile in Britain we were being congratulated by the House of Commons. "This House congratulates Culture Club, the Police, Duran Duran and other British stars on their success in the Grammy awards; and acknowledges the enormous pleasure they bring to millions of people around the world and the exports they and their industry achieve for the United Kingdom."

"Britain Rocks America Again. From the Beatles to Boy George and Beyond." I appeared on the cover of *Newsweek* alongside Annie Lennox. *Newsweek* were celebrating the second British pop invasion of America. In 1983, over a third of U.S. singles and albums chart places were taken by British acts.

Newsweek wrote, "There is such a radical difference between the American and British pop scenes that it is all but impossible to imagine this country producing a phenomenon like Culture Club." Many believed the only reason I was successful in America was because I was imported. The day of the *Newsweek* photo shoot I heard Annie Lennox telling the makeup artist Lynne Easton not to make her look like Boy George. Annie was my female counterpart, the tomboy to my tomgirl. I enjoyed the irony of being photographed with her; I was the fan made good, even if she didn't want Boy George eyebrows.

There was never any time to stop and breathe. Rehearsals began for a spring U.S. tour. Tony wanted us out on the road to capitalize on the success of *Colour by Numbers,* "Karma," and the Grammy. Jon never wanted to tour. We only did short ones. The longest ever was four weeks. He said there was no need to go traipsing around everywhere. We were in the video age. I was convinced the real reason was he didn't want to be trapped in a hotel room with me.

CHAPTER 27

Three thousand fans were waiting at Mirabel airport in Montreal on March 28, 1984, for the start of the A Kiss Across the Ocean tour. It was an incredible rush when we walked into the arrivals hall. A whoosh of screams and swaying arms. I caught my breath. "My God." Roy went, "Blimey. 'Allo." We were all wondering how we were going to get through. An accompanying police officer assured us, "Don't worry. We'll surround you." Tony was insistent. "We can't go through that. Someone will get hurt." He was told there was no other exit and to leave it in their hands. I was led through the surging crowd hemmed in by police. Gary Lee and Billy did their best to protect the others. Limbs occasionally broke through the phalanx, grabbing anything they could reach. By the time I got to the limo I was wearing a quaint off-the-shoulder number and my hair was minus a few fake dreads. They clambered over the top of the car, almost crushing the roof. I went straight in one door and out the other, it was like a *Pink Panther* movie. We were driven off in a van at high speed. Cars trailed us into the city, honking, waving, screaming, cameras flashing. Fans hung dangerously from the windows.

"George, George."

"He looked at me."

"We love you."

Our agent, Jim Rodman, booked us into the hotel under pseudonyms. Mikey was Jerome Calloway, Roy and Alison were Mr. and Mrs. Rex Simi, Jon was Charles Shaw, and I was Edward Beringer. All names of California vineyards. There was fuss from the plane to the limo to the hotel. It was annoying, I felt on edge, pulling my bag away from the bellhop. "It's all right, I can carry it myself. Just give me my key." They'd come to the room, follow you in, and start giving you a guided tour. "This is the bathroom, sir. Over there's the . . . If you need anything . . . " I'd be nodding my head, "Thank you. Thank you," wanting to scream, "Get out!"

By the time I got to my room I didn't want to see another face. It was the only time I could relax. I'd chuck on some comfy clothes and jump straight on the phone.

"Room service, can I help you, sir?"

"A club sandwich and french fries, please."

It was impossible to leave the hotel as it was surrounded by a moat of pop piranhas. They called out our names and waited, day and night, night and day. Some were happy just to get an autograph and leave. Others kept religious vigil and always had something else to sign. Chubby cheruby types with smudged lips and baggy smock shirts, ribbons and clown rouge, plaits and hats and round mirrored specs. They'd push their comical little faces against the van window and kiss the glass. Some fans had to be admired for their ingenuity. Gary Lee always searched the dressing rooms. They would hide in cupboards, under tables, bent in two for hours, holding their breath. Those with cars would follow us everywhere. It made me so angry. "They're bloody detectives, not fans." We tried to go shopping in downtown Montreal. Every time we got out of the car fans charged at us screaming, clicking their cameras, attracting more unwanted attention. I shouted at Billy and Gary, "Tell 'em not to follow us." Gary pulled a persistent fan's keys out of her ignition and chucked them down the street. Photographers sneaked into our sound check disguised as janitors and took blurry pictures. Chambermaids gave details of my wardrobe. How many pairs of shoes, etc., etc. Room service discussed my dinner.

The manager of a trendy designer shop, Greche, offered to open Sunday morning so we could shop in peace. I felt like the

Queen visiting Harrods. He asked if he could take photographs of me in some of the clothes I bought. I sent Gary Lee to the stockroom to negotiate a sizable discount. They gave me $4,000 worth of clothes for nothing.

The Canadian concerts were well received, not that anyone was savoring the content. The fans screamed before, during, and after every song. It was strange playing those large arenas. I found it much easier playing to twenty thousand people than to a hundred. You become detached and go onto remote. It wasn't helped by playing the same set in the same order night after night. Jon said people came to hear the hits. If that was true, we never disappointed them. Culture Club never put on an amazing show. There were moments of greatness, times when we gelled and joy beamed out from the stage. Mostly it was labored, a me and them situation. I didn't know cocaine was being used by the band and crew. Drugs had been on offer from the very first American tour. Liggers turned up bearing strange gifts in small packages.

"Hi, guys. Loved the gig. Want a line?" One of our crew was dishing out coke and hash to the band, making himself a few bob on the side. His peddling made him indispensable and gave him insidious control. The drug taking was well hidden from me. Not that it was difficult. I was never around. The use of cocaine could explain many things—frayed tempers and flaccid members.

From Montreal we flew to Ottawa and then the United States and Buffalo, where we were held up at the border. It was unusual for us to be stopped. They searched the van and body-searched Mikey and Roy. I thought the same was going to happen to me. A Customs officer led me into a room, leaned over me menacingly, and asked. "Can you sign a couple of autographs?" I obliged, happy to get out of there without having to reveal my trade secrets—safety pins, hairgrips, and shoulder pads.

Tempers were frayed after being held up for three hours. Jon and I had a vicious punch-up in the van. As I sat weeping the extended mix of Marilyn's hit "Calling Your Name" came chirping out of the radio. I shouted, "Turn it off." Jon had given me a fat lip and the last thing I wanted was to be serenaded by Marilyn.

Tony Gordon was in a panic because we were late for a *Rolling Stone* photo session. It was no ordinary session either. We were being snapped by the great Richard Avedon for a cover. We arrived too late to fit the session in before the gig. I offered to do it after the show, even though I would be knackered. Tony phoned Avedon to break the news. He refused to wait, ranting that he'd traveled all the way from New York, something he never did. He was deeply insulted by our lack of professionalism. I called him myself. "Hi, it's Boy George. I'm really sorry about all this, but we were held up at Customs. It wasn't our fault. We really want to do the session."

A queenie voice came back, "I'm sorry. It won't do."

"Who is this?"

"This is Avedon's assistant, sir."

"Well, look. We haven't done this deliberately. And there's no need for you to be so fucking pissy." He put the phone down on me. I went steaming to Tony's room. He was chuckling and happy that I'd given them what-for. Susan Blond was in a tizz and *Rolling Stone* were threatening to sue. They were paying Avedon enough money to keep the Third World in biscuits.

Tony was adamant. "Sod Avedon. We're not to blame, and that's it."

I said, "Shall I call him back and give him another mouthful?"

"Yeh," said Tony. "Bloody cheek."

His assistant answered again.

"Listen, Avedon's assistant. Go fuck yourself, and tell Avedon to do the same."

The saga followed us from Pittsburgh to Columbus. Susan was still fretting about being sued by *Rolling Stone*. When she told me Avedon's cancellation fee was $25,000 I laughed my head off and told her, "My mother's never heard of Avedon."

She became more hysterical. "You don't realize what this means. It's terrible, terrible." I told her to send him a bunch of roses. She said, "This is *the* Avedon. You can't send Avedon roses." I sent them myself with a cheeky message: "Dear Dickie, Money isn't everything. Truly sorry. Boy George."

The next day in Detroit I received a signed book of Avedon's photos. "Dear George, Let's start again." I could have died when I flipped through the book. I'd bought postcards of his famous *Vogue* pictures and stuck them on the walls of the squat.

When I finally met Avedon in Miami at the end of the tour he handed me a single rose. He was one of the most unassuming legends I've ever worked with. Those assistants are always more precious than the real thing. The session went smoothly and we got our *Rolling Stone* cover, a brilliant picture with me holding Jon, Roy, and Mikey's heads under my arms. The interview contained more legendary hypocrisy. "I don't think people think I'm gay. Or maybe they do until they meet me." Asked whether my last relationship was with a man or woman, I told them, "Woman. The last time I had a really serious relationship was a long time before the band. Most of my male lovers have been kind of casual things. Men are difficult to have relationships with. You still fall in love, but you don't really hear about two men living a happy life for forty years, do you? Or if you do, it warms your heart. I think the press make light of my sexual feelings. There are certain things that are really sacred. Your relationships are really important, more important than any of this." An even bigger joke was "The problem is, most people who get up here waste their time drinking champagne or staying stoned. I don't do any drugs, I never have. I do not wish to find out what it feels like to stick a needle in my arm."

Ronnie Gurr had his work cut out trying to keep the hacks away from us. We were followed everywhere by the Fleet Street truffle pigs or their American counterparts. The *National Enquirer* sent an old scumbag out from their Miami office to get some dirt under his nails. He asked Ronnie, "What's the story about George and Jon Moss? What's going on there?"

Ronnie was edgy, convinced he was fishing for the gay angle. "I don't know what you mean."

"Well, do they ride motorbikes like Led Zeppelin used to?"

Ronnie told him, "The most exciting thing Boy George does when he checks into a hotel room is take the wrapper off the soap." They used the quote in the *National Enquirer*. It was one of Ronnie's proudest moments.

Jon's big mouth almost got him shot in Columbus, Ohio. He saw an underage girl drinking with her parents in the hotel bar and told them they were irresponsible. The dad told him to go to hell. Jon drank up and left the bar. A few drinks later the man was hunting Jon with a loaded pistol. Hotel security tackled him on our floor and dragged him away.

The fundamentalists were showing Christian generosity at the Brigham Young University in Salt Lake City, Utah. They removed Culture Club records from the college radio station, accusing me of perverting the nation's youth. It didn't stop us filling the venues down South. In Louisville the show was full of lookalikes. I reveled in the animosity and teased the audience, "If I could sleep with you all individually, believe me I would." I danced around like a big girlie in bare feet and teased wig.

"Billy! Billy! Scissors, safety pins, powder puff." Billy Button became my personal dartboard and gofer-quickly. For all the running he did he never lost an inch. Like so many people connected with the band, he enjoyed the ill-gotten perks of Culture Club's fame. He played the teddy bear, but behind my back he was entertaining fans in his room. Helen and Roy used to cup a glass against the wall and listen to the goings-on, pestering him with phone calls. He shouted at Helen, "Leave it out, girl, I've got a tart spinning round on me nob." I had my share of offers, mostly from girls. I found a bottle of champagne on my pillow and nude Polaroids of a shapely girl and a message, "I can make a man of you."

Some boys tried to stick their tongues down my throat. I often saw boys in the crowd that I would have gladly shown my eyelash collection and some real dishes arrived with the room service. I wanted Jon more than anyone else.

We had our own mobile *Peyton Place*. If Roy and Alison weren't fighting, then Jon and I were, and the band split up at least twenty-five times a week. Alison complained if Jon and I were booked into a more lavish suite and there was always something wrong with the room. Roy wasn't averse to a bit of sulking. He kicked up the most fuss about the preferential treatment I received from the media and the record company, using Alison as his mouthpiece. It didn't help when people referred to him as Ron or Reg, though it kept the rest of us in stitches. I could see that no matter how much the band complained, things would never be the way they wanted, unless they all underwent sex changes and called themselves Rowena, Michaela, and Joan. Jon was the band pinup.

When I introduced him onstage he always got the wildest screams. That annoyed Mikey, Roy, and Alison even more.

There was nearly a mutiny when Helen got sozzled on vodka and decided to tell the rest of the session players she was being paid more. I trudged down the corridor in my bathrobe. "What the bloody hell's wrong with you?" Helen was tearful and blamed her biorhythms. Jon and Tony were really happy: they had to give everyone a rise. The sessions were an odd bunch and very twitchy around me. "Watch out, God's about." Ron the trumpet was a Buddhist and into yoga; he would spend hours upside down in the sirsasana position, feeding his brain. To look at him you wouldn't think there was that much going on in his head. He was the most enlightened of us all.

When the tour ended I stopped off in New York for a few days chaperoned by Jim Rodman. Jim's role was confused. Officially he was our travel agent but he was more like a tour dad. He was well connected around the fifty states. He always knew someone who could smooth the ride, get us an upgrade. Tony had a knack of getting everyone to bend over backward for the thrill of being in our company. Jim was a real friend to the band, particularly to me. He looked like a typical West Coast rocker, Cuban-heeled cowboy boots, a ponytail, and *Easy Rider* shades. He had plenty of rock stories to back up his credentials. The travel agent, the roadie, the chauffeur, the makeup artist, the hairdresser, they always had the best gossip. The first question I would ask any chauffeur was "Who's the worst person you've ever driven?" They loved to spill the dirt, tell you about the time when so-and-so had three hookers in the back of their limo.

I hung out in New York with Jim and my photographer friend Bonnie Lippel. Bonnie and I were now firm friends. She came to visit me in London and flew to the West Coast for our tour. The band called her "Superfan" and couldn't understand why I gave her special treatment.

Bonnie drove me around Greenwich Village in her Beetle and I raided the trendy stores, using Jim's gold American Express card. I bought some hats, a top for my little sister, Siobhan, and T-shirts and trousers for Jon. I was always buying presents for him. I loved New York's crazy indigestion, especially now I was getting a chance to look around. I'd traveled the Midwest, the Deep South, the East and West Coast and seen nothing.

Photographer Andre Csillag traveled with us. We'd jump out of the van for quick "we woz here" shots—in front of Niagara Falls, under a Detroit road sign—we never got much of a feel for anything. Tours were so high profile it was impossible to do anything quietly. I could have walked around if I'd been prepared to put up with the constant harassment. It was easier to put up with the air-conditioning.

I arrived back in London to discover Mikey had been busted at Heathrow. Because he tried to sneak in a brand-new guitar they searched his suitcase and found a small vial of hash oil. Mikey claimed a roadie packed his bags and it wasn't his. After a good grilling they gave him the option of going to court or paying an on-the-spot fine. Mikey was lucky that Customs didn't choose to make an example of him. The press were outside, waiting and wondering. My antidrugs stance was well known. Mikey told Customs he would be fired from the band if it was made public. Customs were cooperative and issued a press statement saying Mikey had been stopped for the guitar.

I attended the Sony Radio Awards at the London Hilton where Princess Margaret was guest of honor. I joined the official lineup and received a mean handshake. As the Queen's sister walked away she was heard to say, "Who's Boy George? He looks like an over-made-up tart." The press wanted a reaction. I spat back, "Who cares? I'd rather be photographed with my fans." Much fuss was made of the incident over the following days. One of the most amusing theories was that she said my face resembled one of the masks from the commedia dell'arte and that she was misheard. A likely story.

As a joke I had T-shirts printed with a cartoon of Princess Margaret wearing dreadlocks and a hat, with the caption "Boy George is not a tart." Months later, while I was lunching with Marilyn in a Kensington bistro, I was approached by Margaret's son Lord Linley. He said, "I just want you to know, my mother didn't say anything nasty about you."

I didn't care, I liked the idea of being insulted by a royal. The Royal Family are just a bunch of Sloanes who live off our taxes. They're certainly not my moral guides. I don't go with the idea that they are better than us because of their breeding. Anyone given that amount of privilege could become stately and time has proved how ordinary they really are.

Culture Club turned down two royal events, the Prince's Trust concert and the *Royal Variety Show,* because we didn't need the cornflake seal of approval.

CHAPTER 28

"Go on, make an effort, it won't take you five minutes."
Jon was showing an unusual interest in my appearance. I was already comfortable in the hotel bathrobe and couldn't be bothered to dress up for a party. We were in Hong Kong en route to Japan for our second tour. The one-night stopover was purely to break up the journey—at least that's what Tony had said. When we arrived I was told the record company had arranged a small soiree in our honor. They were presenting us with platinum discs and wanted Boy George there, as well as Jon, Mikey, and Roy. Jon's innocent comments riled me. I was tired and oversensitive.

"Come on, George, don't be such a slob."

"Don't call me a slob."

"Don't be one, then."

"Fuck off, dwarf."

"Slob."

"Dwarf."

"Slob."

"Dwarf."

I grabbed a family-sized Coca-Cola bottle and threw it as a warning shot, I didn't mean to hit Jon but it cracked against his head. He dropped to the floor and was out cold. I flung open the door and screamed at the top of my voice, "Billy. Billy. Quick, I've hurt Jon."

Billy scampered down the corridor pulling up his trousers. "Oh, no, guv'nor, wass 'appened now?" Jon's dying act didn't last long once he had an audience. He sprang up fists flying. Billy and another crew member, Micky Body, had to separate us as we wrestled on the floor.

Downstairs at the soiree Tony, Mikey, Roy, and Alison were awaiting our arrival. Gary Lee whispered in Tony's ear, "You'd better come quick. George has bottled Jon." Tony excused himself and hurried to the room.

"Georgie, Georgie. What's wrong?"

"I've bottled Jon. I don't care if he's brain dead."

"Oh dear."

After a couple of hours in hospital and an X ray Jon was given the okay. He returned to the hotel in a surprisingly forgiving mood, we had great sex, and the tour went on as planned.

Here comes the bride, all dressed in white.

Roy almost stopped playing when I swept onstage for our encore at the Castle Sports Hall in Osaka, Japan, wearing a wedding dress and veil, clutching a bouquet. The crowd roared their approval. I loved it, spinning around and dropping to my knees, acting up for the cameras. We were being filmed for Channel 4's Midsummer Night's *Tube*. "Bloody 'ell" was all Jon could muster when we came offstage. My bridal gown was made by my friend and new costume designer Alan Roberts, sewn together in his tiny Chiswick flat and paraded a week later in front of ten thousand people. My costumes were getting camper and so were the band's. Alan made futuristic Victorian bathing suits for Jon and Mikey, green-and-white-striped vests and skimpy shorts with leggings that clipped on like tights. Roy said no way. I don't know how I got Jon and Mikey in them. They wore them under black tracksuits, which I ripped off onstage. The British press reported in titillating fashion, "First he stripped off their shirts, then pulled off their trousers. Many of the young girls in the audience looked away in horror." Another one of Alan's outfits was a green-and-white-striped smock with a matching kabuki-style mask, which was supposed to come off after the first number. Billy was waiting in the wings to assist me. He fumbled with the strings—my hysterics made it more difficult. "Fucking hurry up, hurry up." Finally I got it off. "Get me a mirror, quick. I think I've smudged me eyebrows." I sacked Billy for the millionth time.

Our second Japanese tour was a media circus. Ronnie Gurr had given British journalists, Christena Appleyard from the *Sunday People* and Dave Rimmer from *Smash Hits,* an exclusive. Tony had unofficially (officially) invited creepy John Blake from the *Sun* and there were various other gentlemen of ill repuke tagging along. It was a nightmare having journalists sniffing around, appearing at all the wrong moments. Dave Rimmer was standing sidestage and heard my tantrum. He was planning his own book and wanted to do as much snooping as possible. A week into the tour Ronnie quit. He could no longer stand the pressure or Tony's interference. Tony was adamant that it was for the best. He preferred nodding dogs to raging Scots.

From Tokyo we flew to Sydney for our first-ever tour of Australia. The mob scenes were reminiscent of Montreal. The four policemen on duty were unable to handle the crowd. Things really got out of hand and the band was almost torn to pieces by the loving throng. In fright Roy and Alison escaped into the Hertz Rent-a-Car office. They were left behind in the confusion and had to catch a cab. They were understandably furious.

Tony blamed Jim Rodman. Tony had sent him ahead to prepare the airport authorities for our arrival. They ignored Jim's request for extra security. Tony didn't care. He fired Jim and sent him back to L.A. I argued against the decision. Tony said it would look bad if he had to reinstate him. Tony needed to show who was boss. He didn't always understand the difficulties of life on the road.

Hordes of fans circled the Sebel Town House Hotel in Kings Cross, Sydney's red-light district. "We want George. We want George." Australian fans were much more robust and hyperactive. I had to stay locked in my room, peering out of my sixth-floor window, itching to explore Sydney. Two hours after arriving we gave a massive press conference. I touched up the cracks on my already madeup face and faced the even more robust Australian press. Marilyn was hot news in Oz and they all wanted an opinion.

"Do you still speak to him?"

"Were you two ever lovers?"

I laughed. "I don't think so."

Marilyn's recent blitz through Australia had done me a big favor. From the moment he arrived he threw tact to the wind, pouting at Customs and asking them to strip him for drugs. They did. He appeared on *The Bert Newton Show* and had an on-air cat-fight with a leading Australian critic because he called him a Boy George clone. Marilyn was hissing, "Did you get the number of that bus that ran over your face?" The queenie audience coaxed Marilyn with their shrieks. He went into auto-bitch and it became boring. Marilyn apologized the next day, but it was too late. He'd already made himself unpopular. He got kicked in the face at a Sydney gay bar by a macho queer. He claimed Marilyn had sneered at him; others said the attack was unprovoked. Marilyn flew back to London with a black eye, saying Australians were animals.

In Sydney I met up with my old squatting friend Kim Bowen, who had moved there with her Aussie husband. Kim was working as a freelance fashion stylist. She told me Marilyn's black eye was a fake, she'd been with him minutes before he left for the airport and watched him apply theatrical bruises. Typical Marilyn. I sneaked out of the hotel and went to hang out at Kim's flat. All seemed calm until the fire brigade came rapping on the door. Some fans had followed us and called them out. Ha, ha.

I did a photo shoot with Kim and another old acquaintance, makeup artist Stevie Hughes. "Hi, Mum." Stevie hadn't changed a bit. He painted me for days and Kim styled me in a peaked military cap and air force coat. Stevie shot me from a ladder so there were no chins. "Purse those lips. One for all the kamikaze pilots that died in your honor." He had me in fits. The photos were later used for "The War Song" single sleeve. I had the most fantastic day. I hadn't seen any normal people for ages. I didn't want to go back to the hotel.

We appeared on the *Countdown* TV show hosted by Molly Meldrum. The audience was full of drag queens. It was brilliant. The press claimed I hand-picked the crowd myself and banned all straights. It was a lie, but one that amused me. Australia was full of transvestites and clones. Their attention to detail was mind-boggling. Most of them looked better than me. Their costumes, hair, and makeup were incredible and they had my movements down to a tee. Moral watchdog the Reverend Fred Nile said I was going against the word of the Bible dressing as a woman: "It says in the Bible that God will punish any man who dresses as woman and that's what Boy George is doing. Boy George puts on an act that he's moral and upright, but if he were, he would really be boy George and not girl George. The frenzy that the Beatles created was a healthy thing but there's definitely something evil about this latest craze."

Catholic priest Father Ron McKiernan, deputy director of Brisbane's Catholic Education Centre, publicly tore up my picture. He told his congregation, "He doesn't know if he is a boy or a girl and makes young people think their sexual identity does not matter . . . Kids may like Boy George for the music, but he's helping many to wallow in sexual confusion. Boy George represents anarchy—an escapism and refusal to face up to the realities of life."

I was incensed and told the press, "A priest's job is to carry the Word of the Lord, not to make comments on society. To cut a long story short, the Word of the Lord is to love your fellow man."

Forty-five thousand people signed a petition for us to play in Adelaide. The petition was the brainchild of three young fans. We couldn't find a big enough venue so we made a public appearance at a shopping mall. Along the route from the airport, schoolkids lined the footpaths for a glimpse. We were given the keys to the city from the state premier, John Bannon, in front of ten thousand people at Rundle Mall. I was dressed in a fuchsia pink wool coat and sang a few lines of "Karma Chameleon." The crowd responded with "Waltzing Matilda." We were also given the freedom of Tasmania.

At the request of the *Daily Sun* newspaper we went on a boat trip to Moreton Island off the Brisbane coast. They wanted to shoot us on the luscious beach. When we arrived and saw it was a sandy old dump we did a quick picture and got back on the boat. Halfway home we hit a storm. It was terrifying. We were in shark-infested waters. Everyone was throwing up and screaming. I went downstairs to the cabin and clung to the bed. Tony's wife, Avi, was in tears. Jon was puking over the side and would have gone overboard had he not been grabbed by Billy. Our new press agent, Jo Bailey, sent out by Virgin to replace Ronnie, clung to a bottle of red wine. She'd been expecting a storm but not one that bad. Arriving safely back at the hotel we all laughed and ordered a hot curry to remind us of home.

We ended the tour with five shows at Sydney Entertainment Centre. The last night was televised live. I was lowered onto the stage inside a glittering heart. Very Gary Glitter. Various celebrities and politicians including the prime minister, Bob Hawke, were filmed as part of the TV special. They made funny little comments about me. Spike Milligan, who was touring Australia, said, "He's not only a good-looking boy, but he's also a good-looking girl." Over two weeks we were seen by more than 100,000 people. Two million were believed to have watched our final show and heard the radio simulcast. Magazines with my face on the cover increased their sales by 20 percent, rivaling the selling power of Princess Diana. The reaction in Australia was phenomenal and unexpected. I believed Australia was full of macho men. There was only one incident of aggression. A fat, slobbering skinhead spat on our car window and gave me the finger.

From Australia I flew to Los Angeles and on to Miami en route to Jamaica for a three-week holiday with Marilyn. I stayed overnight at the airport hotel. I hacked out my dreadlocks and bleached my hair. The next morning I got a few odd stares. "That looks like Boy George. No, it can't be." I looked like Edgar Winter in drag.

CHAPTER 29

Marilyn was waiting at Norman Manley airport. He screamed when he saw my hair. "Sorry, that's my look." We linked arms at the taxi rank and broke into song, "Sisters, sisters, there never were such hideous sisters." Like Egypt, Jamaica was a head-spinning adventure. I leaned out of the taxi window to catch the hot sun rays. Jamaica was so beautiful, swaying palm trees, blue ocean, and reggae music pumping out of the tinny car stereo. Our cabdriver recognized me immediately. "You is Bwoy Gearge?" Marilyn answered for me, "No, it's Randy Crawford." We all giggled like silly fools. Marilyn and I were friends again. He was happy and feeling secure. Things were going well for him in Europe. Away from our competitive pop careers we always had the most fun.

Marilyn had already bagged the nicest room at the villa. He was on first-name terms with the cook and maid, Pansy and Desree, and had worked out the week's menu. The food was amazing. That night we had dinner under the moonlight—jerk chicken, rice and peas, plantain, corn, followed by fresh mango and ice cream. We sat by the pool and smoked a spliff. I laughed when I thought about Australia, the Gary Glitter heart, my fights with Jon. It seemed a lifetime away.

It wasn't long before reality slapped us in the face. Press photographer Alastair Loos had taken up residence on the hotel roof next door. Marilyn and I took all the mirrors from the house and propped them up in the garden, reflecting the sunlight. When I went for a swim I held a full-length mirror in front of me as I side-stepped across the garden. It was comical, but it did the trick. We lobbed coconuts over the wall at him too. Eventually Loos moved into a tree right by our garden wall. Marilyn and I tried to lure him in for a cup of tea. We planned to tie him up in the spare bed-room. Unfortunately he declined our offer.

Our day trip to peaceful Dunns River Falls was a nightmare. I tried to disguise myself, dark glasses, a straw hat, a baggy T-shirt, and a sarong. Marilyn wore his infamous Union Jack shorts and a black see-through nightie. His subtle attire instantly drew crowd attention. Some people thought he was me and shouted, "Look. Boy George."

Marilyn and I had a heated row. He screamed, "We can't go anywhere, everyone's looking at us." I reminded him that he was the one dressed like a Page Three girl.

Marilyn hired a car and we drove to Negril and found a more secluded waterfall and lake where we could swim. Some creep spotted me and a photographer from the local newspaper turned up. I was furious: all I wanted to do was relax. As we jumped into the car to speed off we were approached by a pretty Rasta woman. "'Ello. M'name Sister Pea. You want to go somewhere nice and quiet?" We were hesitant, already sick of people trying to sell us carved jewelry and bamboo-leaf hats. Marilyn asked her, "Where's nice?" With that she jumped into the car. "Jus' drive, I show you." Sister Pea took us far up into the Blue Mountains where she lived with her Rastaman boyfriend, Dr. John, in a wooden shack with an allotment. They were sweet, gentle people and weren't after any-thing. Pea cooked us sweetcorn on a charcoal fire and we smoked strong ganja.

Marilyn kept nagging me to call Keith Richards, who had a villa on the island. I said I didn't know him, but I was too embarrassed. We were hardly from the same rock school. After much arm twist-ing I picked up the phone. Marilyn got his number from a cab-driver.

"Hi, can I speak to Keith?"

"Who is it, please?"

"Boy George."

"Boy George?" I could hear lots of hysterical laughter in the background. Keith came to the phone.

"Is it really the bag lady? How you doing, man?"

I put the phone down.

The next day he rang our villa. He was apologetic and invited us up to his house. Marilyn was jumping for joy.

Andre Csillag was staying with us, taking shots in Jamaica. He was excited by the prospect of a picture of me and "Keef." I said he could only come if he didn't bring his camera.

There was a little party going on at Keith's place. He introduced us to the handful of guests. His dad, son Marlon, a couple of roadies, and a guy called Freddie Sessler, who Keith had known since the sixties. Freddie certainly looked lived in.

Keith was like a ravaged baboon, scratching his head, darting in and out of the room, holding fragmented conversations. Every other word was man, man, man. He called me Boy instead of George. I liked him, though. He reminded me of my old uncle Jim. He had a dangerous twinkle in his eye. He talked about Mick Jagger and said he was "a nice bunch of guys." Keith played guitar and mumbled the blues.

Andre was upset when he found a strange pill fizzing in the bottom of his drink. It looked like a downer. No one would own up to putting it there. Obviously Andre wasn't relaxed enough.

We left at 3 A.M. As we were driving off Marilyn remembered he'd left his sunglasses behind. I went back to knock on the door. I could see Keith through the shutters wearing Marilyn's sunglasses, doing a poofy dance around the living room. "Two-faced cunt." Marilyn got his glasses and we left.

The next day we were taking pictures on a cliff top. Marilyn and I were posing with the waves crashing behind us. Suddenly I was engulfed by a wave and dragged across the sharp rocks. My arms were bleeding and I was drenched. The next thing I saw was Marilyn with his hand across his mouth, laughing hysterically. "You look better wet. Just think, if you'd have gone over the cliff me and Andre could have sold the story. The last two people to see Boy George alive." I had to laugh at this twisted humor. My presence on the island caused a stir. "Karma Chameleon" was pumping out of the radio almost hourly. "Bwoy Gearge in the vicinity. Welcome to Jamaica." Even right up in the hills kids were pointing as we drove by. "Bwoy Gearge" or "Whitey, whitey." Generally people were very warm and sweet to us. There was some animosity. Occasionally we were called "Dirty Babylon" or "Batty Bwoy."

We met the prime minister's wife, Mitzi Seaga. She brought her children over to the villa. She was very down-to-earth and friendly. She invited us to spend the day at Laughing Waters, a private beach where they filmed the James Bond movie *Dr. No.* And we went for dinner at her house. I met Prime Minister Edward Seaga briefly at his parliamentary office. I just shook his hand and let him get on with his work. He was much more official.

When we arrived back in London Marilyn made sure to stay out of the way. The cameras caught my blond image complete with five days' growth and a bullfrog chin. One paper printed a center spread. "Georgie, Porgie, Pudding and Pie," claiming I'd piled it on in Jamaica. They discussed my diet with a dietician. It was so insulting and intrusive.

I could see the attitude of the press was changing toward me, as my attitude was changing toward them. In the beginning I was obliging. They had a job to do, I had a job to do. I thought the two things worked in harmony. I knew they weren't there simply to praise me. They hadn't always been nice but I hadn't really experienced their truly nasty side. I began to realize that when you play the publicity game you don't get a day off. No matter how popular you are, they always have the last word. Their brand of spite was no different to what I experienced in the playground at Eltham Green. "Fatty. Big nose. Poofter." They went for the lowest common denominator and you were expected to take it on the double chin, like a professional.

I was invited to a party for photographer Bruce Weber at Mr. Chow's restaurant in Knightsbridge. I brought Marilyn as my plus one. While I was nibbling spring rolls and chatting to Tina Chow, Marilyn was downstairs causing trouble. Marilyn told someone to fuck off. Bruce Weber, who was unrecognizable with a knotted hankie on his head, had Marilyn ushered into the street. I left with him. The next day the story was twisted, saying we were both abusive.

Bored of being a blond bombsite, I became the fire queen and dyed my hair vermilion. I showcased my new tresses when I took Mum and Dad to see Frank Sinatra at the Royal Albert Hall. I arrived with my drag queen chum Tranny Paul. He looked sensational in his rubber swimsuit, fishnets, and stilettos. We planned it and surmised the headlines. Tranny said he would call himself Coral Reef. "Imagine, 'Good Grief, It's Coral Reef.'" But at the last minute he settled on Jemma. I said, "For God's sake, Tranny, don't open your mouth or you'll give it away." He towered above me in his six-inch heels. In the press Jemma became my "new love" but it didn't take long for the press to catch on that Jemma was actually Paul and that he hid his manhood with the aid of Sellotape.

CHAPTER 30

Philip Sallon had been planning fame since birth. Everyone else was making it in showbiz so he formed his own group, the Mud Men, and began secretly writing songs. None of his close friends knew he harbored any pop-star aspirations. We'd only heard him singing Doris Day songs in the back of Gay Robert's car.

EMI records signed Philip to a one-off singles deal in the hope that he would become the next chart-topping English eccentric. I was pleased for him and relished the idea of Philip Sallon on *Top of the Pops*. For moral support I accompanied him to a meeting in the press office at EMI in Manchester Square. It was amusing to listen to Philip's ideas as his press officer tore her hair out. He wanted to drive down Oxford Street on a float miming to his song "Summer Dreams" and present rubber plants to all the DJs at Radio One. Ronnie Gurr had an easy job.

As we left EMI we ran into a bunch of fat, spotty Duran Duran fans. My dislike of Duran was well known. One of them shouted, "Fat queer," and kicked Billy's car as we pulled off. I stopped the car and jumped out. I carried the struggling mouthy fan into EMI's reception and told the security guard to hold her there or she was liable to get slapped.

The next day she was plastered on the cover of the *Sun*. "Boy

George Punches Duran Fan" with a fabricated picture of her lying battered in the road. I was terrified to leave the house, thinking people would actually believe I hit a sixteen-year-old girl. Other newspapers took up the story. Everyone wanted to hear what I had to say. I told them it was a lie and that I intended to sue the girl for libel if she didn't retract her allegations. Finally the girl's parents made her admit she was lying. That part of the story was buried among the tits and the tattle.

The songs on Culture Club's third album, *Waking Up with the House on Fire,* were catchy but weak. Jon told *Smash Hits,* "We booked three weeks to do the songwriting and didn't use one day of it. We had an argument and left. We tried again three days later and had another argument. We rowed and rowed. George smashed his tape recorder, I threw a chair at him. Then we wrote the album in four days." He was being flippant, but *Waking Up with the House on Fire* was the most disjointed album we ever made. No wonder it fainted at the starting post. When we delivered the album to Virgin they should have advised us not to release it. Perhaps they were pecking at the last bit of flesh.

The success of the first single, "The War Song," which reached number two, gave everyone a false sense of security. Its patronizing lyrics and brain-curdling melody was enough to drive even the most hard-core Culture Club fan into hiding. Held up against anti-war classics by Dylan and Country Joe it shriveled in its own misgivings. I was influenced by Frankie Goes to Hollywood's "Two Tribes" even though I would never have admitted it at the time. I was sick of writing lovey-dovey songs about Jon. I wanted to change the formula.

We had so many ideas and so much energy in the beginning that we managed to make the first two albums without thinking. By the time we recorded *Waking Up* we were out of ideas and out of touch. We'd been traveling around the world almost continually since "Do You Really Want to Hurt Me?" hit the top. Writing songs had become an unnatural process. We never rang each other up to say, "I've got a great song idea. Let's work." It was premeditated and prearranged. Songwriting had become secondary to our fabulous lifestyles. Culture Club was a disaster. We'd lost the ability to communicate with each other. The songs were more bitter but not better:

Laughing at the rumour
That you've been screwing someone.
Laugh, better cry
It could be your turn next time.
Brother what a lover
Beyond the fourth dimension.
He's got an ego
That's bigger than yours and mine.

I flew Stevie Hughes from Australia to shoot the album cover. I gave him free rein, allowing him to style the band however he wanted. It was his first album cover and I knew he was going to do a good job. The others were resistant to the idea, but he made them look good and flattered their fragile egos. Only Mikey fell victim to Stevie's wicked sense of humor. When he eventually turned up at the session Stevie dressed him in a skimpy white Lycra bodysuit, greased his skin, gave him a huge quiff, and perched him on a swing with his pert bottom in the air. Stevie was screaming when he showed me the Polaroids. "It's fierce. Tony Curtis in *Trapeze*." I wondered how he got Mikey to do it. He was obviously too intimidated to argue.

Jon, Roy, and Mikey all wanted to be on the cover. Despite their whining their pictures only appeared postage-stamp size. I dominated the cover with my new flame-red hair. A sensual muscle-bound drawing of myself appeared on the back. Roy hated it—it was too gay for his taste.

Russell Mulcahy's epic video for "The War Song" was its only saving grace. Three hundred schoolchildren dressed as skeletons, tanks, explosions, soldiers, fashion models, and three wig changes. Stevie did the makeup and brought his friend Ray Allington in to do the hair. They had a field day. Russell was never one for holding back the camp. Every time I appeared with a new look he shouted, "That's the one." Both Stevie and Ray were in the video.

They painted their faces, slipped into Antony Price costumes, and came screaming down the catwalk. They gave everyone else a headache, but I loved having them around. It was the perfect video to go out on. If only we'd had the courage and foresight to end it on such a pyrotechnic high.

CHAPTER 31

"oy George is Evil," "If sex is a sin what is Boy George?" The
fundamentalists were back out in force for the beginning of
our third U.S. tour, which began in Dallas. Hundreds of protes-
tors stood outside the hall urging people to turn back. They even
brought along tiny children. And they called me evil? The media
made a big deal of the fact that four thousand tickets of the
19,000 capacity remained unsold. A few other dates were canceled
too, which further fueled the idea that Culture Club were on the
way out. The late delivery of the album to America meant that we
were touring without a hit single and playing unfamiliar songs.
The album was released three days after the tour had begun; normal practice is six weeks before. The tour was being jokingly called
the Waking Up with the Band on Fire tour. Tony squeezed the
promoters, reducing their margins, so their only hope of making a
decent profit was if the shows sold out. He refused to back down
when the promoters realized they were going to lose money. This
increased animosity toward the band. Jon was quick to remind us
that we were never big down South and said it had been a bad
move to start the tour in Dallas. Obviously I was worried. Jon and
Tony normally shielded me from bad news because of my ten-
dency to flap, but I saw reports of our poor ticket sales on local
TV news right before the show. From the stage everything seemed
fine. The crowd reaction was as enthusiastic as ever. But I was nig-

gled by the reports and found myself scouring the auditorium for empty seats.

The tour carried on with mixed reviews. Austin, Houston, San Antonio. On October 31, Halloween night, we played Baton Rouge, Louisiana. My life was threatened by a mysterious caller, and Tony insisted that we go onstage wearing bulletproof vests. I was large enough, and the last thing I wanted was extra padding. I argued that if the threat was real why the hell didn't we cancel the show? I was terrified and uncomfortable onstage. I waddled around weighed down by my protective armor. There were hecklers in the crowd holding up Bibles, shouting, "Devil's spawn" and "God hates queers." I wondered how many of them had actually read that in the Bible. The fear added to the performance. Everyone said it was a great show, though it didn't feel that way from where I was standing. After, I went back to my room and locked myself in. I phoned everyone in my phone book and moaned that I was having a miserable time.

There was more bad press when we visited Graceland, Elvis's Memphis shrine. The *News of the World* claimed I called Elvis a "bighead" in a radio interview. I never insulted Elvis. While we were being shown around the mansion the guide told us, "This room took Elvis ten minutes to decorate. He saw it in a shop window and had to have it." I burst out laughing. It was the tackiest furniture I'd ever seen. I was sure if Elvis could see it now he'd have a laugh himself. I hated Graceland. The place was so plastic and soulless, it depressed me.

I was becoming more defensive and aggressive in my interviews. On November 8, 1984, we were invited onto the *Donahue* show, filmed the morning of our concert in Chicago. I had to keep up the front. "Well, one thing we don't do is take drugs, okay." I returned the attack on Jerry Falwell for accusing me of being evil. "Reverend Falwell says you can make kids homosexual by playing them pop records, which is rubbish. We come here to entertain, to bring happiness. People enjoy the concerts and there's nothing immoral about it at all." Phil Donahue praised me for being drug-free and said parents should be grateful I was held in such high esteem.

A member of the audience offered, "All the groups that are coming in from England, the heavy-metal groups, that are on drugs, that are gay, have spoiled it for any other group coming here."

I asked, "Are you saying that all gay people take drugs?"

"No, no."

Jon laughed. "Or all people that take drugs are gay, maybe?"

"A lot of them do," she replied, not making any sense.

Roy said, "All heavy-metal drugs are gay."

The women kept attacking me for dressing as a woman. I had a go at them back for wearing men's jackets. I told them they would have been branded lesbians twenty years ago.

Donahue couldn't even pronounce Mikey's name properly. He asked "Micky" if his ego was damaged by my getting all the press. We jokingly brushed aside queries about problems within the band. I said, "A blowtorch couldn't separate us now."

Just before we went onstage at the Rosemont Horizon in Chicago I had yet another massive fight with Jon. I refused to go on. Gary Lee was panicking, trying to smooth things over. He grabbed me and pulled me round the back. "You can't do this." I never had any intentions of carrying out my threat. I just wanted to be heard. It had been a long day, I'd spent the afternoon reediting our disastrous *Medal Song* video with director Zelda Barron. I made her fly to Chicago because I was unhappy with her video. She was furious at my interference, but played along to keep the peace. The song and the video were based on the story of Frances Farmer, the rebellious forties actress accused of being a Communist, institutionalized by her own mother, and given a lobotomy. Marilyn showed me the film *Frances,* her life story. It moved me so much that I wrote the song.

I jumbled the story up with other imagery. I had a troupe of Hare Krishna devotees jumping and chanting—they weren't the real thing, we hired a load of bald extras. Jon, Roy, and Mikey were dressed as the Fabulous Furry Freak Brothers. I wore a gold Lurex Chinese skullcap, an Indian sequined shirt, and long false metal nails. The video ended up looking colorful but very confusing. You couldn't tell it was about Frances Farmer.

Our tragic tour culminated in New York with a successful show at Madison Square Garden. I flew the whole family over by Concorde and put them up at the Ritz Carlton. Dad was ill, but didn't want to miss it. His doctors advised him not to travel as he was awaiting a heart bypass operation. He loved New York, as I had predicted, and had to swallow his preconceptions. He said, "This is my kind of place. Always buzzing, always something happening." Mum and Dad could hardly watch the show for adoring fans kissing them and taking their pictures.

Despite all the recent disappointments, it felt like a major achievement to walk out on that stage. The place was packed. Sean Lennon and Andy Warhol were there. Warhol noted in his diary, "Thanksgiving. Went to see Boy George at the Garden with Jean Michel and Cornelia Guest." He bitched, "Boy George is so fat." I wished I'd pulled his wig off.

I was dressed like Grace Kelly with a yeast complaint, in a gold fez with a black chiffon chador around my throat, a long black baggy jacket, matching pleated skirt, and bare feet. My look on that tour was a real disaster, a long way from the cutesy image that made me famous. Jon said my constant image changes were a bad idea, but I had to do something to quell the boredom. My makeup got heavier and heavier as the tour went along. Me and the makeup artist Pearl (Lynne Easton), who I knew from my punk days, had a right laugh. "Chuck it on, girl, chuck it on." Half an hour before the show I decided to have a haircut. Ray Allington gave me a Mohican. Billy and Gary were panicking that I might miss the show. I didn't care. I said the twenty thousand people could wait.

I took everyone out for a meal in a big stretch limousine. The whole family crammed in with Pearl, Nick Egan, and Ray. Ray jumped into the limo and asked Mum, "Have you got a light, dear, or shall I rub two Boy Scouts together?" Mum laughed her head off. The next day Mum was interviewed on *Late Night with David Letterman*. I'd been on the week before to promote the concert, and said jokingly, "My mum's in town next week. You should have her on." I was surprised when they called up. I sent her off to Bloomingdale's to buy a new dress.

Letterman asked her, "What was George like as a boy?"

Mum told him I was like any other boy. She was nervous and matter-of-fact. She recounted the story about the big platform shoes she bought me in Brick Lane.

*　　　*　　　*

I was washed out after that tour and decided to stay in New York and have a relaxing time with friends. However, my plans were quashed by a phone call in the middle of the night.

"Hi, is that George? It's Bob Geldof. I want you to fly back to London now."

"I'm in bed," I said. "It's five o'clock in the morning." I couldn't understand what he was going on about.

I splashed my face and called Tony. He said Geldof had called about some charity record; he said I should do it. When Bob called back he was ranting about starving children in Africa. "You have to come. You have to come." I said I'd try and get a flight first thing in the morning, which meant I would arrive back the following evening, in time for the recording.

I left New York without seeing Mikey and Roy. Tony told them about the event, but they didn't seem too interested. It was only when it hit the news that they were cut up and accused me of disloyalty.

I landed at Heathrow after a seven-hour flight, looking like a battered housewife, carrying three stuffed poodles under my arm. Billy picked me up and drove me straight to Sarm West Studios in Notting Hill. I was surprised when I arrived and saw the crowds and camera crews. Inside it was just as chaotic. There were so many stars milling around—Sting, Bono, the Durans, Status Quo, Bananarama, Midge Ure, Alison Moyet, Phil Collins, Paul Young, Spandau Ballet, Paul Weller. Jon was there with gray highlights in his hair. He was trying to look mature and sophisticated. He didn't pay me much attention; he was too busy schmoozing Sarah from Bananarama.

There were film cameras everywhere. When I went in to do my vocal on "Do They Know It's Christmas?" I was panicking. My God, they're going to film me singing without even a chance to practice. I didn't dare throw a pop-star tantrum.

I was meant to come in after George Michael, who'd already laid down his vocal and left the building. The voice on tape sounded just like Alison Moyet.

"Who's that?" I asked Bob.

"George Michael."

"My God, he sounds camp. But then he is."

Bob and Midge Ure rolled up at the mixing desk and my quip was captured on film and used. I was pleased about that.

The Band Aid event was one of the few times I've felt comfortable around other pop stars. It was as if everybody had deflated their egos for the evening. It all seemed very natural. There was no banquet laid on for the stars, just cups of tea and coffee and bacon and cheese sandwiches.

After the high of Band Aid came Culture Club's first chart flop. Our second single from *Waking Up,* "The Medal Song," failed to enter the Top 30. It was a real kick in the teeth after all the bad luck on the American tour. I was mortified. Jon just shrugged his shoulders. "What can we do? It's just one of those things." I wanted a reason, someone to blame. But Jon was right. Worrying about it didn't change the fact. We had to think about our next move. Old enemies cheered our demise. Frankie's Paul Rutherford said we were "old hat." Pete Burns said, "Poor Boy George. I think I'll send him a wreath." I was glad we had engagements in Europe—I couldn't wait to get out of the country.

We had to choose another single. I didn't want to take another track from the album after it had been given such hateful reviews. There was little choice. We decided to release "Mistake No. 3," ironically our third single and third mistake. The video, directed by David Mallett, was a Busby Berkeley extravaganza with me sat atop a huge revolving cake dressed like Auntie at the wedding in a white silk diamanté cape and a demented topiary-bush taffeta hat made by Stephen Jones. The video was ridiculous. We'd reached the pinnacle of excess.

I wanted Tony and Jon to cancel the up-and-coming U.K. Christmas dates. Jon argued against it. "If we're going to freak out at every obstacle we might as well give up now." That didn't seem such a bad idea. The first date in Edinburgh had slow sales and was pulled with the excuse that we couldn't get our stage set back from America in time.

The tour started instead at Birmingham's NEC. The three dates were a sellout, which lifted our spirits. I upset the band by having several female fans parade the stage during "Mistake No. 3" wearing the wedding dresses from the video. I thought it would look good, but they traipsed onstage like wet lemons. Jon threw a complete wobbler after the show. "You're trying to make us look like idiots." I told him, "I don't have to try." I did feel guilty. It certainly wasn't a malicious gesture, but I have to admit it didn't work.

The following morning Marilyn and Miss Binnie drove up from London to see the second show. Binnie gave me a tarot reading, my first ever. I learned a lot of new things about myself. She said there were two Georges—Boy George, who everyone knew and loved, and Girl Georgina, who no one knew and would be terrified if they did. Girl Georgina was my alter ego, my destructive half. Georgina was the one fighting to get out.

Tony came to my room. We had a screaming row. He agreed with Jon that the previous night's show was embarrassing. I knew he was right, but told him to fuck off anyway. We'd never had such a fight.

Marilyn was surprisingly objective. He said the best thing would be to leave Culture Club, have a break, and do something different. I wish I'd listened to him. The tarot reading was remarkably accurate, but I wasn't ready to take in any new information about myself. By accepting certain truths I would have to admit that I made mistakes. I wasn't open enough to be able to criticize myself, not when everyone else was doing such a good job.

Following Birmingham we played five nights at Wembley Arena. Not every night was a sellout but we didn't do badly, considering the odds against us. The final night was the most enjoyable show I ever performed with Culture Club. For the encore we played "Do They Know It's Christmas?" which by then had reached number one. Elton John, George Michael, Paul Young, and Bob Geldof, who were in the audience, joined us onstage. The crowd couldn't believe it.

I celebrated Christmas at home with Mum and Dad and the family, consoled that, despite everything, I still had a Christmas number one. I was proud of my brief performance on "Do They Know It's Christmas?" I was one of the few who didn't sing flat. We cringed at all the cats' choruses.

CHAPTER 32

I had to find myself a new home. My place in St. John's Wood, though in a secluded mews, opened onto the street. Fans were calling round, morning, noon, and night, beady eyes through the cracks in the curtains, giggling, hammering on the door, and running off. I frightened quite a few of them with my impression of a screaming hag. "Fuck off, you little bastards." It wasn't what they were expecting from their favorite doll-like pop star.

Only a week after moving in I received a hand-mailed letter from a fan taunting, "I know where you live." I sent her a get-well card and told her to rearrange these two words into a well-known phrase—Off Fuck.

Then one day a freelance photographer spotted Marilyn and me shopping in Kensington and followed us home. I went loopy and threatened to put a brick through his car window. He said he wouldn't take photos of the house if I did a roll of shots for him. I had no choice but to agree to his blackmail.

I thought about buying myself a Graceland, complete with electronic gates, security cameras, and Rottweilers. I looked at properties down "Millionaires Row," the Bishop's Avenue near Hampstead. The press caught word of it and the snobby residents drew up a petition. They didn't want a noisy pop star living down their select street. I even thought about moving to the country-side. Philip said I could get somewhere massive for half the price.

"Have your own private disco, like a modern version of the Elizabethan balls."

We went off one Sunday in Marilyn's car, Philip, Tranny Paul, and myself, to look at properties in the Hertfordshire green belt. We drove into the grounds of a house that looked deserted. It had a huge fountain in the middle of the drive. Marilyn went whizzing round. We were all screaming and carrying on. The front door opened sharply, a tall, elegant, and very angry old man came walking toward the car. Philip was the first to speak.

"Sorry, dear, we thought the house was empty. We're looking for a house for my friend."

The elderly gent peered into the car. When he saw me his face lit up. "My, my. Mr. Boy George. Well, I never. You've done so much for us. Why don't you come and have tea?"

Philip was delighted. He liked nothing more than to nose around other people's homes.

A portly chap was sitting in the living room in a dressing gown and slippers decorated with a fancy crest. He looked like an expensive Toby jug, welcoming us with a rosy smile. On the walls were pictures of the two gents with members of the Royal Family and politicians. Philip was excited and whispered, "They're in with the royals. Maybe we'll get invited to the garden party."

Philip's attempts to find out who they were and what they did were brushed aside. "Oh, it's not important, really." They told us they had an apartment in Los Angeles, right underneath the Hollywood sign. Dusty Springfield was their neighbor. They wouldn't talk about themselves, but they were happy to gossip about Dusty. I thought they were extremely hospitable, considering we'd almost mashed up their drive. We stayed chatting for over an hour and then drove off for another adventure.

Philip knew about a Hare Krishna temple in Letchmore Heath and said we should go there for a laugh. I wasn't sure it was a good idea. The previous Sunday, Philip took us to the Bhagwan Rajneesh temple in Belsize Park. They were having a "red" disco, jumping around in spiritual abandonment. Philip started mimicking them and they asked us to leave.

The devotees at the Krishna temple recognized me and were very friendly. Philip said, "Crawlers. They're only after your money." It was a festival day, and the place was overrun with Indian families who were bemused by our freakish presence. We watched a play about Krishna. Philip sniggered because the men were wearing dresses. "Drag queens, they're everywhere." I poked him. "Shut up, have a bit of respect."

After the play we were invited upstairs to a private room for an audience with a Krishna guru bigwig, Sri Dṛṣtadyumna, who was seated on a dais surrounded by attentive shaven-headed disciples and awestruck girls in saris, boys on one side, girls on the other. One of the girls was my old punk hero Polystyrene, who looked like she was floating off to another planet. From the moment Dṛṣtadyumna opened his mouth I knew there was going to be trouble. Philip's questions about their beliefs started a heated discussion. He asked why all the devotees were sitting there like "nodding dogs."

Dṛṣtadyumna replied, "They know all they need to know."

"That's ridiculous," said Philip. "You never stop learning." I had to agree.

Philip grilled him about sex and the movement's attitude to homosexuality. The answers were evasive. Philip was chanting, "Rubbish. Absolute rubbish."

We were served gorgeous vegetarian food, briefly filling the gap in Philip's mouth, a spiritual blessing for all, and left as soon as we could, none the wiser. Dṛṣtadyumna shouted at Philip, "We fed you."

On the way home we stopped off at journalist Jonathan Ashby's house. Philip said it would be a scream, but really he wanted to display his powers of delivery. We bundled into Ashby's house and had tea with the wife, the mother-in-law, and the kids.

Jonathan was a regular at Philip's Mud club. His disco visits were a mixture of business and pleasure. There were always pop stars passing through or passing out. Philip valued his press contacts too. More mentions, more people, more pennies. He liked Jonathan: he was Jewish and could be fed through the cage.

One Sunday we dressed Jonathan up as a woman and took him for a gay night on the town, unfortunately he looked more like a wrestler. He didn't know if we were trying to humiliate him or run him in. I was surprised he played along. It helped that Fat Tony and Tranny were also in drag. Tony was wearing a see-through pink baby-doll nightie with matching marabou-trimmed knickers and slingbacks. Tranny was in leopard-skin Lycra. Philip called them the Rhoea Sisters—Pyor, Diar, and Gonor.

Fat Tony, not to be confused with my manager, Tony Gordon, was by no means your traditional drag queen. His stage name was Diana Dogg, as if to send up the very idea. His look was modeled after Divine in *Pink Flamingos* and *Female Trouble,* and he recited the lines loudly, "Dawn Davenport's eating a meatball sandwich right out in class."

We met in 1980 down the Kings Road. Tony worked on a stall in the Great Gear Market, a fifteen-year-old fishwife with a view on everyone and everything, part tough, part camp, but instantly unforgettable. In those days he was tubby, hence the name, which apparently he gave himself. Over the years, through word of his own mouth, Tony became a more and more infamous DJ, and we became friends.

Our drag evening started with a Chinese meal in Paddington, we had the place to ourselves after clearing it with our dick jokes. I became suspicious when a photographer appeared outside the restaurant. It was hardly Langan's. I knew Jonathan must have tipped someone off. After being chased by the snapper we moved on to gay night at the Kensington Roof Gardens, where Jonathan almost got lucky. A rich old Arab stroked his face and said, "You don't have to wear makeup, you have a beautiful face." Tranny came to the rescue and saved him from a life behind the veil.

The house hunting went on in earnest, from Bishop's Avenue to Berkshire and back again. I wanted an old property with character, a house with many lives. Jon phoned one evening and said he'd found the perfect house in Hampstead. He laughed. "You could haunt the place." He drove me there and I instantly fell in love with it. A nineteenth-century Addams Family–style Gothic monstrosity. We had no appointment to view, but Jon said ring the bell, if anyone can get away with it you can.

"Hello."

"It's Boy George. I was just driving by, I wonder if I could look around."

The place was perfect, secure and set back from the street. A huge hallway with Roman arches, pillars, stained-glass windows, and a sweeping staircase. The decorations were a chrome and hessian nightmare, but I knew I could change them. I had to have it. The owners gave me a brief history of the house. It was previously owned by Marty Feldman, one of my favorite comedians, cowriter of *Round the Horne*. I could just picture him and Kenneth Williams round the kitchen table shrieking over scripts. It gave the place a whole new flavor.

The house was purchased quickly. I hired my brother Kevin to dismantle the offending decorations. He moved in with his tool kit and never left. Kevin was at the tail end of a disastrous marriage. Decorating my new home gave him the perfect escape route.

Kevin married Sheena when he was eighteen. They were the perfect suburban couple with matching perms, a Kev and Sheena windscreen sticker, furry dice, and a liking for jazz-funk.

It was Dad that insisted everybody went to his cousin's daughter's wedding—that's where the trouble started. A fight broke out at the reception between Sheena and the bride, of all the people she could have chosen.

The bride's mother stepped in. "Listen, you little slag, this is my daughter's wedding and you're not gonna spoil it."

Kevin came to the rescue. "What did you call my wife?"

The bride's mother calmly told Kevin, "You're a nice kid, I've always liked yer, but shut your fucking mouth."

Mum stood up, Campari in hand. "Typical O'Dowds. Typical."

A communal punch-up commenced, brothers, uncles, cousins, bruising to the tune of "Una Paloma Blanca."

During the fracas Gerald noticed Sheena and my eldest brother, Richard, leaving the hall together. He sensed skulduggery. After the last second cousin twice removed had been pulled off, he went outside to check. He caught Richard Sheena-handed.

"I'm gonna kill you, you dirty bastard."

Richard legged it down the road, Sheena followed. Gerald went back inside and told Kevin his wife was an old tart and set Richard's wife on her heels after the pair of them.

Things were never the same between Kevin and Sheena. Mum tried to smooth things over—the last thing she wanted was a divorce. But Sheena was frozen out of the family home, Kevin took his Maze albums and left.

When Mum told me the story I couldn't take it in. It was like one of the better episodes of *Coronation Street*.

I hired a firm of interior designers, recommended by Alison Hay, to create a Hollywood-style bedroom and add some other touches to the house. The renovations went on forever and cost a fortune. Dad said I'd been "mugged off." Still, I was pleased with the finished bedroom, a pink and cream starlet's cocoon with a raised four-poster bed and Jacuzzi.

I planned to build an underground swimming pool and garage. I invited the neighbors round to view the proposals, laying on tea and cucumber sandwiches. Philip said it would disarm them. It didn't work. They were a stuffy old lot and saw me as the tacky nouveau riche pop star I was. They scoffed at the plans, which were balmy and would have left me bankrupt.

I went on mad shopping sprees and ended up overfurnished, buying at whim high-tech, fifties retro, and ornate antique; nothing matched. I lined the staircase walls with silver, gold, and platinum discs, interspersed with homoerotica and religious artifacts, all the things that were important to me.

Kevin painted a sky on the kitchen ceiling and hung an upside-down chair from it, his contribution to modern art. The design clashed hideously with the beautiful teak ceiling beams. My decorations were as unsympathetic as the previous owner's.

I invited Bonnie over from New York to house-sit. I thought it would be good to have someone else living there other than Kevin. She could deal with my domestic affairs, phone bills, filling the fridge, buying the lightbulbs, and, more importantly, making sure Kevin didn't throw any wild parties. Kevin was metamorphosing from social worker to social butterfly. "Can I borrow your Gaultier jumper?"

Billy was upset when I hired a car and got Bonnie to drive me. Tony didn't like it much either. He said it wasn't safe for security reasons, but really he wanted Billy keeping an eye. Everyone was suspicious of Bonnie's presence, including my family. What was she after? Jon said, "Be careful, you don't know anything about her." I laughed. "Who do you think she is? Norma Bates?" They all thought they knew what was best for me. It must have seemed ridiculous letting her move in like that, especially when I'd built walls around me to keep people out.

Jon didn't like the fact that I was spending more and more time with Marilyn and my other "bitchy friends." I pleaded with Marilyn to be nice to Jon, but all my attempts to bring them together failed. I held a dinner party at Hampstead: Bonnie, Jon, Marilyn, and myself. There was a clash before I could even dish up the Marks & Spencer chicken Kiev.

Marilyn started teasing. "George, tell Jon about those cute boys we met the other night."

"What boys?"

"Tee hee hee."

Jon took the bait and stormed out.

I don't know how I ever persuaded him to come on holiday with us. Marilyn and I flew out to Jamaica. I phoned home and pleaded with Jon to join us. I invited Gay Robert, thinking he would be a moderating influence and keep Marilyn happy. Marilyn was aware that Robert was arriving with Jon, but pretended he knew nothing of it. He sneered at Robert, "What are you doing here?" Marilyn did his best to be as hateful as he could to Jon and Robert. Within days Robert was moaning that he wanted to go back to London; Jon wanted to drown Marilyn in the swimming pool.

We all went to dinner at a ritzy colonial restaurant. Marilyn started ribbing Jon and flicked a chip across the table. Jon overreacted. "If you do that again I'll smack you." Marilyn flicked another chip. Jon picked up his lobster thermidor and rubbed it in Marilyn's dreadlocks followed by a swift glass of Pimm's. Marilyn started screaming. Not knowing what to do, I laughed. I could hear the other diners: "Good God. That's disgusting."

Marilyn knocked his plate off the table and ran red-faced out of the restaurant. Jon went to go after him. I pulled him back. "Don't. He's been asking for it." The atmosphere at the villa was tense for days.

When Marilyn slipped off a rock and tore open his knee, Robert and Jon had to hold back their laughter. Marilyn was carrying on as if he needed major surgery. We took him to the nearby Couples Hotel. The resident nurse bandaged him up and gave him painkillers, and he sat by the pool like a dying swan.

It wasn't long before he was back to his old self. He told Robert, "If George wants to be with Jon, let him. We're gonna go off on our own." They were out of the villa before we woke. When Jon and I finally caught up with them on the beach, Marilyn was hostile. I couldn't believe his attitude. Robert got bored with Marilyn's game and told him, "We're all here together." Marilyn got bored with Robert and pleaded with me to fly Dencil Williams out. Desperate to create a harmonious atmosphere, I stupidly agreed.

Dencil's presence was a pain. He brought out a side of Marilyn that was best kept secured with an anal plug. All they wanted to do was look for hard drugs. The rest of us were happy to smoke ganja. They made Robert drive them to a shantytown in the hills where they scored cocaine rocks for freebasing. Robert was terrified, convinced they were all going to get their throats cut. When they arrived back Marilyn and Dencil locked themselves in their room. We didn't see them again till breakfast. Marilyn was walking around on invisible stilettos wearing a dried green face pack. He spent hours looking at himself in the mirror while Dencil lay on the bed purring like Eartha Kitt.

Robert got the brunt of their comedown. They gnawed at him so much he took an early flight back to London. Jon was quick to follow, he was sick of Marilyn's company and terrified for his bourgeois skin. Riots had erupted on the streets of Kingston over a rise in the price of petrol.

That holiday was a last-ditch attempt to bring Jon and me closer together. It would have worked if we'd gone alone. I wanted the best of both worlds, fun and love.

Marilyn was much happier after they'd gone. We made friends with the nurse at the Couples Hotel and spent our days on their private beach, sipping rum punch and scoffing the free barbecue. The rough Jamaican boys taunted Dencil as he minced across the sand. "Look 'ow she wiggle 'er pussy. Dirty blad clot." They asked him if he was fucking Bwoy Gearge.

After Jamaica, Dencil went home and Marilyn and I flew to

New York for two weeks. We stayed at the newly opened Morgans Hotel, where all the staff looked like Calvin Klein models. We roamed around Manhattan like a pair of demented unsociablites, running up ridiculous limousine bills and reputations to match. However much of a user Marilyn could be, he had style. If I complained about him taking advantage, he would say, "You know you want me to." I found the unpredictability of Marilyn exhilarating. I guess that's why I paid the bill.

Jon offered no exciting alternative. I would have loved a jet-set global romance, sex on the beach in Tangier, Bali, Barbados, wherever. It was just a dream. We weren't Liz Taylor and Richard Burton. We had nothing in common. He hated my friends. He didn't like clubs, gossip, or fashion, at least that's what he said, but I knew he had more than a few vile designer jackets and a thriving social life which excluded me. He was too embarrassed to bring me into his Jewish circle. A couple of his closest friends knew about our relationship, but it was generally hush-hush.

It wasn't that Marilyn led me astray: he reminded me to laugh, have fun, and not take myself so seriously. He was Sharon, the slag with the three-inch miniskirt, white stilettos, and snakeskin handbag who would jump into a passing car with a bunch of strangers. I was Wendy the frump in the high-collared blouse tugging on her arm, "Don't, Sharon, don't." Back in the old days I was just as willing to take risks, but success had sobered me. I had to think about my public image.

Marilyn would hang out of the limousine and whistle at boys in the street, "Yoo hoo, wanna come to a party? It's in my mouth," sometimes stopping to pick them up, rough Puerto Ricans and college jocks. We'd bring them to the Area club or Private Eyes.

During that trip to New York in January 1985 I dropped my first Ecstasy pill. A friend was handing them round like after-dinner mints. I was wary, but everyone else was doing it, and I didn't want to feel left out.

After half an hour the drug hit me like a sensuous tidal wave. I turned into a tactile temptress and wanted to stroke the whole planet. It gave me untold confidence. I walked up to a gorgeous Nordic blond at Area and asked him to come back to the hotel with me. He did.

The next morning I woke feeling liberated, like I'd opened Pandora's pillbox and found the meaning of life. I wanted to buy a whole bag of E. Marilyn had that told-you-so look on his face: he'd always preached the benefits of drug use. They were mystical and tribal, and put you in touch with yourself. Marilyn had spent too much time under Binnie's oil lamps. That night I managed to buy a few pills, which I shared with Marilyn. It was just as good the second time, the third, and the fourth.

At the height of Culture Club's fame when I should have been out whoring and scoring, I was in my room sipping English breakfast tea, plaiting my wigs. I was shielded from the Spinal Tap realities of the rock and roll world. I never imagined any of it was true until I experienced it firsthand. I didn't have to go looking for drugs, they were everywhere. "Do you wanna E? Do you wanna line?" Offering drugs was a shortcut to friendship with a pop star.

We all went to the Paradise Garage, a sweatbox for the disco-demented down in the West Village. It opened at midnight and carried on thumping until noon. On the way in you had to pass through a metal detector. Knives and guns were handed back on the way out. There was barely a white face to be seen.

Even though the club had a heavy reputation, we were never given any grief. People were surprised to see us in there, but they just smiled and carried on dancing. Dancing was what the Garage was all about; the music was hypnotic, early house and psycho-funk. One of the biggest floor stealers was a track called "Set It Off" by Straffe, which I went to buy on my way home. I even thought about recording it, I loved it so much. I thought, These are the kind of records I should be making.

We made friends with the DJ Larry Levan and hung out with him in the booth overlooking the dance floor. That's where all the drugs were. I took my first line of coke in that dark disco cocoon. I felt hypocritical as I put the rolled-up dollar bill to my nose. There were four lines in front of me, I aimed for the skinniest one and snorted up half of it. I was encouraged, "Go on, finish it." I handed him back the note. "No, it's okay." My eyes were watery, my mouth was dry, I could feel the chemicals slithering down my throat. That toot kept me buzzing for hours. Rabbit, rabbit, rabbit. I didn't need to take any more, though plenty was offered.

I'd always been very wary of drugs, of being out of control, but I also had a secret yearning to know what I was missing. My initiation to drugs was so casual, especially after all the years of pontificating against them. I dropped my first E among friends in a relaxed atmosphere, not in some dingy basement with a bunch of sordid dealers, although I was to meet quite a few of those in the months to come. Coke was a natural progression from E. One led to another like steppingstones across a murky stream.

CHAPTER 33

I already knew what I wanted to call the fourth album. I'd written
a song, "From Luxury to Heartache," which seemed to sum up
the moment.

> From luxury to heartache,
> Such a long way to find that you were mourning,
> From luxury to heartache,
> Such a long way, you gave me little warning.

A two-week songwriting session was arranged in January 1985,
which meant we had to turn our minds back on Culture Club. We
all knew there had to be a change of tactics. Jon was talking about
re-creating "the old magic." Given the dissension within the band
and the failure of the last album, I didn't fancy our chances.

I invited Phil Pickett down to Gaslight Studios in Brixton,
where we were writing, I didn't tell the others. Roy was surprised
to see Phil and thought it was a nice coincidence we were working
in the same place. Phil was embarrassed. I had to take Roy to one
side and explain.

Mikey and Roy were adamant that the weakness of *Waking Up*
lay with the melodies. I wasn't having it. I said all the program-
ming was ploddy and lifeless, the songs were good. Jon mediated:
he said I should listen to their criticisms. They wanted to approach

the songwriting in a different way. In the past all the songs had come from my melodies. They'd work out the basic chords, elaborate, and find new parts. Now they wanted to work the other way round, rhythms and chords first.

Mikey came up with a bass line and I begrudgingly came up with a chorus. "God Thank You Woman," they were the first words that came into my head, probably brought on by Roy's nagging that I never wrote songs about women. "Women are not all devils—you came from one." The fact that I was gay seemed to slip Roy's mind. My reality was a gay reality; it had nothing to do with misogyny. I told everyone "God Thank You Woman" was about my mum, which was a lie. It wasn't about anything, *nada* script; they loved it. They were determined to make the group more democratic, at any cost. I resented them commenting on my lyrics.

We argued about another new song, "Inequality," which I wrote about immigrant slave labor in America. Jon and Roy said the lyrics were patronizing.

What if you're a Mexican,
What if you're an Indian,
What if you're a Puerto Rican.

In retrospect the lyrics were naive. I didn't consider how they would be perceived: they only had to make sense to me. "Inequality" was blanded out and became the sickly sweet "Heaven's Children." Despite the problems, things were looking good after that initial writing session. Jon said it was creative conflict.

That same month I received the Variety Club of Great Britain award for Recording Artist of the Year. I couldn't work out why, but I didn't refuse. I was happy to be collecting an award for anything.

I camped up for the ceremony in an A-line Yohji Yamamoto coat and double false eyelashes, the crowning glory on a frighteningly over-made-up face. I sprayed a fluorescent yellow border around my hairline which made me look like a mad queen bee. Marilyn swaggered behind sporting his new geezer look, short spiky hair, unshaven face. He was method posing as the moody flip side of his former glamorous self. Marilyn told everyone he lopped off his dreadlocks first, a defensive measure; he knew it was a filthy lie. Still, he looked handsome as a bloke; he would have won the prize hands down.

He said, "People are bored of that old drag bullshit." I ignored his advice—he didn't even know what sex he wanted to be. When he came back from America he was Peter. Then he was Marilyn. It was so confusing. The only constant rule was that you never asked for Marilyn when you phoned his mum.

Marilyn became what he wore, whether it was the dizzy blond legend in the Antony Price dress, the sporty sequined pop star, or the new macho incarnation. He always had to have a theme, and he worked it to the last detail. Themes and obsessions kept Marilyn spinning.

CHAPTER 34

One afternoon I went round to Marilyn's flat in Maida Vale. He was lying in front of the TV, glued to a video of Diana Ross in Central Park. He kept rewinding and replaying his favorite bits, cooing compliments. "She's fab, she's brilliant." Then he switched to another video of Diana in Las Vegas. He sang along as she broke into "The Man I Love." He knew every ad-lib; he told me he was going to meet her and that she was going to love him.

To affirm his obsession he recorded an obscure Diana Ross song, "I Ain't Been Licked," as the B-side of his new single, "Baby U Left Me." I joked, "No one will believe that. Licked? You've been chewed and spat out."

February 1985, Marilyn went to New York to shoot the video for "Baby U Left Me" and stir up some interest in his career. He still hadn't managed to secure a U.S. deal, despite having success on the import chart. He had an underground reputation in New York and some of the big cities. He enrolled his journalist pal Sydney Masters as his "American secretary." She wore out her phone, credit card, and feet trying to prove her love and dedication. Sydney met Marilyn in 1983 when she flew to London to interview him for a U.S. pop magazine. She was really mixing business with torture when she innocently offered him a place to stay if he was ever in New York.

Marilyn phoned all excited to say he was performing at New

York's Area club on February 20. He wanted me to be there and read out his VIP list—Joan Rivers, Christopher Reeve, Andy Warhol. I laughed. "Andy Warhol would go to the opening of your legs." I really wanted to go, but I'd promised Mum I'd take her to see Phil Collins's royal performance at the Albert Hall, attended by Princess Di, and it was on the same night. Marilyn called constantly over the next few days. "You are coming, Blanche?" He left endless messages on the answering machine. "I know you're there, Dawn Pigport."

Friday afternoon I decided to cancel Mum. I packed a bag and hurried off to Heathrow to catch the evening Concorde. Had I told anyone I was paying £2,576 to hear Marilyn sing they would have questioned my sanity. Still, I was turned on by the Joan Collins of it all. I arrived in New York at 7 P.M. and went straight to Morgans Hotel. I didn't call Marilyn, I decided to surprise him. I rang my friend Nick Egan and his girlfriend, Ellen Kinnally, and arranged to meet them at the club.

Area was buzzing, press, punters, celebrities, just as Marilyn had predicted. He was about to launch himself on the makers and shakers of New York. There was a fantastic vibe. I arrived just as he took to the stage. Screams, whoops, and whistles filled the air. I stood at the back and watched like an anxious stage mother. He opened his mouth to sing and there was a loud buzz. It was only feedback, but Marilyn lost his nerve. "Fuck this!" he snapped and ran from the stage. I could see people shaking their heads. I made my way over to the sound booth to see what was wrong. DJ Johnny Dynell was operating the sound, he didn't seem to know either.

Several long minutes passed, then the crowd started to disperse. Johnny put on a record and Marilyn became a figment of our anticipation. I was told he'd walked straight offstage into a waiting limousine. People were asking me, "What happened? Is he going to sing?" I was as baffled as they were. I felt like a complete idiot having come all that way.

When I found Nick and Ellen they were laughing in disbelief. "What's he like?" Nick said it wouldn't have been Marilyn without a performance. We all agreed that Marilyn had poo-poo-pe-dooed his big chance. He wouldn't be able to draw a crowd like that again.

When I saw Marilyn later at the Limelight club he started screaming at me. He said Dencil had seen Nick, Johnny, and me laughing when the sound broke down. I told him he was being pathetic, he just needed someone to blame. We didn't speak for the rest of the night.

In a room behind the Limelight Star Bar, a sodden Billy Idol was whacking a drum kit. A bare lightbulb swung above his head illuminating his peroxide tuft and overtanned skin. He was no longer the angelic baby-faced boy that made me gasp at Louise's. A handful of coked-up sycophants were milling around, soaking up his celebrity. It was surreal and tragic, and very New York.

The next morning I awoke feeling lonely and foolish. I met up with Nick and Ellen to go shopping. I wore out my credit card at Charivari buying overpriced Yohji, then we went for lunch at Richoux. Marilyn phoned early evening. He was still on the Johnny Dynell warpath, annoyed that I wouldn't take his side. I told him it wasn't Johnny's fault. I warned him to expect bad press. He was unrepentant. I could hear Dencil in the background, chuckling like Toad of Toad Hall, obviously pleased to have worked Marilyn's nerves.

Marilyn and Dencil were partners in slime, Dencil snooting around in his black spiky fun-fur coat, arse jutting out, nose in the air, acting like he was heir to the Mugabe dynasty. Dencil had an undeniable presence, black as midnight with feline features, a mixture of Lloyd Honeygan and Naomi Campbell. I never understood what motivated him. He was a good-time girl with airs and graces, tripping out on his own fabulousness. Both he and Marilyn knew they were better than me. It was only a matter of time before the world caught on.

It was beyond reason that I would splash out on Concorde just to poke Marilyn in the ribs. But he was convinced of my treachery. Marilyn was now freebasing cocaine regularly, which might have explained his deficient logic. He swore blind that he wasn't basing before he went onstage at Area: "I would never do that, it's unprofessional." Even so, the aftereffects are long-lasting. Whatever the cause, there were more reasons to be friendly with me than not.

The base pipe became our peace pipe. Behind the drawn curtains and DO NOT DISTURB sign at Morgans Hotel I made a deeper connection with my lower self; my first experience of freebasing cocaine, sucking the devil's dick. The rush was orgasmic and desperate. My head and chest full of dirty white toxic fumes. Joy and fear, panic then paranoia. I wanted to grab the pipe and get some more. We all did, Dencil, Sydney, and myself, but Marilyn had a tight grip.

Outside, New York seemed flat as we stood waiting for a taxi to take us to Private Eyes. We were higher than the Empire State, no one said a word, just lots of eyes. We made it to the club despite the temptation to go back and give some more head. At Private Eyes I bought a small vial of coke from a loud lesbian friend to keep the buzz going.

While we were in New York Marilyn persistently tried to make contact with Diana Ross. He discovered she had an apartment at the Sherry Netherland Hotel on Fifth Avenue, and insisted we move there from Morgans. I said he was being ridiculous, but was soon seduced by the adventure. We moved in. Marilyn discovered Diana Ross's code name, Mrs. Blue. He left her repeated messages and couldn't understand why she didn't return his calls. He made excuses: "Oh, she's probably out of town. She'll call." He tried creeping up the back stairs to get to her apartment, but could only get as far as the security gate.

Bored with that, Marilyn suggested we fly to L.A. for the Grammy Awards. He said it would be good for my image. My best interests always coincided with a glamour event. We left Sydney and Dencil in New York and flew out to Los Angeles planning to take in a few days' sun before the event. Jim Rodman booked us into the Bel Air.

That first morning, I received an unexpected alarm call from Jim. "Marilyn's asked me to hire a convertible Mercedes on my AmEx." I laughed, still sleepy. "Cheeky bastard." Marilyn acted all innocent. "Oh, I didn't want to wake you. It was a surprise. I was going to drive us to Palm Springs."

As we were leaving for our day trip I was ambushed in the car park by a creepy paparazzo. "Hi, George, you look great in blue." I pulled my jacket over my head, jumped into the car, and screamed at Marilyn to drive off. Eager to make his money, the photographer trailed us at top speed down Santa Monica Boulevard. I was getting more and more upset. Marilyn broke every road code trying to lose him. Finally, he gritted his teeth, "Watch this." He slammed on the brakes, forcing the rat into our rear with an almighty crash. I was hysterical. "The car, the car." Marilyn didn't seem to care. I leaped out to check the damage. Luckily there wasn't even a scratch on our Merc. His VW Beetle was crumpled, steaming and going nowhere fast. He waved his fist at us. "Assholes. You'll leave L.A. in chains." Marilyn blew him a kiss and we drove off.

Palm Springs was a waste of a journey, nothing but suntanned wrinklies and candy stores. I whistled at two boys and they threw stones at us. Marilyn drove up to Bob Hope's house and urged me to ring the bell. He imagined Bob would open the door and invite us in for tea.

The day before the Grammys we went shopping. On Marilyn's advice I bought myself a classic linen suit from Maxfield's on Melrose Avenue. I was sure it wasn't me, but Marilyn insisted. "It's a fab new look." I bought Marilyn a black pin-striped suit, we were both being boys.

I tried to get Liz Taylor to be my date for the Grammys and Marilyn asked Joan Rivers. Neither of them could make it. Liz was appearing in *The Little Foxes* in London, and she phoned to say she would love to any other time. Joan sent Marilyn a bunch of balloons and invited us to her show.

We considered several other legends, but decided to be realistic. I phoned my friend Pinkie and told her to dress for the cameras. Marilyn invited Monroe lookalike Linda Kerridge; he thought someone might notice he was parodying himself.

We arrived at the Shrine Auditorium in a white stretch limo and were cheered by the crowds. Marilyn and Linda looked like a normal couple, Pinkie and I were mad freaks. I felt so uncomfortable in my man drag. Pinkie was dressed like a mobile gâteau in a tiered bustle dress and massive Busby Berkeley hat.

Inside it was all black tie and turkey-wrap ballgowns. John Travolta waved at me and blew a kiss. I wanted to go and meet him, but the lights went down. A woman behind demanded Pinkie remove her hat. She did so without protest. Underneath was even more view-blocking exotica, a fake dove perched upon a cluster of purple ringlets.

Prince was the main recipient that year. He received three Grammy Awards, yet didn't deign to collect any of them himself, despite being backstage and quite able to trot in his Cuban heels. Various caped members of his entourage collected the awards, thanking God. Prince had sold the most records that year, and the industry was going to kiss his pert bottom. I could see the rest of the proceedings were merely a buildup. Only Tina Turner shone through, singing her comeback hit, "Let's Stay Together." It was touching to see her receive a standing ovation after a long exile in the cabaret wilderness. Some years later Elton John dragged me backstage to meet her at Wembley Arena. I was embarrassed. Elton insisted, "No, she's fabulous, she's a Buddhist." The dressing room was crowded. Elton said, "Tina, this is Boy George." She turned her back. Luckily Faye Dunaway was there, she hugged me and spared my blushes.

After that every time Tina Turner was mentioned I adapted the Buddhist chant "Nam-myoho-renge-cow, Nam-myoho-renge-cow." I detested her for years but forgave her when I saw the movie of her life.

After the Grammys we went to see Joan Rivers at Carlos and Johnny's club on Sunset Boulevard. She was hilariously vile. I was glad I sat at the back, especially when she told her Boy George jokes.

That night on *Entertainment Tonight* they reported on the Grammys. They showed a clip of me arriving with Pinkie and said it was my "close pal" Marilyn. Marilyn was livid: his attempt to promote his new butch self was foiled by a swish of Pinkie's bustle skirt. He called up the TV station and demanded a retraction.

We left the palm trees and returned to New York, setting up camp at Morgans Hotel. The first thing we did was buy a couple of grams of coke and a bag of weed. It was nice to be home and high. Our trip to L.A. had been virtually drug-free, except for a couple of joints and some Valium that I nagged off Jim. I told him I needed it for the flight.

Our main dealer in New York was a fat Mohican guy down on Columbus Avenue. He claimed to be a producer but was more famous for the celebrities he supplied. Marilyn would call, "Are you in?" Then Sydney would go off in a taxi. We told her to be quick, she never was. Another dealer, "Sweaty Roger," offered a door-to-door service. We called him the pizza man. He supplied us with freebase rocks and often joined in our sessions. Roger was all deathly drawn and desperate, setting up the pipe, sucking like his life depended on it.

Once you hit that pipe you can't stop. Each hit is like a mental ejaculation, but you're never sated, so you keep grabbing and grabbing, all eyeing the pipe like it's the last morsel to a pack of dogs. We were like crazed fugitives, suspicious of each other and the furniture. Marilyn was so nutty he Sellotaped the curtains to the windowsill and kept looking in the cupboards, "Shh, what's that?" When room service came we all hid in the bedroom and made Sydney answer the door. "Don't let 'em in."

During one of our daytime sessions Marilyn had an all-powerful revelation. He said he knew how to get Diana Ross to call back. I rolled my eyes. "Why don't you just forget it?" He rang and left a message saying he wanted her to manage him.

Some forty minutes later the phone rang. I couldn't tell if it was the bells in my head or the real thing. I picked it up and waited.

"Hello."

"Yes?"

"Can I speak with Marilyn, please?"

"Who is it?"

"Diana Ross."

I covered the mouthpiece and shouted, "It's her."

Marilyn grabbed the phone, and the room stood still. They spoke for two minutes, then he announced smugly, "Told ya she'd call. I'm meeting her tomorrow."

The next day Diana sent a limousine to take Marilyn out to Knotsberry Farm in Connecticut where she was performing. I took a long bath, brooded over a club sandwich, and waited for him to return with the gossip. He didn't come back until the early hours. He said Diana hugged him on sight, called him beautiful, said he should be a film star, and offered to manage him. Whatever the truth was, that meeting gave his life new purpose. He was talking about his career again, getting a new look together, he was enthused.

I was also full of plans for my resurgence. I talked constantly of leaving Culture Club. When we were high we had ideas coming out of our ideas. We were desperate to be on top of our lives, but were doing everything we could to screw them up.

CHAPTER 35

London was full of rage and disappointment. Whenever I went back I couldn't wait to leave. I was a failure at home, at least in my screwed-up head. Culture Club had been buried, and "Karma Chameleon" was our chirpy epitaph. I kept away from the clubs and the style hyenas.

On top of my shame there was Jon to deal with. I couldn't leave him alone, even though I knew he'd lost all respect for me. I'd call him the minute I landed. We'd end up in bed; the perfect home-coming.

Sex was our unspoken agreement, but it was never enough for me. After the initial excitement of having him, I was left with the same empty feelings that fueled the internal, external wars. The easiest way to avoid it was to fly away, Paris, New York, places where I was still celebrated.

When I couldn't escape I went to visit my friend Alan Roberts in Chiswick. He was a shoulder to moan on. He would cook me curries and listen to my woe-is-me tales.

Alan had been a barman at the Blitz club. He was like so many people I'd seen around for years but never spoken to. In those days you'd dismiss someone for having the wrong haircut. We didn't become friendly until Culture Club were big-time. He was chief designer at a merchandise company we were using. I got him to make stage clothes for the band and we became friends. I still call him my Jewish mother. Every time I went round there he would insist on feeding me.

When I flew to Paris for the menswear fashion collections I took Alan with me. We were so excited—neither of us had ever been to a real fashion show. I didn't tell him I had no tickets; I was sure my eyebrows would get us in. His flatmates, Johnny Rico and Karen Elton, came with us.

It was gray and miserable in Paris. We took a taxi to the Champs-Elysées and booked into the first hotel we could find, the Marriott. We were all in a fabulous mood. I hurried everyone to get ready, then spent an hour deciding what to wear.

We arrived late for the Yohji Yamamoto show. They led us in and gave us good seats. It was the perfect entrance, everyone whispering and staring. There was darkness, somber music welled up, and the models morgued down the catwalk, malnourished boys in pleated skirts and lopsided jackets. All the clothes were for twigs, none of it would have fit me. Alan said he could run it up for half the price.

After the show we mingled with the crowd, I was desperate to get stoned. There were loads of familiar faces from London. I asked around to see if anyone could get me some smoke. I'd become very indiscreet about my cool new habit. A stylist friend pointed out an Algerian photographer and said he supplied the models. I got him to introduce us and we went outside. "How much you want?" he asked. I didn't have a clue, I'd never bought drugs myself. I just bluffed. "Let me see it." He pulled a flat block of hash from his pocket. He wanted 250 francs. I didn't know if he was ripping me off, but I paid him anyway.

"You like 'eroin, Ecstasy?" Without thinking I said yes. He handed me a tiny envelope covered in clingfilm and a white tablet, taking the rest of the money out of my hand, about seven hundred francs. He could have given me anything, cocoa powder, aspirins. I stashed the drugs in my sock.

Next stop was the Jean-Paul Gaultier show at the Cirque de Paris, the place was swarming, even people with tickets couldn't get inside. They let me in, but not the others. I ran around trying to find a sympathetic official face and managed to get the others in just as the show started.

Straightaway I had a run-in with a snotty buyer. "Sit down, sit down. I can't see."

"Shut up, you old cow. Have you ever been fucked with a spiked dildo?" I couldn't believe I'd said it. The sluice gates just opened. She was horrified to hear such language from a cuddly pop star, but it did the trick.

I saw Jeremy Healy in the seats behind. His girlfriend, Lizzie Tear, was in the show. I waved. "Hi, Jeremy." He gave me a Jack Frost stare. I wished I hadn't bothered.

I went backstage afterward, met Gaultier, and eyed up the models. It was a voyeur's paradise, bums and tits everywhere. Gaultier gestured to the boys like they were fruit on a stall. "You like zis one. Yes, very nice." He invited me over to his showroom. He seemed a lovely man.

Stephen Jones was backstage looking pleased, he'd made all the hats for the show. He invited us to dinner at La Coupole. We arranged to meet at 9:30 P.M., then Alan, Karen, and I went back to the hotel.

I locked myself in the hotel bathroom, took the drugs from my sock, and unfolded the small envelope. I rolled up a franc note, held it in my fingers, and took a polite toot. It tasted rancid. I retched, head spinning, eyes streaming, demons in my saliva. I was scared that I'd taken too much.

The nausea quickly turned to serenity. My body was filled with a sense of relief that one day I would know well. I walked dizzily to the bed and lay down with my new sensation. Alan was dozing, I closed my eyes and fell asleep.

Heroin was available so I took it. It could have been any drug. If the guy had given me LSD I would have popped that too. I was well aware of its reputation, that it was habit-forming and could kill. I hadn't forgotten Mitsu's squalid death in the basement of Warren Street, but somehow in the moment it didn't seem to matter.

I woke startled, not knowing where I was. Alan was wrapped in a towel, watching TV. I went to the bathroom and splashed my face, I couldn't be bothered to shower. I stretched and yawned. "I feel weird."

"What, ill?"

"Just weird."

I took another toot in front of Alan. He shook his head, "What's that? Breakfast?"

I shrugged. "Can't take it back to London with me."

It was almost ten. We got dressed quickly, split an E, and went off to La Coupole. It took ages to get a cab. By the time we reached the restaurant the E was coming on.

Stephen and his guests were halfway through their meal. The last thing I wanted was food. The place was packed with models, designers, and fashion freaks. Simon Le Bon, Nick Rhodes, and their glamorous girlies were at another table.

As I was chatting to Stephen I felt the sudden urge to throw up. I stuck my head under the table and vomited over the floor. Everybody looked horrified. Alan ran out of the restaurant. I chased after him. "What's wrong?" He felt ill and wanted to go back to the hotel. I tried to make him stay, but he wouldn't. I felt guilty going back inside, but I was high and wanted to go clubbing.

I shortly found myself in the girls' toilet rolling a joint with the beautiful wife of a fellow pop star. Then we all went off to Le Palais for the Fashion Week party. I borrowed a pair of sunglasses, my eyes were on stilts and the place was swarming with cameras. I didn't get back till 5:30 A.M. The next morning Alan was ashen and apologetic; he said he felt like death. I felt normal. We both laughed about me throwing up over Stephen Jones's shoes. "It's a good job it wasn't one of his hats."

When Culture Club traveled to Austria for a TV spectacular, Alan came under the pretext of wardrobe mistress. Really I wanted to have a friend around—being with the band was so boring. We stayed in picturesque Innsbruck where the only excitement I could find was the local wig shop. I bought myself a Mary Quant bob wig and joked that I was going to wear it on TV. I was modeling it on the way to the dress rehearsal. Alison piped up from the back of the coach, "I don't think so."

"Piss off, pop star's wife. What's it got to do with you?"

Roy jumped out of his seat. "Don't talk to my wife like that."

"You should keep her quiet."

Then Jon started. "Come on, George. You're out of order."

"I like the way you stick up for her, dwarf."

When we arrived I stormed off to the dressing room, quite sure I was in the right. Alison came to make it up. It wasn't long before we were at it again. Alison didn't think Roy was getting enough camera shots and wanted me to tell the producer. I told her to bloody do it herself.

The set was pink. None of my clothes went with it. Alan was sure he could create something suitable in time for the show that evening. He went off with Billy in search of some cloth and a sewing machine. In under six hours he made me a floor-length pink-sequined coat, cut out on the hotel floor and sewn together on a prehistoric sewing machine.

After the show we were invited to Brooke Shields's party. She was in town promoting her new line of clothing. Just before we left the hotel Tony came to my room, he'd received a call from Brooke's agent.

"Were you rude about Brooke Shields?"

"Rude?" Then I remembered. I'd recently been asked by an American magazine to list my ten worst-dressed women. Brooke Shields was one, for wearing Michael Jackson too often. It was only lighthearted, but her agent was worried I might be hostile. I reassured Tony.

Brooke was greeting her guests at the door. I was smoking one of Alan's menthol cigarettes. She said, "You shouldn't smoke. It's bad for you."

I replied, "So is getting fucked up the arse, but I do that every night."

She couldn't hide her disgust, but smoothed it over with celebrity falserity. During the party Roy went to shake her hand and squeezed a shelled boiled egg into it. She shrieked, but was forced to laugh with the rest of the room. She must have thought we were a bunch of monsters.

The next time I saw her was at Grace Jones's birthday at the Palladium in New York. She was with George Michael. Marilyn and I kept whispering in her ear, "He's a poof, he's a poof." She didn't know what it was, but looked worried.

After Innsbruck Alan flew back to London, the band drove through the Alps to Montreux to meet up with producer Arif Mardin at Mountain Studios. The plan was to record two songs to test the waters. None of us wanted to jump into a whole album for fear it might be an expensive disaster.

Tony, Roy, Alison, and Mikey stayed in a plush hotel near the studio. Jon and I stayed in a private chalet, nicknamed "The Bunker," set into the hillside by Lake Geneva. Jon stayed with me as a matter of course. The chalet had several bedrooms, so there was always an escape, and there were plenty of times when he needed to.

Most mornings Jon was gone before I woke up, having breakfast in one of the town cafés or taking a long walk by the lake. We didn't see a lot of each other, which gave the illusion that we were getting on. I made regular visits to the studio, but didn't hang around. As always I found it too boring. The band would busy themselves in the studio, play pool, or watch TV in the roadies' flat underneath. But I had nothing to do and no one to talk to.

Most days I rose in the afternoon, hazy from my late-night dope sessions. The first thing I did was roll another spliff, which didn't help my voice. I lost the top of my range and couldn't be bothered to sing when I was expected to. Arif handled me well. He knew a lot about temperaments, having worked with eccentric Aretha and topsy-turvy Chaka. "No problem," he would say, "there's plenty to do." By avoiding pressure he finally got what he wanted. Arif was a sweet man, like a lovely old uncle.

Even though we liked him, there was conflict. Arif said some of our new songs were weak. We were so beaten down by the failure of *Waking Up* that we questioned our own judgment. We'd never listened to anyone else in the past. Jon was worried that we were giving him too much say. We agreed to wait for the final mixes before we made a decision. I was so stoned everything sounded good to me.

To fill in lots of spare time I bought a word processor and started writing stories about meeting other rock stars and my views on fame. I sat through the night, toking and typing. "The Billy Idol Rich," "The Five O'Clock Shadow," which was about Marilyn.

Club-goers from London to New York spit at the mere mention of his name. We hate Marilyn, we hate his attitude, and attitude is something Marilyn has plenty of. Long before his first hit he was cutting them all to the quick. A hedonistic drag queen that everyone loved to hate.

I read it over the phone to Marilyn. "You'd better be joking. I'll sue." He was shocked by my wheezing and ticked me off for smoking so much. He considered it the most shocking thing I'd ever done. "What about your asthma?" I wasn't a professional, I didn't inhale. It was just something else to break the monotony.

I was so bored I invited Philip Sallon out to Montreux and offered to pay for his hotel. Knowing Philip's attachment to London and his telephone, I didn't think he would come. He phoned back saying he'd managed to persuade Cadillac Graham to drive him over in one of his vintage American cars and would I mind if he brought Tranny Paul and Michael Prew? Typical Philip, he couldn't go anywhere without an entourage. He forgot to mention he'd also invited Linda Queenie.

When they went to collect Queenie from her torture chamber in Old Compton Street she was kicking an Indian punter down the stairs. He moaned, "Madame, I came here for correction, not torture."

"I'll give you correction," she screamed, and he flew out of the door. At Queenie's the customer was always wrong. They could hardly complain to the police.

Queenie left for Montreux in a fur coat and skimpy lingerie, clutching a whip in case of bother. It came in handy on the P&O ferry. A group of schoolchildren were laughing at Philip and Tranny. Tranny was in drag and Philip was wearing a Womble coat. Queenie cracked the whip. "What you little bastards laughing at?" Their teacher hurried them along.

Philip promised to pay for Queenie's meals, but refused when it came to the bite. He said she could share his plate. "You schnorra." She grabbed a handful of chips and legged it across the canteen singing, "You gotta pick a pocket or Jew . . . "

French Customs were startled by five freaks in a Cadillac. Queenie flashed open her coat, "Voulez-vous coucher avec moi?" They were lucky to be waved through. Then halfway across France the car almost blew up. Queenie and Philip had another fight. She

jumped out of the car and offered him out. "Come on, yer bastard, come on." Philip declined the catcall. He knew she'd mince
him. They were all whacked out when they arrived in Montreux.
Only Philip was running on full batteries. I was annoyed that he'd
brought Queenie and that I had to pay for another room. He just
sniggered. "Oh, she's a laugh."

The next morning Alison came with me to their hotel. Queenie
wasn't happy. "What kind of dump is this?" She meant the town,
not the hotel. She said she'd been out at the crack of dawn and
hadn't seen one "schwarze." She was yodeling and spreading her
legs. When we left Alison asked why she was so coarse. I had to let
her into Queenie's secret.

Philip and Co. brought life to Montreux. Our visits to the
casino disco were talked about long after their departure. It was
amusing to watch boys ogling Queenie's breast, deliberately on
display through her lacy bra. Every so often she'd pop them out.

"Get a load of that, luv. National Health, these."

I threw a farewell party at the bunker. Andre set up a makeshift
studio in one of the bedrooms and took portraits. Philip was
dressed up like an Indian goddess. Tranny and Queenie wore as
little as they could. Queenie stuck her hand up Mikey's girlfriend's
skirt and asked, "Are you the one fucking the schwarze? Once you
go black there's no turning back." Mikey and his girlfriend left in
a huff.

After they'd left I invited Mum and Dad out. Dad was conva-
lescing from his bypass operation. I thought the clean air would
do him good. He was pale and drawn and more subdued than I'd
ever known him. One morning I went round to collect them for
breakfast. They were sleeping. I was shocked when I saw the huge
scar down Dad's chest. It brought home how ill he'd really been
and how much he meant to me.

When Mum visited the bunker she picked up a piece of hash
and wanted to know what it was. "This ain't no Swiss chocolate."
I told her it was Jon's. She was tearful when I owned up to smoking spliff. Dad was cool; he wanted to try it. "Don't encourage
him, Jerry."

After a month in Montreux I flew to Paris and met up with
Marilyn, Tony, and Avi for a party in honor of the genius costu-

mier Erté, hosted by actress, singer, and celebrity-snatcher Régine. Tony and I befriended Régine after Culture Club appeared on her TV show. A small tough woman with flame orange hair and viciously plucked eyebrows, her rendition of Gloria Gaynor's seventies gay disco hit "I Will Survive" made her popular with French gays. Her friendship was only sequin deep and waned with my popularity.

I was told to arrive at Régine's nightclub at eleven o'clock for a photo call with Erté, Régine, and Joan Collins, but Marilyn and I got stoned at the hotel. I got the munchies and ordered heaps of room service. Then I couldn't decide what to wear. "I'm too fat, I can't go."

Down in the hotel lobby I bumped into Charlie Watts, Bill Wyman, and Ronnie Wood from the Rolling Stones. I was so excited, they were real legends. Marilyn stropped off and sat in a chair with his back to us. Years later I bumped into Charlie at Heathrow. He asked, "Do you still see that moody little bastard Marilyn?"

The clock was striking the witching hour when we finally arrived at Régine's. Joan Collins was on her way out. She gave me a glare and smiled. "How dare you keep us waiting?" Marilyn and I posed with her for the cameras. Erté had gone to bed—he was ninety-two, after all.

CHAPTER 36

I was so proud when I was invited to appear at the fiftieth anniversary celebrations of the Apollo Theatre in Harlem, New York City. I was scared too: it was my first appearance without Culture Club. I'd been asked to duet "Signed, Sealed, Delivered" with Stevie Wonder and another undecided song with Luther Vandross. As usual Tony elaborated the facts, telling me I was the only white artist on the bill. I discovered that wasn't the case when I arrived at Heathrow and saw George Michael strutting through the Concorde lounge.

I went to New York early, hoping for a rehearsal with Stevie and Luther. Stevie was recording in Los Angeles and wouldn't be flying in until the day of the show, and Luther was probably buying a fur coat. I sang "Signed, Sealed, Delivered" over and over, driving everyone mad. My press agent, Jo Bailey, who had an adjoining room, said she was hearing it in her sleep.

The morning of the show I developed my usual psychological sore throat. I was in a total state. Marilyn arrived at the hotel in a glorious showbiz mood and a full-length white fake-fur coat. He laughed when I said I wasn't going. "All those fab Motown stars are gonna be there and you're not going. Really."

The excitement of arriving in Harlem, already buzzing with the big day, made me temporarily forget my predicament. But a call to Stevie Wonder's dressing room secured the noose. Stevie was hammering away at a keyboard and grunted a quick hello in mock Cockney. I stood rigid, wondering if I'd have to practice in front of his entire entourage. He sang "Signed, Sealed, Delivered." Even raw he sounded brilliant. I hummed along, not daring to sing out. Five minutes of rehearsal convinced me we should try another song. Stevie persisted, "You can do it, you can do it." I knew I sounded weak. I decided to let Tony argue for me. After a bit of managerial wrangling we agreed on "Part Time Lover."

I sat in on the rehearsals and watched Sammy Davis, Jr. He was fantastic, skipping about the stage like a nimble youth. Only his chesty cough gave him away. He shook my hand. "How ya doin', kid?" I went over to meet Patti LaBelle, who was sitting at the back in black shades. She gave me a big hug.

I took pictures of every cute cop on the block. The boys in blue were in every nook, but unfortunately not in every tranny. Andre Csillag was running around looking for legends to snap with me. He dragged me upstairs to meet Little Richard, who was hysterical, eyes popping, hands up to heaven. "Ooh, look at you, boy. You so big and fine, and pretty too." For once I had nothing to say.

I had a "hidgeous" dress rehearsal. Stevie was charitable, but Luther used me as a mop during our rendition of "What Becomes of the Broken-Hearted?" Marilyn, who was watching, heard a couple of Luther's people enjoying the kill. I was relieved to hear Smokey Robinson murdering George Michael's "Careless Whisper"—he sounded like a throttled duck. Rod Stewart sang "Dock of the Bay" casually and soulfully, which made us all look like we had white man's disease. I went to my dressing room and rolled a huge spliff. Not even my floor-length Gaultier dress coat could save me now.

Onstage my white suburban tones were drowned out by Stevie. I shuffled around awkwardly, thankful it wasn't talent night. Tony said I was wonderful. Marilyn's silence spoke the greater truth.

There was venom in the green room for Diana Ross. A former Motown pal snarled, "In my day we saved vegetables for bitches like that." Diana had flown in by helicopter after a live date in Atlantic City and slithered onstage for the finale. Patti LaBelle was onstage too, lifting the roof. The next morning a critic sniped,

"Miss LaBelle hit notes that Diana Ross could only reach by Concorde." Bitchiness was the mood of the day; there was little Motown love flowing around.

Diana invited Marilyn into her double star dressing room. He said it was like an audience with the Queen. Other celebrities kept popping in to kiss her ring. Luther Vandross was one of them. He greeted everyone, then sneered at Marilyn. "Uh. What are you doing here?" Marilyn was devastated, being a huge fan—he was forever playing his records.

We'd both met Luther only a few weeks before. Helen Terry was recording with him and brought him over to Morgans Hotel for a surprise visit. He seemed so down-to-earth even in his ankle-length wolf-fur coat. "Try it on," he said. "I'm sure it'll fit." He was obviously being sarcastic as he was no Slimcea girl himself.

At the after-show dinner, Stevie Wonder grabbed me by the throat, probably rewarding me for my performance. The photographers swooped before I could break free. I was angry that he'd made me ridiculous for a second time and wondered how he'd managed to aim so well. "Bastard, bet he can see."

For Marilyn there was only one star at the Apollo, and it wasn't me. He kept going on and on about Diana Ross. He said if I saw one of her shows I'd change my mind. Two days later I was funding an excursion to Atlantic City, and I wasn't even a fan. We arrived at New York City heliport to discover there were no scheduled flights. Marilyn was like a disappointed child. The only option was to charter one at $900. Our flight was a white-knuckle nightmare, the tiny helicopter blowing everywhere. Marilyn couldn't contain his glee, he kept sticking his nose out of the sliding window, I was tearful. "Stop, stop, we're gonna crash."

When we arrived at the Golden Nugget casino, Diana was in full schmaltz. Steve Wynn, the casino boss, led us to our seats, which were frighteningly close to the stage. I had an unnerving feeling that we were going to be part of the cabaret. During "Reach Out and Touch," Diana made her way over and handed me the microphone. I felt like one of the Muppets warbling a painful refrain. "Ladies and gentlemen, Boy George." Marilyn wouldn't sing, she told the crowd he was shy.

Marilyn was transmarveled by Diana's performance. He kept

going on about how much money she was making. To me, Atlantic City, like Las Vegas, was a glitzy graveyard, the last place I want to end up.

After the show we went backstage. I took pictures of the two stars. I didn't have to ask them to pose. Under Marilyn's orders, I brought my Sure Shot and some black and white film to capture the moment.

Steve Wynn took us all for dinner in the casino restaurant. A croupier came to the table and gave "Miss Ross" a gambling voucher. I couldn't tell whether it was won or owed, but the naughts were mesmerizing. "I'll deal with that later," she said casually, as if it was a £10 bet at the Catford dog track. If she'd done it to show off, it worked.

I was relieved when Diana offered us a lift back to New York in the casino helicopter; it looked a lot sturdier than the Airfix model we arrived in. During the flight Diana and Marilyn sat in the corner canoodling. I didn't dare take a picture of that.

Diana came back to Morgans and rooted through our wardrobes. Marilyn gave her his Egyptian waistcoat as a present. I took a picture of her sitting on the bed wearing it. It was so unsettling having Diana Ross in your bedroom. I found it hard to be natural, lots of frozen moments and embarrassed smiles.

CHAPTER 37

Marilyn and I had to fly back to London. Maz had run out of money, and I had a date with Culture Club at the Montreux Pop Festival. Tony Gordon wanted us to appear, even though we had nothing to promote. It was three days of hell, under the beady eye of Fleet Street and back into the George and Jon sitcom. Seeing him brought back all the pain. I was antagonistic, fresh from my play away in New York. I tried to act like I didn't care, to show Jon he had no power over me. Emotionally I was fluctuating between nonchalance and desperation. I still fancied him like crazy.

We had a punch-up on the first night. I was in the hotel bar with Andre sipping a Brandy Alexander, chatting to a sweet Swiss boy. Jon was laughing and telling jokes to a bunch of rowdy backup singers. I was watching him from the corner of my eye, I could feel myself getting more and more aggravated and jealous. I stormed out of the bar. "Night, slags."

I was just putting my key in the door when Jon sprang out of the lift. "What the fuck's wrong with you?" I tried to escape into the room; I wasn't quick enough. He grabbed my arm. "You don't give a shit, do ya?"

"No. Go away." He pulled me down the corridor. I started shouting, "Tony, Tony!" I could feel the tears. "Just fuck off. Leave me alone."

"You started it."

A door opened and a startled David Wigg, showbiz editor of the *Daily Express,* stuck his head out. "Is everything okay, boys?" I bellowed at him, "Fucking mind your own business." He quickly shut the door. During the scuffle I noticed that my £3,000 antique brooch had fallen from my collar. I forgot the fight and scoured the floor. This made Jon even angrier. "Sod your bloody brooch."

"Tony, Tony," I screamed again. Jon tried to put his hand over my mouth.

Tony's door opened. "Georgie, what's going on?"

Jon had hold of my hair while I was kicking at him. Tony tried to grab Jon and narrowly missed a punch in the face. We bundled into Tony's room still going at it. Avi started screaming at Jon, "Stop it, stop it." She thought Tony was going to get hurt. Jon let go of me. He was raging, "That's it, I hate you. You're a piece of shit," and left.

Tony was shaking his head. "You're going to kill one another if you carry on like this." I went to my room and spent the night alone. I wished I hadn't been so stupid. I wanted Jon so badly I ended up pushing him away.

Mine was a hypocritical and selfish obsession. When I was away from Jon my loyalties were divided. There were always other gorgeous boys to chase after and play games with. We spoke irregularly on the phone, fighting or having long-distance phone sex, but then I might not phone him for two weeks. Jon was as bad. We mirrored each other in many ways.

After Montreux I went back to London for a few days. As soon as I got there I wanted to leave. There was so much domestic crap to deal with. The building work at Hampstead was still dragging on. Dad wanted to take charge, but I wouldn't let him. I acted like it was all under control. It must have been frustrating to watch me being so wasteful and irresponsible.

There was no one strong enough to bring me to heel. I resented advice or any attempts to rein me in. Tony Gordon expressed concern about my finances. I nodded, and carried on, spending like the Sultan of Brunei. Hotel bills for myself and Marilyn, round-the-clock limousines, restaurants, clothes, drugs, and first-class travel. I had no idea how much I was spending, but I was quite sure I wasn't going to run out. My life had no sense of order. The only thing I cared about was having a good time. I no longer had any focus on my career: I knew there were plans to tour and record, but it wasn't something I felt passionately about.

Marilyn and I went back to New York for the grand opening of Steve Rubell's new department-store nightclub, the Palladium. I was lured there by Rubell with the offer of a free penthouse suite at Morgans. He never kept his promise. Still, I was happy to be back in New York. We flew in on the morning Concorde, another £2,576 lost to the speed of sound.

Marilyn took me for an "I say, you pay" lunch at Tavern on the Green in Central Park which was in the Marilyn Guide to Expensive Restaurants. We were chauffeured there in a slate gray limousine. It was a beautiful horny spring day. All we ever talked about was dick and where to eat. Our favorite game was who would you shag in this room. As I was digging into my gorgeous pasta lunch with extra garlic bread on the side, I noticed something equally mouth-watering and Italian, the maître d'.

"I'd cook for him."

Marilyn waved him over to the table and ordered a bottle of Perrier like he wanted it shoved up his arse. I stared at my plate.

"What are you like?"

"Listen, girl, you won't get anywhere with that coy act."

Marilyn gave him the twenty-third degree. Name, age, marital status, what you doing later. He was called Richard, he was about to get married, and it was his night off. Marilyn invited him to the Palladium opening and told him to meet us at the hotel at ten. I was angry when we left the restaurant. Typical Marilyn, hogging everything you fancied. I didn't think he'd show up.

I was painting my face when Richard arrived. I hid in the bedroom, keeping the door ajar so I could hear every word. Marilyn was his usual brutal self. "Have you ever slept with a bloke? Do you lick girls out?" Childish questions followed by salacious cackling. Richard was cool and even more desirable out of his waiter's tux, casually dressed in blue cotton slacks and a baggy jumper, his dark hair slicked back. Sofuckinghandsomeitwasuntrue.

Marilyn and I dropped an E before we left the hotel, which

made the carnival at Area seem even more trippy than the bush kangaroo. Skateboarders zipping around in giant cages, human sculptures, divas and desperadoes. Andy Warhol doing his best to represent the undead; so cool he wasn't even breathing. He took my picture, I took his. There were some faces from London, Stephen Linard and John Maybury. John looked at Richard and whispered in my ear, "Mm, a giant Jon Moss." Richard was straight, but who was to know I wasn't the lucky girl?

By the time we reached the Palladium I was off my trolley and looking for more E. I bought ten Quaaludes off a stranger at the bar. I loved Quaaludes, you couldn't get them in London. Soon I was even more whizzed out. John Maybury and I slouched to a table and drank to our divorces. Mine with Jon, his with David Holah.

Up in the Mike Todd VIP Room I had a mouth-to-mouth encounter with New York debutante of distinction Cornelia Guest, a blond brash socialite. "Are you that vile debutante?" I inquired. She was quick. "Why? Is someone important asking?" We got on like strychnine and rat poison. I helped her polish off her champagne and we exchanged numbers.

Richard and I left the Palladium around three and went off to the Empire Diner. I knew Marilyn would be furious that he'd have to cab it, but I didn't care. We talked for hours, about everything, music, food, love, life. When I told him my hero was Joni Mitchell he called her a Communist. It was almost daylight when the limo dropped him off at the Staten Island Ferry.

An innocent flirtation became a friendship for life. Richard Roesler was one of the most genuine people I met during my drug fest in New York. It was a time full of creeps and users. He liked George O'Dowd not Boy George, even though that was the initial attraction. The fact that we had nothing in common made our friendship more interesting. I went over to Staten Island for dinner with his fiancée, Louise. For a few hours there was sanity in my life.

Marilyn hated my new friend Cornelia, except when he wanted to borrow one of her expensive Halston jackets. He called her "Stuck-up Bitch" and "Unwanted Guest." Cornelia didn't think much of Marilyn. She was only interested in me, and put up with him because she had to.

Cornelia was obnoxious but fun with it, her head stuck up in a gilt-encrusted cloud, privileged, petulant, and perfect. She introduced us to the New York society scene, and we dragged her downtown to late-night leather bars. It was a brand-new adventure for me, escorting a deb to high-society gatherings. For Marilyn, it made a change to get in through the front door. I often wondered what her snooty friends thought of us; their looks often said enough.

Wherever Cornelia went, cameras would be waiting. Marilyn and I were sure she tipped them off, so we devised a plan to make her camera-shy. Outside the Palladium we lifted her upside down, aided by her journalist friend Couri Hay. She screamed hysterically, punching and kicking, almost in tears. When she broke free she swung for Couri. "You bastards." How were we to know she had no knickers on? After a brief sulk and a couple of kir royales she forgave us. We taunted her, "Leave it to beaver. Leave it to beaver." She laughed, but the next day she was up with the cleaners trying to track down the photographers. Luckily no one would print the picture in America, but it appeared in a French magazine.

Couri was a freelance journalist and celebrity slayer, fox-eyed and sulfur-tongued. A small handsome chap with an astrakhan mop and a half-moon smile. Rumor had it he slipped the odd story to the *National Enquirer,* although he sneered at the accusation. He was one of Cornelia's best friends, and so became ours. Marilyn loathed him, probably because he pipped him on the obnoxioscale. They had quite a few confrontations. One time Couri raved demonically at Marilyn, "I'll finish your career before it's started." He really believed he could. Marilyn was unperturbed. "What career?" The silence that followed would have blunted a knife. Couri had his nice sides. Like Cornelia he went with the flow, sometimes creating it. He was older than the rest of us, but had an irrepressible childlike energy. I never attracted his aggression, but then I never felt threatened by him.

Another of Cornelia's friends, Andy Warhol, didn't take to us at all. In his eyes we were uncultured and bratlike, and having the worst kind of effect on Cornelia. I couldn't find anything remotely interesting about Andy, and told her so. It wasn't strictly true. I had a grudging admiration but sensed his indifference to me. I never trusted anyone who didn't react. Andy was so cardboard and creepy: that strange, fearful face, those funny Groucho Marx eyebrows, and that shop-dummy wig. Sometimes he would be really friendly, and I'd change my opinion. Other times he would stare right through me. I tried to squeeze Cornelia for gossip about Andy, especially his sex life, but she wouldn't dish.

Andy and Cornelia were modeling for photographer Francesco Scavullo at a charity fashion show. Couri, Marilyn, and I were in the front row cheering them on. Afterward I suggested dinner at Mr. Chow's. I had a limo outside, but Andy and his friend Benjamin took a cab, which was typical and rude. Andy and Benjamin were solemn at dinner, the rest of us were at full screech. Couri spotted bosomy club goddess Diane Brill at another table and screamed, "Hey, Brill. Get yer pussy over here." We all yelped and whistled as she oozed toward our table. Our noise annoyed the other diners. A waiter asked us to keep it down. Cornelia told him he looked like a dried duck. I couldn't believe she said it. Andy was shocked. Of course it was our influence.

I first met Andy Warhol in January 1985: his assistant Vincent called up Morgans Hotel and invited me to lunch. I was wary and asked who else would be there. "Bianca Jagger," he said, "and some other nice people. But if there's anyone you'd like to invite . . . " Marilyn had a few suggestions, Rob Lowe, Barbra Streisand, himself. I decided on Quentin Crisp as I'd always wanted to meet him. Vincent said Quentin and Andy were good friends, he could arrange it.

I spent the following morning throwing clothes around the hotel room, finally deciding on what I always wore, my baggy black Issey Miyake suit to cover all sins.

We were over half an hour late arriving at the *Interview* magazine offices on Broadway, and I was panicking. Marilyn said, "Oh, please, real stars always keep people waiting." No one seemed to mind.

Andy was seated at the head of the table like some limp voyeur. I shook his hand and sat down. Marilyn sat beside me. Both of us felt intimidated, as if we'd gatecrashed a Freemasons' lodge. Andy introduced me to Quentin: "This is Boy George. He asked me to invite you."

Quentin looked at me and smiled, "How nice," and held out his dainty hand. There was such sadness and beauty in his face. He looked just how I imagined, silvery blue hair, lightly rouged cheeks, and a dashing lilac cravat tied just so. The only other guest I recognized was Bianca Jagger.

I told Quentin my Avedon story. He said, "Oh, Avedon. All that running and chiffon. I don't know how one manages it." Every syllable and pause seemed loaded with significance. Had he not been there, lunch would have been a blank canvas. He held our attention without holding court.

While the rest of us had coffee, Bianca went off to another room to be interviewed by a TV crew about the war in Nicaragua. Marilyn sat in and listened. Bianca was being all serious and political when one of her shoulder pads slipped, giving her a third breast. Marilyn walked over and lifted it back on to her shoulder. She gave him daggers. Afterward he didn't stop slagging her off. "Oh, let her go to Nicaragua in that silk blouse and those heels, she'll be really useful."

As we were leaving, I asked Quentin if I could meet him again. "I'm in the phone book. Call me any time." I didn't see Quentin again until many years later when he gave a talk in Brighton. He was eighty-three and still brilliant. Afterward I lined up to get a signed picture. He was surprised to see me.

"My, my, Boy George, living in Brighton." I told him I'd driven there especially. "That's so kind," he said. "I am honored."

There was no mention of our lunch date in the published Warhol diaries. But Andy mentioned that he and Cornelia had gone to see Culture Club at Madison Square Garden. He hated the show and called me fat. I was angry when I read it and knew there was a reason why I didn't like him. I'd never have had lunch with him had I known, but then I wouldn't have met Quentin.

There were other entries in his diaries, "Boy George and Marilyn like me because they can say mean things and I'm not quick enough to think of a comeback, so I'm no threat to them." He didn't like Cornelia being friendly with Marilyn and me. He described us as "horrible brats."

We were having dinner at the Café Luxembourg with Cornelia, Andy, Benjamin, and artist Jean-Michel Basquiat. There wasn't enough room on the table, so Dencil and Sydney were relegated to the cheap seats. Dencil was furious that we were sitting with Andy. When the food came he started throwing chips across at our table. One of them landed in Andy's wig. He picked it out and carried on eating. I could tell he wasn't amused, but as usual he didn't react. Marilyn was trying not to laugh. I was angry with Dencil for embarrassing me. Cornelia kept a stern face, but laughed her head off afterward.

The next time we went to dinner with Andy, I made sure not to bring Dencil. Andy didn't ask where he was. We were at Elaine's with Cornelia, Andy, and Baby Jane Holzer, one of Andy's trash movie stars. The waiter came to the table and asked, "Is there a Marilyn here? It's Diana Ross on the phone." I was sure it was Dencil setting him up.

Marilyn skipped back to the table, the cat's cream dripping from his lips. "Diana's joining us for coffee." He was well pleased with himself, as anyone would be.

She arrived in ripped jeans and a bubbly mood and was openly affectionate to Marilyn, which surprised us all. Marilyn was unbelievably charming. He saw Diana Ross as his big chance, especially in America. He thought she could do for him what she did for the Jacksons. He admired her too, and loved her voice; he was a genuine fan. The whole saga was intriguing. It was like my schoolboy dreams of being discovered by Bowie or Bolan, only it seemed to be coming true for Marilyn.

Then out of the Mrs. Blue, Diana stopped calling. Marilyn knew it was deliberate because her flag was out in New York. At first, he made excuses, then started wondering what he'd done wrong.

I had my own theory about this new twist. Diana's silence coincided with the publication of a certain picture in the *New York Post*, one taken by me in Atlantic City. The photograph was so glamorous and professional I couldn't resist getting it printed. Marilyn didn't object, so we got Sydney to give it to the *Post*. Diana may have considered it a breach of confidence. Who knows the superstar mind?

Some months later, back in London, Diana was performing at the Royal Albert Hall. Marilyn wanted to get tickets and expected me to sort it out. I phoned the stage door and was surprised to find Gary Lee was tour manager. He said, "Diana doesn't want Marilyn within two hundred yards of the place if he's not with you." So I had to chaperone Marilyn. We attended the show and Diana lived. Marilyn didn't savage her with a carving knife. The next day he sought her out in true Misty fashion. Clutching a bouquet of roses he arrived at the Savoy reception. She invited him up to her suite as if nothing was wrong. Marilyn asked why they weren't seeing each other so much. He said, "What about those songs you sing, 'Reach Out and Touch'?" She replied, "They're just songs, Marilyn, just songs."

CHAPTER 38

Philip Sallon blew into New York on the back of his broomstick. It was his first-ever trip to America, and he was like a little kid cleverly disguised as a mad bag lady. My friend Richard couldn't believe such a creature existed out of the hobgoblin fairy tales. Philip came screaming down the hotel corridor dressed in a silver lamé sari and pleaded with Richard to be the father of his child.

Philip was the perfect British undignitary. We took him round the clubs and he slagged everyone off, "Uch, slimy New Yorkers. They're all so false." He hated Cornelia on sight and was none too pleased when we announced she was joining us for a week's holiday in Jamaica. "Creepy Cornelius, I don't want her breathing my oxygen."

Philip in Jamaica was even funnier than Philip in New York. Ocho Rios was the furthest he'd been from civilization. He kept complaining there were no gay clubs and that everyone was black. "You know I don't fancy schwarzes. I'm bored." Marilyn tormented him throughout the week with anti-Semitic snipes. "Morning, Syphilis. That's a fab Auschwitz you're wearing." We both serenaded him with songs about his fading years. "Old man Philip, he keeps on breathing . . . "

Philip could be just as cruel: "That's about as interesting as your last chart position." He said if I went on the beach Greenpeace would come and rescue me.

One morning I woke to Philip's screaming. "Fuck off, Marilyn, let go, let go." He was being dragged toward the villa swimming pool by his sari and that's where he took his early-morning bath. Philip got his own back when Marilyn tried to pick up three Spanish sailors down at the docks. Marilyn had just primed them when Philip started henpecking. "You can't bring them back without asking George, he'll go mad. You should phone and ask." His nagging frightened the sailors away. Marilyn was raging, "You interfering old Jew. Just cos you haven't got a sex life." I was pretty pissed off too. I wouldn't have minded a bit of seaweed.

The holiday was full of comedy sketches. On our way to Negril we stopped for petrol and a gang of kids surrounded the car. One of them recognized me and shouted, "Bwoy Gearge!" Marilyn said, "No, it's his mother." They asked if Philip was Mick Jagger and pressed their faces against the window to take a good look. One of them shook his head. "Nah, Mick Jagger's good-looking." Philip was furious and took it out on Cornelia. Cornelia saw us bitching at Philip and thought she could join in the sport. Philip turned on her, spitting that she was a crawling bitch and only interested in Boy George for his celebrity. I was furious with Philip for insulting Cornelia, even if it was true.

That evening we went to a local hotel. We dined on salt fish and danced to the corny standards chugged out by the band. Marilyn and I were impressed with the singer, Gem Myers, who sounded like Deniece Williams. I met her after the show and asked if she was interested in touring with Culture Club. She was shocked and didn't believe I was Boy George. I took her number and said I'd be in touch.

Philip flew back to London tired and bruised. The rest of us flew to New York where Marilyn and I checked into the American Stanhope Hotel. It didn't take us long to switch to the butt reality of New York. That night we watched the Gay Porno Awards on cable TV. It was hilarious: all the porn stars were dressed in black tie, taking themselves so seriously, as if it were the Oscars. Marilyn and I recognized them all: Rick Humungous Donovan, Jeff Stryker, and Leo Ford. We thought it was fab that this sort of thing could be on TV. Only in America.

The drug triathlon continued. I was taking at least three Es a week, and on Saturdays maybe even three in a night. Nick Egan knew some old hippies in the East Village who dealt in acid, grass, and E. I would buy handfuls and hand them out to our gang. If everyone was high, I felt less guilty. The E came in fluorescent orange capsules or in white pill form, costing twenty dollars, sometimes more.

Marilyn and I were out clubbing every night, even though most of the clubs were empty and boring during the week. We were two restless spirits constantly in search of action and distraction. Sometimes after heavy binges we would be forced to watch TV for an evening, but it didn't take us long to jump back. To counteract the effects of E, we would dose ourselves up with multivitamins and drink fresh cranberry juice, which we were told was good for the liver. We'd eat things like liver and onions and vegetarian food. It didn't last long, it was just a panic measure.

My diet was hellish and had been for years. I've always loved my food. It was one of the many ways I anesthetized myself. New York was Billy Bunter heaven—Mexican, Indian, Chinese, Japanese, Thai, and all-American. On tour I always used to eat after shows, the worst type of food, burgers, chips, and onion rings. I sent Billy off to Fatburger in L.A. for a triple bacon with extra cheese.

Marilyn liked to eat and be seen. Elaine's, where Woody Allen and other such luminaries could be spotted nibbling, was his favorite. One night he had his photograph taken outside with Shelly Winters.

Marilyn could eat five deep-pan pizzas and a dustbin of ice cream and still stay trim. It used to drive me nuts. He would bring home treacly pecan pies and cartons of Häagen-Dazs and leave them in the fridge to torment me. I said he wanted me to be his fat friend, a bit like those ladies in the Spanish court who went round with monkeys to make themselves look more beautiful. I was secretly pleased when he gave himself a Mohican haircut; it really didn't suit him. It was the ugliest he'd ever looked. Marilyn the Homohican. With the hair came a new persona. He walked around snarling as if auditioning to be an extra in a Billy Idol video. I'm sure he was acting up because he was embarrassed about his self-mutilation. It wasn't a look that you could easily go back on. It raised a few eyebrows. "What the fuck has he done?"

The bad news was it didn't stop him picking up boys. I was sure he could go out covered in excrement and still get lucky.

Our daily routine was that of two dizzy showgirls: we took breakfast as the afternoon rush hour began and fell into bed when the rest of New York was rising for an honest day's work. Sydney was always around, crashing on the sofa, waiting for her daily dose of S&M (slavery and Marilyn). Marilyn ordered her around like she was Diana Ross's maid. He wouldn't do anything for himself. I was just as bad. Sydney took it on the chin, it was her way of keeping in with us and maintaining a motherly control. We subjected her to ritual abuse, tearing off her knickers and bra, tickling her parts with the loo brush. Marilyn tied her to a chair and took Polaroids while I back-combed her hair into a fright wig.

We wouldn't even let the chambermaids in to change the sheets or towels. Magazines, clothes, half-eaten sandwiches, and most of the hotel's coffee and teapots littered the floor. I even moved all the furniture around. No one complained as long as the bill was paid.

Fans were a constant hassle. We had to make sure they didn't follow us back to the hotel. They hounded us at the clubs, wanting to take pictures and get records signed. I couldn't deal with them when I was off my face. Marilyn was always rude whatever state he was in. Some of them thrived on the abuse, it was an acknowledgment of their existence.

All calls had to be announced and if they got through they had to deal with Marilyn. He showed no mercy. "Sorry. We don't know them." Slam.

One afternoon I received a worried call from the front desk. "Mr. O'Dowd, there's a Hare Krishna in reception. He insists on seeing you."

I was intrigued. "Who is he?"

"He says he's married to Annie Lennox." I knew Annie had married a Hare Krishna and I was desperate to see what he looked like. I told them to send him up.

Radha Raman was handsome and a little pushy. He certainly didn't have the wounded innocence of other devotees I'd met. I ordered tea and he ranted about Annie. He told me they had separated, but wouldn't say why. He was so jittery, I couldn't wait for him to leave. I never found out why he came to see me.

The day after Radha's awkward visit I received a phone call from yet another Hare Krishna, Nayana Bhiran, who was PR for their Brooklyn temple. It all seemed rather timely and suspicious. Was this a concerted effort to snatch my soul?

Nayana offered to bring food to the hotel. I was tempted but thought I'd better check with Marilyn. He said, "Uch, don't want that lot over here." I told Nayana it wasn't convenient, but perhaps I'd come to the temple another day. Of course I forgot all about it. The next time Nayana rang it was from the hotel lobby. "Hare Krishna, we're here."

"Oh," I said. "How many of you are there?"

"Just two."

I invited them up, but protected myself by saying I was on my way out.

When I opened the door I had to stop myself laughing, it was a holy peculiar sight.

"Hare Krishna," they said in unison.

"Nayana."

"Latchmee."

It had been raining. Nayana, the smaller of the two, was wearing a brightly colored umbrella hat and a disposable polythene mac over his temple togs. Very Gandhi goes to Woolworth's. He placed an exotic flowered garland around my neck saying, "This is from the deities." I smiled as if I understood. He'd brought one for Marilyn too, but Marilyn was busy customizing a pair of Levi's. It was almost ten minutes before he acknowledged their presence. "Oh, hi."

Nayana offered Marilyn some Krishna food, I was already digging in.

"No thanks," said Marilyn. "I'm saving my appetite for the soft-shell crabs at Elaine's."

Nayana said, "You'll come back as a crab in your next life. Mind you, you're already quite crabby."

Bitchy Krishna, I thought. I could see Marilyn's mind ticking over. "I'd rather come back as a crab than a rotten old lettuce leaf." Even the devotees thought that was funny.

Having avenged himself, Marilyn loosened up. He asked Latchmee to show him how to wear a *dhoti*, the Indian skirt worn by devotees. Latchmee dressed him in a bedsheet, then showed him some Indian dance moves. We drank tea, munched, and talked about all things spiritual. The devotees' presence had a humbling effect on me. I found myself being overly polite and watching my language as if I was with two nuns. Marilyn kept contradicting me. "Don't lie. Yes, you do . . . No, you don't."

It was important for me to know their stance on homosexuality. Their views were no different from the Christians or Jews. God loves us all, but gay sex is forbidden. I was disappointed with Nayana's by-the-book explanations when I could see he was as queer as a satin jockstrap. Still, I liked the devotees, they were gentle people and a lot of what they said made sense. Nayana again invited me to the temple, and I promised I would make it this time.

It didn't take us long to trade in our tickets to heaven. I picked up a blond at Area and gave him a bed for the night. Daley was a stargazer cum hooker, but what did I care? He was cute, and those kind of boys didn't fall out of the sky. He stayed around for a few months, working my nerves and my wallet.

Marilyn had so many boyfriends he could have started his own football team, and they were all drop-dead athletic. One of them, an incredibly handsome Puerto Rican, turned up at the hotel. Marilyn said tell him I'm not here, and hid in the bedroom. I invited him up to the room and made him tea, knowing it would infuriate Marilyn. I was thinking, Have me instead, I'm loyal, loving, and desperate.

On our way to see Madonna at Radio City Music Hall, Marilyn and I stopped off for some food at Jezebel on Forty-fifth Street. We had two spare tickets for the show and were joking about picking up a couple of boys. Marilyn suggested selling the tickets outside and keeping the money, I thought that would be a bit conspicuous. I spotted a cute boy in the restaurant and nudged Marilyn. He'd already seen him. The boy and his friend were with two girlies, obviously on a double date. That didn't deter Marilyn. He went over to get a light and asked if they wanted to come to Madonna with us. I was surprised two straight boys would leave their girlfriends like that, but they did.

We had great seats at the show, I spent the whole time slagging off Madonna's voice. "Uh, cats' chorus." I couldn't watch anything without criticizing. Madonna straddled a ghetto blaster and announced, "Every girl has a box; only mine makes music." Marilyn and I were screaming, "Tart!" When she sang "Like a Virgin," I joked, "She must have a long memory."

Marilyn was friendly with Madonna's makeup artist Way Bandy. He invited us backstage and we met Madonna, still sweaty from her performance. I asked if I could take some pictures of her. I could tell she didn't like the idea, but didn't want to appear snooty. I took pictures of her with the two boys; they were thrilled. Madonna, she was tough, intimidating, and very full of herself. I thought then as I do now that she's a gay man trapped in a woman's body.

The boys, let's call them Paul and Adam, became clubbing companions for a week or so, plenty of time for Marilyn to work his charms, or get bored. He tried every trick to get into Paul's jeans. When he realized he was a no-entry he became hateful. "I don't want to hang out with them. They're wankers." This was always a dilemma for me. I didn't think it was fair to hate people just because they wouldn't swing. There were lots of boys I fancied and pursued, but I didn't turn on them because I couldn't get what I wanted. If they were thick and only good for one night, then fair enough, but not if they were nice, intelligent, and fun to be with. I suppose I never wanted people to think I was horrible. Marilyn couldn't care less. He'd kill the atmosphere at dinner or leave me stranded in a club if he didn't like the company.

I worried about Marilyn's behavior reflecting on me, and it often did. He spotted *Gremlins'* star Zach Galligan at the Limelight club and went over to pout at him. Galligan was unfriendly, Marilyn became abusive. "I thought you were a gremlin." Galligan asked me, "Why do you hang around with assholes like that?" It was a common enough question and one that I often asked myself.

There were times when I could have gladly pushed Marilyn from a moving train. But whatever happened I could never cut him off completely. We had a real racket going. I needed his need as much as he needed mine. I always thought of myself as the victim, but now I realize I was just as manipulative.

In my heart I did everything I could to help Marilyn, but he just didn't trust me. He was convinced I wanted him to fail, that I was operating on some deeply twisted level. My biggest mistake was making him dependent on me, and his biggest mistake was expecting me to run his life.

He asked me to produce a record for him, a cover version of a childhood favorite, "Spirit in the Sky." "You'd be a brilliant producer," he said. "All that Culture Club stuff is you."

Neither of us knew any musicians in New York who could help us make a record. Of course, Marilyn thought he could waltz in to superstar studios and announce, "I'm here." Meeting Diana Ross had raised his expectations. He was full of practical ideas, Luther, Prince. He put in a call to Prince's management, but there was no response. I told him Prince only works with people who are smaller than him.

Things spun around when Sydney introduced us to mutant-disco star Man Parrish, luke-famous for his dance hit "Hop Hop Be Dop (Don't Stop)." Parrish had access to a cheap mobile recording studio and invited us over to his house in Brooklyn to work. He brought in his collaborator, Michael Rudetsky, who knew his way round the studio like an electric current. I quickly realized that Rudetsky was the musical talent and that Parrish was an ideas man. I had enough ideas of my own, and as there was only room for two people in the tiny studio I edged him out. Parrish retreated to his kitchen and Marilyn sat on the steps talking to local kids. Rudetsky and I worked through the night and came up with a spunky dance version of "Spirit." Marilyn was so bored he kept opening the door and moaning, "How far are we now?" But he was happy when he heard the result.

From that night on I developed a strong bond with Michael Rudetsky. It was the first time I'd ever enjoyed being stuck in a studio. Michael didn't doubt my ability. It wasn't like working with Culture Club.

Marilyn and I were so happy with the track we decided to record it properly and tout the finished product. I didn't want to fork out any more money than I had to, so everything was done on deals. Michael got us free "downtime" at New York's Hit Factory when the studios were empty. He also brought in two female country singers willing to donate their services. I was adamant that the backing vocals should have a gospel feel even if I had to pay for it. I called up the Singer Service and they sent along Diva Grey, who was everything her name suggested. During the session she kept stopping to complain that one of the girls was flat, which intimidated all of us. This went on for half an hour, then she beckoned me into a corner. "What kind of sound are you after, boy?" I told her I wanted gospel. "Well," she said laughing, "you are trying to get pear juice out of an apple. These white girls, bless their souls, are not cutting it." She said she would bring in some real singers if we waited a day. I started to panic, knowing we had limited studio time. Michael groveled to the studio manager.

The next night Diva arrived with Brenda White and Jocelyn Brown. I was surprised that Brenda was white, but she passed the soul test, taking all the top notes. Diva kept her promise, the backing vocals were brilliant. Jocelyn sang some of the lead lines. The passion in her voice made Marilyn want to crawl under the carpet, he was so nervous. After a couple of hours and much coaxing we managed to get a decent vocal out of him. Then Michael and I mixed the track, finishing just as the cleaners arrived and our coke ran out.

The finished track sounded like a smash. I took it to Frank Rand at Epic and gave it my best hard sell. He liked it, but said he'd have to play it to the company. Even though he made no commitment, I left there feeling optimistic. That wasn't good enough for Marilyn. He couldn't understand why his advance wasn't in the bank.

A week later I had a second meeting with Rand, this time accompanied by Marilyn. Marilyn says I introduced him by saying, "This is Marilyn. He can be rude and obnoxious, but he's really talented." Whatever I did or didn't say, Marilyn exuded little charm. He was totally unrealistic about what he could expect from a record company. He didn't realize he was back at the starting post.

Through the fog of drugs and clubs, my twenty-fourth birthday was looming. Cornelia, in a champagne state, offered to throw a party for me. I was happy to have a quiet dinner with friends. She had all these grand ideas. I thought she was just blabbing, but

within days it was all arranged. It was going to be the party of parties. Both Area and the Palladium were fighting to host the event.
I was excited, but worried it might be a disaster. Cornelia just
laughed. "It'll be fabulous. Leave it to me."

Couri said he'd host a select preparty dinner at his house. I
thought that was sweet of him, but had to laugh at the guest list he
and Cornelia conjured up. I'd read all about the Khashoggis'
yachts, planes, and jewelry, but I'd never considered myself an inti-
mate friend. I was concerned I wouldn't know anyone, so I phoned
home and tried to rally a few friends and freaks. Philip said he and
Tranny would try and come, but nobody else could afford it.

The dilemma of where to hold the main party was dealt with
ingeniously by Cornelia. Neither of us wanted to upset our club
host friends, Eric Goode at Area and Steve Rubell at the
Palladium, so it was arranged that after dinner at Couri's we would
party at the Palladium and then at 4 A.M. go to Area for breakfast.
Everyone was happy.

I asked Marilyn to premiere "Spirit in the Sky" at the party. He
thought it was a great idea, but said I'd have to lend him some
money to get a new outfit.

The morning of the party, Marilyn was getting cold stilettos. I
told him he'd be brilliant. He was miming, what could go wrong?
I decided I had to have at least one family member celebrating my
birthday with me. I phoned Shooters Hill and invited my sister,
Siobhan, who jetted in on the evening Concorde. Philip and
Tranny flew standby. I arranged a double room for them at the
Chelsea Hotel. They weren't intent on visiting the ghost of Sid
Vicious, they just wanted cheap.

By the time I arrived at the Chelsea, Philip and Tranny had
already enamored themselves with the front desk. Without asking,
they knew who I'd come to see. "Fourth floor." I could hear
Philip's hysterics as I stepped out of the lift. Their door was wide
open, he was lying on the bed with a look of mock shock on his
face. "Hi, dear. You're never gonna believe this."

Minutes after they'd arrived, a drunk strayed into their room.
Tranny, never one to miss an oppor-importunity, was having it off
with him in the shower. What was worse, said Philip, he wasn't
even attractive. Philip was enjoying the decadence all the same.

Tranny emerged shamelessly from the shower and disposed of the clean drunk. I had to agree it wasn't one of his greatest conquests. Tranny was philosophical. "Oh, well. It's a laugh." We had a quick cuppa, then I went to the Stanhope to pick up my clothes and makeup and headed for Cornelia's. She was already dressed and impatient, sipping champagne in a black beaded dress.

Siobhan arrived dazed and excited. It was like I hadn't seen her for years, she was so grown-up. I gave her a hug and she gave me a mouthful. In my dizziness I'd forgotten to arrange a car to collect her from the airport. She'd been waiting there for an hour and a half.

Cornelia gave Siobhan a tour of her high-society wardrobe. None of the ritzy frocks suited her, she looked like a little kid in her mum's clothes. After much rooting, she settled on a fake pony-skin coat which she wore over a gold lamé jumpsuit.

Richard was my official chaperon for the evening. He looked better than the Manhattan skyline. Siobhan cooed her approval. "Blimey, don't tell me he's bent."

Dinner at Couri's was literally staged: his friend from the Metropolitan Opera did up the gardens of his three adjoining town houses—candlelight, scattered rose petals, there was even a mini orchestra playing Vivaldi on the balcony. The guests looked like they'd been picked to match the tablecloths: Nabila and Mohammed Khashoggi, Rupert Everett, Patty Hearst, Nona Hendryx, Divine, Sylvia Miles, Francesco Scavullo, Andy and a smattering of obscure European royalty, Prince Dimitri of Yugoslavia, Prince Egon von Fürstenberg of Austria, and Countess Marie-Hélène du Chastel from Belgium. There were 325 dinner guests and two hundred bottles of Cristal swigged. The mood was soon destroyed when Tranny and Philip came crashing in. "Hi, girl, where's the food?" Tranny lunged at Nabila's diamonds. "Is that paste, luv? Can I try it on?"

I followed dinner with a quick toot which set me on a paranoia trip. I was feeling queasy for the rest of the evening, but that didn't stop me taking more drugs. I popped an E before we left for the Palladium.

The Palladium was jammed. I held on to Siobhan for fear of losing her in the crowd. Everyone was grabbing and kissing,

"Happy Birthday, get us in." I made my way toward the sanctuary of the DJ booth and Marilyn went to the dressing room to prepare for the stage. He performed "Spirit in the Sky" like a true star. I joined Diva and Jocelyn on backing vocals. The crowd loved it. Afterward Madonna came to the dressing room and told Marilyn he had a hit.

Later on Madonna asked Marilyn to dance. He was waiting to sing me "Happy Birthday" and asked her to hang on. He claimed she was really hassling him. Finally he gave in, and she led him to the floor where they danced to "Into the Groove." The photographers were lapping it up. While they were dancing Madonna leaned over to Marilyn and said, "You know how good this is for you." Marilyn was furious and stormed back to the booth. "Naff bitch."

The party continued up in the Mike Todd VIP Room, which was packed with New York faces. Andy Warhol, Keith Haring, John F. Kennedy, Jr., Diane Brill, and a couple of Durans. I sat in the corner with Richard, Nick, and the others, trying to avoid jaw-grinding well-wishers. Philip and Tranny were circling the club, looking for cute boys, appearing every so often like queer cuckoos. Tranny was ranting, and Philip asked him what he was on. Tranny looked at me, "Beecham's powders, girl." Sniff. "We've both got colds, ain't we?" Sniff.

Steve Rubell proclaimed it a great party. I thought it was more a celebration of celebrity than a birthday. Throughout the night I had a feeling of being disconnected, I was there but not really.

At 4 A.M. we moved from the Palladium to Area for breakfast. They'd filled the place with beds for people to lounge on. I had a special king-size bed on a podium, cordoned off with ropes. I was too embarrassed to sit on it. Tranny said it was like being in the court of King Solomon, an orgy without the sex. He could think of nothing else, even over breakfast.

Matt Dillon was there, looking more scrumptious than any piece of crispy bacon. He declined my offer to come and sit on the bed, saying he was with his girlfriend. My quip to a magazine about being "reincarnated as Matt Dillon's underwear" must have given him the willies. At least my fans responded: after I announced my lust for him they sent me hundreds of pinups.

I don't know whether Matt's presence brought on my asthma attack, but I had to be rushed out the backdoor, wheezing and choking. The mixture of coke, Ecstasy, and constant spliffing took its toll. I was panicking because I'd forgotten my inhaler. Luckily another asthmatic was at hand.

I rounded off the morning with a visit to the WPLJ radio studios with Tranny, Philip, and Jonathan Ashby, who arranged the interview. Tranny and I were out of it, babbling and carrying on like a pair of court jesters, Tranny doing impersonations of Carol Channing and Linda Queenie.

I was hammering six-inch nails into my professional coffin. It was the first time I'd ever been interviewed in such a state. I was slurring and hoarse. I handed them an unmixed version of a new Culture Club track, "Heaven's Children," and said I'd get killed for letting them play it.

Years later I heard a recording of that interview. I couldn't listen to it, it was too painful.

After ten days in New York, Philip and Siobhan returned to London. Philip deliberately made Siobhan miss her Concorde flight so that he would have company. I could have killed him—he knew Siobhan was smuggling in an $8,000 fur coat I'd bought for Mum.

The sight of Philip in his pink Womble coat and a sixteen-year-old in sable aroused suspicion at Customs, plus the coat lining was printed TO MUM, WITH LOVE, a dead giveaway. They questioned Siobhan and took the coat. Philip was strip-searched after demanding, "What's wrong with my fur? I demand to be searched." It cost me £500 to get Mum's present back. The first thing she said was, "Where the fuck am I going to wear that? Safeway's?"

With Philip gone, Tranny moved into Marilyn's room at Morgans. The bill was on me. I had the phone blocked so they couldn't dial long distance, but they did their best to clear me out. Marilyn ordered room service on the hour. One afternoon there were five trays of uneaten food outside his door. He'd ordered it and then fallen asleep.

I was staying in the penthouse, where I continued my awkward liaisons with Daley and whoever else I could entice. I had a brief fling with Fidel, a Puerto Rican I met through Keith Haring. Keith was the Puerto Rican Pied Piper. He was always surrounded by gorgeous green-eyed Latinos.

One weekend Cornelia gave me the keys to her plush apartment while she was out of town. I took Fidel there and we abused her hospitality. We spent the weekend in bed watching MTV and snorting lines. The maid nearly fainted when she walked in and found us.

Tranny stayed in New York for six weeks, amazing as he arrived with only £40. I paid for drugs, limousines, cabs, and food for a good part of his stay. But he would have survived alone on the amount of protein he was taking in.

Tranny became my Barbie doll, I bought him clothes, Spandex swimsuits, and cheap tarty lingerie from sex shops. Philip said I only had him around because I couldn't get away with dressing up in women's clothing myself. It wasn't just that; Tranny was superb entertainment. He could mimic anyone's voice within minutes of meeting them. He would send me up on old interviews, "I'd sack my band if any of them took drugs." His impersonations proved useful. He'd dial my limousine service and order cars. It was vile, considering the free ride he was already getting.

At the end of June I flew to Italy to meet up with Culture Club for the San Remo Pop Festival. Tranny moved in with a cocaine dealer and lived on drugs and cat food until his worried mother tracked him down and ordered him home. Marilyn moved into a luxury twenty-eighth-floor apartment on Seventy-ninth and Columbus which I rented to cut down on hotel bills. As was typical I went for the first apartment I was offered without thinking of the cost. Five thousand dollars a month. It was in a snazzy part of town and our next-door neighbor was John Taylor of Duran Duran.

When I arrived at the Grand Hotel Del Mare, the bingeing hit me like a lead handbag. I spent twenty-four hours in bed comatose. My press agent, Jo Bailey, had the clever idea of sending food to my room in an attempt to bring me round. Her gesture proved fateful. The waiter let himself into my room, flicked on the lights, and banged his trolley. "Wake up, signor. Wake up." I was so startled by his intrusion I leaped out of bed and punched him. He ran terrified from the room followed by a silver platter.

I finally came to at six o'clock Saturday evening after much goading and pleading from Billy Button, Jo, and Gilberto from Virgin, Italy. My head was still in New York, I didn't care that we were headlining the show or that not appearing would finish us in Italy.

Tony Gordon and the band were in the bar watching the live transmission, resigned to the impending disaster. Gilberto was receiving hysterical messages from the producers and conveying them in more hysterics to Tony. Finally I appeared and there was a mad dash to the studio. We bounded onstage just as the host had apologized for our absence and the final credits were rolling. They extended the show to accommodate my rudeness; the crowd erupted.

The following day the Italian press accused Virgin of hype, saying they had planned it to maximize effect. If only they'd known. The waiter who was walking around with a bandaged ear was paid off so that he wouldn't squeal to the hovering British hacks. Roy and Mikey nicknamed me "The Irish Labourer."

During the three days in Italy I kept myself together by smoking as much dope as possible, procured by someone in the record company. I sniggered my way through interviews, constantly forgetting my train of thought.

After San Remo I returned to London restless and wretched about facing my forthcoming commitments with the band. Culture Club were about to embark on an awkward world tour, taking in Israel, Greece, Japan, L.A., Puerto Rico, and New York. I couldn't have been less prepared and it was showing.

Jo Bailey told Tony, "George isn't doing his job. I'm sure he's got a drug problem." Tony thought she was sticking her nose in— he already had Billy keeping an eye and reporting back.

With a tour coming up and rehearsals, the band were understandably worried. They elected Alison as spy and minder. She asked if she could come and stay at St. John's Wood because she had some things to do in London. Her job was to make sure I caught the plane to Holland for rehearsals and to try and find out who was supplying me with drugs. She wasn't sleuth enough. The night before we left for Holland I gave her the slip. I went to Heaven and didn't come home until 4 A.M. Between her and Billy, they just about managed to get me on the flight.

We rehearsed in the Commodore Studios in Zelhem, Holland, and stayed across the German border in Elten, close to the River Rhine. Elten, like Montreux, was dull, full of patisseries and bicycles. Every day was like a dreary Sunday.

Jon and I had adjoining rooms at the Hotel Hoch but we couldn't have been further apart. As soon as we were in the same space we reverted to type. Our angry voices echoed round the quiet chalet night after night. Jon didn't have the guts to say it was over, even though it was as obvious as the scars on his face. He kept his options open for the sake of Culture Club.

Ending our relationship would have been messy, like any divorce, only it didn't involve the house, the kids, the car, and the cat. We were talking careers, futures, finances. Knowing that Jon had ulterior motives added to the misery. I foolishly believed if things improved for the band it would reflect on our relationship. Deep down I knew I was fishing in an empty pond.

Even out of it I was able to write songs. I felt marijuana enhanced my songwriting. It certainly made the lyrics more direct and caustic. I didn't bother singing some of my new songs to the band. I knew they would be too blatant for their hetero-sensibilities. "Forgotten Guy" really hit the mark.

Every time he walks out of the bedroom,
Looking brash and buttoning his fly
I always look and laugh and say there's something,
Something wrong with my forgotten guy.
Looking tough is all he ever wanted, looking cool.
But on the other hand,
Love is strange but love is built on something,
Something that is hard to understand.

Trying to maintain a working relationship was hard. We hadn't played together for some time and our egos kept colliding. One minute I was the floppy hippie, the next I was back to form, dictating like a tuppenny Hitler. Gem, the backing singer I'd hired in

Jamaica, was driving us all mad with her timidity. She sat in the corner reading books and wouldn't communicate with anyone. Jocelyn Brown, our other vocalist, came to me in despair and said she was dreading touring with "The Mouse," which had become Gem's moniker. You'd think with all the aggro going on we'd have appreciated Gem's calm. But it was a horrible, pointed silence. Gem didn't fit in, she was a homely Jamaican girl out of her depth.

Alison and I discussed the problem of the mouse that wouldn't squeak. She said, "Send her back to Jamaica." I took her advice and called a band meeting. Jon said we'd never be able to rehearse another singer in time. I asked Jocelyn if she knew anyone, and a big smile erupted. Sensing that Gem was for the chop, she'd already alerted a friend in New York, Wendell Morrison, Jr. When she told him about the job he said, "I'll be by the phone till God gets home." I was excited, we'd never had a male backing vocalist before. Wendell literally arrived the next morning and brought with him a breath of fresh sarcasm, a rangy blacker-than-black man in an African hat and granny glasses. Jocelyn was happy to have a sparring partner, and the mood was relit. Gem the mouse went back to Jamaica, where she squeaked to the press.

During rehearsals I had an unexpected visit from journalist Jonathan Ashby. It was nice to see him, even if the band didn't think so. He came back to the hotel and we stayed up all night spliffing and talking. It must have been weird for him, doing drugs with Boy George and not being able to break the story. Still, I gave him enough freebies, Culture Club tittle-tattle which he sold to Fleet Street. We had a right laugh, stoned, adding horns to a butt of a tale. He proved trustworthy, never printing anything blurted in confidence. The stuff I told him about me and Jon could have bought him his own bagel shop. I didn't tell him everything. He was desperate to know why Culture Club weren't appearing at Live Aid—I suspected that was the reason for his visit. I found it difficult to speak the truth because it was such a worthy cause. I didn't want to appear, even though I'd made half-hearted promises to Bob Geldof and excuses to the band. It was a mixture of fear and loathing. I didn't think we could cut it in front of two billion people and disliked the rock pomposity of it all.

Culture Club flew back to London on the day of Live Aid, July 15, 1985. I watched the concert round at Alan Roberts' flat in Chiswick. Madonna's howling confirmed all my fears. Except for Bowie and Queen I found it boring and self-congratulatory. All my friends went on at me for not being there. Jon, Roy, and Mikey were bitter. I'd ruined their chance of a part in history.

I was desperate for cocaine. I didn't have contacts like in New York. I called Helen Terry and sheepishly asked if she knew where I could score. She was taken aback, "I don't believe you, George." She'd seen me smoke spliff in Montreux, but this was new territory. It was the first time either of us had been honest with each other about drugs. I knew she liked cocaine. She said she knew someone who could sort me out, but I had to promise to keep my mouth shut.

When I arrived at her flat in Islington she had the perfect greeting, "Hello, Mr. Hypocrite."

I laughed. "Fuck off. Where's the drugs?"

Both Helen and her Oriental girlfriend Mimi were smirking as we shared a line. Mimi said, "This would make a great *Smash Hits* cover."

Mimi had baked a scrumptious sponge dope cake. I scoffed more than my share and sat smoking a spliff. I'd never tried dope cake and didn't know it would get me so out of it. Two hours later I was lying on Helen's bed in the fetal position, fearing for my life. I was in tears and wanted it to stop. I knew smack was the only thing that could bring me down. I asked Mimi if she knew anyone. She said she'd call her friend Steve, he was normally "in." A dreadlocks called Steve Luben and his girlfriend, Ginty Feiner, turned up an hour later with supplies. I bought a gram of heroin, which I shared with Helen and Mimi. Helen was embarrassed and made it clear that she didn't do "it" very often. I couldn't wait to get the rolled ten-pound note up my nose. I retched, then felt that warm glow. The smack calmed me right down. We smoked some spliff and watched a video of the Monterey Festival, it was spooky seeing all those dead legends, Janis Joplin, Jimi Hendrix, Brian Jones.

CHAPTER 39

When Culture Club flew to Israel for a huge open-air show in Tel Aviv I carried smack in my underpants. It wasn't much, but it was the first time I'd done anything so career reckless. I didn't consider the possibility of getting caught or my responsibilities to the band. As soon as the seat-belt signs were off, I was in the loo chopping out. I crashed out for the rest of the flight.

At Lod airport I hid behind dark glasses to avoid the flashguns and bright questions. "How do you like Israel?" "I haven't been there yet." The press were surprised by my colorless and sleepy mood.

The Israeli fans were madly excited, jumping in front of the van and surrounding the Daniel Tower Hotel, weeping as if some prophet had arrived. I couldn't share their joy. I needed to sleep it off.

I slithered to my room like a sweaty slug. Jon went off to visit some friends without bothering to ask me along. I sat alone in our barren seventies suite, gazing out at the hazy city, I was rancid and too agitated to sleep. I called the doctor and tried to get some sleeping pills. He was too traditional to understand the needs of a wayward pop star. He gave me antibiotics and impractical advice to stay in bed for a week.

There was anger, jealousy, and rage when I woke to find Jon

had not returned to the hotel. He'd spent the night with his friends, clubbing and having a great time. I was the last thing on his mind. I wanted to go back to London, but didn't have the courage. I had to drag myself into the day. I appeared for the press conference dressed for a night in front of the telly, the only thing that was snappy was my tongue. Inevitably all the questions centered around my wardrobe. I told them, "Things change quickly in this generation although you're obviously a lot slower." After the conference I had some one-to-one interviews with important magazines. I joked to a reporter about sleeping with Jon. The joke was taken as intended, and syndicated around the globe. I'd come close to an admission in a recent interview with *Smash Hits*. They asked me to name the person I'd been having a long relationship with. I said, "I think everyone knows who it is anyway. Most of the fans know. I don't care." Adding, "Unless they invent gay marriages in England I don't think I'll be getting married."

That night we played an open-air concert in Hayarkon Park to 35,000 people, 1 percent of the then population. The crowd loved it, but the press panned the show for its lack of style. Everyone had expected a flamboyant Boy George with dreadlocks and a kosher hat. I knew I'd let both myself and the crowd down. It was a tired performance. During the show Jocelyn sang her hit, "Somebody Else's Guy." It was my cue for a costume change, but I couldn't be bothered, I sat backstage and smoked a spliff. The next morning when I read the reviews I mourned my own behavior. I knew they were right. It was the kick up the arse I needed for the rest of the tour.

I spent the day wandering around ancient Jaffa with Alan Roberts and Andre snapping the journey. Jon and Tony went to Jerusalem to visit the Wailing Wall. Little Hasidic children followed us down the street, pointing and laughing, and old men came out of the shops to stare. I bought a menorah, a Star of David necklace, and worry beads, then had lunch at a falafel bar in downtown Tel Aviv. I'd never tasted anything so scrumptious and greedily ate four portions. The Israeli men were as tasty as the falafels, particularly the soldiers. A Jon Moss on every corner.

From Tel Aviv we flew to Athens, where Culture Club were to play as part of a government-sponsored all-day festival, featuring a whole host of mismatched acts—Depeche Mode, the Cure, the Clash. There was tension everywhere. I was spat at in the street, and Dave Gahan from Depeche Mode was punched in the face. As we were about to leave for the show, word reached us that riots had broken out outside the Panathinaiko Stadium. Two hundred anarchists were demanding free entry, even though the fee was only fifty pence. Tony suggested canceling our appearance. I didn't want to consider it after the disaster in Israel. I was fired up and determined to play.

The moment we hit the stage we were pelted with bottles, cans, stones, and sharpened coins. I taunted the troublemakers, taking it personally. "You Greeks invented homosexuality—what you throwing stones at?" The rest of the sixty thousand strong crowd appreciated my humor, but it didn't stop the missiles. I jumped around shouting, "Missed. Missed." I could see young girls in Culture Club T-shirts crying in terror. Halfway through "Victims" Phil Pickett caught a brick on the head and the show was over. It was a triumph that we managed to stay out there for forty-five minutes. I remained elated throughout; being in battle was a powerful drug.

Robert Smith from the Cure told the press Culture Club deserved to be bottled for making crap records. We waited in the hotel lobby to return the compliment with our fists, but the blob never appeared. I felt let down because I admired Robert Smith and had been a big Cure fan since the punk days. The British press ran front-page stories saying that Culture Club had been booed offstage. Typically they were economical with the facts. It was one of the most hurtful things ever written about the band.

Inevitably Jon and I had one of our official tour punch-ups. Jon autographed the hotel door, and there were fears that we'd have to cancel Japan. He flew back to London to see a specialist. That night I went out to a tacky disco accompanied by Andre, Billy, and Alan. The crowd was bothering me so the club appointed two hunky boxers as bodyguards. I had a great time wedged in between them.

The following day the rest of the band flew on to Frankfurt for a connecting flight to Tokyo. I insisted on going back to London so that I could fly with Jon. I was only there for fifteen hours.

The Japanese tour was a British pop package featuring Culture Club, the Style Council, Go West, and the Associates. It was a difficult tour: word of Culture Club's demise had spread to the land of the Sony Walkman and, but for the Style Council, the other bands weren't famous enough to fill a sushi roll. At Yokohama Stadium we pulled five thousand out of a thirty thousand capacity. The fact that Sting was playing the same night didn't help. The crowd danced and sang in the rain. It was the same all over, the crowds, however small, were enthusiastic.

Despite all the problems, I enjoyed that Japanese tour more than any other. I was no longer a prisoner of my eyebrows. I went out to restaurants and clubs and walked about the streets. There were lots of late-night drinking sessions in the hotel bar with the other bands, Mick Talbot at the piano and the rest of us singing along like English yobbos abroad. Alan's presence on the tour made life more fun: together we played tourist, savoring every aspect and flavor. Of course, Alan couldn't avoid being ensnared in Jon and George politics. Both Jon and I would pump him for information. It drove him mad. He broke down outside the Lexington Queen nightclub in Tokyo. "Fuck you and Jon. I'm sick of it." He stormed off, leaving me in the street.

Yet again I made myself unpopular with the Japanese press by arriving forty-five minutes late for a press conference. The band had been sitting there fidgeting and waiting to be asked questions. After a long awkward silence Roy stormed out and burst into tears. Roy and Mikey were always sensitive around the media; they had a history of being ignored and insulted. Jon held himself together. "It's all a load of old bollocks." Most of the time I didn't notice what was going on for Roy and Mikey, until Alison told me. Aside from the personality differences, there was much to put up with. Jon and I excluded them from just about everything, except our squabbling, which by now had been choreographed to perfection.

When we arrived in Japan we carried on the tradition of sharing a room, but it didn't last long. "Get out. Stay out." Jon packed his case and moved down the corridor. It was the most honest thing he ever did, making it plain that we were well and truly separate.

I kept up a bitching front during the day, I knew how to get

Jon's attention when he was in my range. But at night I was tormented. Where was he? Who was he fucking?

One night he couldn't be found. I woke the whole crew
demanding to know where he was. No one would tell me, probably because they couldn't, but I wouldn't have it. I kicked Jon's
door repeatedly and ordered Billy to get me a passkey from the
front desk. I let myself into his room and rooted through his
belongings looking for clues. It was an act of insanity. I found
nothing. We came to blows in the early hours, and I was left with
a battered face and a bleeding mouth. Jim called the hotel doctor.
I told him, "I didn't fall down. My boyfriend beat me up." I
phoned Tony in L.A. and said that was it, I was definitely leaving
Culture Club. He didn't know what to say. "Oh dear, it's that
bad, is it?"

Whatever my threats I completed the Japanese tour and arrived
in Los Angeles as scheduled. I didn't feel so isolated there. Tony
and Avi provided a nesting warmth and a cup of tea in times of crisis, and there was plenty of work to keep me occupied. On top of
the five live shows we had TV appearances and loaded press days.

I was invited to perform a live duet with Dionne Warwick on
the *Solid Gold* TV show, singing the Aretha classic "Say a Little
Prayer." After my Apollo experience I was wise: I said I wanted to
record it first and mime. The producers said Dionne wouldn't do
playback, but Tony managed a compromise allowing both stars to
get their way. I wasn't sure it would work, but I knew I'd sound
good, and that was enough for me.

However good I sounded, it didn't make up for the fright on
screen. I was bloated and looked like Liz Taylor at her worst.
When I was able to reflect, I called it my Hollywood Babylon
period. Alan hid my voluptions with baggy cuts, bold colors, and
NFL shoulders. My hair was short and black with spidery spikes. A
much more intimidating look than the Boy of old. One critic said
I was trying to be less androgynous to broaden my appeal. When I
looked in the mirror, and I did often, I was appalled. But no matter how much it depressed me to be a singing juggernaut, I couldn't
control the urge to stuff my face.

I appeared with Smokey Robinson on *The Motown Story,* where
I was forced to sing live. We performed "Do You Really Want to

Hurt Me?" together and an old soul classic, "Signed, Sealed, Delivered." It was as if Stevie had popped up to slap me in the face. This time I just got on with it. The other guest on the show was Linda Ronstadt. I let her do most of the singing and meekly joined in the chorus.

Our first concert date at the County Bowl in Santa Barbara was hesitant. We were late going onstage, which left the audience twitchy. Two numbers in, alien voices appeared in the P.A. The culprit was the president himself, Ronald Reagan. He was staying at his Santa Barbara ranch and we were picking up his secret servicemen live and direct. Our radio microphones had to be swapped to plug-in jacks, which further dented the vibes.

While I was busy touring, Marilyn was using my New York apartment as a drug hovel. He spent a healthy part of the summer sucking himself into ill health with his loyal cokehorts Sydney and Dencil at his bad side. Throughout the tour I heard nothing of him, even though he had a tour itinerary which he'd misplaced in an unfurnished apartment.

Out of coke and cash, Marilyn and Co. decided to pay me a visit in L.A. They concocted a story about an evil drug dealer who was sharpening his blade for their throats. Dencil even mocked up a fake stabbing, bandaging his arm for effect.

The three of them arrived at the Bel Air Hotel looking like extras from *Oliver!,* carrying pillowcases for luggage. Avi was the only one at the hotel. She was horrified when she saw the state of Marilyn. "Oh, my God, what's happened to you? Do you need to go to hospital?" The styling worked. She handed him fifty dollars to get a meal.

I was sound checking in San Diego when I received word of Marilyn's presence. I was confused and wondered how and why he was in L.A. When Jim told me Avi had given him money, things became clearer. I called Avi at the hotel. Marilyn had told her I'd left him penniless in New York, as if it was my responsibility to keep him. Avi felt "terribly sorry" for him and was pleading his case, "Poor thing, he's in an awful state. You should help him out." She didn't know the half of it. Before I left New York I gave Marilyn five hundred dollars. I realized it wasn't enough to last, but I wasn't going to start feeling guilty. If Marilyn was resourceful enough to get cocaine, why couldn't he sort his life out? Jim said Marilyn wanted tickets for the show. I banned him—I didn't want him anywhere near me until I knew what game he was playing.

My other visitor that afternoon was much more welcome. My Krishna friend Nayana turned up in San Diego with a bunch of his saffron clan. They brought food, garlands, and tranquility.

After the gig I went round to see Marilyn at his old boyfriend John's house off Hollywood Boulevard. I intended to lop off his head, but when I saw him I couldn't, he was being so pathetic. "You left me in an empty apartment. I would have died if it wasn't for my friends." I told him I had my own life to lead and that if he, Dencil, and Sydney had run up a $3,000 drugs bill, they'd have to pay it. I asked how they could afford to get to L.A. He said Sydney had bought three first-class tickets on her grandmother's credit card. Even in desperation he had style. We argued about my friend Patrick Cox staying in the apartment. He said I'd sent Patrick to spy on him. It was all irrational drug-induced paranoia. Marilyn did his best to transfer guilt. He said, "You know I'll pay you back when I get my deal." I knew that was about as likely as Jon and me shacking up in a semi. I gave him $500 for food, and that was the last I saw of him those twelve days in L.A.

In the morning Nayana took me to the L.A. temple and gave me a tour of the museum and their late founder Prabuphada's private rooms. There was a music box on his desk that played "Raindrops Keep Falling on My Head." It was nice to see that saints have a sense of humor. I felt awkward inside the temple as if I was invading the calm. Dreamy devotees sat cross-legged, chanting "Hare Krishna, Hare Krishna," their minds fixed in devotion. Nayana explained some of the basics of Krishna Consciousness. Part of me wanted to agree, and the other part wanted to run. When I told him the horror stories about Marilyn, he wasn't surprised. He said Marilyn was in the "mode of ignorance" and quoted a relevant passage from the Bhagavadgītā. Afterward I was treated to a vegetarian feast at their restaurant, Govinda's. The food was delicious, but it was the tanned blond behind the juice counter that extracted my attention. He didn't look much like a devotee in his shorts and sleeveless T-shirt. Nayana could see the level of my consciousness.

He said he would send him to the hotel with fresh juices. Of course I told him not to.

The next day the juice boy arrived at the Bel Air by skateboard with watermelon juice and samosas. I was embarrassed and blushed in shame. Thank Krishna he was unaware of my earthly desires.

When Nayana came to visit me at the hotel, security threatened to call the police and have him dragged off the premises. He called me on the house phone and I stomped down to the front desk. I told them he was my guest and that they shouldn't discriminate against people because of the way they dressed. It seemed that only paying freaks were welcome at the Bel Air. This experience of snobbery was nothing new: often when I went to take my first-class seat on airplanes, stewardesses would ask to see my boarding card and the passengers would grimace in disgust.

From L.A. we took an overnight flight to San Juan, Puerto Rico. I traveled in full stage clothes and makeup as Tony had arranged an early-morning airport press conference. Another piece of great organization assuring maximum comfort for the artists. It was sweltering in San Juan, I was tired and didn't feel like being all things to all people. I talked to the press as arranged, but then the eager promoter wanted me to stand around and have my photo taken with everyone and their mother. I was unsubtle. "Fuck this. I'm not Julio Iglesias."

Our show at the Hiram Bithorn Stadium was the best of the tour—such enthusiasm on both sides. The stage was in the middle of a football field with a hundred-yard grass moat separating us from the crowd. They said it was to protect us from Latin passion. Every now and then an eager fan would jump from the stands and make a dash to the stage only to be tackled by the military-style security.

Later that night Alan and I wandered around the streets of San Juan, stopping for a drink in a small crowded bar. No one wanted an autograph but the men shouted as if they were calling a dog to a bowl of water. "Aye, Boy George, faggot, faggot, I want to buy you drink, come." I didn't know how to take their aggressive cheer, but I didn't feel threatened.

We had a free day in San Juan. It was a relief. The sun, palms, and chalky buildings gave it the feel of a holiday, if only for twenty-four hours. There was faint sorrow that the tour was almost over. Jocelyn and Wendell wanted to know when we were doing it again. They didn't realize they were tempting providence.

We finished the tour with two dates on the East Coast— Holmdel, New Jersey, and Jones Beach, Long Island. They were the last live shows Culture Club would ever play. Jersey was a benefit for the Garden State Arts Center. It was a great night. Alison had a punch-up in the stalls. Afterward we all went to an arty party in Asbury Park. Keith Haring and Andy Warhol were there, Andy was his not-very-often-friendly self.

All my friends came for the final date at Jones Beach—Nick, Ellen, Bonnie, Nayana, Couri, Cornelia and her mum C.Z., and Debbie Harry too. As I was about to go onstage a friend popped an Ecstasy in my mouth. I swallowed it and bounced on with a devilish grin. Halfway through the show the E came on. I forgot where I was and started rambling the intro to "Victims." "This song . . . is about somebody I used to love . . . But nothing lasts . . . you know . . . " I stared into the audience for what seemed like ages. Onstage there was mild panic. "Psst, psst, start the song." I didn't care what happened. I was laughing my head off. Nobody in the audience knew what was going on; they just assumed I was in a camper mood than normal.

With the tour over, I moved to Manhattan and stayed at Morgans Hotel while my apartment was being decorated. Jim arranged for Jamie Schevers, our baggage handler, to do the work. The living room was painted saffron, like a Krishna temple, the kitchen canary yellow. Jamie painted into the early hours while Marilyn lay comatose in his bedroom unaware of the transformation. When he finally came round he thought he was in the wrong apartment. "It looks like a hideous Krishna temple. You've got no taste."

"I can't have if I'm letting you live here."

Marilyn was even more disturbed when four devotees turned up carrying a sofa and a bed. Nayana, who was now in New York, had kindly arranged some Krishna removal men to help me out. I had fun decorating the apartment. I bought six-foot framed posters of Marilyn Monroe, Elvis Presley, and James Dean. They stared out of the wall as if to remind us of our mortality.

Marilyn, Dencil, and Sydney were all still breathing, even though Marilyn insisted the dealer was still after their skin. The alleged maniac called the apartment and asked when I was going to pay up. I said, "The name's George. Did I ever buy coke from you? Just fuck off." Nothing ever happened. I still think Marilyn set the whole thing up.

That night I was out at the Paradise Garage with Marilyn, Sydney, Andre, and two bouncers from the Garden City Hilton disco in Long Island. We were all smoking dope and snorting coke—even sensible Andre had a toot. We left the club at 5 A.M., and I had to stop the limo so I could throw up.

Our next event was a party for Randy Jones from the Village People at a small restaurant in SoHo. Cornelia brought me as her plus one and I brought my whole gang. The Village People may have been dried up on the sand as far as the pop world was concerned, but they still had mega kitsch appeal. I said it was like a party for the lava lamp. I wondered whether I would be drawing such a crowd when my shoulder pads had drooped. Journalist Dave Rimmer had predicted in his book *Like Punk Never Happened* that I would end up running a greasy caff in the Old Kent Road. My cozy corner would be called Queenie's, and I would dish up eggs and bacon while reminiscing the glory days. I retorted, "Rimmer by name, rimmer by nature."

Nick Egan brought his friend Alice Temple. I gave her an E. It must have seemed like a weird initiation ceremony, Hi, I'm a pop star, have some drugs. Marilyn leered at her. "Are you a bloke? You look like one." He was right, Alice in her baggy jeans, brogues, Windcheater, and cropped hair looked like a cute little rent boy. We took her with us in the limousine and went off to Indochine, where Cornelia said she could get us free champagne. On the way Marilyn and I took a Quaalude, I gave one to Nick and Alice, which they split. Cornelia didn't need drugs; bubbles were enough to get her high.

· The club must have wondered what hit them, as we did. The 'ludes made us all mental. Alice lost control of her limbs and Nick jumped up on a table, which was more than totally out of character. I was babbling and shouting like a gypsy selling pegs. Cornelia was in hysterics. I spotted Christopher Reeve at the bar and tried to drag him to our table. "Hello, Superman. Where's Lois? Where's Lois?" He was good-natured about my antics, but it wasn't long before he collected his cape and left.

We ended up at the Palladium. I had to hold Alice up on the dance floor like a rag doll, she kept blacking out. Both her and Nick kept asking what I had given them. They didn't believe it was just a Quaalude. I suppose the mixture of drugs had reacted badly. I was fine. We all went back to my apartment and crashed.

From that night Alice became one of the New York gang, joining the disco crawl and drug dementia. I was strangely attracted to her boyish charm. And even stranger than that, she was attracted to me. Nick loved the idea of me going straight and did everything he could to wind it up.

Keeping my promise, I began writing songs for Marilyn. I got Michael Rudetsky to move his Fairlight and keyboards into the apartment, setting up a home demo studio. We threw loads of ideas at Marilyn, but he remained unmoved, moping around wrapped in a sheet, making useless comments. "Umm, don't like that. Nah, nah. Make it more like Diana Ross." Every note was a battle. It was impossible to know what Marilyn wanted. I tried every form of persuasion known to man, egging, begging, bullying, indifference. I couldn't understand Marilyn's lack of motivation. He complained that I was stifling him, but wouldn't do anything to help himself. He had no confidence in his ability, and I had no patience.

On a shopping trip I bought two T-shirts. One said, "Cocaine is God's way of telling you you're making too much money." And the other, which I gave to Marilyn, said, "Never try and teach a pig to sing. It wastes your time and annoys the pig."

The fact that we were doing drugs didn't help. We had our buzzing moments when we thought we'd found the formula, but usually the payoff was lethargy from Marilyn and tyranny from me. Michael remained amenable whatever he was on.

We came up with two great songs, "What Have I Got to Lose" and "Sexuality." "What Have I Got to Lose" had the perfect lyric for the feckless queen.

Don't get up early
Don't have to plan my day
Ain't nothing happening since you went away.

We argued about money all the time. Marilyn said if I was a true friend I would give him a lump sum, then he wouldn't have to keep asking for handouts. I knew that wouldn't work—Marilyn always lived beyond his means. If he had £100 to last a week he would go and buy a £50 pot of Helena Harnick face cream and some Harrods handmade chocolates. I told him, "If you want to live like Joan Collins you'll have to graft like her." And there were times when he proved he could pull on his resources: when I went back to London he set up a P.A. at the Limelight club in New York and pocketed $3,000.

London nightlife was in full sneer with the opening of new club nights like Asylum at Heaven and Taboo at Maximus. New York drug culture had filtered through, and everyone was popping Ecstasy and whatever else they could sniff, smoke, or swallow. With the drugs came trash fashions, primed by new disco celebrities like Leigh Bowery and Trojan, hosts of Thursday night at Taboo. They wore blue, green, or yellow faces, glitter platforms, nipple rings, bumless satin shorts, and called themselves "Pakis from outer space." I was dismissive when I first saw them—"I had a blue face years ago." But I had to admit they did it with unmistakable brilliance. The door policy at Taboo was executed with acute vulgarity by the twizzly Mark Vaultier, all legs, lips, and lip. He would hold up a small vanity mirror and ask victims in the queue, "Would you let yourself in?" When the bouncers confiscated drugs they went straight into his stripy tights.

Though he loathed "pretentious" Leigh and Trojan, Philip Sallon never missed a Taboo. Every week he wandered around counting heads and handing out flyers for the Mud club. "Amateurs, amateurs," Leigh spat back, "Philip Sallon's so brilliant managing all those stairs at his age."

The narcomania went over Philip's Vivienne Westwood crown. He couldn't understand why anyone needed drugs. He questioned my choice of friends and warned they were only after what they could get, forgetting he supplied most of the introductions. I had to laugh at his hypocrisy. People crawled around Philip because he ran clubs, and it wasn't just their money he got his hands on.

I carried on where I'd left off in New York, joining in the debauchery at Taboo, Asylum, the Wag, the Mud, or one-off warehouse parties, ending up at someone's flat, doing more E or chilling out with a fat spliff. For most people Ecstasy was enough; a few did coke if they could afford it or were offered a line, but hardly anyone did heroin and if they did they kept it quiet. Those who took heroin found each other through rumor or circumstance. Contact was in whispers. No one wanted anyone else to know their business, though the rumors hung us all.

Even in the drug world there was snobbery—dopeheads looked down on cokeheads and cokeheads looked down on smackheads and smackheads looked down on everyone. DJ Fat Tony, who was known as the "Snow Queen," would warn me away from certain toilet cubicles. "I can't believe you take that shit." He'd kick and punch friends like Richard Habberley and Paul Lonegan, who shared my stash, and blamed them for my demise. It was more a case of like attracts like.

Paul was Richard's flatmate, a sad-eyed queen with haggard film-star looks and a toxic tongue. Like Richard, he hung around for the pickings. It was mutually beneficial. They got free drugs, I got empathy. Of course, there was more to it than that. Richard and Paul were intelligent, wicked, and wonderful. They'd make me howl with their convulsive sister act, telling everyone, "Yer bitter, yer bitter." Richard once asked me, "Why do you think we take heroin?" I couldn't think of an answer, but it hung on my mind.

I was excessive with everything, sex, food, drama, drugs. A couple of times I took so much E I actually thought I was going to die. I had heart palpitations and sat rigid in a chair for hours afraid to move. I told myself I'd never touch it again, but I continued to challenge my invincibility. I bought drugs like I bought designer clothes, not just one Yohji jacket, but ten; 20 Es, a £70 block of hash, four grams of coke. I bought my Ecstasy from a designer friend who imported it to finance his shoe business and keep himself in Montana. But it wasn't that hard to find in a club.

Buying coke or heroin wasn't so easy. I had to rely on friends to sort me out, no Class A dealer wanted Boy George popping round. I would go to Islington and wait while Mimi did the running. Each time it seemed to take longer and longer, just like the song, "He's never early, he's always late. One thing you know is that you've always got to wait."

My use of heroin became more and more regular. Usually I shared it, but I was still taking far too much. In my mind I had it all under control, I didn't consider that I would ever become an addict. I knew people who were, and even I thought they were scuzzy.

At the end of September, Culture Club went back to Commodore Studios in Holland to try and write some more songs for the fourth album. I flew out in a drug daze and slept for twenty-four hours, waking soaked in sweat, feeling deathly, barely able to lift myself out of bed. For three days I could only stomach sweet foods—fruity yogurts, chocolate bars, and ice cream. I knew I was suffering a minor withdrawal: I had diarrhea, cramps, and severe depression. It was my first real warning, but I ignored it.

Despite the infected atmosphere, things went well. We came up with two new songs, "Alright Tonight" and "Move Away." "Move Away" sounded like the hit we needed. A bitter elegy in pop clothing:

I'm prepared to wear my sorrow
Everywhere we go in town
There's no need to beg or borrow
While you're there to drag me down.

The show rolled on with the occasional dustup between the bearded lady and the dwarf. Jon was full of empty civility, playing the amicable divorcé, darling this, darling that. I was looking for every opportunity to sink my teeth in. I could deal with love, hate, but never indifference. I was in several twisted minds. I wanted to leave the band, but that would have meant defeat. I wanted Jon to leave, but that would have meant losing him forever. I raged with pathetic insincerity, "I hate you, I hate you, get out of my life."

The drive for true democracy was gathering pace. There was lots of talk about how things should be in the future. Roy insisted we get equal billing on the album covers and do interviews as a band. I laughed. "Go and join Duran."

"I wish I bloody could."

Roy felt my excesses had painted us into a camp corner. I preferred poofy, he preferred poncy—designer jackets, tanned skin, and ponytails. Of course I ridiculed every suggestion. "When I want your opinion I'll give it to you." I thought all his talk of strategy was premature as we hadn't even finished the album. The only thing that mattered was the music. If we didn't have a good record no amount of posturing, posing, and planning was going to save us.

I managed to persuade the band to let Michael Rudetsky come and write with us, swinging it by playing the demos of "Sexuality" and "What Have I Got to Lose." Roy thought a Fairlight programmer would give us a more modern sound. I was relieved because Michael's ticket had already been booked and he was supposed to be arriving any moment.

My credibility seeped down the drain when Michael failed to show. It was a total farce with Billy driving back and forth to Schiphol airport and endless long-distance phone calls. Michael said he couldn't leave New York because of other commitments, but I was sure it was to do with drugs.

Back in London, Tony was flapping about a "fantastic" new deal for which we were to be paid unearthly amounts of cash. A superconcert featuring Culture Club and our rivals Duran Duran. From the outset the idea seemed ridiculous, a concert for eighty thousand satellited around the globe. I couldn't see us selling that many tickets, and Duran were about as popular as piles. Whatever the sad truth, Tony had secured a $500,000 deposit so we had nothing to lose. We were all flown to New York by Concorde for a press conference, all expenses paid.

The conference held at the Palladium club was a dull and poorly attended summit, Durannies one end and us the other like warring designer nations. Neither camp could suppress the feelings of superiority. The hacks wanted to know who was headlining. We joked ourselves out of the corners.

The next day I was booked to appear on *Good Morning America* to promote the concert. I stayed out till the early hours, Billy had to pry me out of bed for my 7 A.M. call. I was still out of it. I slapped on some foundation, drew in my eyebrows, and chucked on a large pair of dark glasses. Never had I looked so wretched for a TV appearance. The interviewer kept asking me to remove my glasses. "Oh, no," I told her, "I look like Anne Boleyn's death mask this morning." She commented on my punky hair. "It's my statue of taking liberties look." I was sniffing and wheezing like an old sea dog with emphysema.

Tony didn't know how to confront my drug problem, but he could no longer pretend it wasn't happening. Jo Bailey had warned him some months back, "George is becoming a junkie." In his usual naive way he thought things would sort themselves out. He talked about setting up a Culture Club tour, thinking if he could keep me occupied he could keep me clean, but it wasn't that simple. Anyone who tried to cross the dragon's path would have been scorched. I didn't want help or guidance. As far as I was concerned I was having a good time.

I was using at least three grams of heroin a week and was a junkie by anyone's standards but my own. It was a borderline addiction. If I had to go and work or was someplace where I couldn't get hold of any I could weather the withdrawal. Like in Holland, I would die for a couple of days, but get over it. This way I could pretend I was handling it, the old cliché.

When Culture Club went to Montreux for the final recording sessions for the album, I had a much-needed sabbatical from heroin. I still smoked spliff from morning to night, but I was in a much safer place. As before my voice was up and down. Arif Mardin had to juggle the sessions to find the right moment and again did it with minimal fuss. We used the original demo vocal for "Move Away." Everybody thought it was because of drugs, but the demo had a sad quality that I couldn't recapture. Elsewhere I did have trouble: "Gusto Blusto" and "Reasons" took hours, then days to get. Arif made me work harder than I'd ever worked before and I didn't enjoy it. It was impossible to get angry with him. I respected his history and skill, and he seemed to know when I was at breaking point. "We'll try again tomorrow," he'd say, without any guilt trips.

My sabbatical lasted only eleven days. I was on a plane back to London, insisting I had to appear at Fashion Aid, but any excuse would have done. By now I was scoring for myself from Ginty and Steve. That was my first stop from the airport. I bought two grams and went home to St. John's Wood.

I arranged for Tranny Paul to be my escort and chauffeur and hired makeup artist Carolyn Cowan to make me look my best. The poor girl had no idea what she was undertaking: she had to paint me while I was sweating and nodding off. She remained calm throughout as if this kind of thing happened all the time. Years later she was booked to paint me again for an MTV interview. "You're looking better," she said. Tranny had to trash the Highway Code to get me to the Royal Albert Hall on time. He skipped a traffic jam in Hyde Park by driving down the middle of the road, honking and hollering, "Boy George on board. Gangway!"

Backstage I met Pete Townshend. He looked at me knowingly and asked, "Are you okay?"

I laughed. "Yeh. Why?"

"Are you sure?"

I knew I'd been found out, but I walked away and joined in the screeching. Everyone was running around on Ecstasy and toking spliffs. I was modeling for my friends David Holah and Stevie Stewart from Bodymap. It was my second modeling assignment in a month. I'd modeled Bodymap's summer collection during British Fashion Week. I carried child model Felix Howard in my arms down the catwalk. Madonna, who was in the audience, never one to miss a steal, picked Felix for her next video, *Open Your Heart.*

My catwalk partner at Fashion Aid was Julie Goodyear, Bet Lynch from *Coronation Street.* She was ratty because everyone was calling her Bet. "It's Julie, Julie," she insisted. We were disappointed that she took herself so seriously. David said, "Chuck an E in her beer, that'll shut her up."

I swanked down the catwalk in dolphin-print tights and a baggy shirt covered in planets and stars. There was hardly a murmur, so I kicked my shoe into the crowd and offered my best spin and gurn.

Pete Townshend, who was compere, said, "Boy George. A living legend right before your eyes and you don't notice."

While I was in London Philip was robbed and stabbed at Busby's nightclub, where he ran the Mud. Two guys grabbed the takings, and like a fool he fought them. He had his stomach slashed open by a Stanley knife. He was chasing them up Charing Cross Road before he realized half his guts were hanging out. I rushed straight to the Middlesex Hospital to be at his side. Philip was convinced he wouldn't return from the operating theater, "I'm going to die, I'm going to die." I knew he was all right when he started moaning about the wedding dress he'd lent his friend Melanie. He wanted her to have it dry-cleaned because it was splattered in blood. He told her, "If I die you can keep the dress." I told Tranny, "I can't imagine life without Philip, it would be like losing our mother."

While he was in hospital Philip had more visitors than Lenin's tomb. Even George Michael came by with flowers. We were joking that there was a guest list. Sonia Ducie, one of his clubbing friends, appointed herself as his Florence Nightingale, mopping his brow and vetting the flow of visitors. "Philip's tired now. Could you leave?"

When I returned to Montreux I went to visit Tony and Avi at the Palace Hotel. They'd never seen me in such a bad state, sweaty, scratchy, and nodding out. Neither of them said a word, they were too shocked. When I left them I went to the studio and crashed out under the mixing desk.

Over the weeks I took every opportunity to fly back to London. Tony and Jon tried various tactics to make me stay. They said I was being unprofessional, jeopardizing the record. I was adamant: if there was no work I wasn't going to sit around being bored. As it was I was making on-the-hour calls to New York, leaving long depressed messages or moaning to Marilyn and Alice that the only thing you could score in Montreux was cheese. Alice was living at the apartment while she got her modeling career together. Marilyn squabbled with her as he had with Patrick, she was another "bloody spy."

The day Alice moved into the apartment she found Marilyn and Sydney passed out naked in different rooms. It was like the Manson murders without blood. Pizza boxes, carry-out plastic food trays,

empty bottles, and clothes littered the floor in an orgy of slovenli-
ness. Alice left a note and went to see Nick and Ellen. When she
returned Marilyn was hoovering and the flat was shining.

At the lakeside bunker Jon and I stayed in separate rooms, occasionally colliding in the corridor or between the sheets for a bit of
tie-me-up hold-me-down. It was hard not to bite the doughnut
when it was on the plate.

Jon was having his doughnut and his cake. While I was partying
in London, he was shagging Claudia, a local girl, who I thought
was dating our roadie Micky Body. Certainly they were more
suited: like Micky she was hefty and looked like she could polish
Jon off with one bite. It was unlike me to let a barracuda slip
through the net, but Claudia was a blubber-wrapped surprise. One
evening she cooked us all dinner in the roadies' flat. I complained
about the food just to be vile. I didn't trust any woman who hung
around a band. When I found out about Claudia I phoned her
and threatened death. Jon denied it, but not so I could believe
him. I was mortified. I'd been two-timed for a tree trunk.

I was no angel of abstinence, what with all my dabbling in New
York and a quick squidge with one of Marilyn's exes. I cried,
though my eyes were elsewhere. I'd found myself a new love interest, a full-lipped sparkly-eyed Irish boy called Michael Dunne who
shared a flat with Gay Robert's friends, Mark Malloy and Tony
Vickers. One Sunday night at the Roof Gardens I caught
Michael's eye. I didn't think he'd fancy me and laughed when
Tony said he did. Michael was one of those perfect boys with long
legs and a great haircut. I was too intimidated to follow it
through, but when I got back to Montreux I made sure to call
Tony's flat, casually asking after Michael.

Over the coming weeks Michael and I became close. I kept
commitment at bay as I was still clinging to Jon, and made sure
Michael knew the score. Michael was easy about it, perhaps too
easy. I didn't care, I was so wrapped up in the romance of new
love. Philip and Tranny, who knew Michael, said he was star-struck
and after me for the wrong reasons. Philip spread some particularly
nasty gossip about Michael's past, which resulted in an irate phone
call. I told Philip (as many had before) that he was a bitter old
shriveled-nobbed maid.

With all the coming and going to London, it was a miracle *From Luxury to Heartache* was ever finished. None of us expected recording to drag on so long, least of all Arif, who had to return to New York leaving his engineer, Lew Hahn, to record my final vocals. There was little use anyone screaming when I couldn't sing. I had to be in the mood. I told the others, "It's not like plugging in a bloody guitar."

Jon, Roy, and Mikey held a meeting to discuss my drug problem, deciding they would get me some help once the album was out of the way, although Jon insisted, "I bet in six months George'll be a teetotaler again." It was funny they didn't discuss their own drug problems. One morning I found Roy in the roadies' flat gray and sobbing because Alison was about to arrive and he was still flying on cocaine. Roy had to pacify her with a Cartier watch. Another time in Los Angeles, appearing on *Solid Gold,* Roy was so wired a doctor had to prescribe Valium.

After finishing up in Montreux I briefly returned to London and then jetted off to New York as quickly as I could, taking Richard Habberley as chaperon. I left London blitzed out on E. Alice, Nick, and Ellen were at JFK to meet us and we chugged into the city in a cramped Beetle.

Marilyn wasn't pleased to see Richard or the rest of the crowd that followed us over from London: Fat Tony was deejaying at Bodymap's New York show, and his minipop fag hags Jane Goldman and Juliette Silver were tagging along. Jane and Juliette were only fifteen. Jane's parents traveled with them and stayed in a nearby hotel, keeping a watchful eye. They had no idea of the debauchery that was taking place at apartment 28c. There's still argument over who penetrated who with the stiff end of a L'Oreal blusher brush. Or whose bottom was smeared with chocolate Häagen-Dazs and licked clean. It was the kind of children's party you read about in the *National Enquirer.*

I dished out my money like a gormless pools winner, believing I was only worth what I could offer friends. It was hard to tell who my friends were—I wasn't very selective. I picked up a string of cling-ons who were only too willing to grab a free E and a sushi dinner.

Fat Tony was my wayward mother, pulling me into shape when I wilted in public. I was snorting so much smack I'd become the human equivalent of a nodding dog. Our shopping trip to Bloomingdale's will never be forgotten. Up in the menswear department an eager assistant asked how he could help. I ordered his phone number, two Coca-Colas, and bought twenty pairs of Calvin Klein underpants. Tony couldn't stop laughing when they actually brought the drinks. We moved from underwear to cosmetics, where I bellowed, "Turn off those hideous bright lights." Tony put his hand over my mouth, the assistants were too polite to say a word.

Outside on Lexington Avenue I ranted at shoppers, "I'm Boy George, Boy George." An affluent old granny in fur protested, "You're not Boy George. He's my favorite." I pulled out my American Express. "Look, look." I told her she was senile and should be put in a home. Tony dragged me away. We met up with Nick, Ellen, and Billy Beyond at Trader Vic's, where I slumped into a coconut snowball ice cream. Nick and Tony were poking and kicking me. "Wake up, wake up." I came round and drawled, "Shut up, I'm not asleep." Everything was in slo-mo—getting the sugar into my coffee was like shoveling sand.

After dinner we wandered around Fifty-seventh Street. I bought Ellen a Yohji skirt and Billy a pair of stars and stripes ski boots. Tony heard Billy bitching, "Ellen gets Yohji and all I get is these." I wasn't too out of my head to be hurt. I didn't know Billy that well. He was friends with the Bodymap crew, a doll-like queen with incredulous eyes and porcelain skin. After that, I didn't want to know him.

Ecstasy made everyone touchy-touchy. It wasn't unusual for archenemies under the influence to announce their deep-seated love or for straight boys to kiss queens and queens to kiss girls. That's what happened with me and Alice.

After that night on E we woke fully dressed in innocent embrace. Things were spoiled from then on. I'd stupidly given Alice the impression I could be turned. I didn't think beyond the immediate experience. I fancied Alice, but not like I fancied boys. I liked the sensuality of kissing and touching her, but it could never have gone further. Girls didn't make me hard.

Alice wanted a relationship; I was just having fun. I carried on the kissing and the cuddling, knowing where I wanted it to stop.

It was like girlie relationships in the past, only then it was much more covert. I really believed my own innocence. When Hilda announced her love on the train from Stevenage to London, I felt angry. I hadn't created it, it was nothing to do with me.

Ecstasy loosened my inhibitions and heroin made me bloody-minded. Alice wasn't the only girl I crashed. Sydney and I played doctors and nurses, and I had a grapple with Lindsay Thurloe, the girlfriend of Marilyn's ex, Gavin. I met Lindsay at Area. She was high and gushing about her new boyfriend, Gavin. I knew the world was a tiny place. "Is it Gavin Rossdale?" I asked.

She was surprised. "You know him?"

"Yeh," I said. "He used to go out with Marilyn."

"You're lying, you're lying." The poor girl was flustered. I told her she was being naff. After more drinks and discussion, Lindsay decided I would be a good means of revenge and proceeded to stick her tongue down my throat. I responded, much to the surprise of Marilyn, who told me I was behaving like an Irish brickie. Lindsay, like Alice, was another boyish charmer, sticklike, with college-boy hair and piercing eyes. We dragged each other round the clubs, Area, Palladium, and the Paradise Garage, ending up at Morgans Hotel, where Lindsay tried to lure me upstairs. David Holah came to my rescue and Lindsay stormed off calling me a "naff cunt."

The next morning I spilled the plot to Marilyn. He went mental and phoned Gavin to tell him the good news. I made out I'd done it for Marilyn's own good, but in reality I enjoyed the wicked drama. I was flattered when Lindsay told a friend I was a great kisser. Marilyn accused me of interfering in his affairs. But he was just pissed off he hadn't got to Lindsay first and got her pregnant.

Late one evening our Durannie neighbor John Taylor knocked on the apartment door. I was surprised as we'd never nodded in public. He played some *Power Station* demos, and I played him bits of *Luxury*. Marilyn called it the battle of the superegos. I was off my head and more braggy than usual. I can't speak for John. To liven things up, Marilyn flipped on some hard-core gay porn. John blushed as Rick Humungous potted a piece of trade on a pool table. Bonnie was like a grumpy warden, rolling her eyes, sitting hunched up, scowling at the goings-on.

CHAPTER 40

Shortly before Christmas I returned home to London, skinny, sweaty, and addicted. My fellow passenger on the Concorde flight was Dave Stewart from the Eurythmics. He entertained me with tales of acid and mushroom tripping while I vomited the five-star cuisine into a sick bag.

I called Ginty and Steve from the airport and stopped off to pick up some gear, staying there till three in the morning, chatting and drinking coffee with Ginty. It was always such a relief to get to that warm flat and get sorted, once you made it through the raid-proof door.

Their flat was in the basement of a large Regency house along Westbourne Terrace, covered in scaffolding and decaying rags. You always had the feeling that someone was going to pounce on you from behind a car as you scurried to the door. They lived there with their three-year-old daughter, Kaya. The rest of the house was split into flats. At the very top lived Ginty's ex-husband, Richard, and three children from that marriage, Bridget, Naomi, and Nadia.

Ginty was the daughter of a Belgian Jew, though she looked more like an Irish gypsy, rusty-haired with translucent skin and pitying blue eyes. Not attractive in any orthodox sense, but worth more than the life she was leading.

Ginty still claims she was never a dealer. I don't call her this as an accusation, or to portray myself as the victim, but when I scored heroin, it was always Ginty that weighed and dished it out. I never had much to do with Steve. He was always dogged out in the bedroom or hiding out of the way. He was happy to let her run the shop. Out of the two Ginty had the least excuse. Steve was an addict, but Ginty never touched the stuff, which made it all the more sinister.

It would be too easy to demonize Ginty as a cold-hearted pusher, because she was more than that. She had an alluring maternal quality that drew you in and made you feel protected. Even though she was sucking me for blood and money I thought of her as a friend and developed a strong affection for her, spilling out my heart, lamenting about my habit, which in retrospect was rather naive, a bit like discussing hookers' merits with Jack the Ripper.

In the weeks leading up to Christmas I threw myself around the clubs and took as many drugs as I could get hold of. It was open house at St. John's Wood with friends and strangers crashing where they could. After a night at the Wag, Taboo, or Mud, I'd send whispers that it was back to mine. Mostly the usual crowd, Fat Tony, Richard Habberley, Paul Lonegan, Patrick Cox, Tranny, Cadillac Graham, his sister Jane, and some new faces, Hippie Richard, Warren Steingold, and David Spanbock. Warren, David, and Richard were Mud babies. They became friendly with Philip and moved on to me. There was no big ritual, I liked them, that was it. We had more in common: spliff, E, and the occasional gram of coke. It was a running joke that Philip drove most of his friends to drugs.

I met Warren and David in the summer of 1984 at one of Philip's Sunday-afternoon tea parties at his mum's place in Dollis Hill. They were wearing skimpy vests and cutoff denim shorts that pulled on the eye. I labeled them queer teasers even though they claimed to be on the side of procreation. Warren had one of those ghastly feathered haircuts, a proud nose, and a flash car with personalized plates. David was all black curls and cheeky charm—you only had to quip at him and he'd turn the color of Barbara Cartland sheets. Hippie was later into the picture, an old school friend of Warren, lanky with a box jaw, Oriental eyes, and a shag of corkscrew hair. Philip gave him the nickname "Hippie" and "TV Face"—as usual he was poisonously accurate.

Fat Tony and I were like matrons of a vicious knitting circle, always seeking out a victim, someone we knew and loved, or the innocent rockabilly who had the misfortune to follow Tranny back to one of my parties. "I wouldn't touch her, dear, she's past her shelf life." We all used to wonder where Tranny got the energy after all-night initiations in the boiler room at the Mud. Tranny on E was a scary sight. The woman lost control of what little social grace she possessed.

Like most queens Tranny had a side that was vicious and predatory. He loved me, but had the urge to stick his heel in my back, jealous and frustrated about his bottled-up genius. Tranny wanted to be a star, he could sing really well. What was lacking was discipline, determination, and confidence. In an altered state I talked about helping him fulfill his ambitions in show business, but the way I was going I couldn't help myself.

We were all screeching the night we handcuffed Cadillac Graham to a cupboard at St. John's Wood and removed his jeans to check out his much talked-about piercings. He had a ring through the end of his penis and several through his scrotum. It seemed ridiculous that he would blush after going to such trouble. Cadillac was one of those strange heterosexuals warped enough to be in our company.

Shortly before Christmas I made a visit to a private doctor in Wimpole Street. I said I'd been taking heroin, not much, and was suffering mild withdrawals. He asked few questions and coolly supplied me with DF118, a strong painkiller, and some Valium to help me sleep. I was surprised at how easy it was. Going to the doctor should have been an admission that I had a problem, but I didn't see it. I thought I could handle heroin, I'd just taken too much, that's all.

I spent Christmas Day at Shooters Hill, no heroin, no cold turkey. I used the DFs to stabilize myself and a bit of spliff smoked quietly in the toilet.

Boxing Day evening I threw a party at Hampstead for a bunch of the most mismatched guests ever. Mum, Dad, my brothers and sister, Auntie Heather and Uncle Jim, and most of London's users and abusers. Mum and Dad were now fully aware of my new habits. They surveyed the assembled company for someone to blame. There was no way they could have suspected Ginty, who turned up all mumsie with two kids and her ex-husband. I was off my head, running around with a video camera. Mum cornered me. "What have you taken? It ain't just drink." Without actually saying, she blamed Marilyn. He felt her disapproving glare burn through him.

The party fizzled out around five, a few of us went back to St. John's Wood and carried on. The two Richards, Hippie and Habit, Warren, Tranny, Fat Tony, and my brother Kevin. We finished off the morning with a trip to London Zoo. We looked wilder than any of the animals. Tony tried to stick a long-eared ginger bunny up his jumper. He soon put it back when it bit him. I argued with a waiter in the canteen because he wouldn't serve us beer. "Only coffee, tea, or soft drinks, sir."

That same week we all attended an after-club party at Patrick Cox's new flat in Swiss Cottage, where I played an evil trick on Philip, spiking his freshly squeezed orange juice with a tab of Ecstasy—I don't know why I did it. I'm sure Philip would have some Freudian explanation, but at the time he just went loopy. "Tranny, I don't feel very well, I feel awful." Tranny, who'd been in the kitchen and had seen me spike the drink, told Philip that it was me, not that it wasn't obvious.

I ran down the street after Philip, who was heading for the safety of his own flat where he could die in peace. He shouted that I was evil, sick, and twisted. Throughout the night and following day I kept a phone vigil. Tranny, who was playing nurse, gave me hilarious reports. He spent a good part of the night shaving Philip's chest and legs. Then Philip, in his released state, paid for a friend to ride up in a taxi from Brighton to keep him company.

I realized then and now that it was a terrible thing to do. I was out of it and saw it as a joke. Surprisingly, Philip didn't stop talking to me, but he wouldn't let me make him a cup of tea.

On New Year's Eve 1985 Philip threw *A Night at the Opera* at the Piccadilly Theatre. I dressed Warren up as Marilyn, Hippie as Marc Bolan, and myself as the old Boy George in hat and plaits. We looked like a horror-show Bananarama, but we were so out of it we thought we looked brilliant. I was walking around with a packet of twenty ready-rolled joints and a small bag of E, handing them out along the way.

The fact that I was due at Gatwick airport for a ten o'clock flight to Los Angeles was the last thing on my buzzing mind. My sister, Siobhan, was at the club, along with Billy Button and his girlfriend, Debbie. I invited Siobhan to Los Angeles and told Billy to arrange a ticket. Siobhan finished her Malibu and went straight home to pack her suitcase.

The partying finished at 6 A.M. I managed to get an hour's sleep before being dragged off to Gatwick. I took my smack with me and finished it off in the executive-lounge loo. The next thing I woke at the Beverly Hills Comstock Hotel wondering how I got there. The flight had been an embarrassment. I spent it snoring like a pig, coming round briefly to throw up over myself and eat a lighted cigarette. My poor old manager, Tony Gordon, didn't know what to do, he was just praying that it would be accepted as normal pop-star behavior.

The trip was for a cameo performance in the cartoon action series *The A-Team,* my acting debut, not that you could call it acting—it was more for the $100,000. I spent a good chunk of it hauling my entourage with me, hairdresser Robert, makeup artist Pearl, my sister, Siobhan, and brother David. I couldn't stand the idea of being alone.

In the episode titled "Cowboy George," I was supposed to play myself, but I was handed a Valley Girl script full of cringy lines like "Go for it, Hannibal," "Totally awesome, Mr. T." I had to stay stoned to get through the experience. Jonathan Ashby, who came to cover the story for ABC and Fleet Street, procured me a nice bag of fresh weed. During filming I would often catch Jonathan's eye and we'd break up giggling.

My morning call was at 5:30 A.M. to be on location and in makeup by 6:30 A.M. Robert kept us amused bursting into Hollywood musical pastiche. "Right in the middle of a spicy movie starring Natalie Wood." Or talking like Jean Brody. "Girls. Keep your eyes off the janitor's patch."

Ashby quoted me in the *Daily Mirror.* "This is one of the most boring things I've ever done." There was some fun, hiding from

Mr. T, who would charge into my Winnebago every morning and talk about how wonderful he was. There was a running feud between Mr. T and George Peppard, though Peppard showed more reserve. One afternoon there was a scheduled photo call. Mr. T refused to be in the same picture as Peppard. I just stood there with a blank smile. Afterward, Peppard apologized to me. Both he and his young wife seemed totally down-to-earth. Mr. T was fabulous too, but his ego was twenty-two-carat gold, like the chains around his neck.

Toward the end of filming, Marilyn joined me from New York and Jon, Roy, and Mikey flew in for a cameo. Originally the band had no part in the show but they kicked up a fuss, so Tony had a word with the producers and they wrote them in. Jon said it would look better with the album due to be released. I knew it was just ego.

I hated having Jon around, posing about the set in his tassled Lurex cowboy shirt, creeping around Siobhan and David in the hotel bar. He did his best to be nice, and gave me a music box, but I was too contemptuous to receive it gracefully. Every facial gesture and comment made me want to kill. I formed a "We Hate Jon Committee" and forced everyone to take sides. Of course, Siobhan and David were fiercely loyal; Robert and Pearl couldn't help themselves. One evening we were all taking a midnight dip in the hotel pool. Jon came back with a girl. Siobhan and David shouted, "Closet," and we all ducked under the water. Then Siobhan had a run-in with Jon over breakfast because he was slagging me off.

Being around the band for those few days convinced me the bulb had well and truly blown. I couldn't contemplate coexisting with Jon in an Abba-style nightmare. I wasn't adult enough to carry on and accept him as a friend, although I'm sure he could have coldly carried on drumming. I couldn't cope with constantly seeing what I couldn't have but I didn't have the confidence to walk out. Nagging voices kept saying, "Leave this and you might end up with nothing." Marilyn's advice was to leave. "They need you. It ain't the other way round, Blanche. Look at Diana Ross."

The last day's filming was the pinnacle of cringe. They had me pulling a hair grip from my spiky mop and using it to loosen a lock before kicking down a huge door. I felt and looked like a total prat. For the rest of the day everyone was calling me "Rambo."

With the filming completed everyone else flew home. I stayed on in L.A. with Marilyn for a few adventures. Marilyn was staying with his ex-boyfriend John Cochran-Patrick and wife, Mia. But it wasn't long before he was upgraded to a swanky pad with a pool in the Hollywood Hills. Mia's sister Toni was looking after the place for her movie-producer boss. No one else was supposed to be staying there, but Marilyn turned it into party HQ.

From the moment Marilyn had arrived in L.A. I'd nagged him to get me some heroin. He kept telling me it was impossible to get in L.A. "Let's just smoke grass and have a fab time. You don't need it." He was right, it wasn't my body craving it, it was my mind. Still I kept on and on. I said I needed a treat after all the hard work. He found someone who said they could score for us. I handed over $150 and waited. Five hours later I was presented with a gram of chocolate powder. I threw it down the toilet in a rage. I thought Marilyn had set me up to pocket the cash. When I got over being angry we both made jokes about it. "Any milk or sugar?" It must have been an omen.

That night we went to a warehouse party hosted by Josh, an old punky friend from London. We arrived in a huge black limousine. Josh greeted me with a hug. "Got any drugs?" I asked. Stupidly he handed me a gram of coke. I said I'd take a toot and bring it back. He never saw it again.

There were loads of gorgeous boys there. Marilyn kept pushing me toward them. "Go on, you're Boy George, you can have anyone you want." As we were leaving Marilyn wound down the window and lured five jocks into the limo. We drove around to different clubs desperately trying to get into their Calvin Kleins. One of them, Scott, looked like a hand grenade, his head and neck welded together on top of a tanklike physique. We took them to Motherload, a queer club on Santa Monica, to test their reserve, but the pissy queen on the door refused us entry. He knew who we were. Marilyn leaned over the counter, "Hidge pig," and laughed in his face. We retreated to a nearby kiddies' playground. Marilyn and I smoked a spliff while the boys gave us a muscle display on the climbing frames. It was much better than anything we could have seen in the club. Marilyn whispered, "What's all that about?"

After a couple of days we weeded out the likeliest candidates for conversion, Scott and Tim, and took them on a date to Spago's restaurant. They were impressed that we were sitting next to Linda Evans from *Dynasty*, but it didn't get us what we wanted. Whatever didn't happen, it was fab being seen around town with two fresh pieces of loin steak.

That Saturday I managed to get hold of six acid tabs and planned a night in the ozone. I'd never taken acid before, I couldn't wait. It was early evening, Marilyn was still recovering from Friday. I kept trying to wake him so we could start our trip. I got bored and swallowed my tab. I watched telly for a while and put on my makeup. It seemed like hours and still nothing was happening. I didn't realize LSD took ages to come on. Anxious to get high I took another tab.

Scott and his gang turned up and I shared out the rest of the acid, forgetting about Marilyn. When he finally appeared we were all in giggling hysterics. He was furious when I told him there was none left. Had there been no boys Marilyn would have left me to it, but he realized he had a certain power over the proceedings and took over, entertaining us with impersonations of glamorous supermodels and film legends. He wrapped himself in a red bath towel and balanced a tea tray on his head. "Look, Jerry Hall." Then he turned into Joan Crawford and Bette Davis. We were all convinced he was the real thing.

Later, we all went out to a club. There were loads of police cars outside, and I was convinced they knew I was tripping. We saw Danny Bonaduce, the little ginger boy from *The Partridge Family*. I started laughing at him. "You were much nicer when you were five." He called me an asshole and stormed off. Inside the club I really lost control of my body. Everything was breathing and coming at me. I started shrinking and feeling scared. I had to leave. We headed for the house in the hills. When we got back I turned bitchy. I saw that we were being desperate queens. I shouted at the boys, "Go on, go home. What do you want?" Marilyn told me I was being hideous. I carried on until I emptied the place. Marilyn was furious because he had his claws into one of the boys and I'd ruined his chances, but he soon snapped out of it.

I was tripping so badly I couldn't get myself to the toilet. Marilyn led me to the loo in hysterics and left me staring at the bowl. I caught my melting face in the mirror and started to freak. "I can't go, I can't." Marilyn's laughter echoed round the room. I pissed myself, crying and laughing at the same time.

Next thing we were whizzing down the Pacific Coast Highway in an open-topped MG, Marilyn at the wheel. It was like we were flying. I screamed and screamed, it was brilliant. We stopped off at a roadside diner. Marilyn got himself a burger and chips and lay on the bonnet, he shook his head at me. "You're a mess." We ended up on Zuma Beach watching the sunrise. I was tired and asked Marilyn, "When's it going to end?" We fell asleep cradled together on the sand. I came round at about 9 A.M., Marilyn was watching the waves, families were arriving and looked at us like we were tramps.

Later that day, when Marilyn returned the MG to Toni, Toni complained about the smell and wanted to know if we'd had cats in the car.

Marilyn and I returned to New York, where I met up with Michael and my brother Kevin. There was a moody atmosphere; Alice was hurt by Michael's presence and the fact that she had to sleep on the sofa. I didn't tell her Michael was coming or take time to explain the situation. I expected her just to deal with it. I wasn't much use to anyone in my smacked-out state.

We all hung out together, watching the ice skaters at Rockefeller Center, eating giant pizzas, and dropping E at the disco. After four fun days I had to leave Michael in New York and fly to Milan with Billy Button to meet Culture Club. It was the last thing I wanted to do.

On the way to the airport I visited my friend Larry and scored a gram of smack. I got wasted at the airport and then fell asleep in the loo on the plane. I was in there for half an hour before Billy came and woke me up. I was covered in vomit, Billy helped wipe it off. For the rest of the flight I was out, much to Billy's relief.

When we arrived in Milan I had the clever idea of passing through Customs with the remnants of my gear tucked into my belt. As I got nearer the passport desk I spotted sniffer dogs and quickly dropped the package onto the floor, kicking it away. I was shaking and sweating. After passing through I went to collect my bags. The sniffer dog jumped up on me, sniffing and whining. He could smell the heroin-laced vomit. I was dragged off to an interrogation room, where a squinty official ranted at me in Italian. Neither of us could make ourselves understood. I started to cry, I was tired and terrified. I admitted I'd been taking drugs on the plane but there was nothing left. They searched my bags and pockets, thankfully no strip search, and after an hour and a half they let me go. I cried my way to the hotel, realizing how lucky I'd been.

For the next twenty-four hours I was gone to the world. I came round the following evening and joined the band at Super Studio, where shooting had already begun for the *Luxury to Heartache* album sleeve. We were working with photographer Jamie Morgan, stylist Ray Petrie, and makeup artist Lesley Chilkes, all old friends. The call was unanimous. "Nice of you to show up." I was still feeling dazed. Jamie tried some clothes on me and a couple of wigs, but I was excused from the camera.

That night Jamie, Ray, and I went wandering around the seedy part of Milan. I was desperate to find heroin. Jamie asked, "Is it that bad?" It was. I had to go cold turkey for the rest of the five-day trip. I had the shits and the shakes. Luckily there was plenty of cocaine around, which took the edge off.

In my mind the sessions went well, though poor old Jamie had to fit the day around my wonky clock. Most days I couldn't work until early evening. Jon, Roy, and Mikey were up bright and early and wanting to get going. Jamie decided to work on my time and took on extra fashion assignments to fill out the day.

Throughout the shoot there were tantrums and personality clashes. Everyone was wired, which didn't help. Ray had to play stylist and freelance counselor. Whatever the complications, the pictures looked brilliant. Each of us had an individual portrait taken for the front of the sleeve. Finally Roy's dream come true. I looked like a young Shirley MacLaine in my cropped black wig and the boys looked like they had style. The band shots were left to last because of the difficulty of getting us all in the same place at the same time.

I was as vile as I could be to Jon, vainly disguising my desperation. One evening I returned to the hotel to find the adjoining door between our rooms wide open and my mirror daubed with erotic obscenities. I carefully peeped into Jon's room, thinking he might be waiting behind the door with a machete. He was sprawled on the bed starkers. I crept toward him and he jumped up. We shagged on every available surface and carpet space. The morning after things were back to abnormal.

Within days I was off to L.A. to meet with a Japanese advertising agency to discuss my part in a huge campaign for Suntory "Jun" gin. Arriving in L.A., I was struck by heavy depression, I was full of despair and couldn't stop crying. Tony brought in a drug therapist. I confessed I was a heroin addict. He suggested I book into a clinic straightaway. Of course he was right, but I couldn't face that, I wanted to do the commercial. I was being paid £500,000 and I thought the work would help me through it. Arrangements were made to return to Los Angeles in ten days to begin recording and filming. Then it was back to London to work on two new Culture Club videos, *God Thank You Woman* and *Move Away*. The videos were lumped together in panic, no one knew what would happen to me next.

The morning of the *God Thank You Woman* shoot I freaked out, locking myself in my dressing room. I had to have drugs. I phoned Ginty and asked her to put some gear in a cassette box and sent Billy to collect it. Billy had no idea. Once I got my drugs I emerged ready to do battle. No one said a word, they were just happy to have me on set. The video, directed by Steve Barron, was one of the first of its kind. He filmed the band in straight performance and then superimposed footage of Brigitte Bardot, Raquel Welch, and other film legends dancing around the band. It looked amazing and you couldn't tell I was as high as a skylight.

The *Move Away* shoot was a two-day catastrophe. Ironically the director was called Willie Smax, pronounced Smack. I put him and everybody else through the grinder. Jon and I had several punch-ups. I chucked a vase of water from a window as he was about to go on set in full makeup and costume and then hid in the toilet. Jon exploded, trying to kick down the door and cut me with a broken glass. Nobody could believe what was happening. One scene had Jon and me in a car chase and ended with me ramming him off the road. The second day of the shoot I was a mess, ranting one moment, then nodding out. Getting me on set was impossible. I kept changing outfits. My makeup was sweating off, I had no grip on time or reality.

Band battles and other speculative stories were starting to make their way into the press in early 1986. The *News of the World* reported that I'd sacked Jon from the group, then begged him to stay. Jon was quoted: "George isn't quite himself at the moment. It's very sad. He's feeling terribly lonely." When I read that I wanted to cut Jon's balls off.

Another story in the *Daily Mirror,* headlined "What's the Trouble with Boy?" talked about my dramatic mood swings and erratic behavior in shops. Drugs were mentioned for the first time. Philip Sallon jumped to my defense. "I don't take drugs at all myself, and I don't think George takes any either." I was furious with Marilyn, who told the *Mirror,* "I'm going out to L.A. to help a friend who has a problem. I think I can help him." We had a blazing row on the telephone. "What you gonna help me do, get more drugs?"

The day after shooting *Move Away* I was on my way back to L.A., taking Michael with me. I spent the first part of the trip recording jingles, quirky ditties in Japanese, written by an expat Brit who thought he was Bowie. He kept telling me how he wanted me to sing. After several bouts of artistic temperament Michael and I slipped out of the exit and went for a Chinese meal leaving "Bowie" and the twenty-five Japanese executives in the control room. When we returned to the hotel the Japanese were flapping. I agreed to go back the following day and complete the work—my way.

Shooting started on February 10 at Laird Studios on the old Samuel Goldwyn lot. I felt like Gloria Swanson: I had my own luxury trailer and a Japanese makeup artist cum masseur. Every morning he gave me a shoulder and head massage. It was a heavenly kick start. I needed to be relaxed just to face putting on the costumes—wedged platform slippers, a layered ornate kimono, scarves, jewelry, and a heavy gold jeweled crown. The makeup was equally complex, thick as a brick with stick-on plastic eyebrows and facial gems. I hated the way I looked and kept running into the bathroom to touch up my face.

The sets, based on an ancient Japanese myth, were a million-dollar kabuki-Berkeley extravaganza complete with Oriental chorus line. I was a princess traveling with a pig, a bird, and a monkey. Their makeup and costumes were incredible. I never got to see their real faces because they were being painted from 6 A.M. You couldn't fail to be impressed by the skill and efficiency of the Japanese. It was in diametric contrast to my Western decay. Once in makeup and costume I became a six-foot-seven bucket-mouthed royal bully. I'd swagger onto the set and shout obscenities in Japanese taught to me by the makeup artist: "Show me your cock" or "I am a prostitute." They'd cover their faces with their hands and humor me with giggles.

While we were shooting, Prince was on the neighboring sound-stage shooting the video for *Kiss*. I desperately wanted to meet him but was told it was a closed set. I saw him walking around the lot and gave him a wolf whistle. He sneered over his shoulder and minced on.

From L.A. we moved to Bakersville, a half-horse town in the desert, close to Las Vegas but not close enough. It was more of a truck stop than a town. Our motel room was called a suite, simply because it had the luxury of a bathroom, but there was little else suite about it. Room service was courtesy of the greasy Bun Boy diner across the road, a source of many a joke. The first night we all drove into Vegas, Billy, Jim Rodman, Michael, and myself. We hit the one-armed bandits. Michael had the luck of the Irish: he went there with ten dollars and came back with ninety. Afterward we went to see a drag show called *Boylesque*. When they discovered I was in the audience they threw in a quick impersonation. I wanted to crawl under my seat. One of the turns was a takeoff of Zsa Zsa Gabor. A heckling redneck shouted, "Hey, lady, are you any relation to the tooth fairy?" Turning coolly she said, "I am. Puff, you're a pile of shit." We went backstage to meet the "girls." The Tina Turner lookalike wrapped her legs round Billy; he was in love. "Blimey, guvna, it's enough to turn ya."

The next night I was back in Las Vegas minus Michael—he was suffering from jet lag. I went to see Joan Rivers performing at

Caesars Palace. Her act was so crude grown men were walking out. "Marie Osmond makes Mother Teresa look like a slut. Her legs have been together longer than the Shadow's."

Work wasn't so much fun, traipsing around the desert in full Japanese drag in the sticky heat. The director wanted me to ride a white stallion. When I flatly refused he went to Jim. Jim persuaded me onto the horse with the assurance that it wasn't to budge. It was a lucky decision. The stand-in they used for the riding shots was thrown by the horse when a light aircraft buzzed overhead.

Even though I was miles away in L.A. with Michael, Jon was never far from my mind. All I wanted was for him to feel as bad as I did. I sent him a postcard inscribed with the message "Better to have loved a short man than never to have loved at all." Janet Jackson's poignant groover "What Have You Done for Me Lately?" was pumping out of the radio, peppering my mood.

The trip to L.A. had been another sabbatical, even if it was only ten days off nonprescribed drugs. As soon as I got back to London I was at it again. I knew I was being self-destructive, but I couldn't control my compulsion. The minute I had devil's time on my hands I could think of only one thing. I surrounded myself with people who either partook or didn't question my behavior. Hippie Richard became my main cohort, crashing out on the blue leather sofa at St. John's Wood, wearing my clothes and my lifestyle, signing on the dole in my Gaultier.

Richard was a drifter, an easygoing, easy-listening pothead. I used to joke that he and Warren were the lost love children of Brian Jones and Janis Joplin. Everyone wanted to make Richard the villain. Like Marilyn, he was supposedly leading me down the path of destruction. Nothing is ever that simple. Richard would probably be the last to admit the psychological causes. To him drugs were cool, a useful and recreational tool, nothing to get hung up about. His habit chugged along like a slow train, I was the extremist. It was as if I wanted to see how many drugs I could swallow and snort before I exploded. My problems were screaming in your face.

I would pay for the drugs and Richard would collect them from his greasy biker friends on a council estate. We had other backups: a Mama Cass lookalike in Highbury, who defied all the stereotypes of the drug dealer. She was as gentle as a shaved cactus. Her mother, a Red Indian, turned her on to peyote when she was just seven.

Some weekends I would go through at least five grams of coke, sometimes more. Richard and I would snort through the bulk of it but there were always others willing to lend a snout. Fat Tony provided the entertainment, louder, camper, drunker, wilder than anyone else, pulling old Culture Club costumes from my wardrobe and wearing them the wrong way round, trousers on the head and what have you, running down the mews in biker boots and an oversize Joseph cardigan, pulling it up to reveal bright orange underpants and screaming so loud. The neighbors would bang on the wall or the door and try and have a nose at the mayhem. They lived next to a real rock star.

I had to leave the screamers at home and fly to Stockholm for a royal command performance hosted by Bob Hope. I took my DF118s and promised myself I'd stay clean this time. I was moody and ratty. Arriving at Arlanda airport I had a freak-out at my press agent, Jo Bailey, who'd arranged a photo call without telling me. I called her a cunt at the top of my voice. No one knew where to put their face.

Outside the Sheraton Hotel the street was covered in candles: crowds were holding vigil for Prime Minister Olof Palme, who'd just been assassinated. I got to my room, unpacked my bag, and found a gram of heroin in a pair of trousers. I jumped up and down and broke my promise. I was totally bombed out when I appeared in front of King Carl Gustaf and Queen Silvia.

The following week when Culture Club were back in Los Angeles to appear on *Solid Gold* and *Soul Train,* Jo Bailey resigned in a red-faced fit. She was frustrated and felt that no one was taking my drug problem seriously. Back in London she went to see Richard Branson, who said he'd look into it.

I spotted Janet Jackson at the *Solid Gold* studios and went over to introduce myself. She didn't recognize me without my makeup and treated me like a pestering fan. I just about managed to tell her I loved her last record when she turned away. Later when I was in costume one of her entourage approached me with a video camera and asked me to say hi to Janet. I told him to stick the camera up her arsehole, she was a stuck-up cow. Janet came to my dressing room all tearful and apologetic. I said even if she thought I was a fan, I still deserved basic courtesy. The following year I saw her at the *Top of the Pops* studios in London. I waved at her and she glared right through me. "Miss Jackson, if you're nasty . . . "

Culture Club scored a hit with "Move Away," which peaked at number seven. We were all delighted. There were hopes that success would bring me to my senses. No such luck. The day we appeared on *Top of the Pops* we nearly lost our slot and almost got banned for life because I wouldn't come out of the dressing room. They told me I had an hour and it seemed to zip by really quickly. If anything, "Move Away" was the perfect epitaph.

Another story appeared about me and Alice in the *News of the World*. "Stunning Alice Temple, 18, says the gender-bender pop star made love to her after confessing to a long-term relationship with Culture Club drummer Jon Moss . . . " She told them I was a gentle lover, that I took her virginity. If it took place I was too out of it to remember. I loved her dearly as a friend, I even fancied her a bit, but I was A1 queer. I should have stopped the canoodling long ago but whenever I was high it just seemed to happen. Both Alice and I played out to the media that we were an item. It suited me to keep them guessing. Jonathan Ashby pestered us for ages to give him the exclusive on our romance. We fed him stories. Ashby set up an interview between Alice and the dreadful John Blake, pop columnist on the *Daily Mirror*. Ostensibly the interview was meant to be about our romance, but what they were really after was the drugs story. Alice said she didn't know anything about drugs.

Alice and I fell out for a while. She wrote in her diary, "Saw George at Taboo. Ignored me. I hate him now." She couldn't cope with the pain and chose hatred as the easy option. Things had got difficult between Michael and me. He was jealous of Alice and didn't like reading she was my girlfriend. It was all typical of my perfect selfishness. I hadn't grown out of playing people against each other.

I rushed off to Paris for fashion week with Marilyn, Dencil, Richard Habberley, and Fiona Russell Powell, journalist and good-time ghoul. It was almost like being at Taboo there were so many

London faces, Trojan, who had been unsuccessfully wandering round Paris trying to find a tattooist to write "cunt" on his forehead, Leigh, John Maybury, Helen, Ray Allington, the Bodymap lot. I cornered photographer Paul Gobel at the Gaultier party. "Got any drugs?" When he couldn't sort me out I decided to go home. Marilyn was livid. "You're ridiculous. Just 'cause there's no drugs in Paris you're going home." In London Marilyn huffed off to his flat in Maida Vale and I tore apart St. John's Wood looking for stashed drugs. I hid them all over the place.

Fiona Russell Powell was a friend I kept at bay. She wrote clever bitchy articles for *The Face* and liked to be the first to tell the world your worst business. Richard Habberley shared a flat with her in Old Street when he wasn't crashing out at my place. We first met in 1981 when we both went to audition as a presenter for Channel 4's *The Tube*. Fiona looked like Monroe in mourning, black heels, tight black fifties dress, dead bleached hair, and heavy red lips. She was just down from the north and much friendlier than she became.

Fiona interviewed me for *The Face* the day after arriving back from Paris. She tried to use our intimacy to get me to dish. I was high, my tongue was loose, but not loose enough to wrap round my throat. She kept asking about drugs. I told her I'd punch her in the face if she kept on. She printed my threat. "When was the last time you cried?" she asked. I told her, "Jon Moss has probably made me cry more times than anyone I've ever known in my life. Obviously I'm being evasive about it, but I really love Jon." I also said, "I sleep with men and I would love to go to a premiere in a ball gown on the arm of a man."

CHAPTER 41

In my heroin oblivion I had no idea what was really going on in my life. The backbiting, jealousy, fear, and thieving. The friends who were helping themselves to my drugs were also helping themselves to my money and wardrobe. I drew ridiculous amounts of cash out of the bank and left it lying around, asking for abuse. Bonnie was housekeeper and hawk, watching and hating my friends. She kept vigil while I was sleeping, making sure I didn't vomit and die in my bed. My brother Kevin was also around, trying to reconcile his drug taking with brotherly love.

My mood swings would have confused the most seasoned psychiatrist. I defied the textbook description of a heroin addict. Heroin made me manic most of the time, whizzing around, scratching, talking twenty to the dozen. I'd nod out for a couple of hours and then spring back like *Night of the Living Dead*, holding a logical conversation one minute, the next eating a mud face pack. Then there were the shopping sprees. One morning Hippie and I went down to the chemist in Maida Vale and I spent £100 on toiletries. I'd go to Joseph's on the Kings Road, or Jones in Covent Garden, and buy everything. The one thing I loved about being a junkie was being skinny. I thought everything looked good on me. I would change outfits five times a day, just for something to do.

Trips in the daylight were rare. Most of the time I hid away with the curtains drawn, happy in my drug cocoon. What little food I ate was junk style. Cheese on toast, ice cream, sweets, and Marks & Spencer's mousses and desserts.

Jon continued to haunt me. I knew he was having it off with girls, and even though I had Michael, it killed me. I tormented him by playing appropriate songs on to his answerphone: "Don't You Want Me Baby" and "Drop Dead" by the Banshees. Jon kept in contact with me. Every phone call ended in rage. I would type vile ten-page letters and then throw them in the bin. Jon was jealous of Michael. He rang raving that he was going to beat Michael up, but when they met he was as congenial as chicken soup. I couldn't break free from Jon, physically or, even worse, emotionally. I talked and talked about him in the negative, but I wasn't fooling myself. It must have been strange for Michael: he never said much about it—when he did I'd make some excuse about my career.

Luxury to Heartache was Top 10 in the U.K. and Top 5 in the U.S., selling under a million worldwide, a couple of million less than *Waking Up with the House on Fire*. In my mind selling a million records wasn't that bad, but in business terms it signaled disaster, especially as recording costs were in the region of £500,000. The real problem was nothing to do with statistics; the heart and soul had dropped out of Culture Club. We were art imitating disaster.

Jon, Roy, Mikey, and Tony met to discuss plans for a forthcoming American tour. They all agreed things looked iffy. They decided to cancel the tour, freeze the band, and try to get me into a clinic. Despite all the tough talk, things carried on the same.

I moaned to *Smash Hits,* "I'm fed up with this business, I don't mean music, I love music, I'm just sick of being a pop star. I know I could be famous again if I wanted, I know all the tricks, but I really can't be bothered. In some ways I think everything that happened last year was good. It made me think about what I was doing for the first time in ages. I know I must sound tragedy-struck at the moment, but I enjoy tragedy in a way. Basically I'm a bit of a tragedy queen."

On April 9, another story written by my so-called mate Jonathan Ashby appeared in the *Evening Standard,* "Worried

About the Boy." Within an hour of the paper hitting the stands, Annette Witheridge, a reporter from the *News of the World,* was scratching on my doorstep. Normally I was careful, but I'd been up all night snorting coke and foolishly opened the door. Witheridge told me about the story. I said I hadn't seen it and couldn't comment. She offered to go and buy a copy for me. I was anxious to read it and said I'd go with her. We drove down to Lisson Grove in her MGB Midget and I bought the paper. The article centered around gossip from friends and my appearance on Michael Aspel's show a few weeks earlier. "The Boy was not his usual self. He was sweating heavily under the studio lights and at one point appeared to be drifting off to sleep while Aspel was interviewing his other guest, John Cleese." A "source" had also told him I spent whole days lying in the bath and looked gray without my makeup. I was furious about the piece and got Witheridge to drive me to Fleet Street so I could hit someone. I arrived at the *Express* building and demanded an audience. Spencer Bright, cowriter of this book, was the unwilling stooge sent out to face me. As far as I was concerned, any journalist was fair game and I took it out on him. Spencer told me to go home before I embarrassed myself further. It was too late, Witheridge had her story, which appeared the following Sunday: "Health Fear Over Wild Boy George":

> I witnessed the star's sad plight for myself last week . . . He emerged unshaven wearing mirrored glasses, but in great form. In the next four hours I laughed as jokey George ordered sausage and bacon in a Jewish restaurant, was stunned as a story in a newspaper sent him raving and screaming like a mad man, then *watched* horrified as he turned into a gibbering, sobbing wreck.

Marilyn was sparkling after a comeback appearance at the Hippodrome club. They paid him £5,000, and he was playing the pools winner. "Let's get the first plane to Jamaica. We're a mess." He thought a holiday in the tropics would help us kick the habit. I knew it wouldn't be that easy and I didn't really want to stop.

I told Ginty and Steve we were going to Jamaica. They said they'd been planning a trip to see Steve's family, wouldn't it be great if we were all there together? Marilyn didn't agree. He said we had to get away from Ginty. I knew he was right. The day before we left I went to score, much like any other day. Ginty and I walked round to a travel agent in Praed Street to see if there were any cheap flights. I ended up lending her money to pay for the tickets. My habit had reached epic proportions, and logic had long since flown out the window.

I flew into Jamaica with a two-week supply of DF118s and a gram of coke, which I tucked into my underpants. I often used cocaine to help with heroin withdrawal. It was such a dangerous game, switching from one to the other. I didn't intend to bring the coke through Customs but as we came in to land I decided against throwing it down the toilet. I had second thoughts when they hassled us at Customs and marched us off for an unfriendly chat in Mr. P. W. Williams's office. Mr. Williams was on a power trip, shouting and banging the table. "This is not your passport." I rolled my eyes. "Whose is it then, the Queen Mother's?" All I could think of was the small packet digging into my groin. "Look," I said, "I am Boy George. I'm here for a holiday, that's all." Mr. Williams laughed. "You is not Bwoy Gearge. What is your purpose in this country?" I was starting to feel desperate, afraid he would order a strip-search. I told him, "If you don't let me go I'm going to call the prime minister's office." He laughed and pushed the phone in front of me, "Be my guest." I had Mitzi Seaga's home number from the last trip and dialed, praying she'd be there. She came straight to the phone all sunny and happy to hear from me. When I explained the problem she asked to speak to whoever was in charge. Mr. Williams's face dropped. "I see . . . I see . . . Okay." Seizing the opportunity, I asked if I could go to the toilet. They were off their guard and let me go alone. I flushed the coke away, despairing of my stupidity.

After our ordeal, Marilyn and I were driven to our villa in a government limousine. It was the same place we'd stayed for three years running, up in the hills of Ocho Rios overlooking the sea. Our roly-poly cook, Hyacinth, rushed out to greet us, grabbing hold of my arm, "Lord, you is so thin. Wha' happen?" That evening we were treated to a fatten-up feast of chicken, rice, dumplings, and plantain. I picked at it, unable to hold much of it down. Hyacinth kept shaking her head. She knew something was wrong.

For two or three days we lay by the pool listening to reggae in the gorgeous heat. I was twitchy, even though I had my DF118s. All I could think about was heroin. I couldn't wait for Ginty and Steve to arrive on the island. I'd given them our address without telling Marilyn. When they turned up he couldn't hide his disappointment. Ginty made up some excuse that they were passing by on their way into Kingston. They were with Steve's sister and her boyfriend.

As soon as I saw Ginty I pulled her to one side. "I need something now." I got three grams to cover myself in case she didn't come back and dashed to my room, leaving Marilyn to make awkward conversation. For the rest of the day I stayed locked behind my bedroom door, fan full on, blinds drawn. Marilyn kept knocking. "What are you doing? Come downstairs." Finally I let him in. I was in gold lamé swimming trunks, my hair greased to my head, scratching and pinned, unable to keep steady as I snorted lines of heroin from a tabletop. Marilyn claims he was disgusted, but however disgusted he soon joined in.

A few days later Ginty and Steve came back to the villa and stayed with us. They were carrying excessive amounts of heroin and wanted a safe hiding place. I told Steve I didn't want it in the house in case the worst happened, so he hid it outside in the bushes. There was panic the next morning when Steve stumbled out of bed and saw the gardener burning leaves where he'd stashed the drugs. He ran screaming, shooing the gardener, and rescued his reason for living. Hyacinth and the maids came out to see what the commotion was about. Ginty told them she'd lost some jewelry, but Hyacinth was wiser than that. All day she kept saying, "That's a nasty man, I tell you, a nasty man." She was proved right when one of the maids found Steve wrestling with Ginty. They were both naked, Ginty's face was blue. The maid was screaming, "He's killing her, he's killing her." Later

Ginty cried to me and Marilyn, saying she hated Steve and was going to leave him after she'd sold the drugs and made some money.

While I was in Jamaica I received a letter from Richard Branson.

> *It's beginning to become plain to everyone around you that you have a problem (which you are not willing to acknowledge). So clear that one newspaper is now offering £50,000 to anyone who can prove it. You believe you have this problem under control, but it's patently not true. For instance, last week you threw away a TV appearance in Holland, your management have just cancelled the most important TV in Italy in case the same thing happened again . . .*
>
> *You have a chance of being right back at the top and it would be such a ridiculous waste if you chuck everything away now . . .*
>
> *Before it's too late I'd like to suggest you acknowledge you have a problem and let us help you do something about it.*

I couldn't be bothered to read all of the letter. I thought Branson was interfering and tossed it in the bin.

As zonked as we were, Marilyn and I thought we could do some recording while we were in Jamaica. Steve introduced us to producer singer Chris Stanley, and through him we met reggae legend Big Youth and Tyrone Downey, keyboard player with Bob Marley and the Wailers. I tried writing songs with Tyrone, there were some good ideas, but nothing got finished. Tyrone put together a demo of an old reggae classic, "How Could I Leave," which Marilyn and I both tried singing. The combination of coke, spliff, and heroin left us croaking.

Chris Stanley took us up to Blue Mountain Studios in Kingston. Outside there were loads of Rastas toking and talking in the falling light. They turned their backs and mumbled "batty boy" at us. I wanted to leave, Marilyn said they'd get over it. Later we went to Stanley's faded villa and partied through the night. Stanley's claim to fame was mild success in Jamaica and being Grace Jone's ex-boyfriend. Stupidly, I got overfriendly with him and agreed to appear in a video for his new single. Then one day messing around in the studio he ran at me with a knife, screaming "dirty blood clat." Because of that I refused to sign a release for the video. It made no difference, he used it anyway.

We were hanging with the ruff of the rough, freebasing in the back room of Jack's shabeen, handing out my London number to a psycho-Rasta with diamond teeth. Tyrone kept telling us to be careful. He seemed the only decent one around. He got called a "batty boy" for letting us spend a night at his house.

Marilyn and I would go for late-night spins around the island, nodding at the wheel, almost killing ourselves at every turn. One night I crashed the car in the hills. We were so gone we just fell asleep right there in the ditch. In the morning we were woken by a group of uniformed schoolchildren banging on the window. We had to walk to a village nearby and hire a rescue truck. When we got back to the villa, Hyacinth went loopy, like she was our mum. She said she'd been worrying, no one had called and she'd cooked dinner. Marilyn snapped, "Don't tell me what to do. I'll come and go as I please." I realized we'd been selfish and should have called. Marilyn said it was our food to waste if we wanted to.

Toward the end of the holiday we decided to stay longer. Our villa was booked up so we had to move to the other side of town. Ginty came with us after running away from Steve. She said it was over this time. She would stay with us for the week and then fly to New York to unload her drugs. At the new villa I stayed hidden in my room too paranoid for company. I bought enough rocks to kill myself, and with Ginty around the heroin was on tap. I hardly ate, living on a helter-skelter diet of drugs, freebasing myself into tearful panic, then snorting smack to ease me down. I had body cramps, my heart was pounding like it was about to give out. A couple of times I thought I'd really had it. I just couldn't stop.

Even though Marilyn was thick with Ginty, he was aware she could be the death of us. He said we'd need another holiday to get over Jamaica. I phoned Jim in L.A. and he arranged a ten-day cruise round the Caribbean which we would pick up from San Juan in Puerto Rico at the end of the week.

The last few days in Jamaica we were joined by Bonnie, who nagged me to fly her over, sensing the danger I was in. I treated her badly, ignoring her most of the time and then ordering her to drive me to get more drugs.

When we left Jamaica Ginty padded her knickers and bra with heroin. She seemed absolutely fearless. I told her to keep away from us at the airport, even though I had heroin stashed in my makeup box. We all flew to Miami; Bonnie and Ginty went on to New York, Marilyn and I to Puerto Rico.

In San Juan we booked into adjoining cabins on the Dutch ocean liner, then sat on deck enjoying the tropical breeze as we steered out to sea. "Thank God," said Marilyn. "We're going to be sick for a few days, but it's gonna be worth it." He didn't know about my emergency supply. I planned to take it if things got unbearable but, of course, it was all gone within the first twenty-four hours. After that we both had to face up to cold turkey. We slept for most of the next day, retching, sweating, and crying, asking each other what we were going to do. At night we sat on the deck wrapped in blankets watching the waves.

We made friends with the ship nurse and persuaded her to give us Valium, but it was like putting a plaster on a severed head. We only made it through four stops before desperation and sickness forced us to jump ship in Guadeloupe. We left with only hand luggage, arranging for our cases to be sent on to New York. We took a cab around the island trying to find drugs. The driver, who only spoke French, didn't understand our game of charades. We smoked imaginary spliffs and snorted imaginary lines, hoping he would get the picture. He just shrugged and drove us to a beach. We both screamed at him, "You fucking idiot." Frustrated, we told him to drive us to the airport, where we tried to find the fastest route back to civilization. Our only hope was a sixteen-hour flight to Paris, with two stops. We decided to take it.

I called a friend in New York and asked her to fly to Paris with some heroin. She said, "Are you fucking crazy?" I was hysterical and crying. "I'm really ill, really ill." She said, "I can't." I begged her. She finally agreed, but said I'd have to take responsibility if she got caught. In my desperation I was oblivious to the consequences. Marilyn said, "There must be a quicker way of getting to New York. What century is it anyway?" It was 5 P.M., the Paris flight wasn't due to leave till 9 P.M. Marilyn and I were so ill we didn't know what to do. Every five seconds we would wander up to the information desk and rant. "There must be something, there must be." They told us there was a private airfield up the road. We could fly to Antigua and get an international flight from there. Without bothering to call New York we left the airport. We had to walk half a mile in the spiteful heat. Marilyn was weighed down with baggage, I was too sick to carry anything. An hour later and $300 lighter we were flying triumphantly toward Antigua. As we landed I spotted an American Airlines jet ready to take off—without us.

I ran up the steps and asked the stewardess if they were going to New York. They were, but we had to have a boarding pass. I offered to pay there and then, but they wouldn't let me. "Wait for us, please wait," I said and darted into the main terminal. I had to plead, drop my name, and cry before they agreed to hold up the plane. They issued two tickets, but then as we tried to go through a policeman barred our way. I started to scream hysterically and forced my way past him. He had a gun and could have shot me, but I didn't care. I ran up to the plane shouting and waving the tickets. The steps had been pulled away and the engines were buzzing. I didn't think we had a chance, but I kept waving. By some miracle I caught the pilot's eye and we were allowed on. Never in my life have I been more grateful. I kept saying, "I love Americans, they're so fab."

We'd tried phoning my friend from a credit-card phone on the plane, but it wouldn't work. I counted the hours, I was sure we'd get to JFK before she left for Paris and everything would be fine. When we arrived in New York I ran to information. They told us an Air France was due to leave in ten minutes from another terminal. We got them to page, and then ran sweating and panting to find the flight. My friend was about to board when we found her and couldn't believe we were there. "What the fuck is going on?" Minutes later Marilyn and I were in the men's toilets relieving ourselves of the sickness. Then we hired a limo and headed over the Fifty-ninth Street bridge into the glittering city.

Things were no better in New York. We met up with Ginty, who was staying with friends down in the Village. She started charging us $500 for a gram of heroin, five times what she charged in London. She knew Marilyn and I were sick and had little choice, and there were reports on the news that dodgy heroin was being sold on the streets—someone had died. Ginty's excuse was that I owed her money for drugs I'd had in Jamaica. I'd been stealing off her all the time, but I didn't think she knew. She told Marilyn the big guys in London were threatening Steve because the heroin had been taken on credit and they wanted their money. Ginty and Steve had set up a deal in Jamaica which fell through, that's why Ginty came to New York to try and off-load it. Marilyn sided with Ginty. He didn't think she was doing anything wrong; she'd taken the risk of smuggling the drugs into New York. In five days I gave Ginty almost $5,000 cash. Finally Ginty and I had a massive fight over money. I threw her out of the apartment—she was crying hysterically, but I didn't care. A few minutes later she came back for her coat. She seemed curiously calm: she knew she had the upper hand.

Later that day we ran out of heroin. Marilyn said I'd have to ring and apologize. He'd already called her himself. I said, "Fuck the bitch," but I was beginning to feel like death. I called and crawled, she promised she was on her way, but I lay there for six hours, curled up on the sofa, vomiting bile.

When we were high everything seemed fine, but the clock was always ticking toward desperation hour. No matter how much heroin I bought, it never lasted. Once I was out of it I lost all sense of proportion, snorting more heroin just because it was there. It's by God's mercy I never overdosed. I'd snort it in the back of cabs or nip into doorways on the street. Sometimes late at night I'd wander around New York looking in shop windows, drifting till daylight, watching Manhattan come alive as I withered away. I was so thin no one knew who I was. I spent a lot of time thinking, wondering what to do. I didn't think I would ever be able to stop.

Maybe a trip to the head shop to buy freebase equipment, cigarettes, and skins. Then to Häagen-Dazs to stock up on giant tubs of ice cream. There were late-night supermarket sprees to buy snack food that was either thrown up or thrown away. We moved around in a bubble unaware of our accentuated behavior, shouting when there was no need to shout, laughing when there was nothing to laugh at.

One morning I tried to get out of bed and was involuntarily thrown across the room from a convulsion. It was twenty minutes before I realized where I was. I called Bonnie into the bedroom and told her I was going back to London. I asked her to stay behind and throw Marilyn out of the apartment. When Marilyn caught me packing my bags he freaked out, "D'ya mind telling me what's going on?" I spat all my frustration and hatred out at him. "You're a fucking user. You've got two days to leave the apartment." Bonnie drove me to JFK. I missed the evening Concorde and had to wait hours for the next flight. I didn't care, I was just glad to be going home.

Marilyn's recollection of events is very Tom of Finland meets Norman Bates. Two nights before leaving I cried and pleaded with him, "I love you, don't leave me, everyone leaves me." The next day I came at him with a carving knife, swinging a pair of hand-cuffs. Apparently he disarmed me. Anything is likely and more than probable. There was another story about me keeping him awake all night after I decided to hang pictures in his room using a power drill. He kept moaning that he wanted to go to sleep. I kept him up till five o'clock as a revenge for taking sides with Ginty. I had my revenge on Ginty too. She gave me $1,000 to give to Steve when I got home, but I kept it.

At Heathrow the press were there to greet me. A gaunt picture and a brief interview appeared in the *Daily Mail*. I told the reporter I had amebic dysentery and this was the reason I'd lost two stone. I denied reports that I was a heroin addict. "I'm not guilty . . . I've always tried to tell kids to stay off drugs. I've never taken them myself but people think I've been going round taking everything in sight. It's not true and it never will be true." This time I managed to wangle my way out of controversy, although the rumors were intensifying.

The next morning I went to visit Steve to buy some drugs. I knew I was taking a risk, but my desperation for drugs overcame any logic or fear. Steve looked rabid, like he'd been up for days. He ushered me in and double-locked the door, which put the fear into me. As I came into the hallway I saw a tall African guy with an attaché case disappear into the kitchen. We went into the living room. There was base equipment set up on the sideboard and a big fat plastic bag of coke. Steve lit up the pipe and offered me a hit. I took some, but all I wanted to do was score and get the hell out of there. The base made me double paranoid. Steve was sweating and ranting like a lunatic. He asked me to lend him the money to get a car. I laughed nervously and asked if he had any drugs. He didn't, he said he only had coke. I bought a couple of grams. As I was leaving Steve asked about the money. I made up some excuse about going to the bank and said I'd bring it round in a day or so.

Three days later I was back in America promoting *Luxury to Heartache*. My first stop was Boston, where I performed at the KISS radio birthday celebrations, dueting with Gloria Estefan and Miami Sound Machine on their aptly titled hit "Bad Boy."

I was out of my nut, running around, shouting, demanding attention. I was dressed in a black Vivienne Westwood bondage suit and a Boy baseball cap. The Boy logo emblazoned across my hat was the only way I could be recognized. I was so skinny most people thought I was a fan. I even heard someone say, "That's Boy George?"

Just before going onstage I nipped into the ladies' for a toot. I bumped into Prince's leggy protégé Apollonia and sat talking to her while she did her makeup. When she finished her lips she straddled me and pressed her nose against mine. She was completely camp. I didn't know where to look. I grilled her about Prince. Was he a nice person? She said he was the best and that he thought "Karma Chameleon" was a "bad" tune. I couldn't wait to tell Roy Hay.

Back at the New York apartment Marilyn was mixed up in some madness of his own. Bonnie arrived in Boston with enough evidence to have him certified. One afternoon she'd come back from doing a bit of shopping and found him holding Sydney by her legs out of the apartment window, twenty-eight floors from certain death. Staying calm, Bonnie asked, "What's so interesting out there?" Marilyn said there was a man watching them from the street and talking about them. Bonnie said, "Yeah, he's probably saying look at that fucking idiot hanging out the window." Both Sydney and Marilyn were high on freebase.

After that Marilyn kept pulling imaginary poisonous string from his mouth, the air vents, and the sky. He kept wrapping it around Sydney's hand saying, "Can't you feel it?" At first Sydney and Bonnie thought he was joking, but they soon realized he wasn't.

He said the string had come to take away his looks and disfigure him. It got so bad that he blocked up all the vents with cotton wool and put masking tape around the windows.

When Bonnie finally got rid of Marilyn he moved in with Sydney. Things got worse. He hung bedsheets over the windows and stood in front of the mirror for hours pulling the "poisonous string" from his mouth. He was convinced there was a gunman stalking him and told Sydney, "George is trying to have me killed." He ran upstairs to the neighbors and screamed, "I know you work for Boy George." Then he called out the police. Sydney told them he was on medication and they went away shaking their heads. Finally in desperation Sydney tried to get Marilyn to a hospital. He refused and became violent, so she had two beefy friends remove him from her apartment. From Sydney's he moved to the Chelsea Hotel for a few days and left without paying the bill. Then Lori, a friend of Sydney's, put him up. He was still in contact with Ginty and claimed they became close during that difficult period.

After Boston I flew out to Los Angeles, meeting up with Jon and Mikey to appear at the Disneyland Summer Vacation Party. Roy was replaced by one of our American road crew, John Spangler, because Alison was due to give birth to her first child. She told Roy, "Just for once I come before the band."

The flight to L.A. was internal, which meant no Customs. I was able to carry my heroin and stay gone for the two days we were there. Everyone could see what a mess I was in. Jim Rodman confronted me. "I don't know why you're doing this to yourself." I started to philosophize, I said I was happy and wanted to be a smack addict for the rest of my life. Jim was angry with Billy Button because he felt he was colluding in my drug taking. But Billy was powerless. Even out of my mind I was impossible to steer. All he could do was keep an eye on me and catch me if I nodded out. I was like a blind man on roller blades in a china shop. The TV show was broadcast from inside Disneyland. I wandered around the park in full pop-star drag. Billy and Jim only had to watch the swelling crowds to see where I was.

Despite being hideously estranged, Jon and I had a blissful encounter. Maybe he had one drink too many, I didn't care, I was just happy to have him in my bed. I can't recall ever discussing my drug problem with Jon—we didn't speak that much, except to trade sarcasm. What kind of monster must I have been to create such a space between myself and the rest of the world?

Perhaps Tony should have canceled all my engagements and pointed me toward the nearest drug unit. Jim and the others felt the best cure was to keep me occupied, but I don't think any of them realized how easy it wasn't going to be.

Back in London Mum and Dad were starting to get desperate. They started to educate themselves about drugs by phoning help lines and reading pamphlets. They phoned Tony, asking him what he was doing about it. Tony fixed up a meeting between my parents and Dr. Meg Patterson, who was famous for helping Keith Richards, Eric Clapton, and Pete Townshend. Meg Patterson stressed the importance of getting me into treatment but said without my commitment it would be worthless.

Mum arrived unexpectedly at St. John's Wood to have it out with me. I was angry and told her I wasn't a kid anymore, she couldn't tell me what to do. She pulled me in front of the mirror. "Look at yourself." Even her tears failed to reach me, I was so cut off from my emotions. I just wanted her to leave me alone. She started scrubbing the surfaces in the kitchen and washing up. I shouted at her, "Leave it, Mum, leave it."

There were all sorts of plots being hatched. Mikey and Roy discussed a kidnap plan with Dad. Dad wanted to grab me, tie me up, and take me to a house in the Irish countryside. He'd been watching too many movies. He told Kevin to keep an eye, and find out the names and addresses of dealers, which was a bit like asking a horse to give up its grain sack. Kevin, like Hippie and the others, was up to his nose in it. Kevin never took heroin, but he was still in no position to point the finger.

Ginty arrived home from New York; she was furious I hadn't given Steve any money. They both turned up at St. John's Wood, banging and shouting. Hippie and I hid behind the curtains laughing. It was a nervous laughter: I knew if the neighbors called the police we'd all be in trouble. They were outside the house for ages. Steve started leaving threatening messages on my answerphone.

Marilyn came back from New York and moved in with Ginty. He had no money and nowhere else to go, but I didn't see it like that.

It confirmed that he'd been conspiring with Ginty against me in New York. Ginty told Marilyn that I'd called and told her not to put Marilyn up, which was highly unlikely as we weren't speaking.

"Luckily" I found other places to score, from Babs, my old punk friend, and a couple of unreliable addresses off the Holloway Road. It was always so desperate, people promising to deliver then flaking out, cab excursions to unsavory corners of suburbia, twitchy rendezvous in tube stations and burger bars in Kings Cross. Mimi didn't have a desperate habit like me; if we couldn't find smack she was happy with some spliff and a bottle of Muscadet, but I went to pieces, I just couldn't go without.

Through Helen and Mimi I became close to a skinny boy called Stephen Brennan, who had angelfish lips and a theatrical voice. Everything was "gorgejuss," "geeniuss," and "fabuluss." He shared my drugs and kept me amused with his slippery wit. Like so many of those unique characters, his talents were shadowed out by massive insecurity and self-loathing. Stephen made brilliant collages and badges with warped but very poignant slogans. "She only wanted to look cool in front of her friends" cut out from an antiheroin advert and one he gave me after a row with Jon, "It's far less clear what lovers do." He carried his badges around in a Safeways' carrier and handed them out when the mood took him. One day I was so gone I gave him a load of tenners and fivers, which he cut up and turned into the most ostentatious badges. Everyone tried to grab one. My favorite was made out of a credit-card slip after a trip to Bliss, the late-night chemist in Marble Arch.

Stephen dabbled with drugs, just now and then due to a lack of funds—he would have done it more if he could. He had names and addresses, which were very useful for those times when we were scraping around. Sometimes if I was really impatient I would go with him and wait in the street. Once or twice I met the source, nervous shifty types surprised to see my face.

As well as smack, coke, and spliff, we were starting to take lots of different pills, Valium, Rohypnol, temazepam, DFs, and Tempgesics—all downers of one kind or another. The pills came on prescription or off other junkies. Sometimes we used them for withdrawal, but more often as another way of getting high, defying the warnings not to mix them with alcohol. Getting and taking drugs was a sport, no less dangerous than joyriding or surfing on the roofs of trains.

With my body rattling like a pillbox I took part in the Sport Aid Race Against Time, a sponsored run in aid of Bob Geldof's Ethiopia appeal. I took along my brother Gerald, the athlete of the family. Gerald opted for simple vest and shorts while I went for white sequins and a Boy cap, to avoid going unnoticed. Neither of us did much running, unless there was a camera in sight. We kept slipping off the trail for toots of cocaine, which should have given us the boost we needed. It felt corrupt doing drugs with my brother, but he assured me he wasn't new to the game.

Cocaine was readily available in the pubs and clubs around Woolwich. Gerald, because of his boxing and my fame, had become a local face. He worked it too, even though he claimed it was an embarrassment. He was hanging out with hard nuts and criminals who would happily knock off an enemy for a bargain price. I was too self-absorbed to notice the changes in Gerald, though it was clear to the rest of the family something was wrong.

I should have known when he sold me a dodgy lime green Granada for 250 smackers with no tax, no insurance, and no MOT. He says he didn't want to sell me it, that it was a heap of shit, but I distinctly remember handing him the money.

That car came in useful. Two days later I was ramming it into Jon Moss's garage. The drama exploded after one of those nasty phone calls. I tore round to his house in Primrose Hill. At first Jon hid upstairs with his brass wall hangings, but my "no-dick dwarf" jibes must have got to him. He appeared at the door holding a claw hammer. I lunged, thinking he would never dare use it. I was wrong. He cracked it across my shoulder blades and tried to kick me back into the street. I was crying and screamed, "You're sick in the head." I jumped into the car and drove it straight into his electric garage door. It was deliberate, I knew how much he valued his material possessions, much more than people. When I got home Hippie was waiting. I was so upset I couldn't control myself and kept saying, "He really hates me."

In recent weeks there'd been quite a few flare-ups, but nothing so violent. Jon had a new girlfriend, Shee, short for Sheila. Sheila Lippell was the singer in a band Jon had been working with in between Culture Club projects. I knew quite a bit about her. A friend of a friend had styled the band for a photo session and said she had big feet. Of course, I added my own embellishments and turned her into the pig of pigs. Many a moment was spent assessing her personality and worth. I decided she was obviously a spineless yes-person with nothing going on between her ears.

At first I believed Jon's lies that there was nothing between him and Shee. But one night I was round at Jamie Morgan's, close by Jon's. I phoned and asked if I could pop round. Jon said he was on his way out, but I didn't believe him. Stupidly I went round anyway. Jon kept me on the doorstep, making excuses that he was with friends, that it wasn't cool. As I was about to walk away the mysterious Shee appeared from inside. "Tell him," she said. "Just tell him."

I looked at Jon. "What do you have to tell me?"

Jon snapped at Shee, "Go back inside." The picture was clear; I walked away.

When I got back to Jamie's the phone rang. It was Shee trying to be adult about things. I told her Jon could do his own dirty work and slammed down the phone. That phone call hurt more than the hammer. I felt so invaded. To make things worse, Jon had involved Shee and her grotty band with my friend Alan Roberts, who was now making their stage clothes. A little presumptuous as they never made it that far. Alan, ever generous, kept trying to convince me she was really nice until I warned him it might be the end of a beautiful friendship.

I was determined to pay Shee back after that phone call. I did some detective work and got hold of her phone number and address. Hippie and I, both coked out of our minds, went round to her flat in West Hampstead. I took a large rock from a builder's skip and lobbed it through her window, at least I thought it was her window, then we escaped with Hippie driving the getaway car. You've never heard two people laugh more. When I got back home there was an angry message from Jon. "I know it was you, I'm calling the police." I just laughed and told Hippie, "If the police come I'll just tell them everything. It'll be a crime of passion." I followed up my hate campaign by sending her cabs, plumbers, and pizzas.

Two weeks later Jon and I were forced into each other's company when Culture Club appeared on a Japanese TV show, satellited live from London's Docklands. I turned up off my head and locked myself in my dressing room, refusing to speak to the band. I decided my black bondage suit was boring and sent one of the researchers to get me a ball of string and some cans of shandy. I tied myself up, then couldn't decide if I liked it. The Japanese crew were banging on the door frantically. Mikey and Jon tried to reason. Jon lost his temper, kicking the door, calling me unprofessional. On set things reached a hysterical peak. I had to stand on a giant spinning record deck. You couldn't see me for string.

It was a case of dilated to see you when Hippie and I turned up at the Blitz Designer Gala in aid of the Prince's Trust at the Albery Theatre in Covent Garden. Everyone was there and quite a few of them were out of it on Ecstasy. It was as if the Taboo crowd had been jaunted there from the disco. Backstage was swarming with photographers who didn't seem to notice all the spliffs being passed around. I modeled a Leigh Bowery creation, a classic Levi's jacket customized with gold hair grips. I'd glued pictures of naked men onto my bondage trousers and the peak of my cap. I swayed down the catwalk scratching at my neck. When anyone said hi, I laughed. "Might be." Hippie wanted to kill Stephen Linard when he shouted, "Oi, got any drugs, or have you sold them all to Boy George?"

Clapham Common. 'I'm not a drug addict, I'm a drag addict.' (*Andre Csillag*)

Top: **Me and Kev, recovering at the Limelight Club, 1988.** (*Rex Features*)

Above: **Fat Tony and me down the disco, 1989.**

Main picture: **Leaving Hampstead for my first Buddhist meeting. New Year's Day, 1987.** (*Rex Features*)

Opposite page: **Bow down, mister. Bombay, 1990.**

Kinky, me and Alice. A right pair of geezers at George Michael's party, London, 1991.

Above: **Sydney – Slavery and Marilyn – Masters. Remembering it all, New York, 1994. Taken by me.**

Above right: **Paul Starr, 'a healthy friendship', New York 1994. Taken by me.**

Main Picture: **Me and Stevie Hughes as hookers. 'Generations of Love' video, Soho, 1990.**

Absolutely queer, 1992.
Musician, author, DJ,
right-on sister.

CHAPTER 42

With the press so hot on my trail it was only a matter of time before friend or foe would turn Judas, especially with a rumored £50,000 on my head. Some of my friends had joked about spilling the story and splitting the takings, but I never thought anyone would be so cheap.

I met David Levine in 1983 through his brother Steve, Culture Club's producer. David was just starting out as a photographer and was keen to snap my famous face. Steve invited him into the studio while we were recording *Colour by Numbers*. Straightaway I was impressed by his work; the first picture in his portfolio was a handsome shot of Kirk Brandon, which he'd obviously placed just so.

David and Steve were almost identical except for David's pageboy haircut and nothing style. He seemed more concerned with his work than his wardrobe. I wouldn't say we got on straightaway because there was little to get on with; he was just quiet and eager to please.

Our first session together was for the cover of "Karma Chameleon," the first single taken from *Colour by Numbers*. The session was set up as a trial, working at a cheap little studio in Clerkenwell with none of the usual luxuries. David brought in his friend Pearl, Lynne Easton, to do the makeup. I knew Pearl from the punk days, so it wasn't a difficult introduction. I was so pleased with the pictures that David became the in-house photographer overnight.

In time I got to see a different side of him. I liked and trusted him, even though he was a bit of a brick wall. Even with my straightest friends I developed a campy relationship, but not with David. I just accepted him as he was. I did everything I could to make sure he got his due. If cover shots were used in magazines I got them to pay additional fees. There was no question he was on to a good thing. And, likewise, I got some of my favorite shots out of him. One session we did in Madrid, David made me look like a total woman, I loved him for it. Still, I should have heeded my mother's warning that the quiet ones are the worst, because David was truly the louse that roared.

Our final session together was for an American rock magazine, *Spin,* at Lipstick Studios in Islington. It was meant to be a one-day shoot, but it became a three-dayer—I forgot to show up for the first two. When I finally appeared I was untogether and spent over three hours in makeup. Then when I wasn't disappearing to the toilet, Pearl was trying to keep the foundation on my sweaty face. All day David was moody and complaining how tired he was. He kept nagging Pearl to ask me for cocaine. She didn't want to do his dirty work, but he kept on and on. I told Pearl I'd sort him out, but wondered why he didn't just ask me himself. I called Hippie. He picked up a couple of grams and dropped it off at the studio. I gave David a gram and kept one for myself.

After the session Hippie and I went out clubbing and then back to St. John's Wood. We were up listening to music when the doorbell rang at 7 A.M. I thought a neighbor had come to complain. I shouted through the door, "Who is it?"

"Hello, Boy George, we're from the *Daily Mirror.* Can we speak to you?" Hippie ran upstairs with the drugs and I opened the door. "Do you realize it's seven in the morning?" The two reporters were apologetic. They said they were following up a story that was about to be splashed across the front of the *Daily Mirror.* "David Levine is making allegations that you sold him cocaine." I shook my head and laughed. "I don't believe it." I said I had nothing to say because I knew there was nothing I could say. I went back inside and held my head. Hippie said Levine was an out-and-out cunt, but it didn't change the fact. It seemed as if I'd been well and truly set up.

By 10 A.M. the phone was ringing off the wall, Tony Gordon, Elly Smith from Virgin, and various hacks—I kept cutting them off. Everyone wanted my side of the story. Tony was telling reporters it was all rubbish. He said he'd received a call from Steve Levine almost in tears he was so ashamed. Steve might have known something was wrong. Days earlier he'd received an odd call from David apologizing for missing his birthday. They were never that close; David was prying. "What's all this with George and drugs?" He moaned that I hadn't turned up for an important session. Steve didn't want to get involved and cut the call short.

That afternoon I called John Blake at the *Mirror*, ranting. I was sure he was involved. He was typically smarmy and kept asking me for an interview saying that I could trust him to write the truth. I told him to fuck off. He wrote,

> Boy George rang me up in a fine old paddy when he heard that a friend was poised to tell the world of his fondness for Bolivian go-fast powder. After a ten-minute tirade he finally screamed, "I'm fab, I'm happy, and I get fucked every night, so I just don't care."

I went out that night, defying the impending disaster. I told everyone about the story, making it into a joke. It was my way of avoiding the seriousness of the situation, but inside I wondered what it would mean to my career or what else would blow up out of it. I left the Wag club at midnight and walked down to the paper stand in Leicester Square with Hippie, Fiona Russell Powell, and Richard Habberley. We all bought a copy.

"Drugs and Boy George." Hippie and Richard said it wasn't that bad. But Fiona, being the journalist, said it was just the beginning. We were all reading bits out, "Listen to this, listen to this." Levine was so creepy, pretending to be my guardian angel. I wanted to kill him, I really wanted to kill him.

"Pop star Boy George is destroying himself with drugs, a close friend warned last night." A picture of the worried friend, David Levine, appeared with the piece. Levine claimed I borrowed £140 for drugs after turning up late for a photo session and was quoted, "I truly believe if George doesn't pull out of this fatal nose dive he will become just another rock and roll tragedy."

He moaned that he was only paid £500 for shooting the cover of "Karma." What did he expect? A royalty for a cover? He made out he was so hard done by, as if to justify his betrayal.

By the time the paper hit the breakfast tables on June 10, 1986, I was locked away in my house. Outside, reporters and photographers swarmed. I kept the music loud and ignored their banging.

Hippie and I discussed the possibility of a police raid. I said let them come. The house was as secure as a prison; it would take them ages to get in. We had a bit of coke left and a tiny bit of spliff, nothing that couldn't be disposed of quickly. We just sat there waiting for something to happen. It seemed like the longest day of my life.

By 6 P.M. most of the hacks had left. One or two were hovering up and down the mews and a couple of photographers were sitting in cars. I wondered what the neighbors thought of it all. Tony Gordon called, saying he'd been at Virgin all day. They were worried and wanted me to make a statement. He said, "We say nothing.. Levine is a putz, a bloody putz. It'll all blow over." He warned there was a follow-up story about me and Jon. "Oh, well," I said. "I hope the pictures are nice."

Rumors were that Levine was paid £8,000. The story got exaggerated along the way. Some said £50,000, others £100,000. I was disappointed with £8,000—I'd like to think I was worth more than that. I heard Levine was driving a shiny new sports car, other sources said he was hiding out in New York.

On June 11, a follow-up piece appeared in the *Mirror:* "A Punch, but the Lovers Made Up with a Kiss." This story angered me more than the drugs exposé. Levine, professing an insight into my relationship with Jon: "Whenever they are away from the fans they seem to be forever cuddling one another and pecking one another with affectionate kisses." It was so cringey. Levine added, "When I last photographed them together in London George desperately wanted a picture of the two of them kissing. At first Jon flatly refused, but after an argument and a sulk, he gave in and eventually agreed to pose for an astonishing picture of him kissing

George on the cheek." The "astonishing" picture, taken by Levine, was printed center spread with the piece. If Levine thought that picture was astonishing he should've seen what Jon and I used to get up to with a Polaroid camera.

A day or so after the *Mirror* story broke I could resist it no longer, I rang Levine. No one was home so I left a message. "You're gonna be fucking dead when I get my hands on you. And I really mean that." Levine got straight on to the *Mirror*, probably hoping he could add some extra silver to his fee. They printed my call, word for word under the headline "You're Gonna Be Dead." Levine whimpered, "George put the fear of God in me. I was scared he might come round or send some heavies." He's lucky he didn't find a pig's head in his fridge. The *Mirror* claimed the tape had been played to police at Shepherd's Bush, who were planning to interview me. Roy Hay called when he saw the paper. He was in hysterics. He said it was the headline of the year. I went over to Odyssey Studios, where he was working with his moonlight band, This Way Up. The cutting was taped to a speaker. Roy said I'd better watch out. Like everyone, he hoped the press stories would make a difference.

Nothing changed except the way I carried my drugs. I made sure I could throw them if I had to. I knew the police would be watching me. One night a bunch of us were driving through the West End. I flicked a piece of chocolate wrapper out the window. Two unmarked police cars cut us up. One of the coppers picked up the foil, "Out the car, come on." They thought they had me. I was tempted to sing, "Everyone's a fruit and nutcase . . . " They were disappointed and emptied the ashtrays onto the pavement. When we drove off I pulled a lump of hash from under the seat and started cackling. Hippie had a gram of coke in his back pocket. Philip didn't find it funny. It was all a game to me. I was cocky.

I used my celebrity to get away with murder. I walked into the Wag smoking a joint. The bouncer snatched it and I snatched it back. "Sorry." He didn't know what to do. I didn't think anyone had the right to tell me what to put in my body and I thought I was holding it together. That was never more evident than the day I appeared at the antiapartheid rally at Clapham Common wearing a face pack. I had parcel string wrapped around my forehead. My pinned eyes were hidden behind mirrored specs, under a knitted red, gold, and green topper. My grubby white jean jacket read "Heroin Free Zone" and "Suck My Nob." I groaned through "Melting Pot" and "Black Money" with Helen Terry and left the stage shouting, "I'm a drag addict, not a drug addict." Backstage I mumbled gobbledygook at Sting and Peter Gabriel and fell asleep giving a TV interview. I was bundled into a car by Nick Fisher, Culture Club's old tour manager, and rescued from greater humiliation. It was my most public display of drug disorder and I made the *News at Ten*.

When the previous day's tragedies were related I laughed, I thought I was having a great time. No one dared to tell me I was making a fool of myself. Bonnie and Hippie were concerned, but it didn't stop them laughing with me. "You should have seen Sting's face." Reality was when I ran out of drugs.

After Clapham there was more press speculation and concerned phone calls to Tony's office. It was no longer credible to deny there was a problem. The Levine story was a hitch, but now I was swinging my own noose. Tony was out of his depth. He spoke with Mum and Dad and tried to entice me to a meeting with drugs specialist Meg Patterson. I agreed then disappeared on the day.

Dad started playing detective, surveilling St. John's Wood round the clock. Mum phoned Hippie's parents to see if they would help. They told her that Tony Gordon had put Hippie there to keep his eye on me. They didn't think their son was doing anything wrong. Dad decided to get Hippie arrested. He called Scotland Yard. They were dismissive and put him onto the local police at St. John's Wood. He gave them a description of Hippie and the Granada registration. Dad even tried following Hippie himself, but each time he was outwitted. In frustration, Mum and Dad arranged to meet my bodyguard Stuart Page in Hampstead. They hoped that Stuart's experience as a policeman and some heavy tactics would frighten Hippie off. Hippie had become some kind of ogre. What did they think? That I was tied to a chair being administered drugs against my will? Mum and Dad returned to Hampstead day after day, grilling Bonnie, trying to get her to hand over the keys to St. John's Wood.

Unexpectedly, Hippie turned up at Hampstead and was cornered. Dad threatened to kill him. Hippie said he'd come to see Bonnie because I'd sent him to get heroin and he didn't know what to do. Dad ordered him to stay at Hampstead, took the keys from Bonnie, and made his way to Abercorn Close. He let himself into the house. When I heard his voice I locked myself in the bathroom and shouted, "Get out of my house." He said, "I only want to help you, son." I accused him of breaking in and told him I didn't need his fucking help. He kept saying, "You're killing yourself." I screamed, "If I want to kill myself, it's fuck all to do with you." He said he was going to set fire to the house, we could die together. Everything went quiet for about five minutes. I opened the bathroom door and could smell smoke. I ran downstairs. Dad had set fire to a pile of clothes on the front-room floor. I started to cry. "What are you trying to do?" I ran into the kitchen, grabbed a pot, filled it with water, and doused the flames. Loads of my stuff was damaged, clothes, records, the carpet, and cupboards. I shut myself in the kitchen and kept screaming, "Get out, get out." I felt violated—he was treating me like a child. That old Dad had come back trying to rule my roost. Dad said he only wanted to talk. I said, "It's too late to talk—you set fire to my fucking house." He said he would leave the key, go outside, ring the bell, I could let him in, then we could have a cup of tea and a chat. Of course, when he went outside I wouldn't let him back in.

In my panic I called Jon, God knows why. By the time he arrived, the police were there too. As I tried to let Jon in, one of the coppers barged past. Dad told the police I set fire to the house. I called him a lying cunt. The copper told me not to speak to my father like that. I screamed at him, "Mind your own business. Arrest me or go and catch a criminal." Two policemen came into the house and looked around. Some of the clothes were still smoldering. Dad was hoping they'd arrest me, but they couldn't. In the midst of all the commotion Hippie arrived from Hampstead. I let him and Jon into the house and shut the door. Jon and I hugged. None of us understood what was happening. It was enough to say nothing. I could hear Dad outside trying to convince the police that I was out of my mind. When Jon left Dad accused him of giving me drugs. They nearly came to blows.

Mum was furious about the fire. She knew what Dad had done, even though he angrily denied it. She said it was irresponsible and dangerous. She came with Bonnie to clear up the mess. Dad sat outside in the car. I told Mum to keep him away from me.

All the way back to Shooters Hill Dad was raving, "Those bastards, they're trying to kill George." Mum went to bed exhausted, Dad was up all night. My brother David found him in the morning huddled up on the settee, crying like a baby. Dad begged David to go to the newspapers and tell them everything. David was working as a freelance photographer supplying pictures to Fleet Street and the pop mags. He didn't like the idea. "When George wants to do something about it he will." He knew he'd be risking my eternal wrath. Dad was hysterical, he told David I'd set fire to my house, that I was a danger to myself, both Tony Gordon and Meg Patterson thought it was best to make it public. Mum said it wouldn't help anyone, she didn't approve of the way Dad was carrying on.

When David got to his studio in Greenwich that Wednesday morning he called his friend Nick Ferrari on the *Sun*. Twelve minutes later there was a screech outside. Ferrari said, "What's the deal?" David said the story was his as long as it was clear there was no money paid. So July 3, 1986, the story appeared. "Junkie George Has 8 Weeks to Live." High drama in typical *Sun* style. I had an £800-a-day heroin habit, which would probably mean I had seconds to live.

Thursday morning as the journalists, photographers, and camera crews gathered for the kill, Hippie and I sat smoking a joint with the TV blaring and the curtains drawn, ignoring the banging and calling. "Hello, Boy George, have you seen the paper?" I'd been warned about David's story. A message from the *Sun* pleaded for me to call back before it was too late. I sent Hippie to get the paper. I read it and felt betrayed. What else could I feel?

We watched the breakfast news, the lunchtime news, and waited, like prisoners in our own movie. The phone kept ringing, then cutting off. I got angry and rang my brother's studio. "You cunt, I knew one day you'd take the payoff, arsehole, selfish cunt." I rang again. "Cunt, how much did they pay you?"

I spoke to Tony. He said things had got out of hand. The office

had been plagued with fans crying. He wanted me to do an interview with ITN to show the world that I wasn't dying. There were
even rumors that I had AIDS. With the best of intentions Tony
was shoving me in the lion's mouth. The media didn't care how
long I had, they just wanted more copy. I was being forced to
defend myself when all I wanted was to be left alone.

I took a call from Rick Sky at the *Daily Star*. I told him, "If my
dad's been talking about me, he shouldn't be. What he knows
about me you could fit on a fingernail." Philip rang with more
good news. "Marilyn drugged Dencil. He's in a coma. Are you
going to talk to the press? You should really dress up." Dencil had
taken some of Marilyn's medication and was lying in intensive
care. Philip didn't seem to be taking it very seriously. I hoped
Dencil wasn't going to die.

At 3:30 P.M. I left for Tony's office. The press swarmed around
Billy's car, all shouting at once. I denied everything, it was all rubbish. I did the same with ITN. "I'm fine, I'm trying to work hard,
but everybody is interfering in my life and it's making me sick." It
was a stupid thing to go on TV and lie. It would have been more
dignified to stay silent.

At home the press were still hovering. They scrummed around
me, more questions. "Is it true you're spending £800 a day on
heroin?" "How do you feel about your brother David?" They
can't have heard me. I was quoted as saying, "I know I'm a junkie,
and everyone else seems to know as well. You only have to look at
me—it's obvious I'm dying."

The next morning I was booked to appear on TV-am. Again
Tony was looking for a sympathetic profile. We had a good relationship with Jason Pollock, the showbiz editor. A car came for me
at 7 A.M. I had trouble getting out of bed, then a few image problems. I put on some foundation and the biggest pair of dark
glasses I could find. I was out of it, I didn't want to go. I kept
looking at myself in the mirror, panicking, thinking, why am I
doing this? Presenter Jayne Irving was making live appeals for me
to come to the studio. I finally arrived just before nine as the show
was about to end. When I found out Meg Patterson was also taking part in the show I lost my temper. They were setting me up for
an on-air confessional. Pollock tried to appease me. I said I wasn't

doing it and hid in the dressing room. Tony and I were screaming at each other. He said he didn't know about Meg Patterson, I didn't believe him. Pollock tried to persuade me to prerecord an interview for the following day. I said no.

Reports in the papers turned me into a gibbering wreck, saying I broke down in tears. I certainly threw a tantrum because they'd deceived me. But, like everything, it was exaggerated.

That afternoon Philip arrived at the house dressed in a bridal gown with a garland in his hair. Whatever the crisis, Philip was just Philip. A group of fans had gathered with the hacks, dressed up for a concert carrying flowers, clutching cameras. Bad taste, bad timing. Philip hissed at them, "You're a bunch of morbid crawlers. Fuck off." They dared to answer back. He filled a bucket with water and drowned them.

The press were morbid too: they kept a virtual round-the-clock vigil trying to work out the comings and goings at number 8, photographing and grilling all visitors. Bonnie came in and out with money and food, Marks & Spencer's goodies, and more ice cream. She yelled at the vultures, "Eat shit and go get a life." *Mirror* reporter Gill Pringle collared her. "Excuse me, can you tell me where Bonnie the housekeeper is?" Bonnie answered all her silly questions without letting on. As she was about to drive off, Pringle asked, "Oh, by the way, what's your name?"

"Blanche Dubois."

"That's a bit of a strange name."

"Not if you're in a Tennessee Williams play."

Most of the time I hid away, but I had to get drugs. Leaving the house was a military exercise. Bonnie or Hippie would start the car and I'd run head down, dodging cameras and questions. Sometimes I escaped through the back garden and we'd rendezvous in Hamilton Terrace. *Sun* photographer Dave Hogan caught us one afternoon and made chase in his red Porsche. We raced up around St. John's Wood trying to lose him. I got so angry I made Hippie stop the car. I got out and warned Hogan, "This car's a piece of shit. I'll crash it if I have to." I took over the wheel and screeched off. Hogan was persistent. I braked suddenly and spun round, just missing the front of his precious car. He soon backed off.

Bored with it, I decided to go somewhere they couldn't find me. I left Hippie at the house, escaped out the back, and went to Michael's flat in Hampstead. The Eurythmics were on TV singing their new hit, "When Tomorrow Comes." Seeing Annie looking so slick made me disappointed with myself. That evening Michael and I went over to Helen's. Helen was edgy, she'd had the press on the phone and was worried they might start camping on her doorstep. She couldn't believe what my brother had done. The *Sun* of all people, playing into their filthy Tory hands. I said I couldn't think about it anymore, it just made me want to take more drugs. Mimi and I took a cab down the New North Road to Babs. Babs had seen the paper. She rolled her eyes. "You can't trust anyone." She made coffee and we sat talking. Babs was one of those people who held your attention, even when she was saying nothing. Her big rolling eyes and animated face drew you in. She was no longer a punk Marlene Dietrich, but even after years of drug abuse her beauty and spirit still shone through. In my arrogance I never thought things would get that bad for me. I was just passing through the nightmare.

Friday night and most of Saturday we were at Helen's. I was bored of lying low. Pearl and her new husband, Paolo Hewitt, were having a wedding bash and Philip's *Opera House* was on at the Piccadilly Theatre. Bonnie brought my makeup and a load of clothes in a bin-liner. I bought some peroxide and gave myself a new look. I put on the loudest clothes I could find and plastered my face with makeup. Around 11:30 P.M. Kevin and Hippie collected me in the Galaxy and we headed into the West End. Pearl's party had already fizzled out so we went off to Philip's. I drove us down to Soho. Off Beak Street I took a No Entry and drove arseways into Brewer Street, blocking off the road. Kevin was trying to back out when the police arrived. I had drugs in my pocket, I was praying the copper hadn't read the papers. A lucky amateur photographer snapped me being ticked off and sold it to Fleet Street. It seemed as if the bastards were jumping out of everywhere.

On the way home I picked up the Sunday papers. I nearly died when I saw the *Sunday People*. "Boy George in the Drugs Den." There was a picture of Babs's house and another of myself posing playfully with seventeen-year-old Jackie Biggs, a neighbor passing herself off as a concerned fan. Biggs told how she'd seen me smoking drugs. Babs's name hadn't been mentioned for legal reasons, but the damage was done. The picture of myself and Biggs had been taken some weeks before in Babs's back garden. She was just a little girl playing with Babs's kid. When she found out I was Boy George she ran off to get a camera.

My old spliffing partner Jonathan Ashby had written an oily piece for the *Mail on Sunday* using his insider knowledge. "The reality—as those of us close to him have known for some time—is that he is a hopeless addict, and very close to the end." I wonder if Ashby was at the end of a joint when he wrote it.

For his loving concern I rewarded Jonathan with a wreath with the message, "I thought you were my heroine, not my heroin." It was a horrible thing to do, but no worse than him dancing on my grave. A friend in greed is no friend indeed.

I rang Babs as soon as I got out of bed. She was freaked out. "That little bitch." She said she was going to disappear. I asked if I could see her before she went. We arranged to meet at Helen's later that day. Helen wasn't happy, but she knew I was desperate.

All weekend Richard Branson had been leaving repeated messages at Michael's flat for me to call him at his Oxfordshire home. Michael spoke to him. I said, "Tell him to fuck off." It was just someone else interfering. Michael wanted us to go. He said Branson was just trying to help and had been really nice on the phone. I was stubborn and stupid. Everything was closing in on me, I couldn't stand it.

We went to Helen's and waited and waited. I didn't think Babs was going to show. When she did she looked worn out. She'd been trying to score herself, but all her people were "out." She had a bit of "personal," which she shared with me. I gave her a hug, wished her good luck, and she left promising to call me at Michael's. I felt sad that I'd dragged her into my bullshit.

When Michael and I got back to his flat in Hampstead it was gone midnight. Branson called just as we walked in the door. He told Michael David Bowie was at his house, thinking it might lure me. In normal circumstances maybe, but I was too fucked up to care. I had this horrible vision of Bowie and Branson trying to counsel me. Branson asked us to come to his office in the morning. I said I'd go. Michael called Bonnie and arranged for her to drive us there.

In the morning I cried, I felt ashamed. Going to see Branson was like facing up to it. Michael said, "Just see what happens. He can't make you do anything." I was already high when we arrived at his barge in Little Venice. Branson was gentle and thanked me for coming. He said, "Do you accept that you have a problem?" I said, "Of course." He asked if I would let him help me. A tentative appointment had been booked with Meg Patterson. Branson drove us to her house in Willesden. Meg and I spoke very briefly. She wanted to know how serious I was about getting well. I said I wanted to get well, but I was scared. She explained the treatment and asked if I was prepared to leave immediately. Bonnie went home, packed a suitcase, and within an hour Meg, her son Lorne, who was her nurse, Branson, Michael, and myself were on our way to Oxfordshire. Before we left I went into Meg's toilet and snorted my last bit of smack.

As we got further away from London I could feel myself panicking. Empty green fields stretched out, cutting me off from my security. Michael held my hand, no one spoke. Meg looked stern, a bit spiteful, like she was ready to get the job done. I arrived at Mill End House exhausted by all my thoughts and feelings. I went upstairs and sat alone in the frilly bedroom. Meg came to fit me with her black box. It didn't look like it would do anything, a battery-operated metal box attached to an elastic waistband with an electrode that clipped onto your ear. It worked by sending out subtle electrical impulses to stimulate the endorphins. Patterson developed it after working with acupuncturists in Hong Kong.

I sat wearing the contraption, feeling despondent. I moaned at Michael, "This won't work." I wanted to rip it off and stamp on it.

As the day wore on I started feeling wretched, filled with a sulky sadness. I wandered round the house unable to stay in one place. I was sweating and my joints were starting to ache. I knew what the pain would be like, the fear just made it worse. Every second I felt more rage and resentment. I hated Meg. Every time she asked how I was feeling I wanted to spit at her. I kept asking for medication. She said, "That's not the way we do it, dear." She fiddled with the dial on the box to make the current stronger, but it made little difference. I lay down in front of the TV, too tired to move anymore, my legs juddering, my stomach brewing the bile and the sickness. As the pain grew I sniveled like a frightened child. I wanted medication or I wanted drugs. I cried to Michael, "She must have something, she must." He didn't know what to do or say. Meg and Lorne sat away from us in the kitchen, they spoke in whispers and moved around without making a sound. It added to the distortion. I thought they were creepy and suspicious, but they were only trying to give us our privacy. Now and then Meg would appear at the living-room door and look in. I said she was spying on us. I kept repeating that she was spiteful, that she didn't care about me. I had to blame someone for the way I was feeling.

I searched the bathroom cabinet for pills, then rooted through all the bedroom drawers. I ran a bath but couldn't be bothered to get in it. I curled up in a ball and tapped my head against the cold tiles. I thought about climbing out the window. I rummaged through my clothes thinking there might be some drugs, checking the folds of pockets for traces. Every smell made me retch, food, Meg's perfume, my own skin. I couldn't finish a sentence or keep my eyes in one place. I didn't want Michael near me, I didn't want him to leave.

The real sickness came during the night, I was shitting and puking my guts out. I had to sleep alone, though I got little sleep. I drifted in and out, crying, kicking, and turning, the sheets were soaked. At 4 A.M. I snapped wide-awake. I got dressed and crept downstairs. I tried to watch TV, I couldn't sit still. I went through the French windows into the garden and wandered round to the front of the house and into the street in my bare feet. I walked up the country lane for half a mile and found a phone box. I had no money, I thought I could make a reverse charge call to Bonnie and ask her to bring me some Valium. I picked up the receiver and held it till I lost the tone. I just couldn't call. I went back to the house and sat in the garden under a tree listening to the silence.

The psychological side of withdrawal was far worse than the physical. The sickness, however hideous, kept me away from my thoughts, gave me something to hold on to. Without it I had only my isolation—that was the worst horror.

Outside in the world the press were calling for my head. An editorial in the *Daily Mirror* cried out,

> Boy George is a junkie. What are the police doing about it? . . . His music, his dress, his lifestyle, his drug-taking are all likely to be imitated by the young. Tragically, drug-taking would inevitably lead to their ruin, as it is ruining Boy George. We repeat: What are the police doing about it?

Tory party chairman Norman Tebbit asked whether the BBC should ban pop stars known to take drugs.

Tuesday, July 8, 7 A.M., Operation Culture went into action. The police raided Ginty and Steve, Helen and Mimi, Jon Moss, and my homes in St. John's Wood and Hampstead, where Bonnie and Kevin were sleeping. Bonnie hadn't opened her eyes. The police burst in, shoved her head into the pillow, and ordered her not to move. Then two WPCs strip-searched her while the rest of the mob tore through the house. They took answerphone tapes, personal photographs, phone books, letters, and carted Bonnie off to Paddington Green police station.

The scenes were similar at Hampstead. They scaled the gates and jimmied open the front door. The lights flashed on, startling Kevin out of his sleep. He saw them piling into the garden on the TV security system. It was like the Keystone Kops. One copper shouted right in Kevin's face, "Where's the blond girl? Where is she?" They'd been watching the house for days, seen Kevin's girlfriend, Kathy, coming in and out, and assumed she was delivering drugs. Kevin wouldn't give her name. They smashed down a locked antique bedroom door and threw clothes out of the cupboards onto the floor. There was nothing for them to find—Kevin had given the place the once-over after being warned by Dad of a possible raid. The police had been to see Dad at Shooters Hill and assured him they weren't after me. Dad gave them names of suspected dealers.

At Paddington Green everyone was kept in separate interrogation rooms. They told Bonnie, "We've got all the others and they're talking. Why don't you tell us where George is? We just want to question him." After a good hour of shouting, they moved her to the canteen and gave her coffee. A change of mood and attitude. When they questioned her again they accused her of supplying. Everyone was accused of being a dealer. Tired and intimidated, Bonnie told them about our trip to Jamaica with Ginty and Steve. The police had their first piece of substantial evidence. They kept telling everyone they were only after the dealers.

Helen was already up having breakfast when the police called. She saw them pop out of the bushes, laughed in fear, and ran to the door. Mimi wasn't so calm when they dragged her from bed. "Boy George is a user. He's been staying here? You know you're liable for prosecution." They knew if they spoke they would only hang themselves.

At the station they told Mimi they were charging Helen; she confessed to supplying to protect her. They did the same to Helen, playing one off the other. Helen gave information on Ginty and Steve and told them other things they didn't need to know. I trashed two cars in Jamaica, my house was filthy, that she saw huge tennis balls of dope in my living room. It was her first experience with the police, and she went to pieces.

Ginty and Steve had been lucky to start with. They too were expecting a raid and cleared out all the drugs. The previous day Marilyn, who had moved back in with them, returned home from visiting Dencil at St. Mary's Hospital. The police were waiting in a van and saw Marilyn fishing around in a hedge. He was looking for the flat key. They questioned him at Paddington Green for half an hour, then let him go. He was able to warn Ginty and Steve.

Jon was the unlucky one. The police found cocaine at his house and charged him. He was wrongly suspected of being part of my drugs circle.

Ginty and Steve tried to plead innocence, but the finger had been well and truly pointed. Along with Kevin and Mimi, they were charged with conspiracy to supply. Marilyn and Jon were charged with possession, pending court appearances. The others were held in cells overnight. No charges were brought against Bonnie or Helen.

I watched the drama unfolding on TV. I wept and felt so helpless. My brother Kevin and my close friend Mimi had been charged and branded as dealers; it was all so ridiculous and wrong. The police said, "We would very much like to interview Boy George in relation to these offenses. We are asking that he comes forward." There were even rumors that I'd left the country to hide out in New York.

I was doubled up with sickness and cramp; the last thing I needed was to be carted off to a police station. Branson called directly the news was shown; he spoke with Meg. He was worried there might be a warrant out for my arrest. Between them they decided it was best to contact the police. Branson said I was undergoing treatment, he refused to say where. He asked that I be allowed to complete a month's treatment before any interviews took place. The police agreed.

The press was full of it. "Heroin Swoop," "Boy George Hunt as Police Grab Marilyn," "Give Yourself Up, Boy George." Most papers carried a picture of Marilyn poking his tongue out. It briefly lightened my mood and summed up some of my own emotions. Naive as it may seem, I couldn't understand the hysterics of the media or the police. They'd worked themselves up into an animal frenzy. One headline urged, "Find Him." I felt like a cornered fox. Michael and I sat huddled together, watching and waiting. I knew the press would try and find me: they seemed hell-bent on delivering me to the police. I wondered what I'd done to warrant such hatred. I didn't feel like a criminal. On the lunchtime news they showed scenes outside Marylebone Magistrates' Court. I broke down when I saw Mum. She was clutching a bunch of red roses handed to her by a fan. She looked tired, like she could bear no more of it. When they said Kevin and Mimi had been remanded in custody I wanted to jump through the TV and kill someone. I felt guilty and responsible for everything that was happening to them. I wondered if they were thinking about me, I thought they must hate me. Whatever I was going through was nothing. I wanted to speak to someone, to call Helen, but Meg said it would only make things worse. "All you must do now is get well."

Branson issued a statement at the request of the police. "To avoid further speculation we'd like it to be known that since 10 A.M. Monday morning Boy George has been under twenty-four-hour medical supervision. The police have been fully informed of the position. It would be much appreciated if the press could leave him alone for one month." Once the media was aware of Branson's involvement they started staking out his properties. They gathered outside his office and at the Manor residential recording studio, half a mile from Mill End House, thinking it would be the obvious hiding place.

Tony Gordon had no idea where I was or that I was in treatment. He rang Branson, raging that he had spirited me off without his permission. Branson refused to tell him anything. Both he and Meg had agreed that it was best to keep everyone away from me. After a few telephone confrontations Branson relented. Tony drove up to Oxfordshire straightaway. By now the press were checking out Mill End House. His gold Rolls-Royce gave them a fresh scent.

Tony knew Branson's motives were sincere but felt he was playing God to the media. Why was he giving so many interviews? Why couldn't he keep his mouth shut? An article had appeared in the *Sun*, "The Dotty O'Dowds," describing my family as "a clan of crackpots." They were made to look stupid and incapable while Branson took all the glory. Tony asked Branson to mention my family in interviews, to say they'd done everything they could.

I was too ill to care about any of it; the pain seemed to intensify with each hour. The black box did nothing to ease it. I complained it was a con. All I could think about was heroin—if I could just have a smidgin everything would be fine. I kept asking, "What's the time? What's the time?" Only time could take away the agony.

The press closed in on the house. I couldn't see them, but I could feel their presence. It aggravated me so much I wanted to get a gun, climb up on the roof, and pop them all off one by one. I wondered what kind of people they were. Didn't they have feelings? Were they expecting me to come out and give a speech? We tried to maintain some sense of normality in the goldfish bowl. It was absurd. Michael made a chicken and vegetable stir-fry and we all sat down at the table. It was like dining with extraterrestrials: Meg and Lorne hardly spoke, an awkward silence punctuated by clinking knives and forks. I pushed my food around on the plate, I just couldn't stomach it.

To break the boredom we played tennis. I had no energy and kept falling down. Puzzles, games, nothing could hold my interest. We listened to music, the same stuff over and over. Branson, despite being a record-company tycoon, only had a few albums. My favorite was *Revenge* by the Eurythmics. "Thorn in My Side" took on a whole new meaning. Another by Prince, "Boys and Girls," with its simple chorus, "I love you, baby, I love you so much . . . " reminded me that love was something I hadn't felt in so long. I didn't know if I loved Michael or if he loved me. He'd only ever known me as a junkie and I'd never been straight enough to think about our relationship.

Outside pressure was mounting on the police to haul me in. The press were making accusations of special treatment. Tory MP Geoffrey Dickens said, "A month may give this person time to recover, but it could also provide time to consider what he is going to say to the police and to be advised."

Anthony Burgess wrote a scathing piece for the *Daily Mail*, "The Killing of Boy George":

> The failure of talent has killed bigger men than he—Tony Hancock on one level, Ernest Hemingway on another. But these two artists were brilliant enough to be deserving of the stroke of Nemesis. Boy George was a sham, and as a sham he deserves nothing.

All the papers spoke of my fall from grace with the same arrogance that led them to believe they had created me. They were now writing my epitaph. I scribbled a message onto a piece of card, "Moral Majority. Have you come to return my grace?" I Sellotaped it to a window near the front of the house, hoping it would be seen. The press reported seeing me at the window making a rude gesture and claimed I had bleached hair with a green streak down the back. Black reporter Baz Bamigboye elaborated further, saying I shouted, "Oh, God, it's the African Queen."

Tony decided it was best to move me to a safer place. At 7:30 P.M., the evening of the eleventh, we all crept out the back of Branson's house. We went across the fields into a nearby church graveyard; Branson piggybacked Meg through the long grass. A car was waiting to drive us to Roy and Alison's in Billericay, Essex. Branson's own car was there too. He drove back home as if arriving for the weekend and told the press I wasn't there, inviting them in for a drink to prove it.

Branson's charm didn't work so well with the Metropolitan Police, who were now reneging on their promise, demanding to speak with me. Branson was threatened with arrest if he didn't comply. At that point he had no choice but to hand the problem over to my lawyers, Clinton's. Both Tony and Meg were informed of the situation. Meg was fiercely against my being taken to any police station and asked Branson to do his best to stop it. Branson argued with the police that they were setting an appalling precedent. No addict was going to seek care if they thought they might be arrested. He asked that there be conditions. That Meg be with me at all times and that I would only be interviewed in the presence of my solicitor.

My solicitor, John Cohen, spoke at length with Detective Sergeant David Leader of Paddington Green Drugs Squad and told him I was unfit to face questioning. Leader said the police were under too much pressure. Eight questions had been tabled in the House of Commons, the Home Secretary Douglas Hurd was now involved, and they had no choice but to arrest and question me. John asked what they would do if we did not cooperate. Leader said they would find and arrest me. The police were given Roy and Alison's address, and arrangements were made to meet at ten-thirty the following morning.

When Tony phoned and told me I was going to be arrested I was more angry than sad. Again, it seemed like such a lot of fuss over one small person. That's how I felt, small and insignificant. I knew the police wanted to get me while I was ill. I didn't believe all the crap about the House of Commons. Tony said it was because I was Boy George, they could make an example of me. It was maximum-publicity time.

Michael and I talked about what might happen with the police. We both decided it was best if I kept my mouth shut. I lit one cigarette after another, thinking and thinking. I still had the shakes, diarrhea, and cramps. My asthma and nerves were only aggravated by the smoking, I was wheezing and coughing like I had rotten flu. The fear just made things worse. All night I drifted in and out of sleep, getting up and walking around, making tea, smoking more cigarettes.

I'd been up for hours when Tony and John Cohen arrived. John and I sat and discussed what might happen at the police station. I told him I didn't want to admit to taking heroin, but didn't know where I stood as I was being treated for heroin addiction. He informed me he could not be party to any denial of the truth, but I was free to answer "no comment" to any questions. John made it clear we were only talking about possession for my own use at the worst. There was no question of anything beyond that, dealing in it or selling it to other people. It was a personal habit, which, while serious, was nothing major.

Detective Sergeant Leader and Detective Constable Keats arrived promptly at 10:30 A.M. They were cold and seemed to be looking at me with disgust. We went into Roy's study. I was cautioned, formally arrested, then driven to Harrow police station with John Cohen and Lorne. Tony and Meg followed behind in Billy Button's car.

It was a gray, sad day. The drive to Harrow seemed to take hours. I had no idea why they chose that station. Apparently it had to be in the Metropolitan Police area, and they wanted to avoid the waiting press at Paddington Green. On arriving at Harrow police station they insisted that I be taken in separately through the back entrance while the others went through the front. It was part of the intimidation. They made me empty my pockets and remove anything I might want to hang myself with, my belt, my suspenders, took away the black box, and locked me in a cell. Meg insisted they let me wear the box. She was distressed, they knew I was sick. I don't know how long I sat in that cell, it seemed like forever. They wanted to give me plenty of time to suffer and think. I was starting to shake and feel nauseous. It was an hour before I saw the police doctor. I don't think he cared much for junkies and pronounced me fit for questioning. John Cohen protested that I was not fit to be questioned and asked Detective Sergeant Leader to take a note of his protest. Leader declined, saying it was not party to his inquiry.

My plan was to say nothing. I knew if I said nothing they could do nothing. I'd never felt any affection for the police; in my eyes they were as criminal as the rest of us. I had no reason to trust them.

The questioning went on for two and a half hours. At first they appeared random, like they were trying to confuse me, asking things like, "Does Marilyn freebase? Does he do coke? Have you ever seen him take heroin?" I said, "I don't care what Marilyn does. Don't ask me questions about Marilyn." They kept on about my brother Kevin. I started crying. "You can't honestly expect me to sit here and convict my brother. You must be fucking crazy." I was morose and petulant. I hated the two coppers, especially Leader, who was trying to make out he cared about me, going on about my talent, asking, "Where are your friends now?" Leader knew enough stories to write his own book, all about the trips to Jamaica, Puerto Rico, New York, the color of my sofa. He made out that Marilyn had betrayed me. In his words, "sung like a bird." And that Steve Luben had named me as his financial backer and said that I paid their airfare to Jamaica and funded all their drug excursions. Leader wanted to set me against Steve and insisted, "He doesn't care about you. He's going to save himself." I hated Steve anyway and that hatred was increasing by the second. The information the police had was far too accurate to be guess work. My brother Kevin had told them that Luben was blackmailing me, trying to get £1,000 for a car. They said Mimi had admitted scoring heroin for me from Steve and that Helen had implicated Mimi as a supplier. I couldn't believe Helen would do anything like that.

At first I told them Ginty wasn't a dealer and that as far as I knew Luben was just an addict. Leader bellowed at me, "Come on, you know that's not right."

At 2:46 P.M. I was taken back to the cells for another two hours. I was allowed to see Meg. She held my hand. I was crying too much to speak. I decided I was going to tell Leader everything about Luben. It was him or me. My defenses were down, I'd fallen into their trap. I spoke to Leader and said I would change my story. I told him I only blamed myself. He said he was only looking for the dealers. John Cohen had advised me to admit to nothing.

Q: How long have you taken heroin for?
A: About six months.
Q: How many times have you bought heroin from Steve Luben?
A: Maybe a hundred times.
Q: How do you take heroin?
A: I snort it.

Leader feigned sympathy. "You used to be antidrugs, didn't you?" I told him again, "I only blame myself for what's happened to me. I got myself into this and I'll have to fight."

I said I was only prepared to give evidence against Luben, not Mimi, Kevin, or Ginty. I was still very fond of Ginty. I thought about her kids and little baby Kaya.

John Cohen was disappointed that I made a confession. It was easy for him to be detached. I was the one vomiting and shaking. Without a confession there was no basis for a case. There was no evidence to corroborate their allegations. Leader promised me I wouldn't get convicted. I was charged with possession of heroin, which meant past possession as no drugs were ever found on me or in my home. Meg said they were setting a bad precedent. Did it mean they could go into every drug clinic and arrest everyone? Surely it would stop people coming forward to get treatment. The police said they were forced to charge me because of political pressure and all the publicity surrounding the case. They had to charge Boy George in order to make themselves look good.

After spending eight hours at the police station I returned to Roy and Alison's. We were trailed most of the way by journalists. I thought it was strange that they'd traced me to Harrow. It must have been the police that tipped them off. Meg stayed for a few more days before leaving me to my own devices. I kept the black box so that I could finish the detoxification. Part of me wanted to stay off drugs for good, but heroin was all I could think about. I was so miserable I wanted to numb myself. I wondered if I'd done the right thing owning up to the police. I kept seeing Leader's smarmy face. I wanted to punch it through the back of his head. I managed to get one of Michael's flatmates to roll me a few joints and Bonnie smuggled them in in a bag of clothes. Alison caught me smoking and went mad. "I'm not having drugs in this house.

I've just had a baby." I confined my smoking to the bottom of the garden. Both Roy and Alison were sweet. Alison had enough to deal with with a newborn baby. They proved themselves to be true friends.

Michael and I were finding it difficult to stay with Roy and Alison. We felt in the way. I was bored out of my mind and sick of hiding. I went into Basildon town center with Alison and illegally drove her car while she was shopping. We were spotted in McDonald's and made the local press. I made a convincing case for going back to Hampstead, even though everyone thought it was a bad idea. I felt like shit; I couldn't sit still and was chain-smoking cigarettes. I got Billy Button to drive me to Mum's in Shooters Hill. I told Mum I didn't feel any better. The Meg Patterson treatment hadn't worked. Mum was crying, I was crying. I needed some Valium or something. I went to see Dr. Victor Bloom, a private doctor who'd looked after Culture Club's requirements. I told him I needed some medication because I was scared I was going to take heroin again. He prescribed a small quantity of DF118s and Valium.

Once I was in the West End it was hard not to sniff around for drugs. I rang around, everyone was nervous. Eventually I ended up at Dencil Williams's flat in Mornington Crescent, which was morbid as Dencil was still in hospital recovering from his drug-induced coma. A few people were crashing there, Waka, a punky Japanese girl, and Mark Vaultier, who I knew from Taboo and round at Helen and Mimi's. I bought a block of hash, but what I really wanted was smack. Phone calls were made but I was unlucky, or lucky, that night. I said I'd call back.

I stayed that night at Shooters Hill, and the next day Mum, Dad, Auntie Phyllis, Michael, and I went off to the Surrey countryside, to a rented farmhouse in West Clandon owned by Viv Neves, the first Page Three girl. Tony Gordon had arranged the trip to get me away from London and back into a family atmosphere. It wasn't long before the press were ringing the bell. They took up residence in the local pub and waited for a sighting. Mum tried to surround me with people I was close to, like Auntie Teresa and her family—it was as much for her own sanity. Teresa was the first to cop I was still doing drugs. She came and sat on my bed and cried. "Do you want to die? You know you're killing your-self." I said it was just pills and spliff and spliff wasn't a drug, it's a herb. She said, "You know you're talking a load of old rubbish." I made her a promise I couldn't keep. Dad ranted that there were too many people at West Clandon and called it a "bloody circus." He was sure he could contain the situation better if he had me alone.

With the excuse that I needed more clothes I escaped to London and scored some Rohypnol and a bottle of methadone from outside a doctor's surgery in Holloway. All the junkies used to sell their prescriptions to buy real drugs. I had pills all over the house, under carpets and Sellotaped to the back of picture frames. No one seemed to notice my change of mood. It was easier to hold down food. Mum thought I was getting better. Playing happy families was the hard part. I wasn't used to being watched like a child. I smoked spliff openly. No one liked it. Every time I left the house tears would well up in Mum's eyes. She couldn't stop me—I was up and down to London on mad shopping sprees buying presents for everyone. Mum said she didn't want presents, she just wanted me to get well.

I turned up at the newly opened Limelight club in Shaftesbury Avenue for the *Face* magazine party and the *Sid and Nancy* pre-miere. I looked like my own ghost and drank myself into a stupor, asking everyone for drugs. I was frightened of missing out, being forgotten, I wasn't going to hide away like a leprous slug. I knew people were looking down their noses at me. They were all druggy hypocrites. I was uncool because I got caught.

On July 29 I appeared at Marylebone Magistrates' Court and was fined £250 for possession of heroin. I was high on methadone and brazenly carrying a hash joint in my pocket. Outside the court was like a David Cassidy concert, scores of kids screaming and waving banners. One girl had £16,000 in her handbag—she'd remort-gaged her house in case I needed bail. I had total contempt for the proceedings. I knew I was a scapegoat.

Maybe if my case had been taken to the Crown Court it could have been proved that my confession was taken under duress. Equally it could have resulted in a prison sentence. It was generally decided that pleading guilty, getting a slap on the wrist and a £250 fine would "have it over and done with," Tony Gordon's words. Marilyn had the right idea: he kept his mouth shut, even though there was as much circumstantial evidence to convict him. He pleaded not guilty and his case was dismissed.

Politicians complained that magistrate Geoffrey Noel was far too lenient with me. The media ran stories that his stepson had been jailed for smuggling cocaine. Too lenient, they didn't know the half of it. I was banned for life from Japan, one of my biggest record markets, and lost a million-dollar advertising contract with Suntory whiskey, who were trying to sue me for loss of face. My conviction also meant problems entering the United States and Canada. My just deserts, you might say. The only conciliatory statement came from MP David Mellor, then a Home Office minister. "People do not want a pound of flesh. They want him on the road to recovery."

Leaving court we were trampled and probed. "How do you feel? Are you happy with the verdict?" My statement, "I'm glad it's all over," was cynical to say the least. Mum and Auntie Phyllis got dragged into the middle of the road. Mum was so angry she wanted to punch someone, preferably a *Sun* journalist. A toothless tramp broke the tension when he grabbed her hand. "Are you someone famous, then?" She burst out laughing though she was full of tears.

I was driven back to my solicitor's in the West End for an audience with the BBC, ITN, American ABC News TV crews, and a heart-to-heart with Paul Callan from the *Daily Mirror*. It was ridiculous and typical of Tony to try and make good with the media when they deserved a kick in the eye. I was a drugged mug. I sat preaching abstinence from behind a pair of Ray Bans and made several trips to the toilet, smoking a spliff out the window.

Living precariously had become second nature. Prior to my court case I had a meeting with Detective Sergeant Leader at my solicitor's office. Leader was preparing his case against Feiner and Luben (Ginty and Steve). Originally he wanted me to come to Paddington Green police station, but John Cohen persuaded him to keep it informal. Thank God. I was forty-five minutes late and almost hallucinating, I'd smoked so much grass. John was pacing and looking out of the window. He saw me stumble out of Billy's car and weave through the traffic. The doorman was sent to guide me in. Leader was a different man, sympathetic, even nice. He'd got what he wanted out of me and was brimming about convicting Ginty and Steve. I wished deep down that I could change my statement, that I hadn't opened my big mouth in the first place. Was the world going to be a better place because two small-time dealers got put away? I was still trying not to implicate Ginty though the evidence was mounting against her.

CHAPTER 43

It was quietly accepted that Culture Club was over. There were no meetings with our lawyers and accountants or kind words between the four of us. Plans to release a new single, "Heaven's Children," were shelved everywhere. White labels were circulated to radio stations in Europe, but no one would touch it. It was the same story in America, even though our previous single, "Move Away," had been Top 10.

Radio stations were quick to take a moral stance about "junkie George," while the music of the Doors, the Rolling Stones, Janis Joplin, Jimi Hendrix, and any number of known drug users churned out of the airwaves. In America, DJs were playing a spoof record with the lyrics "I'll shoot up for you" and "Do you really want to bust me?"

Foolishly I started making plans to launch my career as a solo artist. I should have been looking at six months in a clinic and then a long holiday. Richard Branson offered me a free trip to Necker Island in the Caribbean and then reneged, asking me to pay half price. I thought it was a cheek after all the millions he'd made out of Culture Club.

Tony and I met with Virgin, who were happy for me to start recording straightaway, suggesting American producer Stewart Levine, who had produced a number one for Simply Red. They thought it would be better to record the album outside England, somewhere like Nassau or Montserrat. Had anyone at the record company used their eyes they would have seen I wasn't well enough to fry an egg. I let them get on with it. Planning ahead helped me delude myself that I was in control again. My old press officer, Ronnie Gurr, was brought in as album coordinator. I knew I wanted the music to be dancy and persuaded Ronnie to fly my musician friend Michael Rudetsky from New York to write with me.

Michael left New York on August 3, the day Trojan died from a drugs overdose at his boyfriend John Maybury's Camden flat. Everyone was in shock. We'd all been messing around with drugs thinking we were invincible and now someone had died. Trojan's death should have been a lesson to us all. Of course, everyone said Trojan was excessive, careless, and unlucky. It could have been any of us at any time.

There were other omens. Michael's mother kept calling the morning he was due to arrive. Mum thought it was odd carrying on like that about a grown man. My brother Kevin went to Gatwick airport to meet Michael at 9 A.M. He waited three hours and came home fuming. Michael appeared at the Virgin offices that afternoon, claiming he'd been held up at Customs and strip-searched. When he finally reached West Clandon I couldn't believe how fit he looked. He was wearing a tight T-shirt and looked like he'd been pumping iron. He was his same dry, cynical self. "You don't look bad for a corpse." He'd been keeping up on all my wonderful press and said he couldn't wait to start working with Marilyn again. "Let's call him now." We talked about our dodgy days on Columbus Avenue. Michael said he'd been clean for months. I told him I was on methadone. The talk was mainly about Montserrat and getting a suntan.

Early evening Bonnie drove Michael and me to Hampstead as there was no room for him at Clandon. He stayed in my newly decorated Joan Collins bedroom. Bonnie and I tidied the house in preparation for an interview with America's *Spin* magazine and Michael went to change some dollars. Journalist Kevin J. Koffler and I were gabbing till gone midnight. Michael was crashed out on the sofa. Philip Sallon turned up with a couple of boys and was intrigued: "Ooh, who's that? He looks sweet. Shall I have my wicked way?" We went out to the Limelight, then I stayed at St. John's Wood.

Bonnie found Michael puking in the kitchen sink. She asked if he'd been taking drugs, he denied it. We were hours late for our A&R meeting with Ronnie Gurr. We lied our faces off, telling him we had loads of song ideas. We were confident we could get the songs together. Ronnie had set up some writing time at Gaslight Studios in Brixton.

On our way we detoured to a photo lab in Farringdon. I wanted to get some of Andre Csillag's pictures airbrushed and it had to be done right away. Andre was used to my madness. He met us at Virgin and drove us to the lab. We didn't get to Gaslight till gone 8 P.M. Bonnie and I went to get some beers while Michael set up the computer and keyboards. I rolled a joint and took a couple of Tempgesics and Valium. We drank and smoked more than we worked. Michael fell asleep on his keyboard. I got the security guard to help me walk him to the car. Michael was moaning like an old drunk. I thought it was funny. We stopped down the road for fish and chips and ate them in the car. At Hampstead my brother Kevin helped walk Michael into the house and we made him comfortable on the sofa. He was soon snoring. We had a cup of tea, then Bonnie and I drove to St. John's Wood. I had a photo shoot the next day with *Blitz* magazine and had to collect some clothes.

Bonnie was woken at 7 A.M. by rapping on the door. It was a journalist with grim news. Someone had been found dead in my house. "We think it's George or his brother Kevin." Bonnie slammed the door.

Mum shook me out of my sleep at 9 A.M. to tell me Michael had been found dead. "Oh, son, oh, son. What's happening to us?" Mum and Dad had rushed from West Clandon after a panic call from Bonnie. I shut myself in the bedroom. I couldn't cry. I was full of selfish thoughts. I'm fucked, I'm fucked. It was the end for me. I knew the press would soon be gathering on the doorstep. I wanted to run and keep running.

After Bonnie and I had left Hampstead the night before, Kevin had gone to the Limelight club to judge a Marilyn Monroe looka-like contest. That was spooky enough. He came home about 5 A.M.

and sat in the kitchen writing poems. It was ages before he discovered Michael lying facedown on the front-room carpet with his shirt off. Kevin realized something was badly wrong. Michael was cold. He called an ambulance and ran out into the street—he was too freaked to stay in the house. The police arrived soon after the ambulance and the press soon after them. It was national news long before I knew. I didn't cry until I saw Michael's body being carried out on the lunchtime news. It was like a scene from a horror movie, especially coming out of that Gothic house. The reports were grim and fatalistic, implying it was only a matter of time before it was me.

I was taken to West Hampstead police station to give a statement. The press almost crushed me in the car door, shoving their mikes at me and asking idiot questions. "How do you think I fucking feel?" I told the police everything I could remember. I didn't tell them we'd been smoking spliff. They said I had nothing to fear and that no one was holding me responsible. I was. I cried and cried and kept thinking maybe if I was there I could have done something. Maybe if I hadn't been pissed and out of it on pills I would have known something was wrong.

Mum had to call Michael's mother in New York. Mrs. Rudetsky already knew about Michael's death via the American Embassy. They talked for two hours. Mum wanted to fly to New York, but my lawyers advised against it. Mrs. Rudetsky kept on repeating, "Something should have been done." She blamed me, as I have always blamed myself. None of us had any idea that Michael had just walked out of a drugs clinic—that's why his mother had been so worried. Mum said someone should have told us. Michael died of morphine poisoning. There were too many theories on how he got hold of drugs. That he swallowed them in a condom or knew someone in London. He may have taken pills out of my jacket pocket. His system had just been detoxed from heavy freebasing and the smallest dose would have been lethal.

Eight days after Michael's death I flew out to the island of Montserrat with my boyfriend, Michael Dunne. I felt like I was running away, escaping my responsibility. The press were waiting at Heathrow. I kept my eyes to the floor and my mouth shut. It was a relief to be on that plane even though it had been a week-long battle to secure a work permit as a convicted drug addict. This was my new form. I had to accept that wherever I went from now on I would be under suspicion. I wondered what people were thinking about me and was glad Michael was there holding my hand.

We flew to Barbados, where we had to clear Customs before flying to Montserrat. Air Studios manageress Yvonne Kelly was there to meet us and smooth the way. My bags were searched thoroughly and one of each pill taken for examination. Montserrat was heavenly: my whole body relaxed as soon as I stepped off the plane. Everyone was pointing and giggling. We looked like aliens with our white hair and Boy prints.

Air Studios was up on a hill overlooking the island and turquoise Caribbean Sea. It had its own swimming pool and cook, who made the best plantain chips and tuna sandwiches I've tasted this lifetime. The studio was owned by George Martin, so there was no shortage of Beatles videos. Watching the screaming girls reminded me of Culture Club's heyday and how fickle it all was. I got to meet George Martin. It was like meeting royalty, except from my experience he was a lot nicer. I hit it off with producer Stewart Levine straightaway. "Don't worry," he said, "I've got the best band for you." He was obviously nervous, and so was I. I'd flown out to Montserrat with no songs and no ideas. I hadn't met the musicians I was making my album with. What could I do but relax into it with a glass of red wine?

Meeting the band was so intimidating, they were sizing me up, wondering how to behave. At first I was treated like a porcelain figure. I had to make an announcement to get a toke off a joint. I'd been asking for spliff since I arrived; no one would get it for me. The band thought it was really cool that I was still smoking dope, and I was initiated.

The star was guitarist Glen Nightingale, a half-caste with pretty eyes and a brute-force charisma. Glen only ever wore one set of clothes, a pair of khaki trousers and a tight jean jacket. He carried a metal case rammed with demos and could talk you through every hi-hat. Drummer Ritchie Stevens looked like a little water vole. He became the victim of endless sexual innuendos. He wasn't my type, but it became a standard joke that I always slept with the drummer. Ian Maidman played bass and was the sensitive end of the rhythm section, a vegetarian who rolled his own. "Wicksie" on keyboards was the oddest man out. He was older than the rest and didn't always enjoy the roll-out-the-barrel humor, which was never worse than at dinner, a colonial candlelit affair around a long wicker table. Yvonne appeared every night in some sensuous getup. Being the only female was hard work.

Montserrat was an expensive holiday with a bit of recording thrown in. I spent most of my time by the pool or watching TV. For Michael and me it was like a honeymoon away from frantic London and the hangers-on. He was kind and attentive and I saw the softness that made me fall for him. Michael was worried about the amount of pills I was taking and was giving regular reports to Richard Branson in London. My voice was a guttural snarl from smoking dope and three packs of fags a day. I couldn't pitch properly and compensated by overusing my vibrato and doing impersonations of Louis Armstrong. Luckily Stewart's background in the druggy New York jazz scene, playing sax for Woody Herman, had prepared him for any mood swings. Like Arif he used psychology. There was always something else to do. Most of the recording went on without me.

Motown legend Lamont Dozier was flown in to write the hits. I still kick myself for missing the moment and not ticking at my full potential. We sat at the piano, gossiping about Diana Ross, trying for that spark of genius. We came up with "Sold," the title track, and "To Be Reborn," the album's tenderest moment and my final word to Jon:

I could live, I could die,
I could be reborn in your arms.
I could laugh, I could cry, I could sigh
If you're there to keep me warm.

All the songs were introspective and bitter, with titles like "Where Are You Now (When I Need You)," "I Asked for Love," and "Next Time." It wasn't meant to be funny, but it cracks me up now. The bulk of the songs were constructed from jamming sessions in the studio, an expensive process at $2,000 a day. I was happy and convinced myself I was creating perfect pop, but now I realize it was lazy and repetitive. The saving grace was our recording of David Gates's classic "Everything I Own," which was a number one in 1976 for reggae artist Ken Boothe. Stewart had only heard the hippie version by Bread and couldn't imagine it reggae style. The tape op was dispatched to the local radio station to find the old 45.

Stewart was priceless throughout, producer, comedian, protector. When two loony middle-aged American fans arrived on the island, he was convinced they were potential ax murderers and asked them to leave. He smoothed things over with Virgin when I insisted on flying in my friend Jocelyn Brown. I wanted her to sing, but I also needed some extra companionship. The last time I'd seen Jocelyn was in New York when I was falling to pieces. She called me "Pumpkin" and said I was looking good with a bit of flesh on me. Her presence was a real boost. We wrote one of the best songs on the album together, "Keep Me in Mind." Jocelyn had a friend on the island, a mystical type who read shells. He warned me of another death and urged me to find my spiritual path.

The last night of recording was celebrated with a slap-up dinner and some heavy drinking. Some prankster had collaborated with the cook and spiked the chocolate cake with dope. Everyone was giggly except for the young tape op, who thought he was going to die. I had to sit and hold his hand for an hour. The party ended with a crowd of us scouring the island for cocaine. I took too much and ended up scraping the villa walls, thinking I was going to have a heart attack.

On returning to London I was faced with a media tirade from the gloating Marilyn, who had sold his story to the *Mail on Sunday* for £5,000. The piece was classic. "George can be really bitchy and nasty, even towards people he likes. I've never done the same thing back to him and you couldn't induce me to slag the guy off if you tried." Accompanied by a psychotic picture appropriately snapped by Steve Bent. Marilyn said my flat in New York was filthy and that he had to live on hamburgers. Poor thing, he didn't mention the soft-shell crab or the small fortune he'd taken from me and Sydney Masters.

Marilyn had been acquitted while I was recording in Montserrat. His case was dismissed because no one had seen him take drugs (if you don't count half of New York and London). He couldn't be prosecuted purely on his own admission, so I wonder, *How the hell could they prosecute me on my own admission?*

Marilyn wasn't the only fiendish friend talking to the press. A cover story in *Rolling Stone*, "Boy George's Tragic Fall," contained interviews with Fat Tony and Jane Goldman and was pepped up with additional reporting by Dave Rimmer from *Smash Hits*. There were a lot of detailed stories from New York. I was angry and felt there was no one left to trust. I was sure they'd been paid for their dirty deeds. Philip had always called Jane Goldman "Jane Gold-digger," but I expected better from Fat Tony.

The first night back I was out at the clubs. I looked great with my tan, everyone commented. I went to the Wag club and gave a mouthful to Fat Tony. Of course we made up, I was never very good at holding grudges. I took some acid and Ecstasy. I should have been happy, I was laughing enough, but my body was craving heroin. That night I made a lethal connection with Paul "Cod," a pond-life dealer and junkie, and began my second spiral. I bought a quarter of a gram of heroin and snuck off to the toilets. It seems crazy that it could happen so quickly, but that's how it was. Michael stormed out of the club when he saw my pinned eyes. I didn't care, I was back in that cocoon.

I promised Michael it was just a little dabble, that I wasn't going to start taking it again, but I wasn't fooling myself. Within days I was taking frightening amounts, on top of medication and alcohol. I found a dealer in Malden Road, Kentish Town. We'd rendezvous at Gospel Oak train station in daylight and at his flat after dark. I bought three or four grams at a time, as always telling myself I'd make it last. I hunted out old accomplices like Richard Habberley and Paul Lonegan. We hid out in Alice Temple's bedroom in the basement of her parents' house in Holland Park, turning it into a speakeasy den with the right sounds and a packet of Rizlas always at the ready. Alice dabbled with drugs, but not like the rest of us—it was mostly just puff. I felt like a fugitive defending my right to take drugs. I didn't want anyone to catch me, but when I was high I became cocky, riding the tube, going to McDonald's in Oxford Street because Prince had been there, complaining that everyone was staring at me.

One hazy day Richard, Alice, and I had lunch at Fortnum & Mason with Annie Lennox and her new boyfriend. God knows how it came about, but there we were, Alice chirping politely while Richard and I nodded into our soup. She kept kicking us under the table. Annie was cool until I woke up singing "There Must Be an Angel" and staggered across the room to light my cigarette on the flambé. Another time we went shopping in my lime green Granada. I was popping pills and could barely keep the car straight, bumping buses and scraping cars. Alice managed to steer me to a curb. I was crying and refused to hand over the keys with the ever-famous line, "I'm fine. I'm fine." We walked around Covent Garden, where I went on a wobbly shopping spree at the Tea House in Neal Street. I couldn't get the pen on my checkbook. I crashed into Paul Smith, then on to Jones, where they had to shut the shop because I was making such a spectacle. The manager helped me to the car and Alice drove me to Holland Park. The next day a story appeared accusing me of attempting to steal an umbrella from Paul Smith. Even though I was out of it I remember events clearly. It was raining and I asked the pissy shop assistant at Paul Smith to lend me an umbrella to go to Jones just down the street. Neither of us needed the publicity.

The press made a big deal when I refused to take part in the recording of an antidrugs record. I told them, "I don't want to become the Bob Geldof of heroin." I knew it would be hypocritical, and I hate cringey charity records. The *Sun* followed up the furor with a splash headline, "Boy George Is Back on Drugs." I was disappointed but not surprised to discover the source of their information was Dencil Williams, who had snapped out of his coma and was taking revenge on the wrong person. Marilyn claimed he had no part in it, but the following month he, Dencil, and Juliette Silver were caught out when they tried to sell another story to Alastair Campbell of the *Daily Mirror* for the greasy sum of £10,000. Marilyn gloated, "I know the guy better than anyone. It'll be more than bitching, I've got hundreds of stories, hundreds of them." They were to be disappointed, the headline read,

"Marilyn. What a Rat. £10,000 Bid to Ruin Boy George." I sent Bonnie to get it framed and hung it on my wall as a constant reminder.

The circus was in town again. I knew I had to be extra-careful not to carry drugs. I was sure if I wore a big enough pair of sunglasses I could get by. Michael and I appeared for the opening of the new Boy shop in Soho and then modeled on the catwalk at the Limelight club. We were holding hands and Michael was wearing a T-shirt that read "Boy Love." It was my first openly gay display. I was screaming fuck you from every queer cell, there was nothing left to protect. I felt like everyone hated me anyway.

It was a shame I couldn't match that love in private. My relationship with Michael was increasingly moody. He hated my druggy friends and was always trying to stop me buying heroin, standing in front of the door pleading, "You don't need it. Just have some spliff." I dodged him like I dodged Mum and Dad and anyone else who challenged me. If he rang the bell at St. John's Wood or Hampstead I'd pretend to be out. I was fond of Michael. I didn't know if I loved him, I was so cut off from my feelings. I treated him like a possession, thinking I could have him there when I felt like it and run to him when there was a problem. I guess I'd always been selfish. I don't know if I was born that way, but being one of six kids and queer, I soon learned to exist in a solitary, demanding sphere. Fame only added to the problem. I didn't like walking on people, but what can you do when they lie on the floor? The drugs were the final eruption of all that was nasty and vile about me.

I knew I was killing myself. I'd long got over the excitement of fitting into a pair of twenty-six-inch waist jeans. I had no life. I drifted in and out of this awareness. I wanted to stop, but I couldn't see a way out. The only time I smiled was when I had a straw up my nose or a strip of tinfoil in my hand. Every day was spent searching for heroin. So many days I woke up vomiting, wishing I could die then and there, making desperate calls, begging for drugs. Sometimes money wasn't enough.

My latest dealer in Malden Road was busted after I'd been spotted going into his house by a nosy builder. I was asking for trouble shopping drugs in a canary-striped Joseph cardigan. Drugs were found, but I was never questioned by the police. I was scared and moved back to the security of Hampstead. I was sure my phone was bugged and only talked about drugs in fashion-speak: hats for heroin, white T-shirts for coke, and camouflage trousers for dope. Scoring drugs was getting harder: I had to send runners and pay them with a toot. Mark Vaultier was crashing at Hampstead and Stephen Brennan was yo-yoing in and out with his badge machine. Neither of them could say no whether it was a line of smack or a bottle of Lambrusco and ten Valium. Mark was legendary in the Taboo days for confiscating people's drugs and swallowing them. Underneath the sneer he was a sweet and talented soul, classically trained on clarinet and piano. He used to joke about scoring music instead of drugs. He was mad about Debbie Harry and would play "French Kissing" over and over. He claimed Debbie Harry had once said heroin preserved her looks.

Extending your drug map was the only loyalty. I was regularly cabbing it over to Steve Strange's place in Fulham to buy smack. All our bitching came down to nothing, we were now dogs in the same kennel. After one late-night session I discovered my American Express card was missing. I knew it was Steve, though he fiercely denied it. I paid him back by rifling his wardrobe and making badges that read: "American Express. Steve Strange never leaves your home without it." Four years too late I received an apology. I've been meaning to return Steve's Antony Price snakeskin coat.

Steve was no sicker than the rest of us. Mark and I started visiting private doctors in the West End who were only too happy to sell us prescriptions. The worst was Dr. "Silver" in Bentinck Street, who was rumored to have royal connections. I stored the pills and methadone in my dressing-room cabinet. We mixed pills, downed them with alcohol, snorted heroin, and floated through the day. We dyed our hair and spent hours in makeup and wardrobe. I let my photographer friend Paul Gobel shoot a Boy catalogue in my ruched bedroom. It was fab, lots of unsuspecting straight boys cuddling with each other and dribbling cornflakes. Paul was taking so much heroin the shoot went on for days. He was another foul-mouthed genius wrecking himself with drugs.

I first encountered Paul in 1982 during my first visit to New

York when he was a celebrity makeup artist working for Italian *Vogue*. He wanted to paint my face for a cover. I refused and he slammed the phone down on me. When we met a few months later at a TV studio I needed no introduction. I knew the large camp figure in my dressing room was Paul Gobel. I sat down. "Well?" He was dead nervous. "Your foundation and brows are perfect, but the rest, I'm sorry." He worked on my face for ten minutes and made me look amazing.

Paul painted and shot me for the Boy catalogue and the album sleeve for *Sold*. Every picture had to be retouched, but I loved my skinny body, wrapped around models and styled by Judy Blame. The makeup took hours—we were so out of it we were sniffing the blusher.

I was still flying the day of Michael Rudetsky's inquest, held on a gray day at St. Pancras Coroner's Court, over the road from where Trojan died. I couldn't face it without drugs. I was fiercely cross-examined and left feeling I had blood on my hands, despite the verdict of misadventure. That same day I learned that Michael's parents were suing me for $20 million and accused me of administering a lethal injection of heroin. They wanted to extradite me to stand trial in New York. I understood why they hated me. Their son had died in a far-off country and they didn't know how or why. I wanted to write a letter to Michael's mother, but my lawyers advised against it.

I was back in court the following day for the committal proceedings against Kevin and Mimi, appearing as a witness for the prosecution. There was lots of nervous giggling. We were all wearing bright red Boy bondage coats and I powdered my nose on the witness stand. I promised Mimi I'd style her for her trial. Both Kevin and Mimi were acquitted of conspiracy to supply drugs but faced further charges.

The laughter and camp arrogance was all a front. I blamed myself for Kevin and Mimi's troubles. Inside I was terrified about the future. I couldn't imagine anyone buying my records again. Every word written about me was negative. I kept telling myself I had to get well, but I was frightened, more than I'd ever been in my life. I saw Dr. Bloom, this time in tears. I told him I was back on heroin. He said he could put me into the Charter Nightingale

Clinic straightaway, it was up to me. I talked my way out of it. I wasn't ready. He said I'd made the most important step, admitting I had a problem. He gave me methadone and asked me to stick to the dosage. I promised I would. He didn't know I was procuring medication from other doctors, like Dr. Christine Pickard, who visited me and Mark at home in Hampstead.

Mark and I talked a lot about cleaning up. We'd survive for a couple of days on pills and methadone, then treat ourselves with a gram or two of smack. There was no way off the treadmill. I thought I wanted help, but if anything concrete was suggested I'd back away.

Richard Branson rang the bell at Hampstead. I left him outside in the rain. While Michael apologized through the intercom, I was throwing things round the house, ranting that he had no right to interfere. I accused Michael of calling Richard and trying to trick me. He returned the following evening with Harry Eves, a counselor from Broadreach House drug treatment center near Plymouth. They stood outside for half an hour ringing the bell. I eventually let them in. I was trying to pretend everything was perfectly fine even though I couldn't string a sentence together. I was singing new songs to them and rambling on about music. Harry Eves and I sat alone in my bedroom and talked for over an hour. He told me about his clinic and their Minnesota method of treatment which was based on total abstinence. I didn't ask questions. I promised I would go to Broadreach House the coming Monday but I never kept my appointment, I found a hundred million reasons. I told Bonnie I didn't trust "flash Harry," that he was trying to make a name for himself "getting Boy George into his bloody clinic."

I couldn't face Mum and Dad and did everything I could to avoid their calls. Bonnie was talking to them two or three times a day, they were so desperate. My problems were putting a strain on their marriage and the whole family. Mum ran off to a family wedding in Dublin without telling Dad. It was the first time she'd done anything like that. My younger brother Gerald made the headlines, "Rowdy O'Dowd," and appeared in court charged with smashing a pub window. The case was dismissed for lack of evidence, but Gerald was on a bender. He'd been doing cocaine for over a year and had chucked in his athletic lifestyle.

The *Daily Star* ran a three-part exposé on the supposed love tri-angle between myself, Jon Moss, and the dreadful pop wannabe Shee Lippell. By now Jon's ex, she was giving the best vocal per-formance of her life, throwing personal letters into the bargain. The thrust of the revelations was that I'd turned to heroin because Jon had run off with Shee, described as a "blonde beauty." She claimed Jon was a "gentle, considerate, exciting lover" and squealed, "I don't think Jon is gay. It's just that Boy George is an amazing person and Jon just fell under his spell." She was the one with the broomstick.

"My Fear Over AIDS" panicked one headline. "What worries me are all the stories of George sleeping around in New York, and the times Jon has slept with him since. There's got to be a chance of George coming into contact with an AIDS carrier then passing it on to Jon." The only thing Shee Lippell was likely to catch was foot-and-mouth disease.

When Jon appeared in court soon after, charged with possessing cocaine, he dismissed the stories and said, "No one will touch her with a barge pole." It gave me some satisfaction until I found out he was seeing a young Culture Club fan, a pretty Turkish girl called Miffy, who used to sit on my doorstep. I was jealous and angry because Jon had always said it was "too easy" to sleep with fans. So much for not abusing your power. I saw Miffy and her friend Sam at the Limelight on Halloween night and cursed them both with a slap and a free beer facial. Reports that I tried to strangle them were exaggerated, though I did call them a pair of "slags."

Jaws dropped when I appeared in clubs. I was a nine-stone skeleton with dead eyes peering out of a pancake face. I wore a floppy cap covered in pins, badges, and buttons that hung over one eye. I had a funny half-inch beard and stunted eyebrows. I thought I looked good. Heroin numbs any self-doubt: you feel more sorry for everyone else. Poor things, they don't know what they're missing. Trojan had summed it up perfectly when he scraped, "Those below us know nothing" in the lift at Godwin Court.

Sacrosanct was the new club on Wednesday night and one of the few places I didn't stand out. It was the same crowd that had frequented Taboo, only the carefree narcomania had been replaced by a kind of desperation. Taboo shut down shortly before Trojan's death, ironically because a write-up in *You* magazine had mentioned the whiff of marijuana and popping of Ecstasy. The whiff was more a tornado: heroin, cocaine, "Special K" (ketamine), mushrooms, acid, and anything else you might care to shove down your fashion gullet.

Sacrosanct was the last gasp. Quite a few people had developed serious smack and coke habits. Trojan's finale may have made the press, but there were other drug deaths, like shoe designer John Moore and model rep Louise Powell, that were just gasps on the club scene.

After a night at Sacrosanct with Mimi and John Maybury, Mark Vaultier and I were trolling up Tottenham Court Road looking for a cab. A police car drew alongside us. "Morning, boys." They were being friendly, but I could barely stop myself running. I had drugs in my pocket and thought it was my final moment. They didn't stop, they just looked us up and down and drove off laughing. All the way home I was looking out for police cars. For days I thought I was going to be raided. It wasn't just paranoia. The police were biding their time. I didn't leave the house for over a week and promised myself I was going to kick heroin for the last time, even though I still had four or five grams left. I called out a doctor from Dr. Pickard's Medi-Call service who prescribed me a bottle of methadone and some Valium. Two days later Mark and I went to Dr. Pickard's surgery in Camden and got hold of more methadone and Valium. I put the methadone into different-sized bottles and labeled them for days of the week. I was planning to wean myself off, even though I was still ringing around everywhere trying to get heroin.

I had a brainwave and decided to go and hide out at John Maybury's flat in Mornington Crescent, thinking "they" wouldn't find me there. Mark and I arrived at John's flat late Friday. John was there with Mimi and another boy, Mark Batham, who I used to go to school with. We sat up all night smoking dope, listening to Nico and Marianne Faithfull. John's flat was the perfect womblike drug den with its blue lightbulbs and artistic clutter—you could imagine Joe Orton living there and having his brains splattered. The tiny toilet doubled as a library with books on Cocteau, Genet, Brian Jones, and, of course, Orton. Trojan's garish paintings were hung everywhere. My favorite was "Female Trouble" depicting a fish, an egg, and a pair of Y-fronts on a washing line.

About 3 A.M. John's friend Leslie Winer came round with some heroin. I scrounged a couple of lines; the rest was cooked up and injected in the kitchen, the same one where Trojan's body had been found. Leslie left suddenly, saying she had to go home to her baby. I watched her from the bathroom window disappearing down Crowndale Road looking like the Count of Monte Cristo in her flared Azzedine Alaïa coat. Leslie was one of John's crowd. She sneered at me, "You don't know how to get high" because I wouldn't mainline. Leslie was a beautiful, androgynous ex-model, married to Kevin Mooney, who was Jeremy's old schoolfriend and bass player in Adam and the Ants. Kevin later formed a group called Max and wrote the song "Little Ghost" about Trojan, which I later recorded on my album *Sold*. Leslie made her own brilliant album in 1993 called *Witch Witch Witch*. I wrote a song about Leslie called "She Wanted What She Knew Till She Knew What She Wanted," inspired by one of John Maybury's paintings:

She sticks the needle in her arm
The blood runs down like tears.
She's screaming for attention
But don't you ever get too near.
If we could get much higher
We could catwalk on the moon
Reflect our desperation in a silver spoon.

At 8:30 A.M. we decided to go to Mark Batham's flat in Bayswater. Batham was off to New York. Mark Vaultier and I went along out of boredom. Trailing down the street we looked like we'd been left behind by a circus. Vaultier and I had on platform sneakers and were carrying white plastic handbags that were printed with the slogans "Stop Corruption" and "Alcohol Kills." Mark's orange hair was straggling out of a big floppy hat and I was shaved like a Buddhist monk. Mark B. looked like an East End criminal in his camel coat. As we reached the end of Crowndale Road a white police van came whizzing round the corner. I ran into a garden and tried to get rid of a piece of hash that was hidden in my underwear. A policeman chased me. I pretended I was going to the toilet. We were questioned in the street. They asked, "Where have you come from?"

"A friend's," I replied. "What's wrong?"

"Have you been drinking?"

"Why? We're not driving, are we?"

"Have you been taking drugs?"

"No."

Mark said he had methadone and showed them the bottle. I started emptying my pockets, thinking it would look good. I complained, "It's because of that other shit, isn't it? It's because I'm Boy George." They told me to remove my sunglasses and said, "We're not entirely happy. We believe you may be concealing controlled drugs on your person. Are you willing to let us search you in the back of our police van without having to go to the station?" We all refused. They arrested us and we were bundled into the van. I started to panic. "Okay, I'll come clean. I've got hash on me." I knew they were going to find it anyway. They wanted to know where I got it. I laughed. "I'm not telling you. You've got what you want, isn't it enough?"

At the station they found hash on Mark V, Mark B was clean. He kept going on about missing his flight. They kept asking him where the party was. He said, "I don't know the number, but it was on the top floor and the door was a rich pinky color." They let him go.

Mark V. and I were kept in separate cells for six hours before questioning. I didn't see him again until 3 P.M. I was sick and in tears. Mark didn't look well either. I told the police he needed a doctor. They bailed him and let him go home. I wanted to go home too. I was crying and told them I wouldn't answer their questions until they gave me some methadone. As always they made out they were interested in everyone else but me. "Does John Maybury take heroin?" "Don't ask me, ask him." They said they were going to raid my house. I kept on shouting, "Give me my fucking methadone, you cunts." They said I was being unreasonable and tried to put me back in the cell. I started punching out. It took four of them to hold me down.

John's flat was raided and he was arrested for allowing his home to be used for taking drugs. Mimi was taken in and charged with possessing cannabis. They also found a small packet of heroin, my methadone, and some amyl nitrate. John told the police, "The amyl is good for dancing and I know I shouldn't say this but it improves your erection, though it never did much for me." We later found out that the police had been watching us—they'd even given Mark Vaultier a code name, Big Bird.

Mum, Dad, and my brother David rushed to Albany Street police station after being alerted by my lawyer, Gary Lux. Dad overheard a copper talking about raiding my home. They went to Hampstead and helped Bonnie and Kevin strip the house of any contraband. Mum threw all my cakes out of the fridge in case they were drugged and burned everything in a bin in the back garden.

At around 7 P.M. the police brought me back to the house for the search. There were dogs running everywhere. One of them started barking at a clothes rail. They found the roach of a joint and a bit of hash. They ransacked every room, throwing clothes out of the cupboards. I sat in the kitchen with Mum. The police were trying to be friendly, making polite conversation. "That's a nice painting."

Mum snapped at them, "Get on with your dirty work and leave us alone."

That night Mum and Dad stayed with me at Hampstead. Dr. Bloom came and gave me something to sleep. I was out for fourteen hours.

The next day Mum told me Mark Vaultier had died. I started screaming and crying, "No, no," and sank to the floor. I couldn't understand how it happened. Mark had gone back to Mark Batham's flat in Notting Hill and gone on an all-night binge of methadone and Valium. He died of methadone poisoning. Mum was holding on to me, weeping, "It could have been you, son. Don't you see where it all leads? Stop it now, son, please, I don't want to lose you." I think we must have cried for an hour or more. Mimi called. We couldn't even speak to each other. It was one of the saddest days of my life.

Mark's death meant that I had to stop. If I said I wanted to I'd be lying. I wanted to stop because of him, but I couldn't think beyond a second. I was scared of the pain that I knew I would have to face. Dr. Bloom asked if I wanted to go into the Charter Nightingale Clinic. I didn't want to go somewhere public where the press would find me. He said he would arrange a private nurse to come and stay at the house. I agreed but hated the thought of being invaded. Mum and Dad wanted it, I couldn't refuse. Dr. Bloom wanted me to stop all medication cold. I said I couldn't, I had to have something. For the rest of that day all I could think of was escaping and getting drugs. I searched through every piece of clothing in the house more thoroughly than the police sniffer dogs. I found a gram of heroin that I'd hidden in the epaulet of a military jacket. It sounds sick to say I was pleased with myself for outwitting the police, but I was. Worse was taking the drugs after Mark's death, but I couldn't help myself. Maybe it was the final catharsis. It was the last bit of heroin I ever took and I savored it. That day John Maybury came round and gave me a hug. He was off for a holiday in Thailand. I wanted to go with him, but I wouldn't have come back alive. He said, "We can't afford to lose you, girl George."

What followed is impossible to explain. The vomiting and physical pain is nothing compared to the emptiness a junkie feels when the drugs are taken away. Even if you could understand the deluded arrogance of heroin addiction you could never imagine the pitiful withdrawal. At best it takes weeks to quell the physical craving, at worst a couple of months, but the psychological craving goes on and on and seems like it will never stop. There's no logic to the fear, it's just fear. An overwhelming panicky fear that eats away at you and won't let you sleep. I hated my parents almost as much as I hated myself. They were in my way, forcing me to suffer. I vented every bit of anger in my body, smashing anything I could get my hands on. Mum said, "If you want to hit me, hit me. If you want to hate me, that's okay." I had horrendous nightmares where I was drowning or being shot. Michael couldn't stay in the bed with me because I was kicking and sweating so much. I had a permanent cramp in my legs and stomach. My sleeping patterns were erratic, sometimes sleeping all day, then sitting in front of the

TV all night. There were times when I didn't sleep for forty-eight hours. I watched every crappy American and Australian soap like a bored, trapped housewife and even began to look forward to my morning dose of *Santa Barbara*.

Two male nurses, Charles and Hughie, stayed with me round the clock. They were the sweetest, gentlest types you could imagine, late-middle-aged and tempered for every outburst and, believe me, there were plenty. I accused them of spying and hating me. I loathed them for interfering and despised their professional cool. As with Meg I had feelings of nausea, the revulsion at bodily smells, food; a tone of voice or an innocent glance could send me into a rage. I screamed at them to give me stronger medication. I caused such a fuss Dr. Bloom prescribed Largactil, a drug used for seriously disturbed mental patients. The drug had little effect. Charles said my body was refusing the drugs. I said he wasn't giving me enough.

Dr. Bloom was a Nichiren Daishonin Buddhist. He started preaching to me about Buddhism and asked me to chant with him, insisting it would calm my mind and lift my spirits. He came round with two sets of wooden beads and we chanted *Nam-myoho-renge-kyo*. It was a stupid waste of time. I didn't have the guts to be rude. He left me books and pamphlets which I didn't read.

Christmas was miserable, even though I had my whole family around me. I barely ate any food or pulled a cracker. I was so sick. I kept thinking about Mark, hoping I would wake up and find it had all been a gruesome nightmare. He couldn't be dead, he couldn't be dead. Outside, fans were keeping vigil along with a couple of sinister hacks. A black woman was testifying on the steps. I was trapped in my mausoleum. I crept upstairs and called Steve Strange's number. God knows what I was thinking. The phone rang and rang until it seemed like a bad idea.

Boxing Day, Mimi and Helen came to visit, I was so pleased to see them. We took a bottle of wine to my bedroom and cried and laughed together. Mimi smuggled in a joint. Her mum had knitted me a jumper in "moss stitch," which was even funnier after a good toke.

CHAPTER 44

On New Year's Day Michael and I attended our first Buddhist meeting at the home of Denise Golding in Chelsea. Dr. Bloom was thrilled. I only went to break up the boredom—I hadn't been out of the house since my arrest. Everyone was gleaming and shaking our hands. "Great to have you here." I knew they were all thinking I was about to be saved by Buddhism. I was handed a small prayer book. I looked at it and thought, I'll never be able to remember this. There were thirty or more people crammed into the living room, kneeling in front of an altar with gold bowls, burning incense, and a black lacquer box containing a sacred Japanese scroll called a Gohonzon. When everyone started chanting *Nam-myoho-renge-kyo* I wanted to laugh. I thought, If anyone saw me now they'd think I'd lost the plot. Michael and I mumbled along. I closed my eyes and tried to feel it. When it was over we chatted and drank wine. I had to change my original assumption that they were all middle-class and snobby. I was looking for things to hate. The whole religious thing gave me the creeps. I was such an atheist and detested the idea of a superior force sitting in judgment. At that point I didn't realize that Buddhism wasn't a religion in the strict sense. It took a few meetings before I began to understand it. I found it hard to sit still and read the books. I asked lots of questions. Buddhism seemed like a common-sense religion. I liked the idea that heaven and hell existed right here on earth and that we were all potential Buddhas. I was uncomfortable with the fact that they chanted for material things, like cars and jobs. It went against my idea of spirituality. I thought, If I'm going to chant for anything it will be peace of mind—I needed it more than a car. I talked with one of the senior leaders about Michael Rudetsky's death. She told me that while the experience was part of my karma it was a form of arrogance to assume responsibility for someone else's death. I found the concept of karma so difficult, that we bring everything on ourselves, murder, rape—even the Jews in the concentration camps.

To begin with, Buddhism was another designer jacket. I preached my new revelations, but I didn't feel it in my heart. I found the chanting uncomfortable. Michael was the one who learned all the prayers and practiced daily. More important than any prayers, we were immersing ourselves in a new environment. No one wanted anything from me and Michael was treated as his own person. I was hit strongly by the idea that I could govern my own destiny, that everything in life, good or bad, was a lesson.

I was still fragile and sickly. Dr. Bloom was visiting me daily and pleading with me to chant. All I was interested in was getting different pills, the medication wasn't working, I couldn't sleep. I was still thinking about drugs all the time. I wanted to get well, but if I could have got hold of some heroin I would have taken it.

I managed a laugh when I read that Marilyn had been seen begging for coins outside a tube station. I suspected it was one of sweet Dencil's stories. Marilyn was actually laid up at his mum's in Borehamwood, gorging pills and Mars bars after a spell in a psychiatric clinic. He'd been suffering from clinical depression. I decided I was clinically depressed too and asked Bloom for some antidepressants.

I couldn't stop thinking about Mimi, Ginty, and Steve and the impending trial. The clearer I became in my mind the more I regretted saying anything to the police. I thought about Ginty and Steve in their prison cells. Mum and Dad couldn't understand why I didn't hate them. They wanted revenge. I didn't.

At Mark Vaultier's inquest Dad caused a huge fuss, shouting questions at Dr. Christine Pickard. He wanted to expose all the irresponsible doctors who were handing out lethal prescriptions.

The coroner told Dad to be quiet. I felt sorry for Dr. Pickard. I don't believe she was wicked, just a little gullible. Dad really blew his top when a prescription for methadone arrived at Hampstead. It had been delayed in the Christmas post. The *Daily Mirror* took up Dad's cause and condemned Pickard and the other doctors.

I was heartbroken to hear that Mark had blamed himself for my arrest. After he was released from police custody he made three calls to me at Hampstead saying he was sorry. I never blamed him and I'll always hold Mark dear in my heart. His funeral was a private family affair. I knew my presence would draw the press and intrude on their grief. I had a big wreath made with the words "I love you Mark" and took it to his grave to say my goodbyes. For months every time I thought about Mark I burst into tears. I couldn't believe he was gone.

It seemed like I was destined to spend the rest of my life in courtrooms. On February 9 I was back on the witness stand at Knightsbridge Crown Court for the trial of Ginty, Steve, and Mimi. I didn't sleep the night before, I was so worried. Mimi pleaded guilty straightaway and was remanded to Holloway prison pending her sentence. I couldn't believe they locked her up, it was so unnecessary. I told the police over and over she hadn't done anything wrong. Ginty and Steve denied all charges and so the trial began and went on for twenty long, boring days.

In his opening statement, prosecutor David Bate said that Ginty and Steve had turned me into a drug addict and added, "They had a lucrative connection in the selling of heroin to people involved in the pop business." He called them leeches, which was probably nearer the truth. They certainly didn't turn me into a heroin addict. It was weird seeing Ginty and Steve in court, and Marilyn, who couldn't resist the drama of it all. They were all staring me out.

That evening I attended the BPI Awards at the Grosvenor House Hotel and presented an award to the Pet Shop Boys. I got a standing ovation. I was tearful. I still didn't know what people thought of me. I told the crowd of my threat to beat up Neil Tennant when he slagged off Culture Club.

Back in court I was fiercely interrogated by defense barrister Anthony Berry, who kept shouting, "Liar. I suggest you have a vivid imagination, Mr. O'Dowd." When he kept asking irrelevant questions about Marilyn I snapped, "What's that got to do with anything?" Judge Samuel Morton tapped his hammer. "Now, now, George, don't get bolshie on us."

To this day Marilyn claims I pointed at him from the witness stand and snarled, "That's who should be up here." Of course it was rubbish—he'd been watching too many reruns of *Whatever Happened to Baby Jane?*

I was taking tranquilizers and fell asleep on the witness stand. The judge asked, "Are we boring you, Mr. O'Dowd?" I said, "Sorry, I'm ill," and asked to go to the toilet. He allowed me to use the private one in his chambers. When I came out Steve Luben was making gestures, touching his nose, trying to insinuate that I'd just gone for a toot. I stuck my tongue out at him.

Throughout the trial I kept thinking to myself, Why have I done this? Why didn't I just keep quiet? I told the court, "The law blames them, I don't. I'm not covering up for anybody. I don't want anybody else to take the blame for what I've done or what I've been through." I also contended that marijuana wasn't a drug, which the press made a big hoo-ha out of: "Pot's no drug, says Boy George. Dozens of his young fans heard his cannabis is OK message."

The trial was a travelogue of the last two years. All the madness in Jamaica, the degradation in New York. They went over everything in fine detail. The defense tried to confuse me and make me out to be conniving. They kept pointing out contradictions in my statements and going on about how I'd lied to newspapers and on TV. They had to discredit me because it was obvious to everyone and their dog that Ginty and Steve were drug dealers. Helen Terry told the court that she had made a pact with Ginty and asked her not to sell me any more drugs. I wasn't allowed in court for Helen's testimony, but Dad came home raging that she was a "mouthy lesbian." The funniest moment came when Bonnie was quizzed by the defense. She described how I was violently sick in New York after Ginty refused me a fix. Ginty's counsel insisted I was sick because I'd eaten twenty-eight pints of ice cream.

I was at home when I heard on the radio that Ginty and Steve had been sentenced to four years. As they were led away Steve shouted "bastards" at the jury. "You have sent two innocent people to prison." I cried my eyes out. In a way I felt responsible. I couldn't rationalize my feelings. I just wished I could wind back the clock. Now I realize they brought it on themselves. They were dealing drugs long before I came along. In their eyes I betrayed them, but our friendship didn't really go beyond the wheeling and dealing at Westbourne Terrace and the odd cup of coffee. I was fond of Ginty and saw a heart beneath the stone. But she was out for herself, cold and simple. Steve was a bully who seemed to hate everyone, including himself. I wouldn't even wish him on Ginty. Friend of the innocents Darrell Thomas was brought before the judge and sentenced to six weeks for contempt after he'd been overheard in the court corridors plotting to beat me up. The best news came when Mimi was finally released from Holloway and put on two years' probation.

The trial was broken up with various celebrity engagements and a busy workload. I was putting finishing touches at RAK Studios to my album *Sold* and shooting a video with John Maybury for the first single, "Everything I Own." I had to keep busy: still I felt like a painted corpse. The makeup did little to disguise my pasty features. I was in extreme physical pain with cramps in my wrists and arms and having frequent palpitations. I kept thinking I was going to die. Twice I was rushed to the Royal Free Hospital in the middle of the night. They gave me a cardiogram and said nothing was wrong. Dr. Bloom kept telling me it was psychosomatic. I thought he was accusing me of being mad, of putting it on. I argued, "How can it be in my head when I'm feeling pain?" I begged for some sleeping pills, saying I was going insane. I started taking little yellow eggs called Normison, but they worked in reverse and kept me awake, probably reacting with all the other chemicals in my blood. They made me so calm I started taking them in the day, and before long I was having them for breakfast, lunch, and tea. Bloom was anxious to get me off all pills and sent me to a psychiatrist, Dr. Lewis Clein. Clein had a hypnotic voice that sent me off into a daze. Everything was fine until I got home.

When I appeared on *Wogan* to redeem myself with the nation, I had to drink half a bottle of wine I was shaking so much. I was sitting there talking about my recovery while straining not to scream.

My biggest fear was coming across like a pathetic little victim or a preaching hypocrite. I didn't see why I should apologize when I was the one suffering. All the tripe in the newspapers, like "I've been really awful" and "I'm sorry if I've let down my fans," was fiction. Like I told Dylan Jones from *i-D* magazine, "I'm not ashamed of taking drugs. Everybody expects me to say oh I've had the worst year of my life, but that's not true. I'm having the worst time now coming off heroin."

The success of "Everything I Own," which reached number one three days after the trial, was really a national sympathy vote. Everyone felt sorry for poor little George and for a long time I felt sorry for myself. Of course I was overjoyed about being number one. I didn't know whether to laugh, cry, or piss. Dad woke me up at 7:30 A.M. with the news. It was as if everything had turned round overnight. Photographers were hanging outside the studio with a bottle of champagne. I obliged, feeling more than a tinge of satisfaction as they clicked away. Suddenly they were being nice to me, it was that simple. "Back from the Dead" was the headline in the *Sun*. Every Fleet Street paper wanted a resurrection special and they were all offering copy approval. I vowed I would never talk to any of those newspapers again or have them in my house. They could write what they liked about me, and they did, but I wasn't going to help them.

During recording I was taken to Kentish Town police station and formally charged with possession of cannabis; that same week I appeared on *Top of the Pops*—it was batty. Then in a spooky twist of fate I was asked by the *Sun* to lend my vocal talents to their charity record in aid of victims' families following the Zeebrugge ferry disaster. I agreed, believing the cause was more important than any personal feelings, but the headline killed me, "Boy George Sings for the Sun." The chosen song was the Beatles' "Let It Be" and it was the usual hotchpotch of clashing celebrity vocals. I gritted my teeth and smiled for the cameras. I was wearing a white coat emblazoned with gold safety pins and a Judy Blame beret customized with hundreds of Levi's belt loops. It wasn't one of my best looks, but I wore it with my convictions. "What's that on your head?" asked tiny pop star Nik Kershaw. I told him it was souvenirs from all the boys I'd fucked.

I finished the night off with a trip to the Limelight with Jeremy Healy and his girlfriend, Lizzie Tear. We bumped into Marilyn, who was dark-haired and kissy-kissy. I invited him and his friend Eddie Armani to the Hippodrome. I knew the sight of us together would stir things up. Peter Stringfellow rushed over. "It's great to see you guys together." He invited us to a party for Ferry Aid the following night where Princess Diana was to be the guest of honor. I told Marilyn I would call him, but I knew Mum would kill me if I'd taken Marilyn to meet Princess Di. At the party Stringfellow said the princess wanted to meet me. I joined the lineup wondering what I was going to say to her. A royal aide pointed at me, "Sorry, you're not on the official list, you'll have to move." I was so embarrassed I crept over to the bar and bought myself a piña colada. Diana spotted me and broke protocol to come and say hello. There was a huge scuffle when a photographer tried to take our picture. His film was ripped from his camera. Diana seemed shy and made a silly comment about my coat. "Oh, you've got enough safety pins to open a shop." I asked her if she would meet my mum. She said, "I'd love to." Mum was thrilled and I decided Diana was the nicest one out of the royals.

Friday, March 20, 1987, I made my final court appearance, at Highbury Magistrates' Court. I was given a two-year conditional discharge for possessing two grams of hash—it was so small you could fit it under your nail. The magistrate, Lady Moorea Black, praised me for coming off drugs but warned, "Don't think you have got away with it. If you are brought back here for any other offense you will be sentenced for this as well." I nearly choked when my contribution to the *Sun*'s Zeebrugge appeal was brought up in court as proof of my rehabilitation. I thanked Lady Black in my album credits.

It wasn't the law that kept me off drugs, it was fear. I'd been off drugs for three months and still felt like shit. I thought about heroin all the time, but I knew if I touched it I might die. At that point I still couldn't see an end to the misery, but I'd come too far and I couldn't have faced the heavy withdrawal again. I kidded myself that once I got well I could take it now and then, control it. I was drinking loads; alcohol was the best sedative of all. Thank God I didn't like it enough to become an alcoholic. I was eating like a pig too, using food to fill the void. Dad was trying to fatten me up with his curries and shepherd's pies.

When I appeared at the International AIDS Day charity concert at Wembley Arena I was so sloshed I was slurring and shouting down the mike. My face was covered in lipstick kisses like I had the pox. Before going onstage I went into the toilet and could hear the sound of indiscreet snorting. I laughed to myself. It was a joke, especially as there was a policeman standing right outside the door. The other stars included Holly Johnson, Jimmy Somerville, Elton John, and George Michael. I dueted Culture Club's "That's the Way" with George, who later refused to have it aired on TV.

Following the success of "Everything I Own" Virgin were happy enough to send me to Barbados to shoot the video for the next single, "Keep Me in Mind." I decided to make a holiday of it and flew out a week early with Michael, Mum, and Dad, my brother David, and his girlfriend, Kelly. Despite the idyllic surroundings I was too tetchy to relax or enjoy myself. Having nothing to do was no luxury. I was angry with Dad because I wanted to take more pills and he wouldn't give them to me. Every chance I got I would creep into his room and pinch a few extra. I managed to get twenty Valium from the local doctor, but they had minimal effect. I was so desperate to alleviate the pain in my body I phoned Jim Rodman in Los Angeles and asked him to courier me some Valium. He wouldn't do it, so I cursed him and slammed down the phone.

Once preparations for the video were under way I was happy, making phone calls back and forth to Los Angeles plotting with director Leslie Lidman. There was no script as such, just a general desire to have me looking sun-kissed and revitalized. Leslie wanted to bring her own makeup artist, Paul Starr. I wanted Pearl, who was already booked on a George Michael video. I yelled at her agent, "Anyone can put on a fake tan." I grilled Leslie, "Who's this Paul Starr? What's he done?" I was impressed that he'd done Annie Lennox and said, "Okay, bring him, but if I don't like him he can fuck off home," adding, "Is he queer?" I ordered her to have Paul bring some Valium. She said, "I will not." I screamed back, "Then he's not coming."

Tessa Watts, head of video, was flown out to supervise and

make sure the video wasn't camp. She warned Leslie and Paul that I was overweight and not looking up to scratch. Paul put his foot in it straightaway. "You're not that big." He said he wanted to make me look boyish. I knew it was Tessa talking and said, "Sod that, I want loads of makeup and if I don't like it I'll do it myself." I thought he was in cahoots with the record company, who were trying to bland me out. After a facial and a few Pimm's I realized Paul was a sister. We were soon eyeing up the arriving crew, looking for a love fascination. The only cutie was "Herman the German," the lighting man, who was straight though happy to play along.

The video was more than a bit of a disappointment. Full drag and tropical climates were a sticky combination. I looked like I had a palm tree up my arse and was dressed for winter in Helsinki in a black wool jacket decorated and weighed down with keys, buttons, and baubles. I had on thick wool tights, Lycra shorts, and a tassled hat covered with Chanel logos. I kept the crew amused with my self-deprecating humor. After a long day Paul and I joined the crew at Rum Alley and sampled the local fiery brew, then it was off to a soca disco. Michael went back to the villa with Mum and Dad. He couldn't just abandon himself to a situation. I was content to dream over Herman, who was being chased by half the women in the club. One of them followed us back to the hotel. She stormed into cameraman Jay Brown's room and confronted him in the shower. "What's wrong with you guys, you queer or something?"

I must have liked something about Miss Paul Starr because he joined me in Switzerland the following month at the Montreux Pop Festival. I was performing "Everything I Own," which was skanking high in the European charts. It was the hour of Run-D.M.C. and the Beastie Boys, who were eagerly playing to the camera and the pen. Spandau Ballet tried jumping over chairs and throwing bread rolls, but no one cared. I paraded around wearing Nick Kamen badges and purring about Adam Horovitz from the Beasties, telling Radio One, "He's a nice Jewish boy and you know how much I love Jewish boys." I was pudgy like white bread and wearing unflattering clothes, printed Boy tights under Lycra cycling shorts, and an oversized jumper. My hair was shorn except for a fringe of bleached extensions poking out of a Boy baseball cap. Thanks to "Everything I Own" I still looked like a star. Everyone clamored to interview me: they all wanted the definitive heroin story. "How much did you really spend a day? Did you inject?"

We left the Beasties in Montreux and drove to Basel, in Switzerland, where I was appearing on TV with Richard Branson and his hot-air balloon. I knew Richard was upset about comments I'd made to the press about him trying to get a knighthood off my back. I was only repeating Tony Gordon's words anyway. We had dinner with Richard and his new signing, Roy Orbison. I was honored, even though Mrs. Orbison did most of the talking. Richard was preparing his ballooning escapade across the Atlantic and offered me a free ride. I declined, thinking he might cut the rope. Tony told him, "Make sure you pay our royalties before you go." He wasn't joking.

I thought "Everything I Own" had set me up for a renaissance, but my second solo single "Keep Me in Mind" was Z-listed at Radio One. Why? When I'd just been number one. I knew it was as good as the dreadful "Nothing's Gonna Stop Me Now" by Sam Fox, which was sticking its chest out at number fourteen. Virgin said it was the wrong record, so I got on with shooting another video for the right record, "Sold," which they said would be a smash. "Sold" was an antiapartheid rant. The video was shot by Russell Mulcahy and was back to the extravagant days of Culture Club, hundreds of extras, simulated race riots, and burning cars. Our Afrikaner cameraman got very upset when we exploded a dummy head of President P. W. Botha. He called me a bastard and was sacked on the spot. I was pleased with myself and felt like a real militant.

I was enjoying the shoot, not only because of the hordes of pretend soldiers running around. Dr. Bloom had put me on new medication to help with my nerves and I was spaced out in the nicest possible way. As I was getting ready for my close-up shot I started having spasms on the left side of my jaw. I patted my face, thinking it was just tension. Then suddenly my whole jaw locked and I was screaming. I thought I was having a stroke. Shooting had to be stopped and I was rushed home biting a towel. Dr.

Bloom was matter-of-fact, saying it was one of the possible side effects, nothing to worry about. No matter that I had to stop a very expensive video shoot. He gave me another pill to bring me back to normal. It took days to get over the shock, and I looked like a hibernating gerbil.

Just because I was moving, it was assumed I was alive. I was existing day to day, putting up with the niggling cramps in my legs and arms and suffering spells of extreme doom. Thoughts of death were routine. I would shout through the night and laugh to myself. This was no sign of happiness: Dr. Bloom had to put me on antidepressants. When I couldn't sleep I would force myself to stay awake till the following evening to try and catch up. The tiredness and pills made me vicious company. I went down the stairs, shattering my gold discs with a broom, and then regretted it with tears.

Breaking the discs was symbolic. I was once proud to adorn my walls with the trophies of success and pictures of me. Now I was disillusioned. I took them all down and hid them in cupboards. I remembered Chaka Khan telling me she kept her awards in the toilet so that people could piss on them. "Who's to say who's better than who? Fuck that sheeit." At the time I thought it was sad, but now I understood. They were only paint-sprayed bits of vinyl, probably some unsold Mike Oldfield stock.

The final sigh came when my brother Kevin was cleared of conspiracy to supply me heroin. The police offered no evidence after they were warned by the judge that his confessions were unreliable owing to confusion and worry about me. Then Jon Moss was given a two-year conditional discharge after pleading guilty to possessing cocaine. He said he was relieved that he could now go to America and Japan to promote his new band, Heartbeat UK, which Fat Tony renamed "Hard Luck You're Gay." I was surprised Jon didn't get a criminal record when they'd found drugs at his house. I didn't wish him harm, but it was further proof that I was a scapegoat. Outside court Jon said a Culture Club reunion was possible. That annoyed me more.

We had our own brief reunion after I phoned Jon and asked, "Do you want a shag?" I went over to his house a few times for good honest sex. I made him tell me the names of all the girls he'd screwed behind my back. The most important revelation for me was that the new nice Jon was a real turnoff. I enjoyed the sex, but something was missing. It was like a final purge. I knew I was free of him on a physical level, but it was scary to realize that was the easy part. More than anything I had to prove that I could survive without Jon, particularly where my career was concerned. I never forgot his comments about how much I needed Culture Club, that I would have had no credibility without them.

Miss Madonna revved into town and mowed down a photographer at Heathrow. I couldn't bear the unnecessary fuss and adulation just because she was doing three nights at Wembley Stadium. I was watching breakfast TV and heard DJ Paul Gambaccini comparing me to her greatness. I was washed up because I hadn't managed to change with the times. I was hurt because Gambaccini was always so nice to my face. What's more, Madonna was having a big birthday party and the bitch hadn't invited me. Fat Tony was deejaying and everyone else seemed to be on the list. Alice Temple and I took a bag of Boy clothes to the Mayfair Hotel as a thoughtful gesture. When we got there I chickened out and gave the bag to one of her dancers, who said of course we were invited.

Alice and I turned up at the Groucho club high on E, hiding behind Ray Bans. There were so many photographers we circled Soho Square for twenty minutes till I plucked up courage. They shouted at me, "What have you bought for her birthday?" I said, "Soap." We sat in a corner: I was too out of it to socialize. The real party was upstairs—Madonna was cutting her cake with a privileged few. When she blew out the candles she announced, "That's the quickest blow job I've done all year." She came down and twirled around the dance floor. We were introduced and sat talking for a good hour. She was warmer than the last time we met. I asked her if Sean Penn had a big dick and whether she was a lesbian as reported in the press. She punched my arm, "Fuck you, I don't dive."

I know it sounds shocking that I popped Ecstasy so casually after my hideous withdrawal from heroin. I remember the night it happened very clearly. I was at a party in Fulham. Someone gave me a pill. I had it in my hand for about twenty minutes, then I thought, Fuck it. An hour later I was vomiting in the gutter outside. I panicked slightly, then had a brilliant night. I told myself it wasn't as serious as coke or heroin.

No one believed I was clean. People were offering me coke all the time. "All right, Georgie boy, wanna nose up? I won't tell anyone, ha, ha." Heroin was never a worry: I knew I would never touch it again. I was self-destructive, but I didn't want to drop dead.

After exhausting the West End one night, a crowd of us went to an Arab club in the Edgware Road. Fat Tony's boyfriend for the night, Phillipe, offered me heroin in the toilet. I stared at the brown powder for a long minute, then said, "No, I can't." The devil himself was tempting me. It was a lucky escape because I was out of it on E and my defenses were down. It was 9 A.M. when we crawled onto the street. Fat Tony and I looked a right sight trolling up Edgware Road in the shadow of Paddington Green police station, chewing our jaws with the traffic hooting.

That scene was a perfect metaphor on the state of my life, wandering aimlessly, chewing my jaw. In between clubbing and sleeping all day I was making various jaunts around Europe, Germany, Italy, Holland, France, pushing my faded self on the innocent record-buying public. There was no long-term career strategy, only a desperate bid to keep me active and away from drugs, Dr. Bloom's advice to Tony Gordon. I was, and felt like, a sad parody, especially on some of the big German pop shows surrounded by all the new popettes: A-Ha, Mel and Kim, and Rick Astley, who sneered at me when I said hello. My star had plummeted into a pile of cow shit. I knew I deserved better.

On Tony's advice I booked myself into the posh Champney's health farm in Hertfordshire. He said it would do me the world of good and drove me there in his gold Rolls-Royce. Tony didn't know I had three grams of cocaine in my pocket. For four days I stayed in my room listening to Jose Feliciano singing "Ain't No Sunshine" and "Light My Fire." I kept snorting coke, feeling sick, flushing a bit down the toilet, then taking more. Eventually I got rid of it all and felt desperate. I spent a few more days in solitary, then tried to involve myself in the health program by taking massages and swimming when everyone else was having dinner. The overtanned staff made me feel worse by whispering and sniggering every time I walked by. I hated it there.

Michael came to visit with Warren Steingold and we went for a pizza in the local town. Some kind soul called the *News of the World* and a reporter and photographer booked into Champney's. I was snapped on the exercise bike. I looked like a before picture in a Weight Watchers ad. They used a dodgy airport shot and penciled in the chins and another picture of Marilyn carrying a carton of food—they claimed he'd been smuggling in hamburger feasts. I can laugh at it now, but then I was mortified. I blamed Champney's, demanded my money back, and left without settling my bill.

Bonnie drove me straight to another health farm in Surrey, Grayshott Hall. I decided to get my money's worth and forced myself to get out of bed for the 8 A.M. forest walk and joined an aerobics class. It was my first experience of normality for some years, mixing with housewives, bending myself into embarrassing shapes. The food was a salad-and-bean nightmare so I cycled to the local village for fish and chips and cream teas, imagining I was burning off fat on my way back.

Grayshott Hall was a big creaky mansion and less pretentious despite being host to a roll call of British comedy. One evening I answered a knock on my door and found *Carry On* star Joan Sims weeping. I brought her in and gave her a cuddle. She'd just lost a dear friend and was going on about having lunch with Penelope Keith. I wanted to invite myself. Then at breakfast I spotted Jimmy Edwards and got straight on the phone to Mum.

My brother David came to visit me and we talked for the first time about him selling me off. Typically my anger hadn't lasted. I'd always known in my heart that he'd acted out of love. I was upset that he'd set up an interview for Mum with *Woman's Own* and that she'd been paid. I wanted my family back. I wanted them to be normal and to stop trying to be pop stars.

Back at Hampstead the family blood had turned to glue. Dad was still living with me and, despite his good intentions, had turned my recovery into a crusade. I knew I wasn't a hundred percent, but I felt smothered and it was making me withdraw again into myself. Dad didn't trust Bonnie or Michael, believing that there were some things families had to deal with themselves.

Dad wrote a bizarre letter to the police informing them Michael was driving without a license and signed it "Bitchy Queen." Bonnie was chief suspect. It inflamed an already tense situation between her and Michael. Bonnie was questioned by the police, who gave her the letter. She recognized Dad's handwriting. Michael confronted Dad, and Dad punched him in the face. To Michael's credit he never mentioned it. Had I known about it I would have been livid. Now it seems rather twisted and amusing—bitchy queen indeed.

While away at the health farm I called Bonnie and suggested she look for her own flat. What I really wanted was for her to go back to New York. I loved and trusted Bonnie implicitly, but our relationship had become too unhealthy. Her role as housekeeper had been trumped up from the start: she only came to London to be near me. She wanted to hang out much more than she wanted to play Cinderella.

Finally, in a cowardly act I arranged for an airline ticket and had my travel agents do the dirty work. I knew it was for the best, even though I went about it the wrong way. She flew back to New York hurt and confused.

Dad was indignant when I asked him to leave. "Well, if that's how you want it." He said he was there for me not himself. He took it personally and didn't understand that I needed my life back. I started sleeping at St. John's Wood rather than face my rage and his hurt. It was months before he finally left.

I tried to soften the sulk by inviting Dad to join me on my first solo tour of Europe. I wanted him to know that I appreciated his love and concern.

My fourth solo single, "To Be Reborn," was released to coincide with the tour. The video, made by French genius Jean-Baptiste Mondino, was shot back in June and had taken months to finish, costing £90,000. Using pioneering video trickery I was given a porcelain complexion and looked like a Hollywood femme fatale crooning from the turning pages of a book. The video was so innovative that I wasn't surprised when I saw it reworked frame for frame in 1993 for Madonna's *This Used to Be*

My Playground. I was furious and renamed it *This Used to Be My Video*.

The first date on the Boy George Revue was in Vienna. I was using the same band I'd recorded with in Montserrat and three girl singers, Sylvia and Ruby James and reggae singer Carroll Thompson, and a brass section. I was dressed like a Jewish bathroom, gold chains, safety pins, badges and buckles, champagne corks and tassels. The costumes designed by Judy Blame and Leigh Bowery were meant to hide my expanding girth, although it was hard to look thin in an A-line smock with angel wings jutting out the back. Paul Starr was flown in to do the makeup and used his skill to give my flabby features some well-needed definition. I nicknamed Paul the "Champagne Queen." We went through at least four bottles of Cristal a night, only after the show, and it wasn't to celebrate. Paul's company was the saving grace of that tour. We laughed, drank, and ate ourselves silly.

After the show in Vienna we were taken to a local disco by Austrian journalist Peter Hopfinger, who was working for the promoter and acting as my chaperon and interpreter. I was after Peter and trying desperately to pair Paul off with Peter's friend Hubertus, an expensive-looking blond who wanted to be a pop singer. Paul insisted he wasn't his type until I told him he was Prince Hubertus Hohenlohe of Austria. "Oh," he said, "I always wanted to meet a princess." Both boys were straight, but they loved the attention. Peter kept asking, "Is there anything you want?" I told him, "I want you." I was demonic on a mixture of cocaine and Cristal and managed to entice Peter back to the hotel for a kiss and a grope.

I had an 8 A.M. call to catch a flight to Communist Budapest. I felt how I looked. There was a weird hippie guy tapping on my hotel door wielding a camcorder, pleading for an interview. "Hey, Boy, I've got a present for ya." I kicked the door, screaming at him to fuck off, then called security. I stuck the remainder of my coke under the tongue of my shoe and left for the airport. I was nervous all the way and kept thinking I should get rid of it. At the airport we were given the VIP treatment and taken to a private lounge. I was laughing to myself. We'd been there about half an hour drinking tea when two Customs officers marched in. "Up.

Up. Passports." Paul and I were led to an adjoining office. They started unloading Paul's makeup box, sniffing and sticking their fingers in everything. He freaked out. "Get me the American consul. I'm American. You can't do this to me." He was making so much fuss they threw him out of the room. They ordered me to strip. It was especially embarrassing because I was wearing woolly tights and Lycra cycling shorts under my trousers. They were mumbling to each other in German. One of them started shaking my shoe. I started crying, "You're making a mistake. Why are you doing this to me?" By some divine stroke they didn't find the drugs.

I slept all day in Budapest and woke up with no voice. A doctor was called, and he tried to numb my throat with a liquid substance that tasted like cocaine. The show was appalling. Still, the 12,500 strong crowd went loopy. Then next morning I took part in the Hungarian equivalent of *Jim'll Fix It*. It was a little girl's dream to carry my suitcases. I was choked and felt like such a fraud.

The tour came to an abrupt end in Zurich, where I sang with my back to the audience and stumbled off the wrong side of the stage. If Billy hadn't been there to catch me I would have broken my neck. I wanted to go home, I was so miserable. At each show there were fewer people. Tony said canceling the tour would be bad for my reputation, as if the tour wasn't. I took a break and flew to London, where Dr. Bloom shot me up with steroids and I was back onstage in Milan two days later. Dad and Michael came with me. The crowd chanted Michael's name for ten minutes after they spotted him. I was thrilled that they'd accepted my sexuality with such Roman spirit. Dad joined us for the rest of the tour and we nicknamed him "Boy Jerry." He was wearing Boy T-shirts, a baseball cap, and punky studded brothel creepers.

The tour struggled through Italy and into Germany, saved only by the gallows humor of the band and heaps of devil's brew. Certain laddish members were wrecking hotels and shagging everything in a skirt. For once I ignored it—we were all suffering enough, some more than others. Glen Nightingale's title was MD—musical director—but it should have stood for mental disturbance. With every beer he became more demonic, insulting, and cruel. One night he chopped off a roadie's ponytail for a laugh.

The guy was bald on top and had been growing it for years. The crew gaffer-taped Glen to a chair and shaved his head in revenge. Unfortunately it just made him look better. The girls in the band, Carroll, Ruby, and Sylvia, and our new keyboard player, Amanda Vincent, had the worst time. Luckily Paul and I traveled in Billy's car and could avoid the torture. There was plenty for me elsewhere.

Before taking the stage in Düsseldorf I gave a live interview on German TV. I was attacked, "Is your life so boring as a pop star you have to take heroin?" It was the last thing I needed. I sat in the toilet and cried. I felt like I was undergoing an endurance test trying to see how much humiliation I could take. In Hamburg I was struck again with facial spasms, luckily during the last song. Billy rushed me back to the hotel, where I saw an efficient doctor. He gave me an antihistamine injection and advised me sternly to get some rest. On top of the large slices of humble pie, I was gorging my sorrows with colon-clogging junk food, eating because I was bored or to fill the gaps between cigarettes. After Hamburg we came home. Paul tried to get me into a healthier regime, walking on Hampstead Heath, which I hadn't set foot on since I'd lived there, and lunching at the East-West macrobiotic center in Old Street. It was hopeless. Paul was a few rungs up the health ladder, but we both fell apart when we saw a Black Forest gâteau. I knew I had to shape up, but every time I looked in the mirror I wanted cheese on toast.

Two weeks later we were in Paris for the penultimate gig of our European tour. I took too many pills (again) and nodded out while Paul was painting my face. He was terrified and said it was like painting a death mask. When it was showtime I snapped to life and bounded onstage shouting, "*Enculez-moi. Enculez-moi.*" Later we went on a club crawl, ending up at Le Palais. I scored some powered Ecstasy which I snorted like cocaine. I threw a party at the hotel for the band and some stragglers. Our drummer, Ritchie, locked me in the bathroom with him and tried to lecture me about getting my act together. I wouldn't have minded, but he could barely stand up himself. Vic Martin was playfully pulling Amanda round the room, and she ended up with a broken rib. I don't know how any of us managed to get past Customs at Heathrow without getting the rubber glove.

The tour finished at London's Hammersmith Odeon a few days before Christmas. It was packed, the crowd held me up through a poor performance after showing an hour late. I was out of it on cocaine and rasping through my swollen glands. We played under a huge McDonald's sign and the slogan "Eat the Rich and Steal Their Culture," my fuck-off to the press who had been calling me fat a little more often than usual. The fact that I was trying to make a joke of it only proved that it bothered me. The show's one glorious moment came when Helen Terry walked on to duet "That's the Way." The cheering went on for minutes. I had tears in my eyes, a little jealousy, and a lot of pride.

A week later there were more tears in my eyes when I read a review of the show in the *NME* written in my blood by Michelle Kirsch: "Junk Culture." Never had I read anything so unnecessarily vicious. It made Fleet Street read like *Family Circle:*

> Boy looks alone, Boy George is just another swollen drag queen past his prime. That's not important. He may have been voted the world's fourth worst-dressed woman, but his inability to disguise his internal flaws coupled with his marked inability to exploit his insipid traumas has always been far more offensive.

It went on and on and on. I wondered how any stranger could feel such hatred and, to this day, I'd still like to spit in her face. I knew the show was crap and I was suffering my own reflection on a daily basis. I didn't need counseling with a machete.

CHAPTER 45

My outfit for Christmas *Top of the Pops* was tongue in chic and designed for revenge. I wore my gold Puma platforms with a Leigh Bowery frock coat and decorated a hat with the words "Fat Pig" surrounded by a fan of McDonald's wrappers. Paul painted me like a tragic clown and I stepped onto the stage sniggering to myself. The music had just started up when I heard, "Cut!" The stage manager ran toward me waving his arms. "Sorry, you'll have to lose the hat." I laughed, "You're not serious. I've spent hours getting ready." He insisted, "I've had word from upstairs. You can't advertise McDonald's. Come on, you're holding up the show." I could feel the crowd staring at me and the humor drain away. I felt like I was on a black square at Eltham Green. "Fuck you," I said and marched off to the dressing room with Tony flapping at my side. There was more pointless debate before I burst into tears. "I don't have to take this shit, do I?" Tony said, "Right, we're leaving." I cried all the way to Hampstead. I hated the damn BBC, they were always calling me up to cut their birthday cakes and fill in when some guest had pulled out of one of their dull shows. Still they acted like they were doing me a favor.

I was so despondent: it was Christmas, a year since I supposedly cleaned up from drugs, but I couldn't cross the road without taking a sleeping pill. The pills had become a lifestyle on top of the occasional E and spliff. The pains in my body had never gone away. I stopped talking about it, I knew everyone was sick of my complaining. It would have been easier if I'd had a hole in my head.

Dr. Bloom tried every painkiller and tranquilizer in his Mims catalogue, but nothing could make me feel like a human being. I cried in front of him, "You've got to give me something. I can't go on feeling like this." I even thought about having a blood transfusion like Keith Richards. Bloom's insistence that the pain was psychosomatic only frustrated me more. He persuaded me to have my first therapy session with Dr. Max Glatt, a psychiatrist at the Charter Nightingale Clinic. I went reluctantly. I couldn't see how talking would help, but I was desperate.

I arrived for the session in a hostile mood wearing a small badge with "fuck" on it. Dr. Glatt screwed his face. "That's a very small fuck. If you want to say fuck then you should really say it." We both laughed and became friends straightaway. We swapped life stories. Max Glatt was a distinguished, silver-haired Polish Jew who had escaped from a concentration camp. Listening to him was a humbling experience. When I said I wanted to feel normal like people in the street, he said, "That's some ambition. The streets are full of crazy people."

After seeing Max I was lighter and could see some humor in my situation. I continued the therapy despite thinking it was for neurotic Americans. I slowly began to understand psychosomatic illness and the effect of drugs on my nervous system. However much I understood the pain it wouldn't go away, but I stopped thinking I had a fatal disease. Max was like a kindly old man from a fairy tale. He listened and heard what I was trying to say. I felt safe and was persuaded to enter the Charter clinic to try and kick my addiction to sleeping pills.

I had a fit when I arrived and was told that I would have to submit to a search. I pleaded, "I need to be trusted or I can't stay." I had a stash of pills wrapped in a sock and no one was getting their hands on them. I only got away with it because I was Boy George. It was typical of me to pull rank even at a time like that. I hid the pills behind the toilet bowl and played patient.

At first I wasted my time, preferring to watch *Emmerdale Farm* than speak to therapists or join group sessions. When I did I was petulant. The treatment was based on the Twelve Steps program used by Narcotics Anonymous and had religious tones. When they spoke of a higher power my back was up. "Sorry, I don't believe in God and I'm not going to say that." I couldn't bear the thought of discussing my problems with strangers. I took a superior view. I wasn't mental like the rest of them. They were anorexics, bulimics, and manic depressives. An old woman stole a pair of shoes out of my room and they were never found; another kept trying to slash herself.

Happy hour came three times a day when they doled out the pills, which had to be swallowed in front of the nurse. I soon ran out of my contraband and had to stick to the allocation. Some days that's all I thought about. The first week was the hardest; after that I started to join in the exercise classes and yoga and talked to the other patients. I realized most of them were quite normal and, like me, believed they were the only ones with a problem. Opening up was hard, but it was a vital part of the cure. After two long weeks I left the clinic vulnerable and pill-free. The world was screechingly bright, like my eyes had been scrubbed. I felt empty inside. I cried and cried and worried if I could last. I couldn't sleep or still my mind. Max's advice was to take each day as a lifetime.

The best medicine was Paul Starr coming to London and renting a flat in St. John's Wood for a month. I moved in with him and we had a whale of a time stuffing our guts with Lean Cuisine and talking through the night about love, life, and disaster. We had so much in common and formed a friendship that is still vibrant today. Paul was successful and didn't need to feel jealous or insecure. I loved listening to his stories about painting film stars and legends like Little Richard and Sophia Loren. I made him tell them over and over. Each time there were more embellishments. Paul introduced me to brown rice, and we took long daily walks in Regent's Park. I even started reading my first spiritual book, *Out on a Limb* by Shirley MacLaine. These ordinary experiences were a revelation to me. Looking at the animals in London Zoo was like seeing God. We walked the streets and rode the bus. When people asked, "Are you Boy George?" I said, "Sometimes."

One sunny day we saw George Michael in Oxford Street posing at the wheel of a BMW convertible, wearing dark shades and blaring his own music. We were in hysterics and shouted, "Hairdresser." Seeing George was symbolic, it was the end of an era, though I don't think he realized.

The mere mention of George Michael was enough to start me off. I'd known him for years, but he was always so snotty. I cracked jokes like, "George Michael's got no sense of houmous." It was true: the more successful and rich he became the more seriously he took himself. Of course, I was jealous. I hated the way he was portrayed as a serious songwriter while I was treated like a pop joker.

Our war started when I bitched about an article claiming George and my old sidekick Pat Fernandez had been lovers. I said the headline "How Pat Broke My Heart" should have been "How Pat Broke My Hoover" and called her a fag hag. Then I called George a "closet" on Radio One. He was touring Australia and said he was going to kick my arse. I retorted, "Don't you mean fondle?"

I admit it was cheap and cruel to poke fun at George's sexuality, but I'd become almost evangelical about my own. I was learning to be comfortable at other people's expense. I recorded my first openly gay song, "No Clause 28," protesting against the new Tory bill outlawing the promotion of homosexuality by local councils.

Won't you be elated to tamper with our pride
They say to celebrate it is social suicide.

The song was inspired by a tabloid editorial, "When Gays Have to Shut Up," following the murder of a young boy by a gang of sadomasochists; the message was for gays to stop demanding rights and blend gratefully into the background. We were all perverts and spreaders of disease.

Even with Thatcher spreading her hatred it was a great time to be queer. She said, "Children who need to be taught to respect traditional moral values are being taught that they have an inalienable right to be gay." A bunch of lesbians abseiled into the House of Lords and some others stormed Sue Lawley on the *Six O'Clock*

News. I cheered them on my TV. I appeared for the first time at London's Gay Pride rally and sang "No Clause 28." Tony wasn't happy that I was waving the pink flag. He knew it was bad for business and he was right. Tony wasn't homophobic—we'd often have conversations about me settling down with a nice Jewish boy. His objections were paternal. He didn't want people to victimize me or think of me as just a queer.

Amid all the laughter there was sadness too. I discovered my stylist friend Ray Petrie had full-blown AIDS. AIDS had always been a distant threat. Suddenly it was all too real. I was reading stories in the gay press about AIDS sufferers being hounded out of their homes and spat at in doctors' surgeries. It made me angry and more determined to speak up and use the media in a more positive way.

Ray survived AIDS for two years and worked for much of that, battling ignorance with amazing dignity. He couldn't hide his sickness because of the extreme weight loss and Kaposi scars. When he turned up at a Jasper Conran fashion show walking with a stick it was a message for us all. Those that froze Ray out were only putting off facing up to this creative holocaust. The fashion industry was hit without mercy. Ray was one of the first. I visited him in hospital; we smoked a joint and listened to my new reggae song, "Kipsy." He was telling me what to wear in my next video. Typical Ray, styled to death.

By the time I started recording my aptly titled second solo album, *Tense Nervous Headache,* I had a handful of songs but nothing you could call an album. As ever, recording began prematurely using the nucleus of the musicians who had accidentally become my band, Glen Nightingale, Ian Maidman, Amanda Vincent, and Ritchie Stevens. Prince's ex-drummer Bobby Z was producer and cowriter. I jumped at the chance of working with Bobby, hoping some of that Prince magic might rub off. The concept was desperation. I didn't know if I wanted to be Prince, Bowie, or Roy Orbison, who I convincingly impersonated on "Don't Cry," a rumbling string-driven ballad. To add to the confusion I was already getting into the new underground garage sounds via clubs like Spectrum and Future, dancing to the music of Todd Terry and Marshall Jefferson. The charts were heaving with the stolen gay-disco pop of Stock, Aitken and Waterman. I dished them as white trash, but still had a meeting with Peter Waterman to discuss a production. I never followed it through. Virgin left me to it. My A&R woman, Danny Van Emden, was grateful for anything that had a chorus.

A contingent from Virgin America, my new press agent, Audrey Strahl, and Sharon Heyward, head of Black Music, swept into the studio. Their comments, "It's very rock" and "Are the vocals gonna stay like that?" caused further panic. Heyward had her own plans. She wanted to turn me into the New Jack Swing kid on the block and suggested a collaboration with young black producer Teddy Riley. I thought Teddy and I would write together, but he arrived in London with three dusty songs he couldn't palm off on Bobby Brown. The lyrics were all about hugging my girl and not being able to stand it. I agreed to sing them if I could work on the lyrics, which I did with little success. The recording session was torturous. Teddy was nice enough when he got to speak, but his middle-aged partner and daddy figure, Gene Griffin, was hogging the oxygen. Gene was a stocky *Shaft* lookalike in diamond-studded glasses and flared leather pants. He kept saying, "We love ya, Boy," and playing someone else's vocal, "Sing it just like that." Danny had to plead with me not to leave the studio. I convinced myself the fat beats and production would compensate for the lack of substance. I was wrong. When I received the final mixes I went into depression. I told Virgin I didn't want the Riley tracks on my album. They'd invested a ridiculous $75,000 (all recoupable) and didn't care about my artistic integrity.

I started writing my own dance tracks with Vlad Naslas, creator of one of the early house tunes, "The Jack That House Built." I was coming at it the wrong way, trying to find lyrics to fit the groove. I was from the Tin Pan Alley verse-bridge-chorus school and found it hard to write anything meaningful at 120 beats per minute. Dance lyrics were virtually nonexistent, an inane call to get up, get down, and jack your body, baby. I wrote songs that made Stock, Aitken and Waterman look like Dylan.

When Bobby Z returned to the purple promised land, I only had half a record. I carried on with yet another producer, Mike

Pela, who'd worked with Sade. I recorded three new songs, "Something Strange Called Love," "Mama Never Knew," and "Kipsy," a collaboration with white reggae chatter M.C. Kinky. "Kipsy" was a real-life drama about a fashion model who was tried and acquitted for conspiring to deal Ecstasy. Kinky's chatting and lyrics brought the track to life. Finally, and too late, I was feeling the inspiration. Working with Kinky was like the early Culture Club days, spunky and spontaneous.

I met Kinky (Caron Geary), at Fred's club in Soho. She was a mouthy little thing in baby blue Crimplene hot pants, rainbow-striped knee socks, and platforms. Her hair was shaved up the back and sprung over her face in raggedy curls. "Do ya still do reggae and stuff?" she asked. "'Cause I do a bit of chatting." She looked good, so I asked for a tape. When I heard her music I was blown away. It was the dirtiest "slackest" reggae I'd heard since the seventies. I put her in the studio straightaway.

However much I tried to patch it together, *Tense Nervous Headache* was self-indulgent, scatterbrained, and painfully out of touch. The sound and the pose had changed drastically under my feet. Acid house was the new punk in town. The stars were faceless DJs and technobuffs. Everyone was dressing down to get high. There was no point going to clubs like Shoom in a crisp outfit when you were going to drop an E and do acid aerobics.

I started dressing like Eddie Normal, going to dodgy raves in the East End and making requests on the pirate radio stations. "Big shout going out to George in Hampstead." I was saturated and sixteen all over again. My twenty-seventh birthday was the best rave that year with Danny Rampling and Jeremy deejaying. The invites were Smiley T-shirts with the message "If you're not screaming you must be dreaming." Kinky gave me a bag of magic mushrooms and the only ones not on E were Mum, Dad, and Philip. If I need an excuse, it's simply that you can't hang around bulls in a red skirt and remain unscathed. Everyone agreed that you really couldn't appreciate acid house without drugs. The bass lines seemed to pump through your bloodstream. I went to see Prince's Lovesexy show tripping—it was brilliant—and on another trip Fat Tony, Kinky, and I ended up outside Ben from Curiosity's flat screaming, "We want Bros." They were silly and liberating days. Kinky nicknamed me "Chanting Pig" and I called her "Pat Geary" because that's how she looked on acid. Like all my best friendships ours was instantaneous and often psychotic. We argued so much friends used to rib me, "See you got your wife with you." Michael couldn't understand why I spent so much time with Kinky. "She" became another excuse, but we were having our own problems.

At the beginning of 1988, following a series of fierce rows, Michael had moved out of Hampstead and gone to live in Soho with his old flatmates. Our relationship had followed a predictable pattern of punch-ups and drawn-out silences. Neither of us knew how to communicate without throwing an insult or a plate and I had a cruel habit of reminding Michael, "This is my house." It was Dad all over again. Michael was no pillar of stability. He didn't try to assert himself, preferring to moan or curl up in the corner like a lazy cat. He was smoking far too much dope, signing on the dole, and living in his shredded jeans. I hated him doing nothing, but at the same time I was terrified of him having too much of a life and not needing me.

What little I know about Michael's past is like a Roddy Doyle story. He was born in Cork as one of seven children. His dad poisoned himself when Michael was two years old. His mother became an alcoholic. Michael was sent to a Catholic orphanage till he was nineteen. His neediness fulfilled my maternal instincts and my need to control. Ours was a mother-son relationship with a bit of incest thrown in:

I love you
Like the stars love the sky and they're never lonely
I love you
Cos you're weak, incomplete and you're never phoney.

Things improved between us when Michael started working as a runner for the Limelight video production company. He moaned like he was doing eighteen-hour shifts down the coal mines, but his personality glowed and he earned a reputation for being efficient and bossy. Within a year Michael was in charge of his own production company, The Unit, producing small-budget videos for Limelight and scouting young directors. Sadly and suddenly his confidence turned to contempt. Once Michael started making a decent wage and feeling independent he cut me out of his life. He was working long hours on shoots and spending most of his free time with my old drugkick Hippie Richard, who had wangled a job at the Unit. It was as if we'd swapped roles when Michael started taking cocaine. His dilated eyes and snappy temper did little to disguise it. I cursed Hippie as a bad-luck talisman and wrote some bitchy lyrics:

Ah, the phone rings and I hear that voice again
Hello, who is it?
It's me your vacant friend.

Soon Michael was hollering in my face that I was jealous he had a life. The change was frightening, but he was only playing me at my own game. I'd always done what I wanted. I was a gay chauvinist pig. My friends always had preference over Michael. Now I was feeling the chill.

CHAPTER 46

Tense Nervous Headache never made it to the racks. It was shelved in the U.K. after the first single, "Don't Cry," died a lonely death. The album did okay in France and Germany, but I was ready to retire. I didn't want to be a pop oddity anymore. London cabbies had the cure: "You need another 'Karma Chameleon.' Sing some more of them ballads." Tony also said I was making the wrong type of music. The words "Culture Club" were appearing far too often in his conversation. I thought about starting a club or designing clothes. I was having discussions with Steph Raynor, who owned the Boy shops—it had always been a dream to create my own fashion collection. Steph invited me down to his apartment in St. Tropez. I made a holiday of it, bringing Jeremy Healy along. It was lucky I did: Steph was unfashionably dull and the club scene was worse. We didn't talk much business. I was just a photo opportunity for a fashion show he was having at a beach restaurant. Jeremy and I made our own entertainment. We schnorrered champagne at the top nightspot and ended up at a gangster's villa in the hills. Thankfully Mr. Big was away on business. His girl dragged Jeremy into the sauna for a cocaine shagging session and I was left with a French hairdresser who couldn't even say yes in English. Jeremy appeared at the foot of my bed late the following morning, wired and raving that we were going to get shot.

After a good laugh and a sleep we decided to catch a flight to Ibiza and have a real holiday.

Ibiza was full of drugged-out clubbers, cor-blimey lads and birds, Germans in headbands, and showy queers. Everyone was wearing fluorescent clothes and Smiley T-shirts. Jeremy called it "Psychedelic Club 18–30, Bring Your Own Rizlas." I'd never done the package-holiday circuit; it was a new experience for me walking around in shorts and a T-shirt, even with shoulder pads. I was quasi-agoraphobic, I didn't mind open spaces, it was the people in them. I hated being stared at, especially during daylight. For years I'd had the protection of makeup and dark clubs, now I was unleashing my ankles on the free world. It was all part of the new me. We hired an open-top Jeep and sat out in the street cafés drinking caffè latte. We were out clubbing every night. The clubs were open air, the music a Balearic blend of acid house, pop, and Spanish rhythms. Everyone was so friendly. We met glamorous American soap star Tracy Scoggins and her friend Mary Ann in the hotel pool and became a platonic foursome sipping cocktails at the Ku club. The Spanish kids ignored me and hassled her for autographs. I realized I didn't like being too anonymous and penciled in my eyebrows. It became the holiday joke: whenever we wanted to get free drinks Jeremy would say, "Come on, Mr. Eyebrows."

My trip to Ibiza and the casual use of drugs contrasted with my vain attempts to lead a healthy lifestyle. I had employed a macrobiotic cook and was swimming when I could remember. As always, it was a never-ending battle between knowing and doing. My nerves were still shattered because I hadn't given my body time to heal. I couldn't sleep without leaving the TV on and had a numb pain in my left arm. On a friend's advice I went to Devon to see Dr. Barry Childe, a homeopath, who told me my immune system was worn out and to give up all stimulants including tea and coffee, which I was drinking by the gallon. I was politely told that I was overweight and advised to take regular exercise, if only a daily walk. He took a snip of my hair for tests and gave me homeopathic pills and Bach flower remedies. The holistic approach was very subtle; I was used to pills that zapped you straightaway. Dr. Childe explained that homeopathy treated the whole person not just the symptoms. Within hours I was an expert, telling everyone they shouldn't use "normal doctors." I couldn't heed my own advice, though I did cut out coffee and tea, which made me a social outcast.

I always felt guilty when I took Ecstasy and complained it was having no effect. It was more droning than joyful, but I still wanted more. Kinky would nag me to stop: "You look like you're dying, you prat." I thought I looked normal until I saw a scabby picture in the press with the caption, "Who is this? See page five." I looked like *The Scream.* We all joked about how ugly everyone else looked on E, looming into your face: "You buzzing man, you buzzing. Peace." Fat Tony would snap, "Peace, yeh, you stink of it." Clubs like Spectrum at Heaven were full of criminal types wired on E, a nation of football hooligans embracing under the strobes. E was the new love drug and ripe for a send-up. Jeremy and his musical accomplice Simon Rogers obliged by creating "Everything Starts with an E." I supplied a poppy chorus and roped in Kinky to write and perform a rap. Her lyrics mocked the scene's attempt to relive the sixties:

Trip out to Hendrix solos
Excuse me while I kiss the sky.

I was so excited by the track I paid for the recording. I knew it was a hit. I played it to Virgin, who were enthusiastic but adamant it would never get played on daytime radio. That was the ultimate seal of approval. I knew it would be massive in the clubs. I persuaded them to press up some promotional copies to test the DJ reaction and created a fictitious label—More Protein—to give it credibility. More Protein came from oral sex.

Virgin were already setting up their own dance department, like every other record company eager to cash in on the rising club scene. They hired two groovers in the know, Rob Manley and up-and-coming DJ Lisa Loud, girlfriend of top acid-house DJ Paul Oakenfold. Both Manley and Loud were adamant that "Everything Starts with an E" "wouldn't go." They sent it to all the best DJs; the reactions were negative. Manley even suggested removing Kinky's rapping. I wouldn't have it: I was trying to make dance music with personality, Kinky was a star. I insisted the record was released, if only as a gesture. Jon Webster, the new managing director, agreed to print a thousand copies in a sperm-print sleeve.

The dance department were as slow with a release as they were with their confidence. "E" took six months to come out. I carried copies round to the specialist dance shops in the West End and forced it on DJs. I knew all we needed was one genius to pick up on it and we'd have a hit. Our savior was Graeme Park at Manchester's Hacienda club, who said it was the best record he'd heard all year. "E" became huge in the north, then everybody wanted to play it. Paul Oakenfold asked, "What's this Ecstasy record?" I was surprised his girlfriend hadn't serviced him. "Everything Starts with an E" became the official acid-house anthem, finally reaching number fifteen in March 1990 on its third release, and spawned a whole generation of ragga dance tunes.

No one could believe Kinky was white, I loved that contradiction. Like Culture Club chatter Captain Crucial, her patois was frighteningly convincing. When we performed "Kipsy" at the Smile Jamaica hurricane relief concert in October 1988, the crowd was culture-smacked. Both on- and offstage she was the perfect sparring partner, adding a spark to my performance and a ring to my ears. I took her on promo trips around Europe and she joined the Boy's Own U.K. Christmas tour. It was the most fun I'd ever had touring. Paul was doing makeup and playing personal assistant. It was a riot of lips, lashes, and lushing. The tour was treated as my comeback even though I hadn't been anywhere. The first night at the London Palladium was jammed and gave us false expectations. Some nights there were more people onstage. I cursed the disloyal British public as I glugged on a bottle of Rémy Martin. An observant hack described me as "a happy victim, putting a brave face on things." I was far from happy, I could hear myself onstage singing "What Becomes of the Broken Hearted" and could no longer laugh at my own joke. It was the week of the Lockerbie air disaster. Kinky, Paul, and I kept bursting into tears every time we saw the news.

My New Year's resolution was to climb down graciously off the pop cross. Still, 1989 started as I didn't mean to go on. I shot a nasty video for "Don't Take My Mind on a Trip," without lipstick. It was Virgin America's artistic contribution to my career. I went along with it, though I couldn't see how lipstick was going to stop me selling records. In fact, it was laughable when I'd already left an indelible lipstick trail across America. Another Teddy Riley track, "Whether They Like It or Not," was released in Germany. I did the rounds on automatic. It was enough misery to make me finally realize that I knew better. After one last concert for Japanese TV I broke up the band. I decided to forget about making my own records and concentrate on establishing More Protein as a serious dance label—nothing else was exciting me. Tony struck a deal with Virgin and the sperm flowed. The E-Zee Posse was my first signing, then Eve Gallagher, an Amazonian soul goddess with flick-knife nails and a skunk hairdo. The Virgin contracts were typically ungenerous, but I believed we could renegotiate if we had some success. Kinky was the only one who objected to the deal. Signing her was like signing the Magna Carta.

I had grand plans for More Protein. I didn't want to sign faceless dance acts. I was looking at the pop scene and nothing sparkled. The biggest star we had was Kylie (unlikely) Minogue. I wanted to create stars that stuck in your teeth, stars with songs you cared about. Technology was like punk in the way it had given a new access into pop, but many of the bedroom boffins were limited when it came to substance. I wanted to bridge the gap and mix beats and bass lines with strong songs. Unfortunately Virgin didn't share my vision.

I was battling on a daily basis with the A&R department run by Willie Richardson, who looked like Neil from *The Young Ones* and openly admitted hating dance music. During one of our many exchanges he screamed, "Don't tell me about acid, I was taking it in the sixties." I was treated like an impractical irrational artist and patronized by the professionals. My main ally was Andy Woodford, a Boris Becker clone who loved music but couldn't A&R his way out of a record sleeve. He did his best to make the label work, even though he was never allowed to make a decision. One of our early releases, "Love Come Down" by Eve Gallagher, was massive in the clubs, but Virgin dithered, taking weeks to finance the video, and we lost a hit. They drained our budgets by forcing us to use expensive Virgin-owned studios, which meant they could double recoup.

In spite of the difficulties I loved running the label. It seemed we could do no wrong with the DJs and I was regaining respect where I needed it most: on the street. I was writing songs with Jeremy for the E-Zee Posse and learning how to apply heart to the groove. I learned discipline and realized instinct wasn't always enough. I realized I could no longer rely on past glories. Elvis had left the building. I was returning to Go.

I created a new band, Jesus Loves You, and decided to record under the druggy pseudonym Angela Dust, both as a twist and to avoid hasty judgments. It was my way in through the backdoor. I spotted the name Jesus Loves You on a church overlooking the red-light district in Amsterdam. It seemed perfectly placed and tied in with my belief that God does not judge.

Spookily, the first song, "After the Love," was written with Jon Moss. Everyone thought it was about us—it was more sweet confusion. The song was about dysfunctional families and how London was becoming more and more like New York, full of homeless beggars freezing in the shadow of Buckingham Palace.

My collision with Jon was no accident. Throughout the year Tony had been hinting about Culture Club making another album. I was of several minds. We had a cold meeting at our lawyer's office and decided to try writing some songs, no promises. It was a voyeuristic experience not to be missed. That July we holed up at Music Farm Studios in West Sussex. It was more fun than I expected. We drank a lot of wine and surprised ourselves by writing some great songs. It was strange being in a confined space with Jon. I kept thinking about sex. He was affectionately distant and didn't squint at my lyrics, all pertaining to a tragedy gone by.

However good it sounded I still felt intimidated. Since leaving Culture Club I'd gained so much confidence. Those stifling feelings were creeping back. I knew I could never have the complete artistic freedom I craved. I was trying to be anonymous with Jesus Loves You, and it felt right. I didn't want to be sewn back into my doll costume. I worried that it was too late. Some of the songs I'd written with Culture Club were brilliant, but they still had a nostalgic eighties feel to them. My work with More Protein was in the moment. I was collaborating with Sheffield dance producer Mark Brydon, writing songs for Eve Gallagher. We'd just written "Master of Disguise," which had the poignant line "Some people say it's better to change than to walk backwards on your life." It was as if I was trying to tell myself something.

Journalists kept asking me if I missed being as successful as Culture Club. Part of me did: I wouldn't have minded the record sales or the advances, but for the first time in ages I was on steady ground. I was a happy ex–cover girl.

Tony had been hassling me forever to do club dates. I sniffed that it was cabaret, but I was bridge-loaned and mortgaged up to the eye shadow. My initiation was a gig with Boney M in Perpignan, France. I consoled myself that no one would find out. Soon after I took on a minitour of Australia using a mixture of backing tapes and live musicians, Kinky, Jeremy, Amanda Vincent, and vocalist Derek Green. Jeremy was playing DJ, cutting beats and samples into the set like we were Run D.M.C. It was miles away from my first visit to Australia, when Culture Club were mobbed at Sydney airport. This time there was only one fan and a lonely TV news crew to greet me. I phoned Mum and laughed: how soon they forget.

I had a surprise meeting with Nayana, my Hare Krishna friend from New York, who was living in Sydney with his wife and daughter. We strolled on a rainy Bondi beach. He was ecstatic to see how healthy I was and said, "Krishna has been watching over you." We talked about India—I'd dreamed of going since childhood. We promised to meet in Bombay after Christmas.

Kinky, Tony, and I flew to Los Angeles. Entering the States was a piece of piss, literally, as I had to give a urine sample to get my visa. I sang live on *The Arsenio Hall Show* and during my interview announced that I loved Guns N' Roses. I didn't know there was a furor about them being racist and homophobic. Arsenio said I was "dissed hard" and I jokingly spat on the floor to defuse the topic saying, "It's a shame Axl isn't more intelligent." The following night at a Virgin bash I had words with Axl's friend West Arkeen and we ended up throwing bottles at each other. The violence continued when Paul Starr, Kinky, and I went on to the launch of Bobby Brown's new album. I had another fight with a trashy white rapper girl who called me a junkie. Kinky and I chased her round Eddie Murphy's table and threw wine in her face. Two huge guards escorted poor Kinky to the door, claiming Bobby

Brown wanted her to leave. She was shrieking, "Bobby Brown don't know me, I'm from Edgware Road." Paul tried to drive home paralytic and got arrested jumping a red light. His attempts to schmooze the police by showing them pictures of me failed famously. They laughed. "Big deal, Boy George is a fag."

Security was heavy when I did a signing at Tower Records on Sunset Boulevard. Tony was worried I would be served by lawyers working for Michael Rudetsky's mother, who was still trying to drag me to court. Every time I appeared on TV I had the feeling she was watching and hating me. I avoided talking about Michael, though the press were persistent. Even with the extra paranoia I had a brilliant time, cruising in Paul's car, eyeing the male hookers on Melrose Avenue, lunching at Taco Bell, and hop-skipping the stars on Hollywood Boulevard. We went to the trendy China Club and laughed at John McEnroe trying to play rock god.

I met with Culture Club at Roy's flash house in the Hollywood Hills. I had to laugh at the place with its swimming pool and remote control gates. Alison was smoking long thin cigarettes and guided me around her place. We worked on some new songs in Roy's studio. We were all beaming that we'd written a Beatles-style classic, "I Need Love." Jon, Roy, and Mikey wanted to pencil in some recording dates. I thought we should keep writing. A meeting had already been set with Peter Asher, from the sixties group Peter and Gordon, who produced Linda Ronstadt and 10,000 Maniacs. I'd never heard of him but was impressed he managed Joni Mitchell. Somehow it was decided that we would cut three tracks with Asher, which must have been planned all along. Tony said, "It can't hurt. If it's shit you can forget about it." There were lots of blank faces when I told friends in London we were working with Peter Asher. I confused him with Peter, Paul and Mary and kept saying, "Remember that song 'Leaving on a Jet Plane'?" No one seemed impressed, and I was starting to worry.

I was reeling in shock from the reviews of my first Jesus Loves You single, "After the Love," which made Record of the Week in the *NME*. They said it left you hanging from the ceiling, which made a change from a rope. Everyone recognized the voice and respected the lack of desperation. "After the Love" only reached

68, but everyone was telling me I'd made a great record. "Carry On Up the Culture Club" seemed less inviting and the release of *Time: The Best of Culture Club* too timely.

Recording with Culture Club began shortly before Christmas with instant recriminations. No one agreed with Asher's choice of songs and yet we were committing them to two-inch. We recorded and boarded at the Wool Hall Studios in Somerset. Roy and Jon acted like they were Phil Spector and Quincy Jones. Mikey and I were shut out of the recording. I didn't fight, I hated the way it was sounding and couldn't be convinced otherwise. One song, "Life Has Rules," was stripped of its irony. I wanted it to sound like New Order, not Howard Jones. Mikey and I copped off to the local health club whenever we could and discussed our limp roles. He wasn't happy, but neither was the tax man. By the end of recording Jon was calling Peter "a Westminster School git." I wasn't surprised Peter wanted to mix the tracks alone in Los Angeles. I didn't hold out much hope for the new mature Culture Club.

CHAPTER 47

Heads shaved to the bone, Michael and I left for India on Boxing Day. I was excited and terrified as I popped another malaria pill. There was a three-hour delay at Heathrow while British Airways staff searched for a blind man in a wheelchair who'd checked in his bags and disappeared. Everyone had to disembark and identify their luggage. I thought it must be a Sikh terrorist. There were lots of Indians throwing up their hands trying to remember how many boxes and bags they'd put on the plane. The chaos was a foretaste of what was to come.

Bombay airport was rich with color, smells, and regimented anarchy. We were held up at Customs because of my Joan Collins passport picture. I was hot, tired, and praying to any god that I wouldn't be sent home. The official kept shaking his head. I held up an imaginary microphone and smiled sweetly.

Outside, Nayana was waiting with a group of devotees, a car, and some flower garlands. I felt like a spiritual dignitary. Dozens of barefoot beggars hemmed us in, pulling at our clothes. Nayana tried to shoo them away: "*Paise ne, paise ne.*" Michael and I played Mother Teresa, handing out chocolate bars and peanuts we'd taken from the plane.

The journey from the airport was bumpy and sweltering. I could barely breathe with all the free-flowing exhaust fumes. My head was constantly turning, trying to take it all in, the cows in the road, the giant garish billboards, the thousands of peering faces. We drove to the Holiday Inn in Juhu Beach where Nayana had booked us rooms. There were no rooms. Nayana said we were welcome to stay at the Krishna temple, but Michael pulled a face. We drove around and eventually we booked into the Hotel Centor. I was instantly recognized in the breakfast room. The place was full of wealthy British Indians who had come for a society wedding. They looked at my shaved head and Krishna scarf and commented, "Oh, we didn't know you were into that!" Nayana explained that modern Indians hated it when Westerners adopted their culture. I joked, "I've come seeking spiritual enlightenment and they want a Gucci handbag."

Nayana wangled an invite to the wedding ceremony, which was held in the gardens of a flash private villa overlooking the Indian Ocean. Michael and I felt like tramps next to all the silk Nehru jackets. We'd only brought scruffy traveling clothes. The wedding was for the daughter of wealthy arms dealers, the Hindujas, so I was surprised to see former prime minister Edward Heath wandering around in a multicolored turban. He was surprised to see me too. That evening we were chauffeured to the reception in a fat fifties saloon. Decadence was the least of it—I'd never seen so much food in my life. I couldn't reconcile the two extremes of India: tattered rags and glittering saris. We wanted to let the beggars in. I said it would be like *Oliver Twist* with a dash of curry.

India was truly Dickensian and demented. Nothing can prepare you for its color or horrors. Men without legs crawling through the moving traffic, emaciated women cradling newborn babies, swarms of diseased kids with blistered feet and seeping eyes. I kept gasping and stopping to give money. Nayana said I was being suckered, that I would harden to it. I didn't believe him, but it was true. In twenty-four hours I learned sufficient Hindi to fend off the beggars. I never stopped feeling sad. India slapped my face and I loved it, every pong and cranny. I dragged Michael and Nayana up the alleys, buying chintzy bric-a-brac and religious kitsch. The funniest sight was posters of Page Three girl Sam Fox topless next to Mother Teresa, Gandhi, and Krishna.

In the morning Michael stayed in bed while Nayana and I took a 6 A.M. stroll on the beach, ending up at the Krishna temple for the greeting of the deities. The mist from the ocean wafted through the white marble temple room and conch shells trumpeted the rising gods. They looked like cosmic pop stars festooned in sequins, peacock feathers, and sparkling stones. The devotees dropped to the floor and I followed, feeling phony. Nayana led me through the proceedings, explaining this god and that god. It was clear there was no shortcut through Krishna Consciousness. I had an audience with the temple president, Sridhar Swami. Every innocent question was met with an epic story from the Vedas. Krishna battling a serpent on the lake, Lord Nrsinghadeva ripping out entrails. I was dying for a chat about *Coronation Street.*

Michael kept quiet in the temple and avoided being drawn in. He'd had his fill of religion at school. He loved the prasad, coconut idlees, and samosas and was pleased that he could be blessed by stuffing his face. He hated Bombay and kept moaning that we should go somewhere more holidayish. We spent New Decade's Eve in Bombay and on the strike of twelve I handed an old beggar a $100 bill. Nayana said it was a year's wages.

New Year's Day we tried to get on a flight to Goa, Michael's choice. We had a row in the travel agent's. The last thing I wanted was to end up in the Indian equivalent of Ibiza. Luckily all flights were full, so we headed to Trivandrum in the south. The airport was like the stock exchange, hundreds of hot and bothered people aimlessly waving tickets. It took two hours to board the plane. I had a rush of Bombay belly and had to hold it because some pig had done a curry job on the seat.

There was more fighting in Trivandrum, so our taxi driver took us to his friend's hotel and dumped us when we refused to pay. Nayana and I wanted to stay somewhere cheap. Michael wanted soft toilet paper. He yelled at me, "You're just doing this so you can tell your friends you slummed it in India. This is supposed to be a fucking holiday." I gave in and we tried to book into a five-star hotel on the beach. There were no vacancies so Michael sulked on top of his bags. "Stupid. Who goes on holiday without booking a hotel?" We both had to laugh when two of Michael's work friends appeared and said they were staying in a hut on the beach. We weren't so lucky, we found digs close by in concrete rooms that looked like prison cells and stank of disinfectant.

Worse still we were woken at 5 A.M. by loud Muslim wailing that went on for hours. The location was perfect in every other way: the beach was golden warm and the palm trees looked like sculptures. We ate at a little wooden café close by or walked along the beach to the posh hotel for a Western snack and used their pool and showers. Michael was right. I loved the scuzzy rooms— I wanted to see and feel India with as little materialistic baggage as possible. It was weird that I kept seeing people I knew. I spotted a white figure mincing down the beach and screamed when I realized it was Joyce, who worked at Browns in South Molton Street. Nayana was amused to meet a man named Joyce, but he was getting a much-needed education. We then bumped into an old designer friend, Mark, while shopping in the city. He was dressed like Gandhi, rambling on about demons and trying to convince us that it was okay to drink the water. "You only need faith." We knew he was nuts when he claimed he'd been living on the banks of the Hudson River in New York and fishing to feed himself. I ended up lending him money which I knew I'd never see again.

When the Muslim wailing became too much we moved upmarket to the Seaweed Hotel. It wasn't five-star, but it was quiet. The chubby owner kept telling me, "You are famous film star, I know you." Michael got terrible stomach cramps and had to be rushed to the local hospital, where he stayed for three days. They thought he had dysentery, but it was a mixture of rich food and cheap fizzy drinks. Michael was miserable and made me promise to book us into the best hotel when we arrived in Delhi.

Delhi was by far the most Westernized place we visited. The Hotel Imperial was a relic of British colonialism run by a fierce Indian woman who dressed like Imelda Marcos. I had an important cassette tape couriered from London, which was signed for and swiped. I didn't get an apology or compensation. Nayana and I exacted revenge by wandering up and down the hotel lobby chanting Hare Krishna. Nayana enlisted his Muslim friend Muhammad Alexander as our guide. He took us to the Muslim quarter of Delhi, which was like going back five hundred years. The Muslims seemed much friendlier and kept grinning. "You are Muslim?" Nayana and I tried to convert Michael to vegetarianism by showing him the meat market, but he was too busy videoing a man having his teeth pulled out with a pair of pliers.

From Delhi we took a train to Vrindaban, the birthplace of Krishna, and stayed in a big white house next to the temple. It was so peaceful there, peacocks in the garden and monkeys running everywhere. Nayana's wife, Daivi Sakti, cooked for us. It was the simplest and cleanest food we'd tasted. I finally felt like I was in the real India. The local people were gentle and friendly. You knew you were somewhere holy.

We drove to the Taj Mahal in Agra—it was like being in a post-card. Then we visited Radha Kund, the sacred lake of Krishna's consort Radha Rama, reputedly the holiest place in the universe, fed by all the oceans and rivers of the world. Nayana and I bathed in the icy holy water while Michael sunbathed. After swimming I wrote the lyrics to "Bow Down Mister," my homage to India and Krishna. Nayana said it was the blessing of the water, and I didn't argue. I found his spiritual claims loony and intriguing but couldn't deny the sense of calm I was feeling. Vrindaban was so still some-times that all you could hear was your own thoughts. There were no telephones, TVs, or newspapers, no means of escape. I scrib-bled in my notepad, "The search for God is the search for your-self." I stopped feeling embarrassed by the rituals of bowing down and chanting because I realized it was just a way of acknowledging the higher power, thanking that power for the gift of life and food, which made more sense in India. I didn't know whether that power was Krishna, but I had to admit he was the most stylish god in the universe. We met lots of fake saints and slimy sadhus in India. There was one on every corner, like British pubs.

Michael left us in Delhi and jetted home first-class. I couldn't convince him to sample the wonders of Nepal. Nayana stored our luggage at a friend's guesthouse and we left the next evening. On the flight I got chatting to a missionary working for the Seventh Day Adventist Church. He was asking me how to help drug addicts. We got on so well he invited us to a leper colony. Nayana and I gawped. I joked, "Might as well see everything." We gave him our hotel number.

My passport picture caused a riot of giggles in Kathmandu. The bemused official called his colleagues to share the joke. "This is you? Looks like pretty lady." They must have trusted my face because they let me through without paying my entry tax. I've never met such friendly Customs people in my life. It was too dark to see the city, we drove to a little guesthouse on "Freak Street," center of the sixties hippie invasion, and went to bed.

At 5 A.M. I woke to the sound of someone clearing their throat and gobbing outside in the courtyard, it sounded like the choke of a knackered car. It was to become a familiar sound and sight, everyone in Nepal seemed to be projecting their snot and phlegm, their motto "Better Out Than In."

After a bowl of porridge and some lemongrass tea Nayana and I ventured into the heavy morning fog, wrapped up for winter. We walked the streets as the market traders set up. I could see the curled eaves of the pagoda-style roofs as the fog lifted; the buildings were wooden and ornate. It was so different from India, more ancient and remote. The people had weatherbeaten warrior faces, they were skinnier, the girls looked like pretty boys, the men wore colorful hats that looked like upturned boats. It was as busy as Bombay but with a calmer pace. We walked for an hour or so, watching the city come alive. Parts of it were bastardized with ugly Western shops selling sports shoes and electronics. There were lots of remnant hippie types and backpackers. I saw scagged-out Nepalese boys begging outside the hotel, one looked ready to keel.

At five the next morning we were picked up by the missionaries and driven into the hills. We were tired but excited that we'd get to see the Himalayas. I wasn't looking forward to the leper colony. We drove for an hour, then stopped for breakfast at a hotel on a ridge overlooking the city. The view was unreal. I stood outside and took a few deep breaths—I've never seen anything as pretty. I was pulled round when an English tourist pointed at me and said, "Last time I saw you, you were cycling down Oxford Street."

By the time we reached the leper colony it was 8 A.M. Nayana and I were fearful of what we might see. The missionaries were treated like arriving saints. Hordes of children came running and grabbed their hands. I later remarked it was like something out of a creepy Christian promotional film. At first we saw nothing odd. The colony was a large square compound with four barn-type stone buildings. There were men and women working in vegetable

patches. As they stood up I noticed their faces were slightly disfig-
ured and they had pink blotches of skin. It wasn't as bad as I
expected. I asked why the children looked so normal and healthy
and was told that leprosy wasn't genetic or spread by touch, it was
spread by germs and living in unsanitary conditions. The missionaries were building houses outside the compound with proper sanitation to prevent further contamination and to integrate the lepers. Their biggest battle was convincing the local community and
quelling centuries of superstition. Inside the living quarters we saw
the worst cases of leprosy. The lepers shied away, masking their
faces as if to spare us. I felt guilty staring. Their ears, noses, and
fingers looked like they'd melted away. The rooms were like animal pens, tiny spaces you could barely stand up in: there were
whole families living in the roof. They'd been living that way for
generations. I was moved by the work of the missionaries and
happy to pose for pictures for their newsletter. Both Nayana and I
were grateful for the experience.

The education didn't stop there. Nayana took me to Pashu Pati
Nath, a Hindu temple famous for its cremation gods. Sadly, no
Westerners were allowed in the temple so I didn't get to see the
Shiva Lingam, a huge phallus that symbolized fertility. I made
plenty of jokes about it. We sat up on the hill overlooking the
Ganges and watched the funeral processions and bodies being
burned on the pyres. It was a formative experience for me and
brought home the impermanence of the human body.

From Kathmandu we took a small plane across the snowy
mountains to Pokhara, a lakeside resort at the foot of MatuPetrie.
We stayed at the Fishtail Lodge, which was on an island and could
only be reached by a raft. We rode around on bicycles and ate our
lunch at the Happy Belly Café. I laughed when I caught myself
telling stories about Marilyn and Philip. "Here I am in the most
gorgeous place on earth and I'm still talking about those two
cunts."

Nayana had the clever idea to climb a mountain trail, which he
said would take two hours. Six hours later we were struggling to
the top. I thought I was going to die with the altitude, my asthma,
and starvation. Luckily we met a couple of teachers from Newcastle
who had cheese and Marmite sandwiches to share.

During my journey in Nepal I really got to know Nayana. When he offered himself as my Indian guide I had no idea what I was letting myself in for. He drove me crazy at times, pinching my pennies and carting unnecessary amounts of luggage. We had a couple of showdowns and I nicknamed him "Mr. Magoo," but he was stimulating and priceless company. I'd known Nayana was gay from the moment he handed me a samosa in New York. That was why he was attracted to me. We gave each other new understandings. He was my painless introduction to the spiritual world. My Judy Garland from the Shirley Temple.

Arriving back in Delhi was a slap in the face with a wet turban. I had my passport confiscated by an angry Sikh at passport control. He looked at my picture and demanded, "Are you mad, sir?" I was given twenty-four hours to leave the country. I didn't care. I was over India and ready for some baked beans on toast and a night in front of the TV. Nayana took me to see a Hindi film, a pseudoviolent musical that was *Rambo* meets Tommy Steele. It was a sign of the new India and the growing Western influence. Nayana warned that when I returned India would be a different place. We finished off the evening at a newly opened burger diner. There was more head shaking from Nayana as we watched the well-heeled teenagers chowing down burgers in their stone-washed jeans.

The flight home was terrifying. It felt like Kali was kicking the cabin. I was crying, chanting Hare Krishna, and downing gin and tonics. As soon as I reached London I was missing India—it was gray and boring in comparison. I was glad I'd stocked up on incense, but I knew I wouldn't eat a curry for some time. India was a 180-degree never-ending spin of torment and tranquility, from the shit on the toilet seat to the freshly made garlands. It puts you through your paces and that for me was the spiritual experience. I couldn't wait to tell everyone my stories and wondered if I seemed different. Everyone joked that I was the only person who ever went to India and stayed the same weight.

It was back to reality when I joined the rest of Culture Club at a small studio in Camden Town to do some more writing. I sang them some of the songs I'd written in India, "Mogul Tomb" and "Bow Down Mister," which everyone agreed was a "Karma

Chameleon." I said they could have publishing if they could change it and make it better. Nothing they did was an improvement. We worked for three days till I had a stupid row with Jon about incense. He called me selfish because I lit up two sticks and he was choking. Somehow it escalated into a political debate. I said I was leaving. Jon laughed. "Leave, then." It was a familiar wolf cry, only this time I meant it. I stomped out into the street and grabbed a cab, quickly forgetting my rage when I saw how cute the driver was. He looked like a fifties pinup and was playing moody jazz. I closed my eyes and drifted off in the music. Even though I was mortified I knew I'd done the right thing. Finally I'd been true to myself. When the cabbie dropped me at Hampstead he refused to take the fare saying, "It's a pleasure to meet you." I skipped off thinking, Yeh, it is, wishing I'd invited him in for a cup of tea.

EPILOGUE

For the past three years I've been pulling myself apart, opening windows and trapdoors, trying to work out what is important to me. I'm practicing Marxist theory by having more than one job—pop star, author, DJ, record-company executive, and producer. I feel free to live my life as I choose and making mistakes is all part of that. Too much time has been spent blaming others. Do you really want to hurt me? The victims we know so well. These days I can maneuver through Sainsbury's, picking up my mooli and organic mushrooms without raising too many eyebrows. I even battle the tube sometimes or the 24 bus if I feel like it. Inevitably people will comment, "Wassa matter, Georgie, down on your luck? Thought you'd 'ave a roller." People are always asking me if I'm still making music. If I'm in a good mood I might bother to explain that I'm still big in Europe and that England is a very small dot. They won't believe me when I tell them I'm more successful now than I've ever been; they want proof like record sales and radio play. I certainly enjoy myself more these days and get to do unusual things, like gigs in Istanbul, Transylvania, and Argentina. Recently I was flown to New York on Concorde to model for Italian *Vogue*. I smiled all the way. I hosted my own New Age pop show *Blue Radio* on the defunct satellite channel BSB and I was good too. I've been asked several times to host a chat show on national TV, but that would be too Establishment, admitting defeat. I've fathered a child by immaculate conception and had to appear at the Inner London Family Proceedings Court. The claim, made by an imaginative woman in L.A., was thrown out due to lack of evidence.

My greatest satisfaction was securing a Top 20 U.S. hit with "The Crying Game" and going back to New York after a seven-year absence. It was great to see it through clear eyes. I feel that my music has become much more focused and personal. I finally met my perfect musical accomplice in guitarist John Themis, a self-taught Greek Cypriot genius who could adapt himself to any of my moods or musical styles. I love singing and writing songs and there's so much I still have to say, sorry. I enjoy my work and all the luxuries that go with it. I no longer take it for granted or make everything a drama. I've somewhat come to terms with the deep-rooted jealousies that have driven me for most of my life. I even speak to George Michael now. Recently we had dinner with Keren and Sarah from Bananarama and he was funny and friendly. I now try to look beyond the veneer of everyone I meet. No one or nothing is ever what it seems.

I'm always asked, "How is the rest of Culture Club?" "Do you ever see them?" Jon and I are on truce terms. We speak occasionally, but I still haven't managed to convince him to have therapy. Mikey I haven't seen this decade. Roy and Alison are the only two remaining friends. And Roy and I still collaborate on music when we get the chance. Alison was one of the few people prepared to stand up to me during my reign as the Attila of Culture Club. I just can't help falling in love with ball-breaker women.

These days my relationship with Mum and Dad and the rest of my family is brilliant—we're like friends. I discuss my boyfriend problems with Mum all the time. She keeps telling me I need someone older and more sensible. Dad has become a bit spiritual. Of course, I always knew he was, somewhere underneath that raging bull. I respect them both for their bravery and the love they have shown me.

I have an especially close relationship with my little sister, Sionhan. I've come a long way from tipping sugar over her head. She works as my PA and housekeeper and gives me a good slap when I need it.

These last few years have seen my personal and career struggles come to some kind of fruition. I can't believe I've been banging my head against the same brick wall all these lifetimes. I've been a cunt and a cow, sometimes sacred, often sacrificial, but I've been in good company.

I've played murderer and Mum to my collaborator Spencer, cooking him vegetarian meals on our various jaunts into the British countryside to meet our many deadlines. His wife, Chrissy Iley, knew the score early on when she taunted us by pinning up a picture of a mouse on a treadmill. I don't know if the mouse was me or Spencer, but I have my suspicions.

There were so many things I didn't want to face, least of all have committed to history. The only reason I didn't become bulimic was because I kept all the food in. The asthma and panic attacks increased as I came round from my amnesia. This book has been a mental and physical trial-athlon. I started writing ten years ago in Switzerland under a cloud of ganja. The first chapter, "Watching Paint Dry," was about my loathsome schooldays. It was libelous, vicious, and great fun to write. I took my sharpened pencil and poked it into every damn teacher, drawing what little blood and guts they had. I bitched into the early hours and couldn't wait to jump back on the typewriter. Culture Club were in Montreux making *Luxury to Heartache;* writing relieved the boredom. The rights to the book were later bought by Crown publishers of New York. I still have comical and tragic visions of my then editor Ronni Stolzenberg turning up in her fur coat at Morgans Hotel. Shuffling through my meager scribble while I pretended to be Hemingway on an off day. Once the book became a serious proposition I couldn't take it seriously. I was too busy getting high. Marilyn would read excerpts and leave angry notes. "You better not write that about me. Who do you think I am, Philip Sallon?"

The deal with Crown fell by the wayside along with everything else during my heroin addiction, but drugs left me with a more interesting book to write. In 1988 I signed a new deal with Sidgwick & Jackson in London, which included a three-year clause to give me eons of time. Two years on I had some more anarchic prose. It was then Spencer Bright entered the picture at the suggestion of Sidgwick's. I didn't argue, I knew I would never finish it by myself. I vaguely knew Spencer from Philip and hanging around the Limelight Star Bar—he hadn't written anything bitchy about me yet. We sat in my kitchen using up twenty-four hours of microcassettes to try and get some shape and continuity. Then Spencer got to meet every freak from Hollywood to Stevenage and beyond. Some wanted cash, others wanted anonymity. There were veiled threats of violence from some of those straight boys and pleading phone calls, "It's not true, George didn't suck my cock. It's all in his mind." Believe me, it was all in my mouth. I was surprised to find friends like Patrick Lilley still holding grudges about stolen Giros. I've since paid him back as life has paid me back. Everyone had their own version of history. Some were just bad liars and losers, others knew how to color a story until it was even better than the real thing. I gulped reading the transcripts. Did Kim Bowen and Tranny Paul really say those things about me?

Spencer was a brutal detective, leaving many in tears. The Batphone was ringing fast and furious. What was I going to do, tell the truth? Helen Terry got into a panic, forgetting how much I loved her and always will. The facts became flying saucers, loaded up with stolen cash and ruined careers. Even Marilyn, who was the only person paid for his information, had no need to worry. I've always had a twisted sense of morality, and money really does grow on trees. Marilyn and I are still friends, much to the horror and disbelief of many. There is some past-life karma involved, she's been the hardest drug to kick. Spencer challenged me to challenge myself, to look beyond my own sharp tongue and ask how things really were. Then two years into the book I went into therapy, as if writing wasn't therapy enough.

There I was strolling down Regent Street on a lovely spring day when a sharp voice called out to me. At first I didn't recognize the Sloane Ranger in the Burberry mac and sensible shoes. "Sonia? You've gone all posh." It was Sonia Ducie, my old bitching partner from the New Romantic days. She looked so different back then in her rubber and silly hats. We went for tea at Country Life, a Christian vegetarian restaurant, and were soon chatting about all things cosmic. Sonia was into reflexology and healing. I tried not to mock, I was open-minded. I'd already dabbled with Buddhism, tried hypnotherapy, flotation, homeopathic medicine, and been to India.

Sonia and I started hanging out, meditating and cooking soup together. She was a psychic in Sainsbury's. "No, no, I don't like the energy of this broccoli." She kept tuning in and seeing auras, mine was off-white and cracked. Sonia's transformation was due in part to a therapy course called the Turning Point. She enthused that it had changed her life and could do the same for me. I went to an open night at a hotel in Russell Square. They gave us name stickers and I sat there uncomfortably. I left early, saying they were all weirdos in corduroy. It was a good eighteen months before I was persuaded to hand over £225 and "give a hundred percent" to the Turning Point.

I had to admit my life was in a mess, even though everyone kept telling me how marvelous I looked and how great it was that I'd kicked drugs. Michael and I were strangers. I felt more like his landlord than his boyfriend. I'd read every book from *Heal Your Life* to *The Road Less Traveled* and *The Psychology of Romantic Love*. It all made perfect sense, but I couldn't put it to domestic use. I wanted to be closer to Michael, but everything I tried just pushed him further away. The fact that Michael was high or low on cocaine most of the time didn't help. I gave him an ultimatum: give up or get out. I sent him to see my old drugs counselor Dr. Glatt, and for a while he was clean and brighter. Max warned me of the dangers of being around Michael; he wasn't happy about it.

Through Sonia I started weekly sessions with Paul Vick, a cranial osteopath and therapist. After much coaxing I persuaded Michael to join me for couples' therapy. It was amazing to hear how similar our frustrations and resentments were. "You never listen to me" and so on. I hoped Paul would mend us and we'd be the perfect loving couple. I thought I could transfer my dreams onto Michael. I wanted to fix him when I could barely fix myself. I was so happy when Paul talked Michael into doing the Turning Point course with me.

We were both skeptical when we arrived at the bright school hall in Wood Green, North London. There were all types milling around, wearing nametags, and a handful of knowing helpers, including Sonia, who was beaming like a proud mother. We sat at the back and hoped no one would home in on us.

The teacher, Grahame Brown, was a small, fiery Australian who burst into the room with the sun in his pocket. "Well, are we ready?" He was rubbing his hands and talking like a politician, raising and lowering his voice to create waves of effect, strolling in and out of the chairs. "Are you with me, Jane? Get that, George?" I couldn't decide whether I trusted or liked him at all.

Like school there were several rules designed to push your buttons. We had to raise our hands and ask permission to go to the toilet; no chewing or eating in class; all watches to be removed and all medication handed in, which included my asthma spray. I could feel the animosity welling up in the room and my bronchial tubes tightening. I was a joker from the start, constantly butting in, asking questions and trying to be the center of attention. I was told quite a few times to try listening. I argued, "I've paid £225 and I want my money's worth." By the end of the weekend I'd learned the hard way that my constant chatter was a survival technique and often "very boring" and was told, "Shut the fuck up, George."

Grahame said everything was choice, life, death, our parents, even the color of our eyes. It wasn't far from the Buddhist concept, but it still made me question. "Okay, then, do you choose to be gay?" Grahame looked at me straight and said, "Do you?" I had the group in stitches with my pitiful tales of never being chosen for the school football team. It seemed the world was a huge mirror onto which we projected ourselves. I had carefully picked my own life experiences, tears, queers, and fears, and the universe had never let me down. The cure, however corny, was to love and value ourselves and others unconditionally. We had to learn to forgive even the worst atrocities against us because without forgiveness we could have no integrity. At times Grahame's sincerity left me hungry for blood. I expected Lionel Richie to jump out and sing "Hello." The most powerful thing was opening up and being vulnerable with a group of total strangers. We punched pillows, screamed our lungs out, and had fun in the "process."

Michael went through his own powerful experiences. He was

regressed back to a little boy and spoke of his pain and rejection. Watching him crying and opening his heart was scary: I could see how much we had in common and why I loved him so much. I realized I wasn't as tough as I thought. I couldn't always be mother, I needed to be able to fall down sometimes, to be cushioned and loved. So many friends and lovers were attracted to my strength only to twist the blade when they discovered my weaknesses. I was lonely so much of the time and felt that no one was there for me.

After the course we were both shell-shocked and full of religious zeal. Everyone needed therapy; they all had to take the course before it was too late. Michael was the best advert, no one could believe the change in him. He was a true Gemini, cracking jokes and making conversation, and he was even more handsome. It frightened me. I got jealous of his friendship with a male course member and knocked him back. Sadly, Michael couldn't handle the power of being in the light and scurried back to the shade and his drug dealer. We fought night and day. I searched the house for drugs and threw them down the toilet. I was turning into my mother and reliving my own drug addiction. The saddest thing was that Michael hadn't learned anything from my suffering.

Five months after the Turning Point, Michael and I took a second therapy course, Point of Choice. I bullied him into being there and wasted my money. He broke a major condition by taking drugs—his commitment wasn't as ready as the sulk on his face. Mum and Dad were in the course, adding to the discomfort. Some weeks earlier I had tricked them into taking the Turning Point by saying I'd already paid the deposit. Now they were bravely facing round two. I was beginning to see how much Michael and I were like Mum and Dad. I'd known for years that I was a gay version of my father. I didn't realize how much Michael was like him, that same defensive anger and coldness. We were all mixed up. I was Mum loving against the odds and somehow unable to show love. When she broke down at the end of the course I could feel every sob in my heart, yet remained numb.

After Point of Choice, Michael said therapy had ruined everything. "There are some things people don't need to know." I told him he was refusing to take responsibility for his life and he screamed, "Don't give me that Turning Point shit." If I'd learned anything it is that you can't run other people's lives, especially where addiction is concerned. Love is not enough. It didn't stop me trying. Looking back at my own situation I know I despised all the people who tried to help me. It took worldwide publicity and two deaths before I was able to stop. Even then it was an hourly battle.

For a long time after kicking drugs I refused to preach against their use. I didn't want to be a hypocrite or lose my cool. I hated talking about it because that's all anyone did. Every journalist thought they could get the ultimate drugs story. I was still in too much emotional and physical turmoil. There weren't many days when I didn't think of Michael Rudetsky or Mark Vaultier. I said no to antidrug soundbites for radio or TV because it felt creepy. Now I feel very differently about drugs, but I still think you teach best by example. Preaching doesn't change anything. At best you can show people that there is a way out of the dark hole of addiction.

I HATE DRUGS. DRUGS ARE A CON. I uphold a hundred percent people's right to destroy themselves if they want to. I don't have any answers. I'm split on whether drugs should be legalized, whether we should have cannabis coffee shops like Amsterdam. In court I stated that I didn't consider dope to be a drug. It's certainly less harmful than alcohol, but I have to contradict the notion that harmless puffing doesn't lead to heroin because it did in my case. Of course, it's not that way with everyone, but once you're open to the drug experience you naturally become curious. The drug debate is as complex as the argument for legalizing prostitution. It's good not to live in fear and have clean sheets—but have you been to the red-light district in Amsterdam and seen the misery that beckons you from the windows? It isn't any better than Soho. Legalizing prostitution and drugs would wipe out street crime and get rid of dealers and pimps. Then the government would be free to rake in the revenue as it does with legal drugs like cigarettes, alcohol, and sugar. Would that be any less cynical?

Drugs are a symptom of a much deeper cause—social, emotional, spiritual—and there isn't any one reason why people take them. People used to ask me over and over, "Why, why, when you seem so bright?" If I could answer that question I could probably solve half the world's problems. People assumed that I started taking drugs when Jon left me and my career took a nosedive. That's all too simplistic, like an episode of *Eastenders*. I was spiraling toward drug addiction long before I learned to say, "Don't leave me, I love you." Drugs help you cut off. God knows, there are a million things that people want to run away from. I have spent a lifetime anesthetizing myself with one drug or another—food, sex, drag, fame, drugs, religion. Food is probably the most lethal drug on the market. Running to the fridge is no different from running to the dealer, except one might kill you quicker and the other leave cellulite.

During the acid-house days I realized something watching all the football hooligans running around out of their minds. For a brief moment, two, three hours, maybe all night if they dropped enough Es, they released some of that Rottweiler anxiety and were free to tell strangers they loved them. Many would argue that drugs are useful for that very reason. It's hard to contradict that view when you see people loved up and E'd out of their minds, but I see so many friends badly fucked up on drugs. Brilliant, sparkling human beings that have been reduced to sniffling repetition. They're not using drugs, drugs are using them. It isn't glamorous or liberating.

I don't look down on anyone for taking drugs. How could I? I just feel a massive sigh in my chest. I suppose I'm like one of those annoying Christians at Speaker's Corner who want to tell you about Jesus. I have found a different sort of light. It's true the road of excess leads to the palace of wisdom. We all have to go down that road and take our chances.

Watching Michael sink deeper and deeper into his addiction was a humbling experience for me. I was on the phone to Dad, telling him how worried I was. There was a brief silence, "Well, son, you know how we felt." These things make you realize how much you love someone and who your friends are. I know I hated my brother David when he took my drug problem onto national TV. I didn't see the interview until 1994, when it was used as part of the BBC Omnibus documentary, *The Boy Next Door*. It rumbled my insides. You see, when you love someone, all the liberal bull-shit flies out the window. Michael's always been trouble, but I know he's got a good heart and those big lips just make me weak. A love addiction is like a drug addiction, you have to take it one day at a time.

One thing about growing old is that you can no longer avoid death. It's worse being gay, with AIDS wiping out the butterflies. The fabulous Leigh Bowery passed away on New Year's Eve 1994, and London lost another mirror ball. No one knew Leigh had AIDS because he didn't want them to. He said, "I want to be remembered as a person with ideas, not AIDS." He refused a funeral, claiming he was the son of Satan and ordered his close friends to tell everyone he had gone to live on a pig farm in Bolivia. Devious to the last breath.

The same year we lost another club queen in Galinda Kostiff, who ran London's most colorful club of the late eighties, Kinky Gerlinky. She died suddenly of a brain hemorrhage while waiting to go out in her sequins.

From the funeral pyres in Kathmandu to the Royal Free Hospital in Hampstead I have seen my own mortality. It was as if God was sending a message when he transferred a young dying fan, Mandi Doward, to the Royal Free Hospital at the end of my road.

I first met Mandi in 1987 when she won a competition on Radio One. She kept writing to me. Hers was one from hundreds of letters that somehow got my attention. She decorated her envelopes with caricatures and made brilliant hand-painted T-shirts. When I discovered she'd developed leukemia I did my best to keep in touch. Michael and I took turns visiting her at her home in Essex and later when she was hospitalized. Mandi's brav-ery was unsettling and made me realize how stupid it was messing with drugs. Her mother, Anne, was by her bed night and day. Her pain was too great even to imagine. Michael and I held Mandi's hand as she lay in a coma. Michael was so sweet and caring. He attended to Mandi and Anne when I had to leave town and was there when they turned off the life-support machine. Mandi died on Valentine's Day 1989, five weeks after her twenty-first birthday. I questioned God after that. I never could get to grips with the karma theory, it just seemed so cruel. Krishna devotees told me that life in the physical body was the worst suffering of all. Surely God didn't put us on earth just to suffer. I had to console myself that death brings peace and Mandi was happily painting in heaven.

Finding peace made more sense when my makeup artist friend Stevie Hughes died of AIDS in 1992. There had been rumors for ages that he was sick. No one wanted to believe it. He seemed fine when I bumped into him in South Molton Street spinning around in flip-flops and a sparkly Indian shirt, telling stories about Pete Burns in the gym, "Pumping iron, Mum, in full makee. She's not a well woman." It wasn't until Stevie was in St. Mary's Hospital in Paddington that we actually spoke about his illness. He told me, "Everyone's known all along. I could have saved myself a lot of bother." He was shaking his plasma bag, "Wipe out a nation, Mum, wipe 'em out." When I told him to stop smoking a joint he reasoned, "What are they going to do, kill me?"

Toward the end Stevie was so focused, practicing meditation and visualization. He fulfilled a dream by swimming with the dolphins in Miami and showed off his crystal when he came to a party at my house. He never lost his witchy sense of humor, balancing spirituality with a wink at a well-hung stranger. I got him to direct Eve Gallagher's first video for "Love Come Down" and he made her look like a goddess.

Stevie and I were never that close, but there was a thread that had kept us in contact over thirteen years. God, she had an evil tongue on her, but, like Philip, and unlike Marilyn, he was funny when he was pulling you apart. I always knew his bitching, like my own, was just a survival technique. He was so much more than that, a talented, genius soul. I never got the chance to say good-bye because Stevie slipped into a coma, but I wrote a song in his honor, "Il Adore," probably the best song I've ever written:

Mother clutches the head of her dying son,
Anger and tears, so many things to feel.
Sensitive boy, good with his hands,
No one mentions the unmentionable,
But everybody understands.
Here in this cold white room tied up to these machines,
It's hard to imagine him as he used to be.

Laughing, screaming, tumbling queen.
Like the most amazing light show you've ever seen.
Whirling, swirling, never blue.
How could you go and die?
What a lonely thing to do.

A radiant black Hare Krishna devotee took hold of my hand: "Lord Chaitanya is going to lift you up to heaven. This is nectar." I laughed apprehensively. I was sure the Krishnas wouldn't like my song "Bow Down Mister," but they were cheering every line and beaming with approval. It was American producer Bruce Forrest's idea to blend chanting Krishnas with a Christian choir. We were going to use session singers but Bruce said, "Nah. We have to have the real shit on here." He was right. When the devotees started chanting I could feel a holy presence in the studio.

I'd been toying with spirituality since my first Buddhist meeting and all the way to India. I know I'm searching for something, inner peace or the answer to life's jigsaw. I used to think of myself as an incurable atheist, but drugs have definitely put things in perspective. Journalists often jibe that I'm the new George Harrison, that I've taken the classic route, fame, drugs, God. Well, I haven't found God in any obvious way, I'm not spouting any doctrine. I just believe there is something out there that matches us step for step. It might be Krishna, Allah, Jehovah, an energetic force. Maybe it's the orthodox Christian God. No one knows, that's the only thing that's certain.

Religion is like a beautiful flower with sharp teeth. The tranquility is always matched with moral goose stepping. Once people have rigid beliefs they inevitably tend to look down on others and act like they've got God in their handbag. All religious philosophies are basically saying the same thing, give or take a few atrocities. Live in harmony with your fellow man and nature and don't enjoy sex unnecessarily.

"Bow Down Mister" swept me up in a spiritual whirl and I became an unlikely queer envoy for Krishna Consciousness. It was a strange dilemma, because much of my lifestyle seemed wholly unholy. To me religion was a breeders' club. I joked privately, "Michael and I have tried for a baby, but we haven't had much luck." None of the Krishnas ever made an issue of my sexuality even though they clearly saw it as a fallen quality. I was, after all, a useful fairy in terms of publicity. The devotees got to dance and chant the holy name on TV shows and onstage, bringing the message to millions. Promoting Krishna was above all else. Their official line on homosexuality was similar to Catholicism: sex purely for procreation or complete celibacy. Noncommittal homophobia. The reality materialized when I played a gay club in Krefeld, Germany. The devotees panicked and would only allow the women to dance onstage. I thought it was slightly presumptuous on their part—some of them weren't lookers. Then a swami, who I was very fond of, told me it was harder for homosexuals to enter the gates of heaven. I replied, "Especially if you keep them shut." I discovered later that other devotees had grilled my tour manager, Stuart Frame, asking, "Is Boy George still gay? You know we don't approve of it."

It's hard to know where I stand or lie down on the subject of God and gays. I pretty much agree with Quentin Crisp: "God created he, she, me." I don't see homosexuality as a curse or an affliction, though it is a cross of sorts. You're never going to convince everyone that you're happy defying God's so-called law and, anyway, it's all down to personal interpretation. Some devotees are obviously uncomfortable about my association with Krishna Consciousness. Others treat me with utmost respect and kindness. I've made some really invaluable friendships, Jayadeva, John Richardson, who used to be the drummer in the seventies glam group the Rubettes. Jayadeva is the best advertisement for the spiritual life. Even my most cynical friends have taken to him. He and his family have always shown Michael and me total warmth and his wife, Satchi, makes killer prasadam.

There are many Krishna concepts that I'm uncomfortable with and others that ring true like vegetarianism. I do believe that as long as we're slaughtering animals we will also be slaughtered. Like George Bernard Shaw said, "Cruelty begets its offspring war." I enjoy the rituals of offering obeisances to Krishna and chanting, especially when there are hundreds of devotees jumping and banging drums. At that moment it seems like the human ego is truly transcended. I do find the sexual attitudes far too rigid, though I admit the cycle of desire is fraught with anxiety and disappointment. I don't choose to cut off from it, maybe I enjoy the pain.

Homosexuals are certainly lust-driven creatures. For most of us, sex is the ultimate fix. We need it just to feel that we exist. A lot of our sex is casual and impersonal. We argue that we don't have to mimic the his-and-her stereotype and be like straight couples. The truth is, most of us find it hard to commit ourselves to relationships, we fear intimacy and always think the dick is bigger on the other side. Philip and I were laughing recently about how much our lives never change. We were getting a lift down to Heaven in the back of a rancid Mini. Philip asked his skinny friend Sean, "So when did you get out of prison?" I chuckled to myself.

I've been in damaged relationships for as long as I can remember. I hang in, hoping something will give, always blaming my partners for being cold and selfish. Now I realize like attracts like. Recently I came across a box of Jon's letters (Yes, she keeps everything) and I was enlightened to some of my own demons. I know now that you can't take out of a relationship what you don't put in, and you always meet the partner that suits your needs. So don't complain, bitch, get the Windolene out and clean that mirror.

Glue for the broken toy,
Wings for the saint,
A Buddha, a false God and some war paint.

Washing your wisdom, yes,
But who can you trust.
Love holds a mirror up to us all.

"Cheapness and Beauty," 1995

INDEX